A Taste of Mexico

The Complete Mexican Cookbook with More Than 500 Authentic Mexican Recipes

MARISSA MARIE

TABLE OF CONTENTS

Beef and Pork ___ 229

MEXICAN COOKING FUNDAMENTALS

Cooking Mexican food in an authentic way can seem like a daunting task, but like everything else in life, some guidance and a bit of practice is all you need. I'll take care of the guidance part, and I will leave it to you to take care of the rest!

Mexican food has an insane variety, and the taste easily covers a wide spectrum of flavours. Most American cooks can cook great Mexican food, but are sometimes a little off the mark from authentic Mexican flavour. The primary objective of this book is to enable an average non-Mexican cook to cook authentic Mexican food using the tools and ingredients easily available in any corner of the world.

In this section, we will look at some of the ingredients, equipment, and techniques you will need to know about before you can achieve great results with Mexican cooking. Keep at it, and you'll be preparing full-course Mexican dinners in no time!

THE FLAVOURS OF MEXICO

All regional cuisine has its distinct flavour, and Mexican food is no exception. You can tell when Mexican food is cooking nearby just by the smell. Mexican food gets its distinct flavour from the combination of ingredients that are commonly used in Mexican food. A few of these ingredients are: cilantro, cumin, chiles, garlic, etc. Once you get a hang of the Mexican flavour and ingredient combinations, you will be able to give a Mexican twist to pretty much every recipe in the world!

Latin markets are great places to stock up on supplies for cooking Mexican food. If you're in the USA or UK, you probably have such a market in close vicinity. You can easily find nearby markets using Google. If there is an ingredient, you're having problem finding, amazon.com is always a great last resort.

I will try my best to keep things simple, and will only use ingredients that are easy to source.

MEXICAN STAPLES

In order to achieve close to authentic Mexican flavour, you will need to have full understanding of the ingredients that make food taste Mexican. In this section we will talk about a few of the Mexican staples that you will absolutely need to include in your kitchen pantry, if you're serious about Mexican cooking.

Feel free to buy canned/preserved versions of the ingredients if you can't find fresh ones.

CHILE

Chile is an indispensable ingredient for Mexican cooking, and we use a wide variety of these here in Mexico. The recipes in this book call for wide variety of these, so make sure you know where to source them. A nearby Latin market or store is a great place to look, or you can always find these online on www.amazon.com , or www.mexgrocer.com .

ANCHO

This dried poblano sports a deep, smoky flavour that couples great with beef and appears in an quite a few Mexican soups and salsas. It needs to be reconstituted.

ARBOL

Less hot, but just as flavourful as the habanero, this brittle, dried chile doesn't need reconstituting when added to soups, pots of pinto beans, or tequila.

GUAJILLO

Fragrant, earthy, and rather spicy, this dried chile is essential to moles and is commonly used as a purée in red chile sauces.

HABANERO

Deliciously fruity and super spicy (up to 350,000 Scoville units), this usually orange, lantern-like pepper is an essential ingredient of bottled hot sauces, tongue-singeing sauces, soups, and salsas.

JALAPEÑO

This most common of chile peppers is picked while green and usually used fresh in pretty much everything Mexican.

MORITA (DRIED CHIPOTLE)

This slightly fruity, dried chile is a smoke-dried jalapeño. When dried, it needs reconstituting. When canned and sold as chipotle en adobo, both the chile itself and its amazingly useful sauce can lend smoky depth to the recipes it is used in.

POBLANO

This mild, dark-skinned chile pepper turns into ancho when dried. When fresh, it can be roasted or turned into a vessel for Chiles Rellenos.

SERRANO

Smaller and hotter than a jalapeño, this important fresh pepper is commonly included raw into relishes and salsas. It is sometimes used roasted.

HERBS AND SPICES

ACHIOTE PASTE

Made using super-hard annatto seeds, this paste adds a smoky, peppery flavour to marinades and sauces. It's usually diluted using sour orange and serves as an important ingredient in quite a few Mexican recipes.

ALLSPICE

These peppercorn-looking berries are usually toasted and ground to impart warmth to salsas, moles, and stews. To save time, buy it ground.

BAY LEAVES

Thinner than other varieties, Mexican bay laurel adds its amazing flavour to marinades, soups, and stews.

CILANTRO

This self-seeding annual is used fresh across Mexican salsas, rice dishes, soups, and moles. It's also commonly used to garnish tacos.

CINNAMON

Mexican cinnamon, or Ceylon cinnamon, is quite unlike the cinnamon normally used in the United States—it's headier and warmer than its American counterpart. It can be found in Mexican markets as sticks or ground. If you can't find Mexican cinnamon, use whichever version you have on hand.

CUMIN

Strong, earthy cumin seeds, for which there is no equivalent, are commonly toasted and ground and used in stews and soups.

MARJORAM

Usually used with thyme and oregano to flavour stews, this fragrant herb also appears as a component of pickled vegetables.

OREGANO

Different from the Mediterranean variety, the Mexican herb is often used dry in pozole and tomato-based soups, or in main dishes.

SESAME (AJONJOLÍ)

An important ingredient in moles, these nutty seeds are also used in baked goods, including on sandwich rolls.

THYME

This aromatic perennial is often used to pickle vegetables and to dry and use in combination with oregano and marjoram for flavouring stews and other slow-simmered dishes.

OTHER INGREDIENTS

AVOCADOS

This mild fruit finds is a common ingredient in many Mexican recipes. Simply halve, pit, and peel.

CAJETA

Similar to dulce de leche, this caramel sauce is a common ingredient in multiple desserts and is used to top ice cream. Look for Coronado brand, which is made from goat's milk and has a full, rich flavour. Cow's milk versions can also be used.

CHEESE

Cheese is a staple in the Mexican kitchen. A few of the popular kinds of cheese in Mexico are: cotija, queso Oaxaca, queso fresco, and Chihuahua.

CHOCOLATE

Mexican chocolate is indispensable for moles. Unsweetened cocoa is great as a background note for sauces and stews, because it lends wonderful depth.

CORN

Sweet corn is indispensable for on-the-cob elotes, as well as in salads and soups.

GARLIC

Whether roasted or used raw in salsas, these cloves are a vital ingredient in Mexican Cooking.

HOT SAUCE

Popular hot sauces among Mexican cooking newbies are: mild Tapatío or Valentina; Cholula; and El Yucateco's Salsa Picante de Habanero.

LIMES

Keep plenty of limes on hand—they're indispensable for adding a spritz of citrusy brightness to finished dishes, as well as to salsas and cocktails.

ONIONS

Red and white/yellow onions are vital ingredients in Mexican cooking. Red ones are used for pickling and using fresh, while white/yellow ones are used in blended salsas as well as soups, stews, and pretty much everything else savory.

TORTILLAS

You can buy these or make your own. I will show you how in the next section.

VINEGAR

White, apple cider, and sometimes sugarcane vinegar add acidic pungency to pickled vegetables, vinaigrettes, and one-pot meals. Fruit vinegars are called for in quite a few Mexican recipes too.

EQUIPMENT

Improvisation is a talent every good cook has. Don't have an ingredient or appliance that a recipe calls for? Just improvise! However, too much improvisation can take a toll on the final result, which is why I will recommend having at least a few basic things in your kitchen if you are serious about Mexican cooking.

THE ESSENTIALS

COMAL

Any old cast iron or non-stick griddle will do the job. If you don't have any of these, you can get a comal, which is the traditional Mexican griddle used to make tortillas, sopes, quesadillas, etc. It is also a handy tool for dry roasting.

DUTCH OVEN

This little appliance is great for slow-cooking, and if you don't have one yet, you would do well to invest in one. If you don't know where to look, just pick up one from amazon.

MOLCAJETE

Mexican recipes sometimes require you to crush stuff. Might as well do it using a traditional Mexican tool. If you don't wish to invest in one, any old crushing tool will do the job.

STEAMER

Quite a few Mexican staples such as *tamales* require steaming. There are many ways of steaming if you don't have a steamer and don't wish to invest in one, just google them.

TORTILLA PRESS

If you ever get tired of rolling out tortillas and other stuff using a rolling pin, just remember that you can always make your work much easier by investing in a tortilla press. These are cheap, and easily available online, and in stores.

THE TIME-SAVERS

All the appliances in this section exist purely to save time. If you have a lot of free time on your hands, feel free to skip to the next section.

BLENDER OR IMMERSION BLENDER

Mexican sauces, drinks, salsas, etc. call for quite aa lot of puréeing and pulsing. Having an electric appliance that does the job at the press of a button sure helps.

FOOD PROCESSOR

Mexican food has a LOT of chopped up stuff. If you don't wish to do the chopping manually, invest in an electric food processor.

PRESSURE COOKER

Pressure cooking is the most efficient cooking method known to man. It is quick, cheap, and doesn't allow for much wastage of energy. It would be a good idea to invest in an electric or traditional pressure cooker if you don't have one already.

SLOW COOKER

Slow cooking really allows the flavours to be incorporated into the dishes, and is a great tool to have in your kitchen.

BASIC TECHNIQUES

If you've been cooking for a while, you will know all the basic techniques mentioned in this section. If you're a newbie, read through this section, and also watch a few videos on YouTube if you don't understand the procedure.

BLISTERING

To blacken and blister chiles, roast them directly over a gas flame for approximately five minutes, turning using tongs until charred and blistered. Another method is to broil them 4 inches beneath a preheated broiler for approximately ten minutes. Then, place them in a bowl, and cover the bowl using a kitchen towel to steam. After about five minutes, remove and discard the stem and seeds, and peel away and discard the blackened skin.

BRAISING

Using an enameled cast iron Dutch oven, which retains and uniformly distributes heat, sear seasoned meat on all sides in shimmering-hot oil on moderate to high heat to accomplish deep caramelization. If sautéing vegetables, remove and reserve browned meat before this step (and return it to the pot once done). Deglaze the pot by pouring in the braising liquid, using a wooden spoon to scrape the browned, tasty bits from the bottom of the pan, as they will enhance the flavour of the dish. Place the meat back into the pot, along with any juices that accumulated while it was resting. Bring the liquid to a simmer, cover the pot, and move it to a preheated 325°F oven to finish cooking until it becomes fall-apart tender.

DRY ROASTING

Dry roasting means applying heat to "dry" foods, such as unpeeled garlic, tomatoes, tomatillos, onions, or chiles. It can be done using a skillet, cast iron skillet, or comal.

GRILLING

Grilling is called for in quite a few Mexican recipes. The process is simple, as long as you have a grill. Keep it clean, well oiled, and preheat it before you throw the food on it.

GRINDING

You can do this in three ways. The most popular method is to pulverize them using a mortar and pestle, or molcajete, a kitchen tool you can also use to bruise herbs and mash ingredients for guacamole. The second way is to use a spice grinder, perfect for larger jobs. Finally, a third option is a Microplane, great for grating nutmeg, cinnamon, chocolate, citrus zest, and garlic.

RECONSTITUTING

Dried chiles have an incredible depth of flavour, and they're something you'll use a lot when cooking Mexican recipes. While ground, dried chiles may sometimes be used as a substitute, just follow this procedure. For up to eight peppers, fill a small saucepan with water and bring to the boiling point over high heat. Take the pan off the heat, and immerse the peppers in the hot water. Let them reconstitute for about half an hour. Drain, discard the water, and use in recipes as required.

STEAMING

My favourite steaming method is using a covered Dutch oven or pot with a tight-fitting rack placed inside. To steam tamales, use a large covered pot outfitted with either a rack or a perforated steamer basket that sits above the water line. Bring the water to the boiling point, place the tamales in the basket, cover, and steam until the masa dough becomes firm and easily pulls away from the corn husk. The process takes approximately ninety minutes.

TOASTING SPICES

This technique enhances the flavour of spices, while mellowing them out at the same time. In a skillet over moderate heat, toast spices just until aromatic, shaking the pan once in a while to avoid burning. Then, move them to a mortar, or molcajete, for grinding.

SALSA, SAUCES, & SEASONINGS

Fresh homemade salsa is the best salsa. Restaurants may or may not use fresh ingredients, and store-bought ready to eat salsa is hardly salsa, as it is laden with preservatives.

So, if you're preparing a full-course Mexican meal, make sure you make your own salsa. In this section we will cover a few of the most popular Mexican sauces and seasonings. Let us dive straight into the recipes!

Achiote Paste (RECADO COLORADO)

This spicy red seasoning is perfect for adding punch to your meat recipes!

Yield: Approximately ¾ Cup

Ingredients:

- ¼ cup olive oil
- ½ cup freshly squeezed lemon juice (about 5 lemons)
- ½ cup freshly squeezed orange juice
- ½ teaspoon whole cloves
- 1 tablespoon black peppercorns
- 10 garlic cloves
- 2 tablespoons salt
- 2 teaspoons cumin seeds
- 3 habanero peppers, seeded
- 5 tablespoons achiote (annatto) seeds
- 8 whole allspice berries

Directions:

1. Use a food processor to pulse-grind the achiote seeds, peppercorns, cumin, allspice, and cloves until thoroughly powdered. Put in the orange juice, habaneros, garlic, and salt and blend until the desired smoothness is achieved. Mix in the lemon juice and olive oil until a paste is achieved.
2. Cover tablespoon-sized portions of the paste using plastic and place it in your freezer for no more than a month.

Ancho and Chile De Árbol Salsa

An insanely delicious rustic salsa from Mexico's interior!

Yield: About 2 cups

Ingredients:

- 1 ancho chile, toasted and rehydrated, 1/3 cup of the soaking water reserved
- 1 teaspoon agave nectar or sugar
- 1 teaspoon salt
- 1 tomato (about 1/2 pound), roasted
- 1/2 cup finely chopped white onion
- 1/2 pound tomatillos, husked and rinsed
- 4 chiles de árbol, toasted and rehydrated

Directions:

1. Put the tomatillos in a small deep cooking pan, submerge them in water, bring them to its boiling point, and simmer until they are tender but not falling apart, about five minutes. Drain and save for later.
2. Finish the salsa. Put the chiles in a blender and put in the reserved 1/3 cup of soaking water. Put in the tomatillos, tomato, agave nectar, and salt to the blender and blend until thoroughly puréed. Pour the salsa into a serving dish and mix in the onions.

Ancho Chile Jam

This jam has a complex sweet & spicy flavour. It can be enjoyed mixed into soups, as a chutney with meat recipes, and much more!

Yield: 2 ½ Cups

Ingredients:

- ½ teaspoon salt
- 2 cloves garlic, peeled
- 2 ounces ancho chiles, approximately 5
- 2 tablespoons honey

- 2 tablespoons white or red wine vinegar
- 6 tablespoons any kind of red jam or jelly

Directions:

1. Use scissors to cut the ancho chiles open, discard the stems, and shake out all the seeds. Put the chiles in a container and add sufficient boiling water to immerse the chiles. Put a small plate on top of the chiles to immerse them. Soak for half an hour, then drain, saving for later 1 cup of the chile soaking water.
2. Put the chiles, garlic, jam, honey, vinegar, and salt in a blender. Put in the 1 cup reserved chile soaking water and pulse on high speed to blend for a minute. Move the jam to an airtight container and place in your fridge for maximum half a year.

Ancho Chile Sauce V2

This delicious spicy sauce goes with pretty much everything!

Yield: Approximately 2½ Cups

Ingredients:

- ¼ cup chopped onion
- ¼ cup raisins
- ½ teaspoon ground cumin
- 1 tablespoon vegetable oil
- 1 teaspoon dried or 1 tablespoon fresh oregano
- 2 ancho chiles
- 2 cups chicken broth
- 2 tomatoes, chopped

Directions:

1. Take the stems and seeds of the chiles and soak them in hot water for about ten minutes. Take the chiles and cut them.
2. In a big deep cooking pan, heat the vegetable oil using high heat. Put in the chiles and onion and sauté until tender, about five minutes. Put in the broth, tomatoes, raisins, oregano, and cumin and bring to its boiling point. Lower the heat and allow to simmer until the tomatoes are cooked, another ten minutes.

3. Cautiously pour all of the contents into a food processor or blender and process until the desired smoothness is achieved. Serve instantly, or store in a firmly sealed container in your fridge for maximum one week.

Arizona-Style Salsa

This salsa from the Mexican state of Sonora goes great with chips or antojitos!

Yield: About 1 cup

Ingredients:

- 1 (8-12 ounce) tomato, roasted
- 1 dried Anaheim (California) chile, or a mild, dried New Mexico chile, toasted and rehydrated
- 1/2 tablespoon rice vinegar
- 1/2 teaspoon salt
- 3 chiles de árbol, toasted and rehydrated

Directions:

1. Throw all ingredients into your blender and pulse for a couple of minutes, or until the desired smoothness is achieved.

Banana Salsa

Tastes great as an appetizer on its own, or as a dip with chips!

Yield: 2 Cups

Ingredients:

- ¼ cup chopped fresh cilantro, leaves and tender stems
- ½ teaspoon salt
- 1 red bell pepper, stemmed and seeded
- 1 serrano chile, thoroughly minced, including the seeds
- 1 whole green onion, minced
- 2 firm yellow skinned bananas

- 2 tablespoons light brown sugar
- 2 tablespoons minced fresh ginger
- 3 tablespoons freshly squeezed lime juice

Directions:

1. Peel the bananas and cut along the length into long strips. Cut across the strips so that the banana is in ½-inch cubes. Mince the red bell pepper and green onion.
2. Mix the bananas with the bell pepper, green onion, cilantro, ginger, chile, lime juice, brown sugar, and salt in a medium container. Press plastic wrap directly across the surface. The salsa can be made twelve hours before serving and placed in the fridge in an airtight container. Allow to reach room temperature and stir before you serve.

BANANA SALSA VARIATION 1: MANGO SALSA

Substitute the bananas with 3 perfectly ripe mangoes. Remove the skin of the mangoes. Cut off the flesh in big pieces, and then cut coarsely to yield 2 to 3 cups. Mix the mango with the rest of the ingredients as directed in the "Banana Salsa" recipe.

BANANA SALSA VARIATION 2: PAPAYA SALSA

Substitute the bananas with 2 firm, underripe Hawaiian papayas or a 3-inch-thick slice of Mexican papaya. Peel, seed, and cut the fruit to yield 2 to 3 cups. Mix the papaya with the rest of the ingredients as directed in the "Banana Salsa" recipe.

BANANA SALSA VARIATION 3: TROPICAL SALSA

Replace the bananas with a mix of chopped fruits— avocado, papaya or mango, strawberries, and kiwi—to yield 2 to 3 cups. Mix the mixed fruit with the rest of the ingredients as directed in the "Banana Salsa" recipe.

BANANA SALSA VARIATION 4: PINEAPPLE SALSA

Replace the bananas with 2 to 3 cups chopped fresh pineapple. Omit the lime juice. Mix the pineapple with the rest of the ingredients as directed in the "Banana Salsa" recipe.

Cebollas En Escabeche (PICKLED ONIONS)

Yield: About 2 cups

An insanely delicious garnish and relish from Yucatán state, this recipe goes great with tacos, seafood, meats, and poultry.

Ingredients:

- 1 (12-ounce) red onion, cut into 1/3-inch rings
- 1 bay leaf
- 1 clove garlic, peeled and smashed
- 1 small habanero chile, cut in half (not necessary)
- 1 teaspoon dried leaf oregano
- 1/2 cup rice vinegar
- 1/2 tablespoon extra-virgin olive oil
- 1/4 cup water
- 1/8 teaspoon salt
- 1/8 teaspoon whole dried thyme

Directions:

1. Make the onions. Put all the ingredients apart from the onion in a big deep cooking pan and simmer for about three minutes.
2. Put the onions in a nonreactive container and pour the hot liquid over them.
3. Allow the onions to sit at room temperature for about two hours, stirring occasionally. Place in your fridge.

Chile Pequín Salsa

Yield: About 1 cup

Don't put too much of this fiery salsa into your mouth in one go. This salsa goes great with steak, seafood, and pork.

Ingredients:

- 1 big or 2 small cloves garlic, minced
- 1 big tomato (approximately eight ounces)
- 1 tablespoon chile pequín
- 1/2 cup chopped white onion
- 1/2 teaspoon rice vinegar
- 1/2 teaspoon salt
- 1/8 teaspoon ground cloves

Directions:

1. Bring sufficient water to cover the tomato to its boiling point and put in the tomato, onion, and garlic. Simmer for about ten minutes, or until the tomato is fairly tender.
2. Peel the tomato and discard the skin. Put the tomato, onion, and garlic in a food processor, put in the rest of the ingredients, and pulse until puréed. Allow about fifteen minutes for the chiles to rehydrate, and process again before you serve.

Chile-Tomatillo Salsa

Poblano chile and tomatillo is an insane combination!

Yield: 2½ Cups

Ingredients:

- ¼ cup packed fresh cilantro, leaves and tender stems
- ½ teaspoon salt
- 1 poblano chile
- 1 serrano chile
- 3 cloves garlic, peeled
- 8 small green tomatillos, husks removed

Directions:

1. In a dry, heavy frying pan on moderate to high heat, mildly char the tomatillos. Char the poblano and rub off the blackened skin. Then discard the seeds and stem. Chop the tomatillos into quarters. In the same dry, heavy frying pan using high heat, mildly

brown the garlic and serrano chile. Chop the garlic and chiles a few times so they are in slightly smaller pieces.

2. Put the poblano chile, tomatillos, garlic, serranogarlic mixture (including the seeds), cilantro, and salt in a blender. Blend until the desired smoothness is achieved. If you don't like this method, if you have the time, finely cut the salsa ingredients by hand for a more interesting texture. Taste and calibrate the seasonings for salt. This can be stored for three days refrigerated in an airtight container. Allow to reach room temperature before you serve.

Chimichurri Sauce

Yield: About 3/4 cup

An Argentinian sauce with a Mexican twist! This sauce goes great with meat dishes!

Ingredients:

- 1 tablespoon dried leaf oregano
- 2 teaspoons chile flakes
- 4 teaspoons red wine vinegar
- 6 cloves garlic, very finely chopped or put through a garlic press
- 1/2 cup extra-virgin olive oil
- 1/2 teaspoon salt
- 1/4 cup finely chopped parsley
- 1/4 teaspoon freshly ground black pepper

Directions:

1. Put the olive oil, garlic, oregano, and chile flakes into a small microwave-safe dish and microwave to approximately 135°-150°F on an instant-read thermometer, approximately half a minute on High. You want to heat the garlic just sufficient to release its flavour, but not so much that it actually cooks or makes the oil turn cloudy. Let the oil cool to room temperature.
2. Mix in the vinegar, salt, pepper, and parsley and let the flavours meld for a couple of hours before you serve.

Cranberry-Jalapeño Jelly

Adjust the amount of jalapeño to adjust the hotness of this fiery recipe to your taste!

Yield: 1-1¼ cups

Ingredients:

- 1 cup fresh cranberries
- 1 small jalapeño, stems and seeds removed, very finely chopped
- 1/2 cup sugar
- 1/2 cup water
- 1/4 cup finely chopped dried apricots
- Grated zest from 1/2 orange
- Pinch of salt

Directions:

1. Cook the water and sugar on low-moderate boil for five minutes.
2. Put in the cranberries, apricots, salt, and jalapeño and cook them on low-moderate simmer for about six minutes, at which time the cranberries should be breaking apart. Put in the orange zest and carry on simmering, stirring, until thick, approximately one minute.

Dog's Snout Salsa

A hot and tangy salsa from Yucatán state!

Yield: About 2 cups

Ingredients:

- 1 habanero chile, stemmed, seeded, veins removed, and very finely chopped
- 1/4 cup finely chopped cilantro
- 1/4 heaping teaspoon salt
- 1-1/3 cups chopped tomatoes
- 2/3 cup finely chopped red onion

- 4 tablespoons sour orange juice, or substitute 2 tablespoons freshly squeezed lime juice and 2 tablespoons freshly squeezed orange juice

Directions:

1. Lightly toss together everything apart from the salt. Let the salsa marinate, stirring intermittently, for a couple of hours at room temperature. Mix in the salt before you serve.

Fresh Tomatillo Salsa

This salsa is a bite of pure freshness, and looks absolutely amazing!

Yield: About 1-1/4 cups. Nutrition information is for 1 tablespoon.

Ingredients:

- 1 heaping teaspoon salt
- 1 medium-sized serrano chile, stem removed, finely chopped
- 3 tablespoons chopped cilantro
- 3 tablespoons chopped white onion
- 3/4 pound fresh tomatillos, husked, rinsed, dried, and cut into quarters

Directions:

1. Put all the ingredients in a blender and pulse just until the sauce is dense and lumpy but not thoroughly puréed.

Guacamole

Yield: 2 to 3 Cups

Easily one of the most popular Mexican recipes in the world, Guacamole is easy to prepare, but also just as easy to screw up. The avocado is the most important ingredient in this recipe, so make sure it is fresh and ripe, and preferably Mexican.

Ingredients:

- ½ teaspoon salt

- 1 serrano chile, minced, including the seeds
- 2 cloves garlic, minced
- 2 tablespoons chopped fresh cilantro, leaves and tender stems (not necessary)
- 2 whole green onions, chopped
- 3 ripe avocados
- Freshly squeezed juice of 2 limes

Directions:

1. Chop the avocados in half and remove the pits. Use a spoon to scoop out the flesh. Then purée the avocados using the tongs of a fork. Mix the avocados with the green onions, garlic, chile, cilantro, lime juice, and salt in a medium container. Taste and calibrate the seasonings for salt, lime juice, and chile.
2. If making this more than an hour in advance, squeeze some lime juice over the surface, then secure the surface using plastic wrap. The guacamole will stay perfectly green for a couple of days stored this way in your fridge.

VARIATION

Decorate using crumbled goat cheese, queso fresco, or crema.

Habanero Salsa

An easy to make salsa from Yucatán packing some serious heat.

Yield: About 3/4 cup

Ingredients:

- 1 teaspoon salt
- 1/2 cup cider vinegar
- 1/2 cup pineapple juice
- 4 cloves garlic, unpeeled
- 5 habanero chiles, seeds and veins removed, roughly chopped

Directions:

1. Put the chiles, vinegar, and pineapple juice in a small deep cooking pan, bring to its boiling point, and simmer, covered, for about twelve minutes. Let the liquid and chiles cool.
2. Roast the garlic. Put the garlic in a small frying pan on moderate heat and cook, flipping frequently, until it is slightly charred on the outside and very tender inside, 8-ten minutes. When the garlic is sufficiently cool to handle, peel and roughly cut it.
3. Pour the chiles and their cooking liquid into a blender, put in the garlic and salt, and blend to a purée, approximately one minute. Allow the sauce to cool and the acids to tone down the chile's heat for two to three hours before you serve. Serve with Yucatecan dishes.

Jalisco-Style Pico De Gallo

Famously enjoyed with fajitas all over the world!

Yield: About 3 cups

Ingredients:

- 2 tablespoons freshly squeezed lime juice
- 1/2 cup peeled, seeded, and chopped cucumber, 1/2-inch pieces
- 1/2 cup mango, chopped into 1/2-inch pieces
- 1/2 cup pineapple, chopped into 1/2-inch pieces
- 1/2 cup orange or tangerine segments, cut into 1/2-inch pieces
- 1/2 cup peeled and finely chopped jícama
- 1/2 cup thinly sliced red onion
- 1 teaspoon pure ancho chile powder, or 1/2 teaspoon powder made from chile de árbol
- 1/8 heaping teaspoon salt

Directions:

1. Make the salsa. Mix everything apart from the salt and chile powder.
2. Mix in the salt and chile powder and place in your fridge for thirty minutes to let the flavours blend before you serve.

Manual Salsa Mexicana

This salsa takes time to make, and only works if you have vine-ripened tomatoes on hand.

Yield: 4½ Cups

Ingredients:

- ¼ to ½ cup coarsely chopped fresh cilantro, leaves and tender stems
- ½ teaspoon salt
- 1 to 2 serrano chiles, minced, including the seeds
- 2 whole green onions, minced
- 3 cloves garlic, minced
- 4 cups chopped vine-ripened tomatoes, including skins and seeds

Directions:

1. In a large container, mix the chopped tomatoes with the cilantro, green onions, chiles, garlic, and salt.
2. Taste and calibrate the seasonings, especially for salt and chile flavour. This can be made three days ahead and placed in the fridge in an airtight container.
3. Allow to reach room temperature before you serve.

Mexican Chile Sauce

This sauce tastes insane with grilled meat!

Yield: 3 Cups

Ingredients:

- ¼ cup lightly packed light brown sugar
- ½ teaspoon ground cumin
- ½ teaspoon salt
- 1 serrano chile
- 1 teaspoon dried oregano, or 2 teaspoons minced fresh oregano, preferably Mexican
- 1½ ounces guajillo chiles, approximately 6
- 2 big vine-ripened tomatoes, 12 to 16 ounces

- 4 cloves garlic, peeled

Directions:

1. Chop the stem ends off the guajillo chiles and shake out the seeds. Put the guajillos in a container and cover with boiling water (put a small plate on top of the chiles to immerse them). Soak for half an hour, then drain, saving for later 1 cup of the chile soaking water.
2. Chop the stems off the tomatoes and slice them in half horizontally. Put a dry cast-iron frying pan on moderate to high heat. When hot, mildly brown the garlic, tomatoes, and serrano chile, five minutes. Discard the tomato skins.
3. In a blender, put in the guajillo chiles, garlic, tomato, serrano, brown sugar, cumin, oregano, salt, and the 1 cup reserved chile water. Blend until liquefied. Taste and calibrate the seasonings. This can be stored safely in a fridge for about ninety days stored in an airtight container.

Pasilla Chile Salsa

This salsa goes great with seafood and grilled meat!

Yield: About 2 cups. Nutrition information is for 1 tablespoon.

Ingredients:

- 1 teaspoon canned chipotle chile, or to taste
- 2 teaspoons extra-virgin olive oil, or cooking spray to coat the garlic
- 2 very big pasilla chiles, or 2½ medium to big ones, toasted and rehydrated
- 3 cloves garlic, unpeeled
- 2/3 cup minced white onion
- 1/4 teaspoon dried leaf oregano
- 1-1/4 pounds tomatoes, roasted (about 2 big or 3 medium)
- 3/4 teaspoon salt

Directions:

1. Preheat the oven to 350°F.
2. Brush or spray garlic with some of the olive oil, wrap in foil, and bake until soft, about forty minutes. Peel and reserve the garlic.

3. Combine the ingredients. Put the rehydrated pasilla chiles, the chipotle chile, one of the tomatoes, the oregano, garlic, and salt in a food processor and pulse until a smooth purée is achieved. Put in the rest of the tomato and pulse until it is blended with the other ingredients, but leave the salsa with some texture.
4. Put the rest of the olive oil in a frying pan on moderate heat, put in the onions, and sauté until they are just starting to become tender. Mix the onions with the rest of the salsa in a container.

Pico De Gallo Salsa

Pico de gallo translates to "beak of the rooster." This recipe is a Mexican favourite and has hundreds of versions. This is probably the most popular version out there. Serve it as a side with tortilla chips!

Yield: 4 Cups

Ingredients:

- ½ medium onion
- 1 jalapeño pepper
- 1 packed cup coarsely chopped fresh cilantro, stems cut
- 1 teaspoon freshly ground black pepper
- 1 teaspoon ground cumin
- 1 teaspoon salt
- 2 garlic cloves
- 2 limes
- 2 pounds Roma or vine-ripened tomatoes

Directions:

1. Cut the tomatoes into little cubes and put them into a large container.
2. Use a food processor to pulse the onion until it is finely chopped (make sure you don't over-process or it'll become gooey). Scrape it into the container with the tomatoes.
3. In the same processor, put in the cilantro and pulse until chopped. Put in to the container with the tomato and onion.

4. Chop the jalapeño in half, along the length, discarding the stem (discard the seeds and veins if you think it'll be too spicy). Pulse the jalapeño and garlic using your processor until thoroughly minced. Scrape into the container with the other vegetables.
5. Chop the limes in half and squeeze their juices into the tomato mixture. Put in the cumin, black pepper, and salt, adding a little extra salt to your taste. Toss together before you serve.

Ranch-Style Salsa (SALSA RANCHERA)

Salsa Ranchera has multiple versions floating around in the world. This version doesn't have an overly strong flavour, and goes great with eggs and meat.

Yield: About 2 cups

Ingredients:

- 1 big guajillo chile, stemmed, seeded, toasted, and rehydrated, 1/2 cup of the soaking water reserved
- 1 clove garlic, minced
- 1 pound tomatoes (about 2 medium to large), roasted
- 1 tablespoon extra-virgin olive oil
- 1/2 teaspoon salt
- 1½ cups chopped white onion

Directions:

1. Combine the tomatoes and chiles. Put the chiles, tomatoes, and the 1/2 cup chile soaking water in a blender and purée thoroughly, a couple of minutes.
2. Heat a big deep cooking pan on moderate heat, put in the oil and onions, and sauté them until they are tender but not browned, about five minutes. Put in the garlic and cook one more minute.
3. Pour the tomatoes and chiles into the deep cooking pan with the onion and garlic and mix in the salt. Bring to a simmer and cook for five to ten minutes, or until the sauce holds together. If it becomes too thick, put in some more water.

Red Enchilada Sauce (SALSA ROJA)

You will never buy enchilada sauce from a store after you make your own!

Yield: 2½ Cups

Ingredients:

- ¼ cup chili powder
- ¼ teaspoon ground cinnamon
- ¼ teaspoon sugar
- ½ teaspoon salt
- 1 tablespoon flour
- 1 teaspoon dried or 1 tablespoon chopped fresh oregano
- 1 teaspoon ground cumin
- 2 cups chicken broth
- 3 tablespoons garlic powder
- 3 tablespoons vegetable oil
- Two 5-ounce cans tomato sauce

Directions:

1. Heat the vegetable oil in a moderate-sized deep cooking pan on moderate heat. Put in the flour and stir, smoothing it out to make a roux, and cook for about one minute. Put in the chili powder and cook for an additional half a minute. Put in the broth, tomato sauce, garlic powder, oregano, cumin, salt, sugar, and cinnamon and stir until blended.
2. Raise the heat and bring to its boiling point, then decrease the heat to moderate and cook until the flavours deepen, an additional fifteen minutes.
3. Turn off the heat and use in your favorite enchilada recipe, pour over burritos to make them "wet," or to make tamales. If you're not using the sauce immediately, store it in a glass jar with a firmly fitting lid in your fridge for maximum one week.

TOMATE VERDE *(SALSA VERDE)*

One of the most popular tomato-bases salsa out there!

Yield: 3 Cups

Ingredients:

- 1 bunch fresh cilantro, stems cut
- 1 jalapeño, stemmed and halved
- 1 small (or ½ medium) onion, quartered
- 1 teaspoon salt
- 1½ pounds (12 to 15) tomatillos, husked and washed
- 4 or 5 garlic cloves

Directions:

1. Preheat your broiler.
2. Chop the tomatillos in half and place them, cut-sides down, on a foil-lined baking sheet. Put under a broiler until the skins are fairly blackened on top, about eight to ten minutes.
3. Cautiously pierce the tomatillos using a fork and put them in a food processor or blender. Put in the onion and garlic and pulse until blended. Put in the cilantro, jalapeño, and salt and pulse until puréed.
4. Go ahead; taste it before you serve and add a little extra salt, if required.

Roasted-Tomato and Pumpkin Seed Salsa

A simple and delicious salsa that tastes insane with grilled meat!

Yield: About 2½ cups

Ingredients:

- 1 medium to big serrano chile
- 1 teaspoon salt, or to taste
- 1/2 cup toasted and ground pumpkin seeds (pepitas) (from 2/3 cup raw hulled pumpkin seeds)
- 1/2-inch slice of white onion
- 2 cloves garlic, peeled
- 3 or 4 tomatoes, for a total of about 1½ pounds

Directions:

1. Put the tomatoes and chile on a baking sheet as close to your broiler as possible and broil until the tomatoes have become tender and barely start to char, about ten to

fifteen minutes. Put in the onion and garlic and carry on cooking until the onion is slightly charred and the garlic is soft, an additional five to ten minutes. Ensure that the tomatoes are thoroughly cooked and fairly tender. Take the vegetables out of the oven, put them in a food processor, put in the salt, and pulse until the sauce is smooth.

2. As the vegetables broil, heat a nonstick frying pan on moderate heat and toast the pumpkin seeds, stirring regularly, until most of them have popped. Don't allow them to scorch. Grind the toasted seeds to a powder in a spice or coffee grinder. Put in 1/2 cup of the ground seeds and the salt to the processor and pulse with the other ingredients until everything is well blended.

Romesco Sauce

Insanely nutritious and delicious, this sauce goes with pretty much everything.

Yield: About 1 cup

Ingredients:

- 1 cup cherry tomatoes
- 1 small to moderate canned chipotle chile, seeded and chopped
- 1 tablespoon sherry vinegar (or freshly squeezed lime or lemon juice)
- 1/2 heaping teaspoon salt
- 1/2 teaspoon sweet smoked Spanish paprika
- 1/3 cup extra-virgin olive oil
- 2 tablespoons minced parsley
- 2 tablespoons roasted and skinned whole almonds
- 3 garlic cloves, peeled and cut in half along the length

Directions:

1. Dry roast the tomatoes, nuts, and garlic. Heat an ungreased frying pan on moderate to high heat until it is very hot. Put the tomatoes, almonds, and garlic in the frying pan and cook, stirring continuously, until the tomatoes are blackened and just beginning to deflate. It is okay if the nuts and garlic seem burned; that just augments the flavour. Do make sure that the garlic is thoroughly cooked.

2. Finish the sauce. Put the tomatoes, almonds, and garlic in a food processor, put in the rest of the ingredients, and process in pulses until the sauce is thick but still has some texture.

Salsa De Chile (Chile Sauce)

One of the most versatile salsa recipes in this book, chile sauce will go with pretty much everything.

Yield: About 2½ cups

Ingredients:

- 1 tablespoon extra-virgin olive oil
- 1 teaspoon dried leaf oregano
- 1 teaspoon rice vinegar
- 2 bay leaves
- 3/4 teaspoon salt, or to taste
- 4 cloves garlic, chopped
- 8 mild to moderate-hot New Mexico dried red chiles, 12 guajillo chiles, or 4 medium-sized ancho chiles, stemmed, seeded, toasted, and rehydrated, 4 cups soaking water reserved

Directions:

1. Combine the sauce ingredients. Put the chiles in a blender, put in the garlic, oregano, and 2 cups of the reserved chile soaking water, and blend for a couple of minutes, or until comprehensively puréed. Put in the rest of the 2 cups chile soaking water and blend one more minute.
2. Cook the sauce. Heat a big deep cooking pan on moderate heat, put in the olive oil, and mix in the blended sauce ingredients. Put in the vinegar and bay leaves, bring to its boiling point, and cook on a moderate simmer until the sauce is barely sufficiently thick to coat the back of a spoon, or the consistency of a very thin milkshake, about fifteen minutes. If the sauce becomes too thick, put in some more water. If it is too thin, cook it a bit longer. Put in the salt and simmer one more minute.

Salsa De Molcajete

A traditional Mexican salsa. Salsa doesn't get more authentic than this!

Yield: About 1 cup

Ingredients:

- 1 chile de árbol, toasted in an oil-filmed frying pan until crisp but not burned
- 1 small jalapeño chile, roasted and peeled
- 1 tomato, broiled and peeled
- 1 very small pasilla chile, toasted in an oil-filmed frying pan until crisp but not burned
- 2 chiles pequín, toasted in an oil-filmed frying pan until crisp but not burned
- 2 cloves garlic
- 2 tablespoons finely chopped white onion
- 2 teaspoons toasted sesame seeds
- 2/3 of 1 small ancho chile, toasted in an oil-filmed frying pan until crisp but not burned
- 3/4 teaspoon salt
- Water as needed to get the consistency you want

Directions:

1. Put in the salt to the molcajete.
2. Put in the ingredients one at a time, grinding each one to the texture you want before you put in the next.

Salsa Fresca

A great all-round salsa!

Yield: About 1 cup

Ingredients:

- 1/2 teaspoon salt
- 1/4-ounce serrano chile (about 1-1/4 inches) long, cut into 1/3-inch pieces
- 1/4 cup loosely packed, roughly chopped cilantro
- 1/4 cup very finely chopped white onion

- 1/4 cup water (not necessary)
- 4 ounces tomatillos, husked, rinsed, dried, and cut into 3/4-inch pieces
- 6 ounces Roma tomatoes, cut into 3/4-inch pieces

Directions:

1. If you have a meat grinder, grind together into a container the tomatillos, tomatoes, chile, and cilantro.
2. Mix in the onion and salt. If you are using a food processor, put the tomatillos, tomatoes, chile, and cilantro into the work container, put in 1/4 cup water, and pulse until everything is finely chopped (as if it had been put through a meat grinder).
3. Mix in the onions and salt.

Smoky Chipotle Salsa (SALSA CON CHIPOTLE)

This moderately spicy salsa tastes great with a side of chips.

Yield: Approximately 5 Cups

Ingredients:

- ½ teaspoon freshly ground black pepper
- 1 onion, chopped
- 12 garlic cloves, sliced
- 2 tablespoons freshly squeezed lime juice
- 2 tablespoons olive oil
- 2 tablespoons salt
- 3 cups chipotle peppers in adobo sauce
- 8 Roma tomatoes, coarsely chopped

Directions:

1. Heat the olive oil in a big frying pan using high heat. Put in the garlic and onion and allow them to brown, stirring only a couple of times (about 2 minutes). Put in the chipotle with adobo sauce and the tomatoes and cook for another three to four minutes until thoroughly heated.
2. Cautiously pour the mixture into a blender or food processor. Put in the salt, lime juice, and black pepper and blend until the desired smoothness is achieved.

3. Serve instantly or save it in your fridge for a few days.

Tangerine-Serrano Salsa

Are tangerines in season? This is the salsa to try!

Yield: 3 to 4 Cups

Ingredients:

- ¼ cup chopped fresh cilantro, leaves and tender stems
- ¼ cup freshly squeezed lime juice
- ¼ cup lightly packed light brown sugar
- ½ cup chopped red onion
- ½ teaspoon salt
- 1 serrano chile, minced, including the seeds
- 1 tablespoon finely grated tangerine zest
- 2 tablespoons minced fresh ginger
- 3 cloves garlic, minced
- 4 tangerines, peeled, segments separated and chopped

Directions:

1. Mix the tangerine zest and segments, onion, cilantro, chile, garlic, ginger, lime juice, brown sugar, and salt in a medium container.
2. This can be made one day in advance and placed in the fridge in an airtight container. Allow to reach room temperature before you serve.

The Ultimate Mojo De Ajo Sauce

Mojo de ajo (garlic sauce) is enjoyed with seafood all over Mexico.

Yield: About 3/4 cup. Nutrition information is for 1 tablespoon.

Ingredients:

- 1½ tablespoons dried cilantro

- 3 chiles de árbol, seeded and coarsely chopped, or substitute a finely chopped canned chipotle chile
- 4 sun-dried tomatoes (not packed in oil), very finely chopped
- 1/2 cup extra-virgin olive oil
- 1/2 tablespoon freshly squeezed lime juice
- 1/2 teaspoon salt
- 1/4 cup minced white onion
- 1/4 heaping teaspoon freshly ground black pepper
- 1/4 cup garlic chopped into 1/8-inch or slightly larger pieces

Directions:

1. Make the sauce. Put the chiles, tomatoes, garlic, onion, salt, oil, and pepper in a small deep cooking pan on moderate to low heat and cook until the oil just starts to bubble. Keep adjusting the heat so that the mixture cooks at the barest simmer, with just a few bubbles.
2. Cook until the garlic is very tender and just starting to brown, about forty minutes, stirring every five minutes or so. Put in the cilantro and lime juice and simmer an additional ten minutes, or until the garlic just starts to take on a golden hue.

Watermelon Relish

A refreshing, crunchy, and spicy relish!

Yield: 3 Cups

Ingredients:

- ¼ cup freshly squeezed lime juice
- ¼ cup lightly packed light brown sugar
- ½ serrano chile, minced, including the seeds
- ½ teaspoon salt
- 2 tablespoons chopped fresh cilantro, leaves and tender stems
- 2 tablespoons chopped fresh mint leaves
- 2 tablespoons minced fresh ginger
- 3 pounds seedless red watermelon

Directions:

1. Remove all the rind from the melon and chop the melon into ½-inch cubes. You should have about 6 cups. Put 4 cups of the watermelon in a blender. Put in the ginger, chile, lime juice, brown sugar, and salt. liquefied. Move to a big deep cooking pan. Bring to a rapid boil on moderate to high heat and boil until reduced to 1 cup. Move to a container and let cool to room temperature.
2. Mix in the rest of the 2 cups chopped watermelon, the cilantro, and mint. This can be made 2 days ahead and placed in the fridge in an airtight container. Serve at room temperature.

Yucatán-Style Tomato Salsa

A tomato salsa spiced up with habanero chiles!

Yield: About 1-1/4 cups

Ingredients:

- 1 habanero chile, cut in half
- 1 pound (about 2 medium-sized) tomatoes
- 1/2 cup chopped white onion
- 1/8 heaping teaspoon salt
- 1½ tablespoons extra-virgin olive oil
- 2½ cups water

Directions:

1. Bring the water to its boiling point and put in the tomatoes and chiles. Simmer for about four minutes, or until the tomatoes are starting to become tender. Take the tomatoes and chiles from the pan; let the tomatoes cool down a little then remove and discard their skins and put the tomatoes in a food processor with the steel blade. Reserve the cooking liquid for a future cook. Reserve the chiles separately.
2. Cook the onions and purée the sauce. Heat a frying pan on moderate heat, put in 1/2 tablespoon of the oil and the onions, and sauté, stirring regularly, until the onions barely start to turn golden. Put the onions in the food processor with the tomatoes

and process for a minute. Put the sauce through a strainer or food mill to remove the seeds.

3. Cook the tomato sauce. Heat a small deep cooking pan on moderate heat, put in the rest of the tablespoon oil, the sauce, and the salt. If you think the sauce needs more heat, put in back the habanero halves. Bring the sauce to its boiling point and simmer until it is thick enoigh to hold its shape, about three minutes. If you used the chiles, remove and discard them.

Three Zigzag Sauces

Here are three amazing Mexican sauces that are more versatile than a swiss knife. These are commonly used to garnish dishes, topping them in a zig-zag manner. What you do with these is completely up to you!

Chipotle Chile Zigzag Sauce

Yield: ¾ Cup

Ingredients:

- ¼ teaspoon salt
- ½ cup crema, mayonnaise, or sour cream
- 1 chipotle chile in adobo sauce, minced
- 1 clove garlic, minced
- 1 tablespoon freshly squeezed lime juice
- 2 teaspoons finely grated lime zest

Directions:

1. Mix all of the ingredients together in a small container or an electric mini-chop.
2. Store in your fridge in an airtight container and use within one week.

Cilantro Zigzag Sauce

Yield: ¾ Cup

Ingredients:

- ¼ teaspoon salt
- ½ cup crema, mayonnaise, or sour cream
- ½ cup fresh cilantro, leaves and tender stems
- 1 tablespoon freshly squeezed lime juice
- 1 tablespoon thoroughly minced fresh ginger

Directions:

1. Mix all of the ingredients together in a small container or an electric mini-chop.
2. Store in your fridge in an airtight container and use within one week.

Orange-Ginger Zigzag Sauce

Yield: 1 Cup

Ingredients:

- ½ cup crema, mayonnaise, or sour cream
- ½ serrano chile, minced, including the seeds
- ½ teaspoon finely grated orange zest
- ½ teaspoon salt
- 1 clove garlic, minced
- 1 tablespoon freshly squeezed lime juice
- 1 tablespoon Grand Marnier
- 2 tablespoons chopped fresh mint leaves or cilantro leaves and tender stems
- 2 tablespoons minced fresh ginger
- 2 teaspoons Worcestershire sauce

Directions:

1. Mix all of the ingredients together in a small container or an electric mini-chop.
2. Store in your fridge in an airtight container and use within one week.

OTHER MEXICAN SEASONINGS

All-Purpose Marinade for Chicken, Pork, and Seafood

Rub this all over your meat before you cook, and enjoy the ultimate Mexican flavour!

Yield: ½ Cup

Ingredients:

- ¼ cup extra-virgin olive oil
- ½ teaspoon salt
- 1 tablespoon freshly ground black pepper
- 1 teaspoon ground cinnamon, preferably Mexican
- 1 teaspoon ground coriander or cumin
- 2 teaspoons finely grated lime zest
- 2 teaspoons finely grated orange zest

Directions:

1. Mix the pepper, zests, coriander, cinnamon, and salt in a small container.
2. Rub the spice blend over the surface of the meat or seafood.
3. Next, rub the olive oil over the entire surface as well.
4. Proceed with grilling or roasting, as desired.

Refried Beans

These are a Mexican staple that can be used to give texture and flavour to main course meals.

Yield: 2 Cups

Ingredients:

- ½ teaspoon salt
- 1 cup dried black beans
- 1 medium yellow onion, diced
- 2 cloves garlic, minced
- 3 tablespoons lard

Directions:

1. Spread the beans on a plate and pick through the beans to remove any pebbles. Rinse the beans, then cover with cold water and soak overnight.

2. Drain the beans and put in to a deep cooking pan. Put in 4 cups hot water to the soaked beans. Simmer on moderate heat until tender, approximately 1½ hours. Remove and reserve 2 cups of the cooking water. If you don't like this method, follow the quick-cooking directions on the bean package.

3. In a big frying pan, melt the lard on moderate heat. Put in the onion and cook until the onion becomes golden, approximately ten minutes. Put in the garlic and cook for 1 more minute. Put in the salt and beans. Mash the beans using a fork, adding just sufficient of the reserved cooking water to make the beans smooth. If you don't like this method, put in a food processor and process until the desired smoothness is achieved. The beans can be made up to four days in advance. Let cool and then place in your fridge in an airtight container.

DRY RUBS

These dry rubs are great on any meat that can be grilled or oven-roasted. Each rub makes about 6 tablespoons, sufficient to season 8 of your favorite steaks, or 8 chicken breasts, or 3 pounds of fish. Just rub the dry rub into the surface of the meat or seafood, then rub the meat with extra-virgin olive oil. As another option, after rubbing the meat with the dry rub, we like to rub the meat with Chinese mushroom soy sauce or Chinese dark soy sauce. This is not authentic Mexican, but it is delicious! Remember, the rub has to be massaged with vigor into the meat fibers. Then when you brush the meat with a marinade or olive oil before cooking, the rub will not dislodge from the meat during grilling.

ANCHO DRY RUB

Yield: Approximately 6 TABLESPOONS

Ingredients:

- ¼ cup lightly packed light brown sugar
- 1 (2-inch) cinnamon stick, preferably Mexican
- 1 tablespoon ancho or chipotle chile powder
- 1 tablespoon coriander seeds

Directions:

1. Put all of the ingredients in a clean electric coffee grinder or spice grinder. Grind into a fine powder.
2. Move to an empty glass spice jar, label, and store in your spice rack for maximum half a year.

CARAWAY DRY RUB

Yield: Approximately 6 TABLESPOONS

Ingredients:

- 1 (1-inch) cinnamon stick, preferably Mexican
- 1 tablespoon caraway seeds
- 1 tablespoon coriander seeds
- 1 tablespoon crushed red pepper
- 1 tablespoon cumin seeds
- 1 tablespoon salt
- 1 teaspoon whole cloves

Directions:

1. Put all of the ingredients in a clean electric coffee grinder or spice grinder. Grind into a fine powder.
2. Move to an empty glass spice jar, label, and store in your spice rack for maximum half a year.

ESPRESSO DRY RUB

Yield: Approximately 6 TABLESPOONS

Ingredients:

- 1 tablespoon coriander seeds
- 1 tablespoon crushed red pepper
- 1 tablespoon curry powder

- 1 tablespoon espresso powder
- 1 tablespoon rainbow peppercorn mix
- 1 tablespoon salt

Directions:

1. Put all of the ingredients in a clean electric coffee grinder or spice grinder. Grind into a fine powder.
2. Move to an empty glass spice jar, label, and store in your spice rack for maximum half a year.

APPETIZERS

Mexicans love appetizers to nibble on, simply because there are so many awesome appetizers available to them to nibble on.

FLAMED CHEESE (QUESO FLAMEADO)

Yield: Servings 6

This robust mexican version of a cheese fondue is best served with picante tomato sauce and a stack of flour tortillas.

Ingredients:

- 1½ dozen flour tortillas
- 12 ounces (340 g) chihuahua cheese or muenster, thinly cut
- 6 ounces (180 g) mexican chorizos, skinned, crumbled, and fried (not necessary)

Directions:

1. Put the cheese in two layers in a shallow, flameproof dish.
2. Melt the cheese either on top of the stove or in your oven, drizzling the chorizo over it.
3. Heat the tortillas and serve instantly, with the sauce on the side.

FRIED PUMPKIN (CALABAZA FRITA)

Yield: about 5 cups (1.25 l)

A delicious recipe for all pumpkin lovers out there!

Ingredients:

- ⅓ to ½ cup (85 to 125 ml) olive oil (not extra virgin)
- 1 green pepper, seeded and finely chopped (1 scant cup/235 ml)
- 1 small white onion, finely chopped (½ cup/125 ml)
- 12 ounces (340 g) tomatoes, finely chopped (about 2 cups/500 ml)

- 2 pounds (900 g) unpeeled pumpkin, cut into little pieces
- Salt to taste

To serve

- ⅓ cup (85 ml) finely grated queso seco de chiapas or añejo or romano cheese

Directions:

1. Place the pumpkin pieces into a big pot, cover with water, bring to its boiling point, reduce the heat, and cook, covered, until still slightly firm, approximately twenty minutes depending on the kind of pumpkin. Drain, peel, and slice into ½-inch (1.5-cm) cubes. Set aside.
2. Heat the oil in a deep flameproof casserole; put in the onion, pepper, and tomatoes with salt to taste and cook on moderate heat, stirring occasionally to prevent sticking, until well seasoned and still slightly juicy—approximately eight minutes.
3. Put in the cubed pumpkin and mix thoroughly. Carry on cooking over low heat while stirring occasionally to prevent sticking, putting in a little water if mixture is too dry, for approximately fifteen minutes. Examine for salt, then set aside to season for minimum 30 minutes.
4. Serve sprinkled with the cheese and accompanied by tostadas.

7 LAYER DIP

Yield: Servings 8 to 10

Although not a traditional Mexican dish, this recipe is loaded with Mexican ingredients, and make a great appetizer!

Ingredients:

- ¾ teaspoon chili powder
- 1 (fifteen ounce) can black beans, drained but not washed
- 1 pound pepper Jack cheese, shredded (4 cups)
- 1 recipe (3 cups) Chunky Guacamole
- 1½ cups sour cream
- 2 garlic cloves, minced

- 2 jalapeño chiles, stemmed, seeded, and minced
- 2 tablespoons plus 2 teaspoons lime juice (2 limes)
- 3 tablespoons minced fresh cilantro
- 4 big tomatoes, cored, seeded, and chopped fine
- 6 scallions (2 minced; 4, green parts only, cut thin)
- Salt

Directions:

1. Mix tomatoes, minced scallions, jala peños, cilantro, 2 tablespoons lime juice, and ⅛ teaspoon salt in container. Allow to sit until tomatoes start to tenderize, approximately 30 minutes. Drain mixture, discard liquid, and return to container.
2. In the meantime, pulse beans, garlic, chili powder, remaining 2 teaspoons lime juice, and ⅛ teaspoon salt in food processor to crude paste, approximately fifteen pulses. Spread bean mixture uniformly into 8 inch square baking dish or 1 quart glass container.
3. In clean, dry workbowl, pulse 2½ cups pepper Jack and sour cream until the desired smoothness is achieved, approximately fifteen pulses. Spread sour cream mixture uniformly over bean layer. Top uniformly with remaining 1½ cups pepper Jack, followed by guacamole and, finally, drained tomato mixture. (Immerse can be placed in your fridge for maximum one day; bring to room temperature before you serve.) Drizzle with cut scallion greens before you serve.

AGUAS FRESCAS

Yield: 8 cups; serves 8 to 10

These delicious non-alcoholic beverages are usually made by blending fruits, grains, seeds, or flowers with sugar and water.

HIBISCUS AGUA FRESCA

Keep the flowers placed in the fridge in an airtight container.

Ingredients:

- 1 cup sugar
- 2 cups dried hibiscus flowers, washed

- 8 cups water
- Pinch salt

Directions:

1. Bring 4 cups water to boil in medium deep cooking pan. Off heat, mix in hibiscus flowers, cover, and allow to steep for an hour. Strain mixture into 2 quart pitcher; discard solids.
2. Mix in sugar and salt until blended, then mix in remaining 4 cups water.
3. Place in your fridge until completely chilled, approximately 2 hours. Serve over ice. (Agua Fresca can be placed in your fridge for maximum 5 days; stir to remix before you serve.)

WATERMELON LIME AGUA FRESCA

If you can't find seedless watermelon, remove as many seeds as you can before processing.

Ingredients:

- ⅛ teaspoon salt
- ⅓ cup lime juice (3 limes), plus extra as required
- 2 cups water
- 2 tablespoons agave nectar or honey, as required
- 8 cups seedless watermelon, cut into an inch pieces
- Mint leaves (not necessary)

Directions:

1. Working in 2 batches, process watermelon and water in blender until the desired smoothness is achieved, approximately half a minute.
2. Strain mixture through fine mesh strainer into 2 quart pitcher; discard solids. Mix in lime juice, agave, and salt into watermelon mixture. Mix in extra lime juice and agave to taste.
3. Serve over ice with mint, if using. (Agua Fresca can be placed in your fridge for maximum 5 days; stir to remix before you serve.)

BEAN AND BEEF TAQUITOS

Yield: Servings four to 6

These large tortillas taste absolutely amazing with Avocado Sauce!

Ingredients:

- ½ cup water
- 1 (8 ounce) can tomato sauce
- 1 big egg, lightly beaten
- 1 cup canned pinto beans, washed
- 1 cup plus 4 teaspoons vegetable oil
- 1 onion, halved and cut thin
- 1 teaspoon chili powder
- 1 teaspoon ground cumin
- 12 (6 inch) corn tortillas
- 2 jalapeño chiles, stemmed, seeded, and minced
- 3 garlic cloves, minced
- 3 tablespoons minced fresh cilantro
- 8 ounces 90 percent lean ground beef
- Salt and pepper

Directions:

1. Heat 1 teaspoon oil in 12 inch nonstick frying pan over moderate high heat until just smoking. Put in ground beef and cook, breaking up meat with wooden spoon, until no longer pink, approximately five minutes. Drain beef in colander. In separate container, purée beans to paste with potato masher.
2. Heat 1 tablespoon oil in now empty frying pan on moderate heat until shimmering. Put in onion and cook until tender and mildly browned, five to seven minutes. Mix in jalapeños, garlic, cumin, and chili powder and cook until aromatic, approximately half a minute. Mix in tomato sauce, water, cilantro, ½ teaspoon salt, ½ teaspoon pepper, drained beef, and mashed beans. Cook while stirring frequently, until mixture has thickened and starts to sizzle, approximately ten minutes. Sprinkle with salt and pepper to taste, move to container, and allow to cool for about twenty minutes.
3. Adjust oven rack to middle position and heat oven to 200 degrees. Coat rimmed baking sheet using parchment paper. Set wire rack in second rimmed baking sheet.

Stack 6 tortillas, wrap in damp dish towel, and place on plate; microwave until warm and flexible, approximately one minute.

4. Working with one tortilla at a time, brush edges of top half with beaten egg. Spread 3 tablespoons filling in tight row across lower half of tortilla, fold bottom of tortilla over filling, then pull back on tortilla to tighten around filling. Roll firmly, place seam side down on parchment covered sheet, and cover with second damp towel. Microwave remaining 6 tortillas and repeat with rest of the filling. (Taquitos can be covered with damp towel, wrapped firmly using plastic wrap, and placed in the fridge for maximum one day.)

5. Put in remaining 1 cup oil to clean, dry 12 inch nonstick frying pan and heat over moderate high heat to 350 degrees. Using tongs, place 6 taquitos, seam side down, in oil. Fry taquitos until golden on all sides, approximately eight minutes, turning as required and adjusting heat as required to maintain oil temperature between 300 and 325 degrees. Move to prepared wire rack and place in oven to keep warm while repeating with remaining 6 taquitos and serve.

BLACK BEAN DIP

Yield: about 2 cups

Black beans are a staple in the Mexican kitchen, and can be use to make some insanely delicious and smooth dips, such as this one.

Ingredients:

- ½ onion, chopped
- ½ teaspoon ground cumin
- 1 garlic clove, minced
- 1 tablespoon extra virgin olive oil
- 1 teaspoon minced canned chipotle chile in adobo sauce
- 1 teaspoon minced fresh oregano
- 2 (fifteen ounce) cans black beans, washed
- 2 tablespoons lime juice
- 2 tablespoons minced fresh cilantro
- Salt

Directions:

1. Mix lime juice, garlic, and oregano in small container; set aside for minimum fifteen minutes.
2. Pulse beans, onion, oil, chipotle, cumin, ¼ teaspoon salt, and lime juice mixture in food processor until fully ground, 5 to 10 pulses. Scrape down sides of container with rubber spatula. Continue to pulse until uniform paste forms, approximately 1 minute, scraping down container a couple of times.
3. Move dip to container, cover, and allow it to sit at room temperature for minimum 30 minutes. (Immerse can be placed in your fridge for maximum one day; bring to room temperature before you serve.) Mix in cilantro and sprinkle with salt to taste before you serve.

CHILE-SEASONED PORK (CHILORIO)

Yield: enough to fill twelve tortillas

Ingredients:

*   ⅛ teaspoon cumin seeds, crushed
*   ¼ teaspoon dried mexican oregano
*   ⅓ cup (85 ml) mild vinegar; make up to ½ cup (125 ml) of liquid by putting in water
*   2 pounds (900 g) pork shoulder, without bone but with some fat
*   2 teaspoons salt
*   8 ancho chiles, seeds and veins removed
*   8 garlic cloves, roughly chopped
*   Lard as required
*   Salt to taste

Directions:

1. Chop the meat into 1-inch (2.5-cm) cubes and cook with salt as for <u>carnitas</u>. When the water has vaporized and the fat has rendered out of the meat but the meat hasn't browned—about forty-five minutes—take the meat out of the dish and pound it in the molcajete until it is completely shredded, or shred it finely using two forks.
2. In the meantime, make the sauce. Cover the chiles with hot water. Soak for about ten minutes and drain.

3. Place the diluted vinegar into your blender jar with the garlic and spices and blend as smooth as you can. Slowly put in the chiles and blend after each addition. The sauce must be thick, more like a paste. You will have to keep stopping the blender to release the blades. Only put in more liquid if required to release the blades of the blender.
4. There must be about ¼ cup (65 ml) of fat in the dish in which the meat was cooked; if not, make up to that amount with lard. Put in the meat and blend the chile sauce thoroughly into it. Cook using low heat for fifteen to twenty minutes, or until the meat is well seasoned and the mixture rather dry, scraping the bottom of the dish to prevent sticking.
5. Chilorio will keep for months in your fridge.

CHILIED PEANUTS (CACAHUATES ENCHILADOS)

Yield: approximately 1 cup (250 ml)

These fiery little snacks are commonly enjoyed in Mexican bars with tequila.

Ingredients:

- 1 cup (250 ml) raw shelled peanuts, with or without brown papery skins
- 1 tablespoon vegetable oil
- 1 teaspoon salt, or to taste
- 1 to 1½ teaspoons powdered chile de árbol, or to taste
- 10 small garlic cloves

Directions:

1. In a frying pan just big enough to accommodate the peanuts in a single layer, heat the oil. Put in the peanuts and garlic cloves and fry for approximately 2 minutes, flipping them over continuously.
2. Reduce the heat a little, put in the powdered chile and salt, and cook for one minute or two longer, stirring occasionally to prevent sticking; take care that the chile powder does not burn.
3. Set aside to cool before you serve with drinks.

CHUNKY GUACAMOLE

Yield: about 3 cups

A chunky version of the classic guacamole which goes great with homemade chips!

Ingredients:

- ¼ cup minced fresh cilantro
- ½ teaspoon ground cumin
- 1 jalapeño chile, stemmed, seeded, and minced
- 2 garlic cloves, minced
- 2 tablespoons finely chopped red onion
- 2 tablespoons lime juice
- 3 ripe avocados
- Salt

Directions:

1. Halve 1 avocado, remove pit, and scoop flesh into moderate container. Put in cilantro, jalapeño, onion, lime juice, garlic, ¾ teaspoon salt, and cumin and purée with potato masher (or fork) until mostly smooth.
2. Halve, pit, and dice remaining 2 avocados. Put in cubes to container with mashed avocado mixture and gently purée until mixture is well blended but still coarse. (Guacamole can be placed in your fridge for maximum one day using plastic wrap pressed directly against its surface.) Sprinkle with salt to taste before you serve.

DRIED SHRIMP FRITTERS (BOTANAS DE CAMARÓN SECO)

Yield: about 24 botanas

Ingredients:

- ½ cup (125 ml) finely chopped white onion
- ¾ cup (190 ml) small dried shrimps, cleaned
- 1 cup (250 ml) cold water
- 1 egg white
- 4 ounces (115 g) flour (approximately 1 scant cup)
- 5 serrano chiles, finely chopped

- Salt to taste
- Vegetable oil for frying

Directions:

1. Combine the flour, water, and salt together for a couple of minutes and leave the batter to stand for minimum 1 hour.
2. Wash the shrimps to remove surplus salt. Cover with warm water and leave them to soak for approximately five minutes—no longer.
3. Beat the egg white until stiff and fold it into the batter.
4. Drain the shrimps (if large, cut into 2) and put in them, with the chopped onion and chiles, to the batter.
5. Heat the oil in a frying pan and drop tablespoons of the mixture into it, a few at a time. Fry the botanas until they become golden brown, flipping them over once. Drain them on the paper towelling and serve instantly.

EMPANADAS

Yield: 24 empanadas

These filled pastries are a quite popular all over Mexico.

Ingredients:

- 1 recipe filling, chilled
- 1 tablespoon sugar
- 1¼ cups ice water
- 1½ teaspoons salt
- 12 tablespoons unsalted butter, cut into ½ inch pieces and chilled
- 2 tablespoons extra virgin olive oil
- 3¾ cups (18¾ ounces) all-purpose flour

Directions:

1. Process flour, sugar, and salt together in food processor until blended, approximately 3 seconds. Spread butter pieces over flour mixture and pulse until mixture resembles coarse cornmeal, approximately 16 pulses. Move mixture to big container. Working with ¼ cup ice water at a time, drizzle water over flour mixture and, using stiff rubber

spatula, stir and press dough together until dough sticks together and no small bits of flour remain (you may not need to use all of water).

2. Turn dough onto clean, dry counter and softly push into consistent ball. Split dough into 2 even pieces. Turn each piece of dough onto sheet of plastic wrap, flatten into 6 inch disks, wrap firmly, and place in your fridge for an hour. Allow the chilled dough to sit on counter to tenderize slightly, approximately ten minutes, before rolling.

3. Adjust oven racks to upper middle and lower middle positions and heat oven to 425 degrees. Coat 2 baking sheets using parchment paper. Roll 1 dough disk into 18 inch circle, approximately ⅛ inch thick, on mildly floured counter. Using 4 inch round biscuit cutter, cut out 12 rounds, discarding dough scraps. Put 1 tablespoon filling in center of each dough round. Brush edges of dough with water and fold dough over filling. Push to secure, and crimp edges with tines of fork. Move to 1 prepared sheet, cover, and place in your fridge Repeat with the rest of the dough disk and rest of the filling. (Filled empanadas can be wrapped firmly using plastic wrap and placed in the fridge for maximum one day or frozen for maximum 1 month. After empanadas are completely frozen, approximately eight hours, they can be moved to zipper lock freezer bags to save space in freezer. Move back to parchment paper covered sheet before you bake. Increase baking time by about five minutes.)

4. Brush tops of empanadas with oil and bake until a golden-brown colour is achieved, twenty minutes to half an hour, switching and rotating sheets midway through baking. Allow to cool for five minutes before you serve.

EMPANADA FILLINGS

These fillings should be chilled at the time of using, and hence should be prepared in advance. Each filling makes enough for 24 empanadas.

BEEF AND CHEESE FILLING

Ingredients:

- ⅛ teaspoon cayenne pepper
- ⅛ teaspoon ground cloves
- ½ cup beef broth
- 1 onion, chopped fine
- 1 tablespoon extra virgin olive oil
- 1 tablespoon tomato paste

- 1 teaspoon ground cumin
- 1 teaspoon minced fresh oregano or ¼ teaspoon dried
- 12 ounces 85 percent lean ground beef
- 2 tablespoons minced fresh cilantro
- 3 garlic cloves, minced
- 4 ounces Monterey Jack cheese, shredded (1 cup)
- Salt and pepper

Directions:

1. Heat oil in 12 inch frying pan on moderate heat until just shimmering. Put in onion and cook until tender, approximately five minutes.
2. Mix in garlic, tomato paste, oregano, cumin, clove, and cayenne and cook until aromatic, approximately one minute.
3. Put in ground beef and cook, breaking up meat with wooden spoon, until beef is no longer pink, approximately five minutes.
4. Mix in broth, bring to simmer, and cook until mixture is moist but not wet, approximately eight minutes. Sprinkle with salt and pepper to taste.
5. Move mixture to container, allow to cool slightly, then cover and place in your fridge until completely cool, approximately 1 hour.
6. Mix in Monterey Jack and cilantro. (Filling can be placed in your fridge for maximum 2 days.)

POBLANO AND CORN FILLING

Ingredients:

- ¾ cup frozen corn, thawed
- 1 teaspoon ground coriander
- 1 teaspoon ground cumin
- 1 teaspoon minced fresh oregano or ¼ teaspoon dried
- 12 ounces (2 to 3) poblano chiles, stemmed, seeded, and chopped fine
- 2 garlic cloves, minced
- 2 tablespoons unsalted butter
- 3 scallions, white parts minced, green parts cut thin
- 4 ounces pepper Jack cheese, shredded (1 cup)
- 4 ounces queso fresco, crumbled (1 cup)

- Salt and pepper

Directions:

1. Melt butter in 12 inch frying pan on moderate heat. Put in poblanos and scallion whites and cook until tender and mildly browned, approximately eight minutes.
2. Mix in garlic, oregano, cumin, coriander, and ¼ teaspoon salt and cook until aromatic, approximately half a minute.
3. Mix in corn and sprinkle with salt and pepper to taste. Move mixture to container, allow to cool slightly, then cover and place in your fridge until completely cool, approximately 1 hour.
4. Mix in pepper Jack, queso fresco, and scallion greens. (Filling can be placed in your fridge for maximum 2 days.)

FRESH MARGARITAS

Yield: approximately four cups; serves four to 6

The best Margaritas are those made at home!

CLASSIC MARGARITAS

It is a good idea to steep for full one day, if possible. If you need to serve margaritas instantly, omit the zest and skip the steeping process altogether.

Ingredients:

- ¼ cup superfine sugar
- 1 cup 100 percent agave tequila, if possible reposado
- 1 cup triple sec
- 2 cups crushed ice
- 4 teaspoons finely grated lemon zest plus ½ cup juice (3 lemons)
- 4 teaspoons finely grated lime zest plus ½ cup juice (4 limes)
- Pinch salt

Directions:

1. Mix lime zest and juice, lemon zest and juice, sugar, and salt in 2 cup liquid measuring cup; cover and place in your fridge until flavors meld, minimum 4 hours or maximum one day.
2. Split 1 cup crushed ice among four to 6 margarita or twofold old fashioned glasses. Strain juice mixture into 1 quart pitcher or cocktail shaker; discard solids. Put in tequila, triple sec, and remaining 1 cup crushed ice; stir or shake until meticulously blended and chilled, 20 to 60 seconds. Strain into ice filled glasses and serve instantly.

STRAWBERRY MARGARITAS

The strawberry flavor in this variation makes the zest and steeping process redundant.

Ingredients:

- ¼ cup superfine sugar
- ½ cup Chambord
- ½ cup lemon juice (3 lemons)
- ½ cup lime juice (4 limes)
- 1 cup 100 percent agave tequila, if possible reposado
- 1 cup triple sec
- 2 cups crushed ice
- 5 ounces strawberries, hulled (1 cup)
- Pinch salt

Directions:

1. Process strawberries, lime juice, lemon juice, sugar, and salt in blender until the desired smoothness is achieved, approximately half a minute.
2. Split 1 cup crushed ice among four to 6 margarita or twofold old fashioned glasses. Strain juice mixture into 1 quart pitcher or cocktail shaker; discard solids. Put in tequila, triple sec, Chambord, and remaining 1 cup crushed ice; stir or shake until meticulously blended and chilled, 20 to 60 seconds. Strain into ice filled glasses and serve instantly.

GROUND MEAT MARINATED IN LIME JUICE (CARNE COCIDA EN LIMÓN)

Yield: Servings 4

A great snack to go with drinks!

Ingredients:

- ½ cup (125 ml) fresh lime juice
- 2 tablespoons finely chopped white onion
- 4 ounces (115 g) tomatoes, finely chopped (⅔ cup/165 ml)
- 4 serrano chiles, finely chopped
- 8 ounces (225 g) freshly ground sirloin, absolutely free of fat
- Salt to taste

Directions:

1. Combine the lime juice well into the ground meat and set it aside to "cook" in your fridge for minimum 4 hours in a nonreactive container.
2. Stir in the remaining ingredients and set the meat aside to season for minimum 2 hours more.
3. Serve with crisp tortillas, either toasted or fried.

HOMEMADE BAKED TORTILLA CHIPS

Yield: 2½ ounces; serves 2 to 3

Tortilla chips for when you're looking to cut your oil intake.

Ingredients:

- 5 (6 inch) corn tortillas
- Kosher salt
- Vegetable oil spray

Directions:

1. Adjust oven rack to middle position and heat oven to 350 degrees. Spray both sides of tortillas liberally with oil spray, then cut each tortilla into 6 wedges. Sprinkle with salt and spread into single layer on baking sheet.

2. Bake tortillas, stirring once in a while, until golden and crunchy, fifteen to twenty minutes. Remove chips from oven and allow to cool before you serve. (Cooled chips can be stored at room temperature for maximum four days.)

HOMEMADE FRIED TORTILLA CHIPS

Yield: 4 ounces; serves 4

These super crisp tortilla chips are exactly how they are meant to be enjoyed.

Ingredients:

- 5 cups peanut oil
- 8 (6 inch) corn tortillas
- Kosher salt

Directions:

1. Cut each tortilla into 6 wedges. Coat 2 baking sheets with several layers of paper towels. Heat oil in Dutch oven over moderate high heat to 350 degrees.
2. Put in half of tortillas and fry until golden and crisp around edges, 2 to 4 minutes. Move fried chips to prepared sheet, drizzle lightly with salt, and allow to cool. Repeat with remaining tortillas and serve. (Cooled chips can be stored at room temperature for maximum four days.)

LITTLE PIECES OF BROWNED PORK (CARNITAS)

Yield: Servings 6

This succulent and delicious recipe is loved all over Mexico!

Ingredients:

- 2 teaspoons salt, or to taste
- 3 pounds (1.35 kg) boneless pork shoulder, with fat

Directions:

1. Chop the meat, with the fat, into strips about 2 by ¾ inches (5 by 2 cm). Barely cover the meat with water in a heavy, wide pan. Put in the salt and bring to its boiling point, uncovered. Reduce the heat and allow the meat to carry on cooking briskly until all the liquid has vaporized—by this time it must be thoroughly cooked but not falling apart.

2. Reduce the heat a little and carry on cooking the meat until all the fat has rendered out of it. Keep turning the meat until it is mildly browned all over—total cooking time is approximately 1 hour and ten minutes.

3. Serve instantly for best flavor and texture.

MEXICAN STYLE SHRIMP COCKTAIL

Yield: Servings 6

A cool, stylish, and mildly spicy appetizer for all the shrimp lovers!

Ingredients:

- ¼ cup chopped fresh cilantro, stems reserved
- ½ cup ketchup
- 1 avocado, halved, pitted, and slice into ½ inch pieces
- 1 cucumber, peeled, halved along the length, seeded, and slice into ½ inch pieces
- 1 small red onion, chopped fine
- 1 tablespoon hot sauce
- 1 tablespoon sugar
- 1 teaspoon black peppercorns
- 1½ pounds medium shrimp (41 to 50 per pound), peeled, deveined, and tails removed
- 2 cups Clamato juice
- 2 tablespoons lime juice, plus lime wedges for serving
- 3 tomatoes, cored and slice into ½ inch pieces
- Salt and pepper

Directions:

1. Mix shrimp, 3 cups water, cilantro stems, peppercorns, sugar, and 1 teaspoon salt in big deep cooking pan. Put deep cooking pan on moderate heat and cook, stirring once

in a while, until shrimp are pink and firm to touch, about eight to ten minutes (water must be just bubbling around edge of deep cooking pan and register 165 degrees). Remove deep cooking pan from heat, cover, and let shrimp sit in cooking liquid for a couple of minutes.

2. In the meantime, fill big container with ice water. Drain shrimp into colander, discarding cilantro stems and spices. Instantly move shrimp to ice water to stop cooking and chill meticulously, approximately 3 minutes. Remove shrimp from ice water and meticulously pat dry using paper towels.

3. Mix tomatoes, cucumber, onion, Clamato juice, ketchup, lime juice, and hot sauce together in serving container. Mix in shrimp, cover, and place in your fridge for minimum 30 minutes. (Shrimp cocktail can be placed in your fridge for maximum one day; allow it to sit at room temperature for about ten minutes before you serve.) Mix in avocado and chopped cilantro and sprinkle with salt and pepper to taste and serve.

MOLLETES

Yield: Servings 6

A popular snack common in Mexican restaurants and coffee shops, as well as many street food stalls.

Ingredients:

- ½ cup finely chopped onion
- ½ cup fresh cilantro leaves
- 1 (16 inch) loaf French or Italian bread
- 1 cup refried beans
- 1 garlic clove, minced
- 1 jalapeño chile, stemmed, seeded, and minced
- 2 tablespoons lime juice
- 3 tomatoes, cored and chopped
- 4 tablespoons unsalted butter, softened
- 8 ounces mild cheddar cheese, shredded (2 cups)
- Salt and pepper

Directions:

1. Toss tomatoes with ¼ teaspoon salt in colander and allow to drain for half an hour As tomatoes drain, layer onion, cilantro, jalapeño, and garlic on top. Shake colander to drain off and discard surplus tomato juice. Move mixture to container, mix in lime juice, and sprinkle with salt and pepper to taste.

2. Adjust oven rack to middle position and heat oven to 400 degrees. Coat baking sheet with aluminum foil. Slice bread in half horizontally, then remove all but ¼ inch of interior crumb; reserve removed crumb for future use. Spread butter uniformly inside hollowed bread and place cut side up on prepared sheet. Bake until mildly toasted and browned, approximately eight minutes.

3. Allow the bread to cool slightly, spread refried beans uniformly inside toasted bread and top with cheese. Bake until cheese is just melted, five to seven minutes. Move bread to cutting board, top with salsa, and slice crosswise into 2 inch pieces. Serve warm.

PEPPERED OYSTERS (OSTIONES PIMENTADOS)

Yield: Servings 6 to 8

I know I know, oysters are best enjoyed raw, but hold your judgments until you try this recipe!

Ingredients:

- ½ teaspoon salt, or to taste
- 1 tablespoon fresh lime juice, more if you wish
- 2 mexican bay leaves
- 2 tablespoons olive oil
- 2 teaspoons whole peppercorns
- 4 dozen oysters, shucked, shells and liquid reserved
- 6 garlic cloves

Directions:

1. Heat the liquid from the oysters to the simmering point, then put in the oysters and poach until the edges start to curl, approximately 2 minutes. Drain the oysters, saving for later the broth.

2. Crush the peppercorns with the salt in a molcajete or mortar. Pound in the garlic and progressively put in the lime juice. Last of all, put in about 3 tablespoons of the reserved oyster broth. Mix thoroughly.
3. Heat the olive oil in a frying pan. Put in the bay leaves and the peppercorn mixture and cook using high heat for approximately 3 minutes. Take away the pan from the heat and put in the oysters. Adjust the seasoning, then put in a squeeze of lime juice and slightly more of the oyster liquid if you wish.
4. Serve warm or at room temperature in half shells.

PICKLED PORK RIND (CHICHARRÓN EN ESCABECHE)

Yield: Servings 6

Ingredients:

- ¼ cup (65 ml) vegetable oil
- ½ teaspoon dried mexican oregano
- ½ teaspoon salt, or to taste
- 1 avocado, peeled and cut
- 1½ cups (375 ml) vinegar, mild or diluted with ½ cup (125 ml) water, roughly
- 2 jalapeño chiles en escabeche, cut into strips
- 2 medium purple onions, thickly cut
- 3 sprigs fresh thyme or ⅛ teaspoon dried
- 6 garlic cloves, left whole
- 8 ounces (225 g) chicharron (Fried pork belly), the thinner the better, broken into two-inch (5-cm) squares
- Freshly ground pepper

Directions:

1. Heat the oil and lightly fry the onions and garlic without browning for approximately 2 minutes. Put in the vinegar, oregano, thyme, salt, and pepper to the pan and bring to its boiling point. Put in the chicharrón pieces and chiles and cook over quite high heat while stirring occasionally to prevent sticking, until the chicharrón has tenderized and absorbed almost all the vinegar—about five minutes. Set aside to cool, then serve, topped with slices of avocado.

2. To my mind, chicharrón en escabeche is best served the moment it has cooled off, but it will keep indefinitely in your fridge (although it congeals and must be brought up to room temperature before you serve).

PUMPKIN SEED DIP (SIKIL P'AK)

Yield: about 3 cups

A classic hummus-like dip that is enjoyed in the Yucatán peninsula.

Ingredients:

- ¼ cup extra virgin olive oil
- 1 habanero chile, stemmed, seeded, and chopped
- 1 onion, chopped
- 1 pound tomatoes, cored and halved
- 1½ cups roasted, unhulled pumpkin seeds
- 2 ounces queso fresco, crumbled (½ cup)
- 2 tablespoons chopped fresh cilantro
- 2 tablespoons lime juice
- Salt and pepper

Directions:

1. Adjust 1 oven rack to middle position and second rack 6 inches from broiler element. Heat oven to 400 degrees. Wash pumpkin seeds under warm water and dry meticulously. Spread seeds on rimmed baking sheet, place sheet on lower rack, and toast seeds until a golden-brown colour is achieved, stirring once in a while, twelve to fifteen minutes. Set aside to cool down a little and heat broiler.
2. Coat second rimmed baking sheet with aluminum foil. Toss tomatoes with 1 tablespoon oil and position cut side down on prepared sheet. Put sheet on upper rack and broil until tomatoes are spotty brown, 7 to ten minutes. Move tomatoes to blender and let cool to room temperature.
3. Put in onion, lime juice, habanero, pumpkin seeds, and remaining 3 tablespoon oil to blender and pulse until smooth, approximately 1 minute, scraping down sides of blender as required. Move dip to serving container and place in your fridge until

completely chilled, minimum 2 hours or maximum one day. Sprinkle with salt and pepper to taste. Drizzle with queso fresco and cilantro before you serve.

QUESO FUNDIDO

Yield: Servings 6 to 8

An insanely delicious table dip of Mexican table cheese served with toppings.

Ingredients:

- ½ small onion, cut thin
- 1 poblano chile, stemmed, seeded, and cut thin
- 1 teaspoon vegetable oil
- 4 ounces Mexican style chorizo sausage, casings removed
- 6 (8 inch) corn or flour tortillas, warmed and slice into wedges
- 8 ounces queso de Oaxaca, cut into ½ inch pieces

Directions:

1. Adjust oven rack to lower middle position and heat oven to 375 degrees. Heat oil in 12 inch nonstick frying pan over moderate high heat until shimmering. Put in chorizo and cook, breaking up meat with wooden spoon, until fat starts to render, approximately one minute. Mix in poblano and onion and cook until chorizo and vegetables are thoroughly browned, five to seven minutes. Drain chorizo mixture in colander.
2. Spread queso Oaxaca uniformly into 9 inch pie plate, then drizzle with drained chorizo mixture. Move pie plate to oven and bake until cheese is just melted, about eight to ten minutes. Serve instantly with tortillas.

RICH WELL-FRIED BEANS FROM JALISCO (FRIJOLES PUERCOS ESTILO JALISCO)

Yield: Servings 6

My personal favourite variation of the classic frijoles puercos.

Ingredients:

- 1 chorizo, approximately 3 ounces (85 g)
- 2 jalapeño chiles en escabeche
- 2 tablespoons finely grated queso ranchero or romano
- 20 small, pitted green olives, chopped
- 6 strips bacon
- 8 ounces (225 g) pinto or pink beans, cooked—3½ to 4 cups (875 ml to 1 l) with broth
- Lard as required
- toasted tortillas or totopos

Directions:

1. Skin and crumble the chorizo, and cut the bacon. Cook in a frying pan using low heat, covered, until most of the fat has rendered out. Be careful not to allow them to burn. Remove chorizo and bacon and save for later.
2. There must be about ⅓ cup (85 ml) fat in the pan. Take out or make up to that amount with lard. Put in the beans and broth and cook them using high heat, mashing them. If they start to dry out and cling to the pan, put in slightly more lard.
3. Once the beans are mashed to a coarse texture and are almost dry, ready to roll, put in the bacon and about two thirds of the olives, chiles, and chorizo.
4. Roll the beans, then turn onto the serving dish and top with the rest of the olives, chiles, and chorizo.
5. Drizzle the roll with the cheese and serve with the toasted tortillas or totopos.

ROE SNACK (CAVIAR DE CHAPALA CARP)

Yield: Servings 6

A delicious Mexican appetizer usually served with hot tortillas other small sides to nibble on.

Ingredients:

- ¼ cup (65 ml) vegetable or olive oil
- 1 garlic clove, finely chopped
- 1 pound (450 g) carp roe
- 1 tablespoon salt
- 2 tablespoons finely chopped white onion

- About 6 ounces (180 g) tomatoes, finely chopped (approximately 1 cup/250 ml)

The toppings

- ⅓ cup (85 ml) finely chopped cilantro
- ⅓ cup (85 ml) finely chopped green, unripe tomatoes or <u>tomate verde</u>
- ⅓ cup (85 ml) finely chopped serrano chiles or any other fresh, hot green chiles
- ½ cup (125 ml) finely chopped white onion

Directions:

1. Place the salt and enough water to cover the roe in a shallow pan and bring to the simmering point. Put in the roe and allow it to simmer for eight to ten minutes, depending on thickness, then remove and drain. When it is sufficiently cool to handle, take off the skin and crumble the roe.
2. Heat the oil in a heavy pan. Put in the tomatoes, onion, and garlic and fry over quite high heat while stirring occasionally and scraping the bottom of the pan, until the onion is tender and the mixture is almost dry. Put in the crumbled roe with salt to taste and carry on frying the mixture on moderate heat, flipping it over continuously, until dry and crumbly, approximately five minutes.
3. Serve hot, accompanied by the onion and the other finely chopped toppings, in small different bowls, and a pile of hot corn tortillas.

SEAFOOD COCKTAIL (MARISCOS A LA MARINERA)

Yield: Servings 6

Any seafood ingredient of your choice will do the job here: raw clams or scallops, abalone, conch, or cooked shrimps.

Ingredients:

- ½ cup (125 ml) fresh lime juice
- 1 big avocado, cubed
- 1 small white onion, finely chopped (about ¼ cup/65 ml)
- 2 heaped tablespoons finely chopped cilantro
- 3 dozen big raw clams or scallops or medium-size cooked shrimps

- 3 tablespoons olive oil
- 3 to 4 serrano chiles or any fresh, hot green chiles, finely chopped with seeds
- About 12 ounces (340 g) tomatoes, finely chopped (about 2 cups/500 ml)
- Salt and freshly ground pepper to taste

Directions:

1. If you are using clams, open them or have them opened for you, saving both the clams and their juice. If you are using scallops, allow them to marinate in the lime juice for about 1 hour or so.
2. Mix the clams (and their liquid) or other seafood with the remaining ingredients, tweak the seasoning, and serve slightly chilled.

SHREDDED CRABMEAT AND VEGETABLES (SALPICÓN DE JAIBA)

Yield: enough to fill 12 small tortillas

This salpicón makes a scrumptious filling for small tacos and can also be served with plain white rice.

Ingredients:

- ¼ cup (65 ml) vegetable oil
- ⅓ cup (85 ml) finely chopped white onion
- ½ cup (125 ml) finely chopped celery
- 1 cup (250 ml) cooked, shredded crabmeat
- 3 tablespoons finely chopped cilantro
- 5 serrano chiles, finely chopped, with seeds
- Salt to taste

Directions:

1. Heat the oil in a frying pan and cook the onion gently until translucent.
2. Put in the celery, chiles, and crabmeat and fry until they barely start to brown mildly. The mixture must be rather dry. Finally, put in the cilantro and salt and cook for a minute more.

3. Serve with hot tortillas.

SHRIMP AND LIME CEVICHE

Yield: Servings 6

Usually served with crispy tortilla chips or used as a topping for tostadas, this simple and delicious seafood appetizer is quite uplifting.

Ingredients:

- ¼ cup extra virgin olive oil
- ½ cup lemon juice (3 lemons)
- ½ teaspoon sugar
- 1 garlic clove, minced
- 1 jalapeño chile, stemmed, seeded, and minced
- 1 pound extra big shrimp (21 to 25 per pound), peeled, deveined, tails removed, and halved along the length
- 1 teaspoon grated lime zest plus ½ cup juice (4 limes)
- 1 tomato, cored, seeded, and chopped fine
- 3 tablespoons minced fresh cilantro
- 4 scallions, cut thin
- Salt and pepper

Directions:

1. Mix tomato, lemon juice, jalapeño, lime zest and juice, garlic, and ½ teaspoon salt in medium container. Mix in shrimp, cover, and place in your fridge until shrimp are firm and opaque throughout, forty-five minutes to an hour, stirring midway through refrigerating.
2. Drain shrimp mixture in colander, leaving shrimp slightly wet, and move to serving container. Mix in oil, scallions, cilantro, and sugar. Sprinkle with salt and pepper to taste and serve.

SINALOAN SHREDDED BEEF (MOCHOMOS SINALOENSES)

Yield: about 6 cups (1.5 l)

An insanely popular dish from Sinaloa, made of carne machaca, or machacada.

Ingredients:

- ½ cup (125 ml) lard or vegetable oil
- 1 poblano chile, charred, peeled, cleaned, and cut into little squares
- 1½ tablespoons coarse sea salt
- 2 pounds (900 g) round steak (with some fat on)
- 8 ounces (225 g) white onions, roughly cut

Directions:

1. Chop the meat into 1-inch (2.5-cm) cubes. Put the meat in a single layer in a big pan. Put in the salt and water to barely cover. Bring the water to its boiling point, reduce the heat, and cook slowly, uncovered, until the water has vaporized and the meat is soft but not too soft—thirty-five to forty minutes. Continue drying the meat out using low heat so that it is dried and slightly crusty on the outside. Let cool.
2. Put 3 pieces of the meat into a blender and blend at moderate speed until meat is finely shredded. Continue in similarly until all the meat has been shredded.
3. Heat half of the lard in a frying pan, put in the onions, and fry for a short period of time for approximately 1 minute—they must be crisp and still opaque. Take away the onions using a slotted spoon and drain. Set aside.
4. Put in the rest of the lard to the frying pan, heat, put in the shredded meat and chile, and stir until the meat is well thoroughly heated and just browning—5 to 8 minutes.
5. Mix in the onions, heat through, and serve instantly.

STUFFED JALAPEÑOS

Yield: Servings 6 to 8

The only thing better than jalapeños are stuffed jalapeños.

Ingredients:

- 1 big egg yolk
- 1 teaspoon ground cumin

- 12 jalapeño chiles, halved along the length with stems left undamaged, seeds and ribs removed
- 2 scallions, cut thin
- 2 tablespoons panko bread crumbs
- 2 teaspoons lime juice
- 3 tablespoons minced fresh cilantro
- 4 ounces cream cheese, softened
- 4 ounces mild cheddar cheese, shredded (1 cup)
- 4 ounces Monterey Jack cheese, shredded (1 cup)
- 6 slices bacon
- Salt

Directions:

1. Adjust oven rack to upper middle position and heat oven to 500 degrees. Set wire rack in rimmed baking sheet. Cook bacon in 12 inch nonstick frying pan on moderate heat until crunchy, 7 to 9 minutes. Using slotted spoon, move bacon to paper towel–lined plate. When bacon is sufficiently cool to handle, cut fine and save for later.
2. Season jalapeños with salt and place cut side down on prepared rack. Bake until just starting to tenderize, approximately five minutes. Remove jalapeños from oven and reduce oven temperature to 450 degrees. When sufficiently cool to handle, flip jalapeños cut side up.
3. Mix cheddar, Monterey Jack, cream cheese, scallions, cilantro, panko, egg yolk, lime juice, cumin, and bacon together in container until meticulously blended. Split cheese mixture among jalapeños, pushing into cavities. (Filled jalapeños can be covered and placed in the fridge for maximum one day.)
4. Bake jalapeños until soft and filling is mildly browned, 9 to 14 minutes. Allow to cool for five minutes and serve.

TOMATILLO AND PINTO BEAN NACHOS

Yield: Servings four to 6

Try this recipe when you're in mood for a crunchy vegetarian snack!

Ingredients:

- ½ cup sour cream
- 1 (fifteen ounce) can pinto beans, washed
- 1 cup Fresh Tomato Salsa
- 1 cup frozen corn, thawed
- 1 onion, chopped fine
- 1 tablespoon vegetable oil
- 1 teaspoon ground coriander
- 1 teaspoon salt
- 1½ cups Chunky Guacamole
- 12 ounces pepper Jack cheese, shredded (3 cups)
- 12 ounces tomatillos, husks and stems removed, washed well, dried, and slice into ½ inch pieces
- 2 jalapeño chiles, stemmed and cut thin
- 2 teaspoons minced fresh oregano or ½ teaspoon dried
- 3 garlic cloves, minced
- 3 radishes, trimmed and cut thin
- 8 ounces tortilla chips
- Lime wedges

Directions:

1. Adjust oven rack to middle position and heat oven to 400 degrees. Heat oil in 12 inch nonstick frying pan on moderate heat until shimmering. Put in onion and cook until tender, approximately five minutes. Mix in garlic, coriander, salt, and oregano and cook until aromatic, approximately half a minute. Put in tomatillos and corn, decrease the heat to moderate low, and cook until tomatillos have released all their moisture and mixture is nearly dry, approximately ten minutes. Allow to cool slightly.
2. Spread half of tortilla chips uniformly into 13 by 9 inch baking dish. Drizzle 1½ cups pepper Jack uniformly over chips, then top uniformly with half of tomatillo mixture, followed by half of beans and, finally, half of jalapeños. Repeat layering with remaining chips, pepper Jack, tomatillo mixture, beans, and jalapeños. Bake until cheese is melted and just starting to brown, 7 to ten minutes.
3. Let nachos cool for a couple of minutes, then drizzle with radishes. Drop scoops of guacamole, salsa, and sour cream around edges of nachos. Serve instantly, passing lime wedges separately.

BEEF NACHOS

Yield: Servings four to 6

The name pretty much says it all!

Ingredients:

- ⅛ teaspoon salt
- ¼ teaspoon cayenne pepper
- ½ cup sour cream
- ½ teaspoon ground coriander
- ½ teaspoon ground cumin
- 1 cup Fresh Tomato Salsa
- 1 garlic clove, minced
- 1 pound cheddar cheese, shredded (4 cups)
- 1 small onion, chopped fine
- 1 tablespoon chili powder
- 1 teaspoon minced fresh oregano or ¼ teaspoon dried
- 1½ cups Chunky Guacamole
- 2 big jalapeño chiles, stemmed and cut thin
- 2 scallions, cut thin
- 2 teaspoons vegetable oil
- 8 ounces 90 percent lean ground beef
- 8 ounces tortilla chips
- Lime wedges

Directions:

1. Adjust oven rack to middle position and heat oven to 400 degrees. Heat oil in 12 inch frying pan on moderate heat until shimmering. Put in onion and cook until tender, approximately 3 minutes. Mix in chili powder, garlic, oregano, cumin, coriander, cayenne, and salt and cook until aromatic, approximately half a minute. Put in ground beef and cook, breaking up meat with wooden spoon, until beef is no longer pink, approximately five minutes.

2. Spread half of tortilla chips uniformly into 13 by 9 inch baking dish. Drizzle 2 cups cheddar uniformly over chips, then top uniformly with half of beef mixture, followed

by half of jalapeño slices. Repeat layering with remaining chips, cheddar, beef mixture, and jalapeños. Bake until cheese is melted and just starting to brown, 7 to ten minutes.

3. Let nachos cool for a couple of minutes, then drizzle with scallions. Drop scoops of guacamole, salsa, and sour cream around edges of nachos. Serve instantly, passing lime wedges separately.

YUCATECAN PICKLED LIMA BEANS (IBIS ESCABECHADOS)

Yield: about 3 cups (750 ml)

Ibis, both fresh and dried, are common ingredients in the food of the yucatán peninsula. They are quite similar to lima beans.

Ingredients:

- ¼ cup (65 ml) bitter orange juice or fresh lime juice
- ⅓ cup (85 ml) tightly packed, finely chopped cilantro
- ½ habanero chile, finely chopped
- 1 cup (250 ml) loosely packed, thinly cut white onion
- 12 ounces (340 g) ibis or lima beans (about 2½ cups/625 ml)
- Boiling water to cover
- Salt to taste

Directions:

1. Cover the onion with the boiling water and leave to soak for a minute. Drain, put in salt to taste, and mix in the bitter orange juice and chile. Set aside in a nonreactive container at room temperature to macerate while you cook the beans.
2. Put enough water into a small deep cooking pan to cover the beans. Bring the water to its boiling point, put in the beans, and cook on moderate heat until just soft—about ten minutes. Drain, and while still warm put in to the onion. Mix in the cilantro and put in salt as required. Serve at room temperature.

YUCATECAN PICKLED POTATOES (PAPAS ESCABECHADAS)

Yield: about 2⅔ cups (665 ml)

A popular snack serve in Mexican bars, usually free of charge.

Ingredients:

- ¼ cup (65 ml) bitter orange juice or fresh lime juice
- ⅓ cup (85 ml) tightly packed, finely chopped cilantro
- ½ habanero chile, finely chopped
- 1 cup (250 ml) loosely packed, thinly cut white onion
- 12 ounces (340 g) waxy potatoes, cut into ¾-inch (2-cm) cubes
- Boiling water to cover
- Salt to taste

Directions:

1. Cover the onion with the boiling water and leave to soak for a minute. Drain, put in salt to taste, and mix in the bitter orange juice and chile. Set aside in a nonreactive container at room temperature to macerate while you cook the potatoes.
2. Put enough water into a small deep cooking pan to cover the potatoes. Bring the water to its boiling point, put in the potatoes, and cook on moderate heat until just soft—approximately eight minutes. Drain, cool off a little, and peel—but while still slightly warm put in to the onion. Mix in the cilantro and put in more salt as required. Serve at room temperature.

YUCATECAN SHREDDED MEAT (SALPICÓN YUCATECO OR DZIK DE VENADO)

Yield: Servings 6

Any meat can be used in this recipe. This recipe is a great way to use any leftover meat you might have from a previous meal.

Ingredients:

- ½ cup (125 ml) seville orange juice
- ⅔ cup (165 ml) radishes cut into fine strips
- 1 cup (250 ml) cooked and shredded meat

- 3 tablespoons very finely chopped cilantro
- Salt to taste

Directions:

1. Mix all the ingredients and allow them to season for approximately 30 minutes before you serve.

TACOS, TOSTADAS, TAMALES, AND MORE

TACOS

When people from all over the world think of Mexican food, the first thing that comes to their mind is "Taco". To the world, a taco is a tortilla bent in half, stuffed with veggies, meats, sauces, etc. Tacos can be soft and they can be fried to a crunchy.

Now, I won't waste too much of your time describing the taco to you, as you've probably eaten more of these than you can count.

TOSTADAS

A tostada is basically a toasted of fried tortilla, and is usually flat or container shaped. This little description doesn't really do justice to the tostada through, as you will see the variety in the recipes that follow.

TAMALES

A tamale is a classic Mesoamerican dish, made of masa or dough, which is steamed in a corn husk or banana leaf.

Now that we're done with the intros, it is time to dive right into the recipes!

HOMEMADE TACO SHELLS

Yield: 8 Taco Shells

For the best results, use the taco shells instantly.

Ingredients:

- ¾ cup vegetable oil
- 8 corn tortillas

Directions:

1. In 8 inch frying pan, heat vegetable oil to 350 degrees. Using tongs, slip half of tortilla into hot oil and immerse using metal spatula. Fry until just set, but not brown, approximately half a minute.

2. Flip tortilla. Hold tortilla open approximately two inches while keeping bottom submerged in oil. Fry until a golden-brown colour is achieved, approximately 1½ minutes. Flip again and fry other side until a golden-brown colour is achieved.

3. Move shell, upside down, to paper towel–lined baking sheet to drain. Repeat with remaining tortillas, keeping oil between 350 and 375 degrees and serve.

DRESSED INDIANS (INDIOS VESTIDOS)

Yield: Servings 6

Ingredients:

The sauce

- ⅓ cup (85 ml) finely chopped white onion
- 1¼ pounds (565 g) tomatoes, broiled
- 2 canned chipotle chiles en adobo
- 2 tablespoons vegetable oil
- Salt to taste

The filling and frying

- 1 big avocado, thinly cut
- 1 pound (450 g) shredded, cooked pork (approximately 1⅓ cups/313 ml), or 8 ounces (225 g) queso fresco, crumbled (approximately 1⅓ cups/335 ml)
- 4 tablespoons finely grated queso añejo cheese
- 5 big eggs, separated
- About ½ cup (125 ml) all-purpose flour
- Salt to taste

To serve

- twelve tortillas, cut into halves
- Vegetable oil for frying

Directions:

1. Heat the oil in a big frying pan and fry the onion gently until translucent. Combine the unskinned tomatoes with the chiles, then put in to the pan, together with the salt. Cook the sauce over quite high heat for approximately 3 minutes so that it reduces a little. Season. Turn off the heat and keep warm.
2. Place a little of the filling onto each piece of tortilla. Fold in half and fasten using a toothpick, then dust mildly with flour.
3. Heat the oil, approximately ½ inch (1.5 cm) deep, in a frying pan.
4. In the meantime, beat the egg whites and salt until stiff but not dry, then put in the yolks, one at a time, and carry on beating until they are well blended. Immerse the tortilla "packages" into the beaten egg—they must be lightly but thoroughly coated—and fry until a golden-brown colour is achieved. Drain thoroughly, then put onto the serving platter, pour the heated sauce over, top with the avocado and cheese, and serve instantly.

SOUR CREAM TACOS (TAQUITOS DE NATA)

Yield: 12 tacos

Ingredients:

The filling

- ½ cup (125 ml) nata sour cream, commercial or homemade, at room temperature
- 1 fresh jalapeño chile, cut into fine strips
- 1 garlic clove
- 1 tablespoon vegetable oil
- 1½ to 2 cups (375 to 500 ml) cooked, shredded, and well-salted chicken
- 12 ounces (340 g) tomatoes, broiled
- 2 tablespoons finely chopped white onion
- 2 tablespoons vegetable oil
- Salt to taste

To serve

- ⅔ cup (165 ml) finely chopped white onion
- twelve tortillas

- Vegetable oil for frying

Directions:

1. Combine the tomatoes with the onion, garlic, and salt and split into two parts. Heat the oil in a frying pan and fry the shredded chicken and chile strips for one minute or so over quite hot heat while stirring occasionally to prevent sticking, until they barely start to brown. Put in half of the tomato puree and carry on cooking and stirring until almost dry. Set aside and keep warm.
2. Heat the oil in a different frying pan and fry the rest of the puree over quite high heat for approximately 3 minutes, stirring occasionally. Turn off the heat and mix in the sour cream. Set aside and keep warm.
3. Heat the oil in a frying pan and lightly fry the tortillas, a few at a time, on both sides.
4. Preheat your oven to 375° f (190° c).
5. Place a little of the filling on each of the tortillas, roll up, and place side by side on the serving dish. Pour the sauce down the center of the tacos and bake for about ten minutes. Drizzle with the onion and serve instantly.

BAJA FISH TACOS WITH PICKLED ONION AND CABBAGE

Yield: Servings 6

Ingredients:

- ¼ cup cornstarch
- ¾ cup all purpose flour
- 1 cup beer
- 1 cup fresh cilantro leaves
- 1 cup Mexican crema
- 1 quart peanut or vegetable oil
- 1 recipe Pickled Onion and Cabbage (recipe follows)
- 1 teaspoon baking powder
- 18 (6 inch) corn tortillas, warmed
- 2 pounds skinless whitefish fillets, such as cod, haddock, or halibut, cut crosswise into 4 by an inch strips
- Salt and pepper

Directions:

1. Adjust oven rack to middle position and heat oven to 200 degrees. Set wire rack in rimmed baking sheet. Pat fish dry using paper towels and sprinkle with salt and pepper. Whisk flour, cornstarch, baking powder, and 1 teaspoon salt together in big container. Put in beer and whisk until the desired smoothness is achieved. Put in fish to batter and toss to coat uniformly.

2. Put in oil to big Dutch oven until it measures about ¾ inch deep and heat over moderate high heat to 350 degrees.

3. Remove five or six pieces of fish from batter, allowing surplus to drip back into container, and put in to hot oil, for a short period of time dragging fish along surface of oil to stop sticking. Adjust burner, if required, to maintain oil temperature between 325 and 350 degrees. Fry fish, stirring slowly to stop pieces from clinging together and turning as required, until a golden-brown colour is achieved and crunchy, approximately eight minutes.

4. Move fish to readied wire rack and place in oven to keep warm. Return oil to 350 degrees and repeat with the rest of the fish, working with five or six pieces at a time. Serve with warm tortillas, cilantro, crema, and Pickled Onion and Cabbage.

PICKLED ONION AND CABBAGE

Yield: Servings 6

Ingredients:

- 1 cup white wine vinegar
- 1 small red onion, halved and cut thin
- 1 tablespoon sugar
- 2 jalapeño chiles, stemmed and cut into thin rings
- 2 tablespoons lime juice
- 3 cups shredded green cabbage
- Salt and pepper

Directions:

1. Mix onion and jalapeños in medium container. Bring vinegar, lime juice, sugar, and 1 teaspoon salt to boil in small deep cooking pan.

2. Pour vinegar mixture over onion mixture and allow it to sit for minimum 30 minutes, or place in your fridge for maximum 2 days.
3. Move ¼ cup pickling liquid to second medium container, put in cabbage, ½ teaspoon salt, and ½ teaspoon pepper and toss to blend.

BEEF TACOS (TACOS DE RES)

Yield: 12 tacos

Ingredients:

The filling

- ½ cup (125 ml) thinly cut white onion
- 1 pound (450 g) cooked and shredded beef (about 2 cups/500 ml;)
- 1½ tablespoons vegetable oil
- 12 strips of jalapeño chiles, with seeds

To serve

- ¾ cup (185 ml) prepared sour cream
- 1 cup (250 ml) salsa ranchera
- 3 ounces (85 g) queso fresco, crumbled (about ½ cup/125 ml)
- twelve tortillas
- Vegetable oil for frying

Directions:

1. Heat the oil in a big frying pan and fry the onion gently until translucent. Put in the meat and chiles and cook on moderate heat, stirring occasionally, until it is mildly browned. Set aside to cool a little.
2. Fill the tortillas and fry until mildly crunchy on the outside. Drain, then serve instantly topped with the sauce, sour cream, and cheese.

CARNITAS

Yield: Servings 6 to 8

Ingredients:

- ⅓ cup fresh orange juice, spent orange halves reserved
- 1 (3½ to 4 pound) boneless pork butt roast, fat cap trimmed to ⅛ inch thick and slice into 2 inch chunks
- 1 onion, peeled and halved
- 1 teaspoon dried oregano
- 1 teaspoon ground cumin
- 18–24 (6 inch) corn tortillas, warmed
- 2 bay leaves
- 2 cups water
- 2 tablespoons lime juice
- Fresh cilantro leaves
- Lime wedges
- Salt and pepper

Directions:

1. Adjust oven rack to lower middle position and heat oven to 300 degrees. Mix pork, water, onion, lime juice, oregano, cumin, bay leaves, 1 teaspoon salt, and ½ teaspoon pepper in Dutch oven (liquid should just barely cover meat). Put in orange juice and spent orange halves to pot. Bring mixture to simmer over moderate high heat while stirring once in a while. Cover pot, move to oven, and cook until meat is tender and falls apart when prodded with fork, approximately 2 hours, turning pieces of meat once during cooking.
2. Take the pot out of the oven and turn oven to broil. Using slotted spoon, move pork to container; discard orange halves, onion, and bay leaves (do not skim fat from liquid). Staying cautious of hot pot handles, place pot using high heat and simmer braising liquid, stirring frequently, until thick and syrupy, about eight to twelve minutes; you should have approximately 1 cup reduced liquid.
3. Move pork to cutting board and pull each piece in half with the help of two forks. Return pork to container, fold in reduced liquid, and sprinkle with salt and pepper to taste. Spread pork in even layer on wire rack set in rimmed baking sheet. Broil pork until thoroughly browned (but not charred) and edges are mildly crunchy on both sides, ten to 16 minutes, turning meat midway through broiling. Serve with warm tortillas, cilantro, and lime wedges.

CHICKEN TAMALES (TAMALES DE POLLO)

Yield: about 30 3-inch (8-cm) tamales

Ingredients:

The filling

- About 6 cups (1.5 l) well-seasoned chicken broth to cover
- One 3½-pound (1.575-kg) chicken cut into serving pieces, with skin and bone
- The chicken giblets

The sauce

- ¼ teaspoon cumin seeds, crushed
- 1 big garlic clove, roughly chopped
- 1 cup (250 ml) thinly cut white onion
- 1½ pounds (680 g) tomatoes, broiled
- 3 tablespoons vegetable oil or melted chicken fat
- 4 whole cloves, crushed
- 6 peppercorns, crushed
- Salt to taste

The masa

- 1½ pounds (675 g) tamale dough
- 8 ounces (225 g) pork lard
- About ½ cup (125 ml) of the reserved chicken broth, warm
- Salt to taste

To assemble the tamales

- 30 corn husks, soaked to tenderize and shaken dry
- 30 pitted green olives
- 30 strips of fresh jalapeños

Directions:

1. Make the filling: put the chicken, giblets, and broth into a big deep cooking pan, bring to a simmer, and carry on cooking using low heat until nearly soft—about 30 minutes. Take away the chicken and allow to cool. Strain the broth. There must be about 3 cups (750 ml). Shred the chicken roughly.

2. Make the sauce: place a few of the tomatoes into a blender jar with the garlic and spices and blend meticulously. Put in the remaining tomatoes and blend to a textured sauce.

3. Heat the oil in a big frying pan, put in the onion, and fry on moderate heat until translucent—about three minutes. Put in the mixed ingredients and cook over quite high heat until reduced and seasoned—about five minutes. Mix in the chicken pieces, adjust salt, and set aside to season.

4. Using an electric mixer, beat the lard about five minutes until well aerated—it will become very white and opaque. Slowly beat in the masa alternately with the warm broth as required (depending on how dry the masa), put in salt, and beat again for approximately five minutes or until a small ball of the mixture floats on the surface of a glass of water.

5. Bring a tamale steamer to heat.

6. Assembling the tamales: spread a big tablespoon of the dough finely over the inside of a corn husk. Put some of the sauced chicken down the middle with a strip of the chile and an olive. Fold the husk so that the masa is fully covered and turn the pointed end up to the back of the tamale—this will tighten up the seam.

7. Stack the tamales in the top of a tamale steamer, steam for approximately 1 hour, then test. If the dough separates easily from the husk the tamale is cooked.

CLASSIC GROUND BEEF TACOS

Yield: Servings 4

Ingredients:

- ¼ teaspoon cayenne pepper
- ½ cup canned tomato sauce
- ½ cup chicken broth
- ½ teaspoon dried oregano
- 1 onion, chopped fine

- 1 pound 90 percent lean ground beef
- 1 tablespoon vegetable oil
- 1 teaspoon ground coriander
- 1 teaspoon ground cumin
- 1 teaspoon packed light brown sugar
- 2 tablespoons chili powder
- 2 teaspoons cider vinegar
- 3 garlic cloves, minced
- 8 taco shells, warmed
- Salt

Directions:

1. Heat oil in 10 inch frying pan on moderate heat until it starts to shimmer Put in onion and cook until tender, approximately five minutes. Mix in chili powder, garlic, cumin, coriander, oregano, cayenne, and 1 teaspoon salt and cook until aromatic, approximately half a minute.
2. Mix in ground beef and cook, breaking up meat with wooden spoon, until no longer pink, approximately five minutes. Mix in tomato sauce, broth, vinegar, and sugar and simmer until it becomes thick, approximately ten minutes. Sprinkle with salt to taste. Split filling uniformly among taco shells before you serve.

CORN TORTILLAS

Yield: approximately 12 (6 inch) tortillas

Ingredients:

- ¼ teaspoon salt
- 1¼ cups warm tap water, plus extra as required
- 2 cups (8 ounces) masa harina or Maseca Brand Instant Masa Corn Flour
- 2 teaspoons vegetable oil

Directions:

1. Mix masa, 1 teaspoon oil, and salt together in medium container, then fold in water using a rubber spatula. Use your hands to knead mixture in container, putting in extra

water, 1 tablespoon at a time, as required, until dough is tender and tacky but not clingy, and has texture of Play Doh. Cover dough using a damp dish towel and allow it to sit for five minutes.

2. Cut sides of 1 quart zipper lock bag, leaving bottom seam undamaged. Line big plate with 2 damp dish towels. Split dough into 12 equivalent portions (1½ ounces each); keep covered. Working with 1 piece at a time, roll into ball, place on 1 side of zipper lock bag, and fold other side over top. Push dough flat into 6½ inch wide tortilla (approximately 1/16 inch thick) with the help of a tortilla press or pie plate; leave tortilla between plastic until frying pan is hot.

3. Heat remaining 1 teaspoon oil in 8 inch nonstick frying pan over moderate high heat until it starts to shimmer Use a paper towel to wipe out frying pan, leaving thin film of oil on bottom. Take the plastic off on top of tortilla, flip tortilla onto your palm, then remove plastic on bottom and lay tortilla in frying pan. Cook tortilla, without moving it, until it moves freely when pan is shaken and has shriveled slightly in size, approximately 45 seconds.

4. Turn the tortilla over and cook until edges curl and bottom is spotty brown, approximately one minute. Turn the tortilla back over and carry on cooking until first side is spotty brown and puffs up in center, thirty to 60 seconds. Lay toasted tortilla between damp dish towels. Repeat with the rest of the dough. (Tortillas can be placed in your fridge for maximum 5 days.)

CRISP-FRIED TORTILLA PIECES (TOTOPOS)

Totopos, squares or strips of crisped corn tortillas, are used as a topping for soups, added to scrambled eggs, and much more. Cut into bigger triangles, they are used as scoops with guacamole or refried beans.

It is a good idea to prepare your own totopos, since the commercially packaged ones, known as "fritos" in the USA, are too thin and highly seasoned. First, cut your corn tortillas into the required shapes and spread them onto a rack to dry out overnight—so they will absorb less oil in the frying process. Heat vegetable oil to the depth of approximately ½ inch (1.25 cm) in a smallish frying pan and fry a small quantity of the totopos until crunchy and a deep golden-brown in color. Drain thoroughly using paper towels. They are best used instantly, but if you have leftovers, freeze them and reheat using your oven.

SIMPLE CHIPOTLE CHICKEN TACOS

Yield: Servings 4

Ingredients:

- ½ cup orange juice
- ¾ cup chopped fresh cilantro
- 1 tablespoon Worcestershire sauce
- 1 teaspoon yellow mustard
- 1½ pounds boneless, skinless chicken breasts, trimmed
- 12 (6 inch) corn tortillas, warmed
- 2 teaspoons minced canned chipotle chile in adobo sauce
- 3 tablespoons unsalted butter
- 4 garlic cloves, minced
- Lime wedges
- Salt and pepper

Directions:

1. Melt butter in 12 inch frying pan over moderate high heat. Put in garlic and chipotle and cook until aromatic, approximately half a minute. Mix in ½ cup cilantro, orange juice, and Worcestershire and bring to simmer. Nestle chicken into sauce. Cover, decrease the heat to moderate low, and cook until chicken records 160 degrees, ten to fifteen minutes, turning chicken midway through cooking. Move chicken to plate and cover.

2. Increase heat to moderate high and cook liquid left in frying pan until reduced to ¼ cup, approximately five minutes. Remove the heat, whisk in mustard. Using 2 forks, shred chicken into bite size pieces and return to frying pan. Put in remaining ¼ cup cilantro and toss until well blended. Sprinkle with salt and pepper to taste. Serve with warm tortillas and lime wedges.

GORDITAS

Yield: 12 gorditas; serves four to 6

Ingredients:

- 1 recipe filling, warmed
- 1 teaspoon salt
- 1¾ cups hot tap water
- 2 cups (8 ounces) masa harina (Dried corn dougn)
- 2 cups vegetable oil

Directions:

1. Mix masa harina and salt in medium container, then fold in water using a rubber spatula. Use your hands to knead mixture in container until tender dough forms, one to two minutes. Cover dough using a damp dish towel and allow it to sit for five minutes.

2. Cut twenty four 8 inch squares of parchment paper. Knead dough for a short period of time, then split into 12 equivalent portions, roll into balls, and place on baking sheet. Cover dough using a damp dish towel.

3. Working with 1 piece dough at a time, press flat into 3½ inch wide disk between 2 pieces parchment with the help of a pie plate. Remove top piece parchment, softly push in edges to make a little thicker and smooth out any cracks, then flatten slightly to level; edges must be smooth, flat, and a little thicker than center. Move to plate, leaving bottom piece parchment in place, and cover using a damp dish towel; tortillas can be stacked.

4. Heat eleven-inch straight sided sauté pan on moderate heat until hot, two to three minutes. Put 1 tortilla parchment side up in your palm, remove parchment, then gently lay tortilla in hot, dry pan; repeat with 2 more tortillas. Cook until lightly golden on both sides, four to six minutes, turning midway through cooking; move to baking sheet. Repeat with remaining tortillas, lowering heat as required to stop scorching. (Gorditas can be stacked between parchment paper, wrapped using plastic wrap, and placed in the fridge for maximum 1 day or frozen for maximum three months; thaw completely before continuing.)

5. Coat second baking sheet with several layers of paper towels. Cautiously add oil to now empty pan and heat over moderate high heat to 375 degrees. Working in batches, fry tortillas, turning often, until they puff, two to three minutes. Move to readied baking sheet and allow to cool slightly. Use a paring knife to cut puffed tortillas open midway around edge. Stuff each tortilla with filling before you serve.

GRILLED CHICKEN TACOS

Yield: Servings 4

Ingredients:

- ¼ cup vegetable oil
- ½ cup chopped fresh cilantro
- 1 jalapeño chile, stemmed, halved, and seeded
- 1 onion, peeled and slice into ½ inch thick rounds
- 1 pound tomatillos, husks and stems removed, washed well and dried
- 1½ pounds boneless, skinless chicken breasts, trimmed
- 12 (6 inch) corn tortillas
- 2 tablespoons water
- 3 tablespoons lime juice (2 limes)
- 5 cloves garlic, minced
- Salt and pepper
- Sugar

Directions:

1. Whisk 3 tablespoons oil, 1 tablespoon lime juice, water, 1 teaspoon sugar, 1½ teaspoons salt, ½ teaspoon pepper, and half of garlic together in medium container. Put in chicken, cover, and refrigerate, turning once in a while, for half an hour Brush onion, jalapeño, and half of tomatillos with remaining 1 tablespoon oil and sprinkle with salt. Halve remaining tomatillos; set aside.
2. **For a Charcoal Grill:** Open bottom vent fully. Light big chimney starter filled with charcoal briquettes (6 quarts). When top coals are partly covered with ash, pour uniformly over grill. Set cooking grate in place, cover, and open lid vent fully. Heat grill until hot, approximately five minutes. **For A Gas Grill**: Set all burners to high, cover, and heat grill until hot, approximately fifteen minutes. Leave all burners on high.
3. Clean and oil cooking grate. Put chicken and oiled vegetables on grill. Cook (covered if using gas), turning as required, until chicken records 160 degrees and vegetables are mildly charred and tender, ten to fifteen minutes. Move chicken and vegetables to cutting board and tent with aluminium foil.
4. Working in batches, grill tortillas, turning as required, until warm and soft, approximately half a minute; wrap firmly in foil to keep tender.

5. Chop grilled vegetables coarse, then pulse with remaining tomatillos, cilantro, remaining garlic, remaining 2 tablespoons lime juice, ½ teaspoon salt, and pinch sugar inside a food processor until slightly lumpy, 16 to 18 pulses. Slice chicken thin on bias and serve with tortillas and tomatillo salsa.

GRILLED FISH TACOS

Yield: Servings 6

Ingredients:

- ½ cup orange juice
- 1 jalapeño chile
- 1 pineapple, peeled, quartered along the length, cored, and each quarter halved along the length
- 1 red bell pepper, stemmed, seeded, and slice into ¼ inch pieces
- 1 tablespoon ancho chile powder
- 1 teaspoon dried oregano
- 1 teaspoon ground coriander
- 18 (6 inch) corn tortillas
- 2 garlic cloves, minced
- 2 pounds skinless swordfish steaks, an inch thick, cut along the length into an inch thick strips
- 2 tablespoons minced fresh cilantro, plus extra for serving
- 2 tablespoons tomato paste
- 2 teaspoons chipotle chile powder
- 3 tablespoons vegetable oil
- 6 tablespoons lime juice (3 limes)
- Salt

Directions:

1. Heat 2 tablespoons oil, ancho chile powder, and chipotle chile powder in 8 inch frying pan on moderate heat, stirring continuously, until aromatic and some bubbles form, two to three minutes. Put in garlic, oregano, coriander, and 1 teaspoon salt and carry on cooking until aromatic, approximately half a minute. Put in tomato paste and, using

spatula, purée tomato paste with spice mixture until blended, approximately twenty seconds. Mix in orange juice and 2 tablespoons lime juice. Cook while stirring continuously, until meticulously mixed and reduced slightly, approximately 2 minutes. Move chile mixture to big container and allow to cool for fifteen minutes.

2. Put in swordfish to chile mixture and stir slowly to coat. Cover and place in your fridge for minimum 30 minutes or maximum 2 hours. Brush pineapple and jalapeño with remaining 1 tablespoon oil.

3. **For a Charcoal Grill:** Open bottom vent fully. Light big chimney starter mounded with charcoal briquettes (7 quarts). When top coals are partly covered with ash, pour uniformly over grill. Set cooking grate in place, cover, and open lid vent fully. Heat grill until hot, approximately five minutes. **For A Gas Grill:** Set all burners to high, cover, and heat grill until hot, approximately fifteen minutes. Turn all burners to moderate high.

4. Clean and oil cooking grate. Put fish, pineapple, and jalapeño on grill. Cover and cook until fish, pineapple, and jalapeño have begun to brown, three to five minutes. Using thin spatula, turn fish, pineapple, and jalapeño. Cover and cook until pineapple and jalapeño are thoroughly browned and swordfish records 140 degrees, three to five minutes; move to platter and cover using aluminium foil.

5. Working in batches, grill tortillas, turning as required, until warm and soft, approximately half a minute; wrap firmly in foil to keep tender.

6. Chop pineapple and jalapeño fine and mix with bell pepper, cilantro, and remaining 4 tablespoons lime juice in container. Sprinkle with salt to taste. Using 2 forks, pull fish apart into big flakes and serve with pineapple salsa and tortillas.

GRILLED SHRIMP TACOS WITH JÍCAMA SLAW

Yield: Servings 6

Ingredients:

- ¼ cup thinly cut red onion
- 1 cup Mexican crema
- 1 pound jícama, peeled and slice into 3 inch long matchsticks
- 1 tablespoon minced fresh oregano or 1 teaspoon dried
- 1 teaspoon garlic powder

- 1 teaspoon grated orange zest plus ⅓ cup juice
- 18 (6 inch) corn tortillas
- 2 pounds extra big shrimp (21 to 25 per pound), peeled, deveined, and tails removed
- 2 teaspoons chipotle chile powder
- 3 tablespoons chopped fresh cilantro
- 3 tablespoons vegetable oil
- Lime wedges
- Salt

Directions:

1. Mix jícama, orange zest and juice, onion, cilantro, and ½ teaspoon salt in container, cover, and place in your fridge until ready to serve.
2. Whisk oil, oregano, chile powder, garlic powder, and ½ teaspoon salt together in big container. Pat shrimp dry using paper towels, put in to spice mixture, and toss to coat. Thread shrimp onto four 12 inch metal skewers, alternating direction of heads and tails.
3. **For a Charcoal Grill:** Open bottom vent fully. Light big chimney starter mounded with charcoal briquettes (7 quarts). When top coals are partly covered with ash, pour uniformly over grill. Set cooking grate in place, cover, and open lid vent fully. Heat grill until hot, approximately five minutes. **For A Gas Grill:** Set all burners to high, cover, and heat grill until hot, approximately fifteen minutes. Leave all burners on high.
4. Clean and oil cooking grate. Put shrimp on grill and cook (covered if using gas) until mildly charred on first side, approximately 4 minutes. Flip shrimp, pushing them together on skewer if they separate, and cook until opaque throughout, approximately 2 minutes. Move to platter and cover using aluminium foil.
5. Working in batches, grill tortillas, turning as required, until warm and soft, approximately half a minute; wrap firmly in foil to keep tender.
6. Slide shrimp off skewers onto cutting board and slice into ½ inch pieces. Serve with tortillas, jícama slaw, crema, and lime wedges.

GRILLED SKIRT STEAK AND POBLANO TACOS

Yield: Servings 6

Ingredients:

- ½ teaspoon ground cumin
- 1 tablespoon vegetable oil
- 1½ pounds poblano chiles
- 18 (6 inch) corn tortillas
- 2 pounds skirt steak, trimmed
- 3 garlic cloves, minced
- 4 onions (3 cut crosswise into ½ inch thick rounds, 1 chopped coarse)
- 6 tablespoons lime juice (3 limes)
- Lime wedges
- Salt and pepper

Directions:

1. Process chopped onion, lime juice, garlic, cumin, and 1 teaspoon salt inside a food processor until the desired smoothness is achieved. Brush onion rounds and poblanos with oil and sprinkle with salt and pepper. Pat steak dry and sprinkle with salt and pepper.

2. **For a Charcoal Grill:** Open bottom vent fully. Light big chimney starter filled with charcoal briquettes (6 quarts). When top coals are partly covered with ash, pour uniformly over half of grill. Set cooking grate in place, cover, and open lid vent fully. Heat grill until hot, approximately five minutes. **For a Gas Grill:** Set all burners to high, cover, and heat grill until hot, approximately fifteen minutes. Leave primary burner on high and turn other burner(s) off.

3. Clean and oil cooking grate. Put poblanos on hotter side of grill and onion rounds on cooler side of grill. Grill (covered if using gas), turning as required, until poblanos are blistered and blackened and onions become tender and golden, 6 to twelve minutes. Move onions to platter and cover to keep warm. Move peppers to container, cover, and allow to steam while cooking steak and tortillas.

4. Put steak on hotter side of grill. Grill (covered if using gas), turning as required, until thoroughly browned on both sides and meat records 120 to 125 degrees (for medium rare), four to 8 minutes. Move steak to 13 by 9 inch pan and poke all over with fork. Pour pureed onion mixture over top, cover, and allow to rest for five to ten minutes.

5. Working in batches, grill tortillas, turning as required, until warm and soft, approximately half a minute; wrap firmly in aluminium foil to keep tender.

6. Peel poblanos, then slice thin. Separate onions into rings and cut coarse, then toss with poblanos. Take the steak out of the marinade, slice into four to 6 inch lengths, then slice thin against grain. Serve with warm tortillas, poblano onion mixture, and lime wedges.

GROUND PORK TACOS WITH ALMONDS AND RAISINS

Yield: Servings 4

Ingredients:

- ⅛ teaspoon ground cloves
- ¼ cup slivered almonds, toasted
- ½ cup canned tomato sauce
- ½ teaspoon ground cinnamon
- ½ teaspoon minced canned chipotle chile in adobo sauce
- 1 cup chicken broth
- 1 pound ground pork
- 1 small onion, chopped fine
- 1 tablespoon cider vinegar
- 1 tablespoon vegetable oil
- 2 garlic cloves, minced
- 2 tablespoons chopped raisins
- 8 taco shells, warmed
- Salt and pepper

Directions:

1. Heat oil in 12 inch nonstick frying pan on moderate heat until it starts to shimmer Put in onion and cook until tender, five to seven minutes. Mix in garlic, chipotle, cinnamon, and cloves and cook until aromatic, approximately half a minute. Mix in pork and cook, breaking up meat with wooden spoon, until no longer pink, approximately five minutes.
2. Mix in broth, tomato sauce, raisins, vinegar, ½ teaspoon salt, and ½ teaspoon pepper and simmer until it becomes thick, approximately ten minutes. Mix in almonds and

sprinkle with salt and pepper to taste. Split filling uniformly among taco shells before you serve.

GUACAMOLE AND SOUR CREAM TOSTADAS (TOSTADAS DE GUACAMOLE Y CREMA)

Yield: twelve tostadas

Ingredients:

- 1 cup (250 ml) prepared sour cream
- 1½ cups (375 ml) finely shredded lettuce
- 12 corn tortillas
- 2 cups (500 ml) guacamole
- 4 to 6 jalapeño chiles en escabeche, cut into strips
- 8 ounces (225 g) chihuahua cheese (or any other cheese of your choice if you can't find it), cut into thin slices
- Vegetable oil for frying

Directions:

1. Heat the oil in a frying pan and fry the tortillas until crunchy. Drain thoroughly.
2. Cover the tortillas with the cut cheese and melt under a broiler or in your oven. Top each tostada with a big spoonful of the guacamole, a little sour cream, some shredded lettuce, and some chile strips. Serve instantly.

INDOOR STEAK TACOS

Yield: Servings 4

Ingredients:

- ½ cup fresh cilantro leaves, plus extra for serving
- ½ teaspoon ground cumin
- ½ teaspoon sugar
- 1 (1½ to 1¾ pound) flank steak, trimmed and cut with grain into 4 pieces

- 1 jalapeño chile, stemmed and chopped coarse
- 1 tablespoon lime juice
- 12 (6 inch) corn tortillas, warmed
- 3 garlic cloves, chopped coarse
- 3 scallions, chopped coarse
- 6 tablespoons vegetable oil
- Lime wedges
- Salt and pepper

Directions:

1. Pulse cilantro, scallions, garlic, jalapeño, and cumin inside a food processor until finely chopped, ten to 12 pulses. Put in ¼ cup oil and pulse until mixture is smooth, approximately fifteen seconds, scraping down container as required. Move 2 tablespoons herb paste to moderate container and mix in lime juice; set aside for serving.
2. Using dinner fork, poke each piece of steak ten to 12 times on each side. Put steaks in big baking dish, rub meticulously with 1½ teaspoons salt, then coat with remaining herb paste. Cover and place in your fridge for 30 minutes to an hour.
3. Scrape herb paste off steaks and drizzle with sugar and ½ teaspoon pepper. Heat remaining 2 tablespoons oil in 12 inch nonstick frying pan over moderate high heat until just smoking. Cook steaks, turning as required, until thoroughly browned on all sides and meat records 120 to 125 degrees (for medium rare), four to six minutes. Move steaks to cutting board and allow to rest for five minutes.
4. Slice steaks thin against grain, put in to container with reserved herb paste, and toss to coat. Sprinkle with salt and pepper to taste. Serve with warm tortillas, extra cilantro, and lime wedges.

LITTLE TACOS (TAQUITOS)

Yield: 12 tacos

Ingredients:

To prepare the tacos

- ¾ cup (185 ml) frijoles refritos (Mexican Refried Beans)
- 1 small avocado, cut into 12 slices
- 12 5- to 6-inch (12.5- to fifteen-cm) tortillas
- 12 thin slices white onion
- 4 ounces (115 g) chihuahua cheese or muenster (approximately 1 cup/250 ml)
- 4 to 6 canned chipotle chiles, each cut into 3 pieces
- Salt to taste

To serve

- 6 big radishes, thinly cut
- 6 romaine lettuce leaves, shredded
- Approximately 3 tablespoons roughly chopped cilantro sprigs
- Vegetable oil for frying

Directions:

1. On each tortilla place a slice of avocado, some strips of cheese, a piece or two of chile, a tablespoon of beans, and a thin slice of onion. Drizzle well with salt, roll the tortillas up, and secure using a toothpick.
2. Fry until golden but not too crunchy. Drain using paper towels and serve topped with the lettuce, radishes, and chopped cilantro.

MICHOACÁN FRESH CORN TAMALES (UCHEPOS)

Yield: 20 uchepos

Ingredients:

- ¼ cup (65 ml) milk (if required)
- 1 tablespoon natas, or crème fraîche or thick cream
- 1 tablespoon sugar
- 1 tablespoon unsalted butter
- 1 teaspoon salt
- 5 cups (1.25 l) white starchy field corn kernels
- About 20 fresh corn husks

Directions:

1. Prepare a tamale steamer. Put half of the corn into the container of a food processor, and pulse until the corn has been reduced to a textured consistency—approximately 1½ minutes. Put in the remaining corn and carry on grinding until you have a finely textured puree—about 2½ minutes more, putting in the milk only if required to blend. Put in the remaining ingredients and mix thoroughly.

2. Shake the husks once again to get rid of any surplus water. Put 1 heaped tablespoon of the mixture down the center of the husk, beginning just below the cupped top and extending approximately two inches (5 cm) down the husk. Being careful not to flatten the mixture, or allow it to ooze out, roll, rather than fold, the husk over so that it overlaps the other side completely.

3. Fold the point end up to the back of the uchepo and instantly place it horizontally in the top of the steamer. (because of the loose consistency of the mixture they have to be cooked instantly and cannot sit around while you finish making them.)

4. To make sure that the bottom layer will not be squashed flat, steam for approximately ten minutes before you put in the rest. Don't forget to stir the mixture well before you continue with the subsequent layers. Steam for 1¼ hours and then test. The uchepos should barely separate from the husk. Set the uchepos aside to firm up for approximately 2 hours before you use.

MUSHROOM TACOS (TACOS DE HONGOS)

Yield: 12 tacos

Ingredients:

The filling

- ¼ cup (65 ml) finely chopped white onion
- 1 pound (450 g) mushrooms or cuitlacoche, roughly chopped (approximately four cups/1 l)
- 12 ounces (340 g) tomatoes, finely chopped (about 2 cups/500 ml)
- 2 garlic cloves, peeled and chopped
- 2 sprigs epazote or parsley, finely chopped
- 3 serrano chiles, cut into strips, with seeds and veins

- 3 tablespoons vegetable oil
- Salt to taste

To serve

- Prepared sour cream (not necessary)
- twelve tortillas
- Vegetable oil or melted lard for frying

Directions:

1. Heat the oil in a big frying pan and fry the onion and garlic gently for a few seconds; do not allow them to brown.
2. Put in the tomatoes, chiles, mushrooms, and salt. Cook on moderate heat, uncovered, stirring the mixture occasionally until the mushrooms are tender and the juices reduced—about fifteen minutes.
3. Put in the epazote and cook for a minute more. Set aside to cool a little.
4. Place a little of the mixture onto each of the tortillas, roll them up, and secure using a toothpick. Heat the fat and fry the tacos until they are just crisping but not hard. Drain them well and serve them instantly, either plain or with a little prepared sour cream.

NORTHERN BEAN TAMALES (TAMALES DE FRIJOL NORTEÑOS)

Yield: about 33 4-inch (10-cm) tamales

Ingredients:

The bean filling and chile sauce

- ¾ teaspoon cumin seeds, crushed
- 1 cup (250 ml) meat broth or water
- 2 garlic cloves
- 3 big ancho chiles, seeds and veins removed
- 3 tablespoons pork lard
- 4 peppercorns, crushed
- 8 ounces (225 g) flor de mayo or pinto beans

- Salt to taste

The masa

- 1 pound (450 g) tamale dough (about 2 cups/500 ml)
- 3 tablespoons reserved chile sauce
- 4½ ounces (130 g) pork lard (½ cup/125 ml, plus 2 tablespoons)
- About ⅓ cup (85 ml) meat broth or water
- About 36 halved corn husks—about 3 inches (8 cm) wide at the top, softened in water, drained, patted dry
- Salt to taste

Directions:

1. Prepare a tamale steamer.
2. Pick through the beans to ensure there are no small stones. Wash in cold water and skim the surface of any flotsam. Place the beans into a big deep cooking pan or slow cooker, cover with fresh water, and bring to its boiling point. Cook until the beans are fairly soft and most of the water has been absorbed—you should have approximately four cups (1 l).
3. In the meantime, prepare the chile sauce. Place the chiles and garlic into a small deep cooking pan, cover with water, bring to a simmer, and cook for approximately five minutes. Drain and save for later. Put ½ cup (125 ml) of the broth or water into your blender jar, put in the cumin and peppercorns, and blend well. Tear the chile into pieces and add, with the garlic and another ½ cup (125 ml) of the broth or water, to the blender jar and blend to a quite smooth sauce.
4. Heat the 3 tablespoons of lard in a deep frying pan, put in the beans, and purée on moderate heat to a rough-textured consistency. Mix in all but 3 tablespoons of the chile sauce and salt to taste and carry on cooking on moderate heat, stirring occasionally to prevent sticking until reduced—the bean paste should just plop off the spoon—and well seasoned, approximately fifteen minutes. Set aside to cool. You should have about 3½ cups (875 ml).
5. In a big container, combine the masa with the lard, the reserved 3 tablespoons chile sauce, and about ⅓ cup (85 ml) of the broth or water—with either your hand or an electric mixer—until all the ingredients are well blended. Put in salt as required.

6. Coat the top of the steamer with some of the corn husks and place an inverted soup plate in the center. Set on moderate heat.

7. Spread 1 rounded tablespoon of the dough super slimly over the whole width of the top of the corn husk and for approximately 4 inches (10 cm) down the husk. Put some of the bean paste down the center of the dough and fold one edge of the husk over the other to make a slender tamale—the overlapping masa will stick and help to close the husk more securely. Double the point of the husk up to cover the seam.

8. Stack the tamales in circular layers, the first layer supported at a gentle angle by the top of the plate. Cover the steamer and cook using high heat for approximately 50 minutes. The tamale is cooked when the dough separates cleanly from the husk.

NORTHERN PORK-FILLED TAMALES (TAMALES DE PUERCO NORTEÑOS)

Yield: about 33 4-inch (10-cm) tamales

Ingredients:

The meat filling

- ¾ teaspoon cumin seeds, crushed
- 1 pound (450 g) stewing pork with some fat, see note above, cut into ½-inch (1.5-cm) cubes
- 2 garlic cloves
- 3 big ancho chiles, seeds and veins removed
- 4 peppercorns, crushed
- Salt to taste

The masa

- 1 pound (450 g) tamale dough (about 2 cups/500 ml)
- 3 tablespoons of reserved chile sauce
- 4½ ounces (130 g) pork lard (½ cup/125 ml, plus 2 tablespoons)
- About 36 halved corn husks—about 3 inches (8 cm) wide at the top, softened in water, drained, patted dry
- Salt to taste

Directions:

1. Prepare a tamale steamer. Place the meat into a big deep cooking pan, cover with water, put in salt, and bring to a simmer. Carry on cooking until the meat is soft—thirty-five to forty minutes. Drain the meat and save for later. You will require minimum 2½ cups (625 ml) of broth; put in water if required to make up to that amount.

2. Place the chiles and garlic into a small deep cooking pan, cover with water, bring to a simmer, and cook for approximately five minutes. Strain and save for later.

3. Put ½ cup (125 ml) of the broth into your blender jar, put in the cumin and peppercorns, and blend well. Tear the chiles into pieces and put in to the blender jar together with the garlic and another ½ cup (125 ml) broth. Blend to a quite smooth sauce.

4. Place the meat into a frying pan, put in all but 3 tablespoons of the sauce and 1 cup (250 ml) of the broth, and cook on moderate heat, stirring occasionally, until well seasoned and the sauce is slightly reduced—to a medium consistency—about fifteen minutes. Adjust salt and allow to cool.

5. In a big container, combine the masa with the lard, the reserved 3 tablespoons of chile sauce, and about ⅓ cup (85 ml) of the rest of the broth with your hand, or an electric mixer, until all the ingredients are well blended—about five minutes. Put in salt as required.

6. Coat the top of the steamer with some of the corn husks and place an inverted soup plate in the center. Set on moderate heat.

7. Spread 1 rounded tablespoon of the dough super slimly over the whole width of the top and for approximately 4 inches (10 cm) down the corn husk. Put a few pieces of the meat and some of the sauce down the center of the dough and fold one edge of the husk over the other to make a slender tamale—the overlapping masa will stick and help to close the leaf securely. Double the point of the husk up to cover the seam.

8. Stack the tamales in circular layers, the first layer supported at a gentle angle by the top of the plate. Cover the steamer and cook using high heat for approximately 50 minutes. The tamale is cooked when the dough separates cleanly from the husk.

PANUCHOS

Yield: 12 panuchos; serves four to 6

Ingredients:

- 1 cup refried beans
- 1 recipe topping, warmed
- 1 teaspoon plus ¼ cup vegetable oil, plus extra as required
- 1¾ cups hot tap water
- 2 cups (8 ounces) masa harina
- Salt

Directions:

1. Mix masa harina and 1 teaspoon salt in medium container, then fold in water using a rubber spatula. Use your hands to knead mixture in container until tender dough forms, one to two minutes. Cover dough using a damp dish towel and allow it to sit for five minutes.
2. Cut twenty four 8 inch squares of parchment paper. Knead dough for a short period of time then split into 12 equivalent portions, roll into balls, and place on baking sheet. Cover dough using a damp dish towel.
3. Working with 1 ball at a time, press dough flat into 4½ inch wide disk between 2 pieces parchment with the help of a pie plate. Remove top piece parchment and gently smooth out any cracks. Move to plate, leaving bottom piece parchment in place, and cover using a damp dish towel; tortillas can be stacked.
4. Coat baking sheet using paper towels. Heat 1 teaspoon oil in 12 inch nonstick frying pan over moderate high heat until just shimmering. Put 1 tortilla parchment side up in your palm, remove parchment, then gently lay tortilla in hot pan; repeat with 2 more tortillas. Cook until lightly golden on both sides, approximately 6 minutes, turning midway through cooking.
5. Flip again and press tightly around center of each tortilla with wad of paper towels until puffed; move to prepared sheet. Repeat with remaining tortillas, putting in 1 teaspoon oil to pan between batches and lowering heat as required to stop scorching.
6. Use a paring knife to cut 2 inch opening around edge of tortillas. Ladle 1 generous tablespoon beans inside each tortilla then softly push on tortilla to spread out beans. (Panuchos can be stacked between parchment paper, wrapped using plastic wrap, and placed in the fridge for maximum 1 day or frozen for maximum three months; thaw completely before continuing.)

7. Heat remaining ¼ cup oil in now empty frying pan over moderate high heat until it starts to shimmer Working in batches, fry panuchos until golden and crisp on each side, five to seven minutes, turning tortillas and putting in extra oil to pan between batches as required. Return to baking sheet and sprinkle lightly with salt. Ladle topping onto center of each panucho before you serve.

PIGS' FEET TOSTADAS (TOSTADAS DE MANITAS DE PUERCO)

Yield: twelve tostadas

Ingredients:

To prepare the pigs' feet

- ¼ teaspoon dried mexican oregano
- ⅓ cup (85 ml) thickly cut white onion
- 1 small mexican bay leaf
- 2 fresh pigs' feet, split in half
- 2 garlic cloves
- 3 sprigs fresh thyme or ⅛ teaspoon dried
- 6 peppercorns
- Freshly ground pepper
- Salt to taste

To serve

- 1 cup (250 ml) thinly cut purple onion
- 1 small avocado, cut
- 1½ cups (375 ml) finely shredded and dressed lettuce
- 1½ cups (375 ml) salsa ranchera, omitting the onion
- 3 tablespoons finely grated queso añejo
- The pigs' feet jelly
- twelve tortillas
- Vegetable oil for frying

Directions:

1. Put all the ingredients for the pigs' feet into a big deep cooking pan and immerse in cold water by ½ inch (1.5 cm). Bring slowly to its boiling point, then reduce the heat and simmer for approximately 2½ hours. (the meat must be soft but not too tender.) Set aside to cool in the broth.
2. When the pigs' feet are sufficiently cool to handle, remove all the bones cautiously and cut the meat, gelatinous gristle, and rind together into little pieces and put in a shallow dish and sprinkle with salt and pepper (bearing in mind that cooked foods served cold need to be more highly seasoned). Strain the broth and pour 1⅓ cups (335 ml) of it over the meat. Set the dish in your fridge until tightly set—approximately 1 hour.
3. Heat the oil in a frying pan and fry the tortillas until crunchy. Drain thoroughly.
4. Chop the pigs' feet jelly into little squares and put 2 to 3 heaped tablespoons onto each tostada. Cover with lettuce, some slices of avocado, sauce, cheese, and last of all the onion rings.

POTATO TACOS (TACOS DE PAPA)

Yield: 12 tacos

Ingredients:

The filling

*   ½ medium white onion
*   12 ounces (340 g) cooked unpeeled and diced red bliss or other waxy potatoes (about 2¼ cups/563 ml)
*   4 ounces (115 g) queso fresco, crumbled (about ¾ cup/190 ml)
*   Salt to taste

To serve

*   ⅔ cup (165 ml) prepared sour cream
*   1 cup (250 ml) salsa ranchera, omitting the onion, warmed
*   1½ cups (375 ml) shredded lettuce
*   12 5- to 6-inch (12.5- to fifteen-cm) tortillas

- Jalapeño chiles en escabeche
- Vegetable oil for frying

Directions:

1. Combine the potatoes with the remaining filling ingredients.
2. Fill each tortilla with approximately 2 tablespoons of the mixture and secure with toothpicks.
3. Heat the oil and fry until the tortilla is just crisp on the outside. Drain thoroughly.
4. Serve instantly, topped with the sour cream, warm sauce, and lettuce. Serve the chiles separately.

SHREDDED BEEF TACOS

Yield: Servings 6

Ingredients:

- ½ cup cider vinegar
- ½ teaspoon ground cinnamon
- ½ teaspoon ground cloves
- 1 big onion, cut into ½ inch thick rounds
- 1 recipe Cabbage Carrot Slaw
- 1½ cups beer
- 18 (6 inch) corn tortillas, warmed
- 2 tablespoons tomato paste
- 2 teaspoons dried oregano
- 2 teaspoons ground cumin
- 3 bay leaves
- 3 pounds boneless beef short ribs, trimmed and slice into 2 inch cubes
- 4 dried ancho chiles, stemmed, seeded, and torn into ½ inch pieces (1 cup)
- 4 ounces queso fresco, crumbled (1 cup)
- 6 garlic cloves, lightly crushed and peeled
- Lime wedges
- Salt and pepper

Directions:

1. Adjust oven rack to lower middle position and heat oven to 325 degrees. Mix beer, vinegar, anchos, tomato paste, garlic, bay leaves, cumin, oregano, cloves, cinnamon, 2 teaspoons salt, and ½ teaspoon pepper in Dutch oven. Position onion rounds in single layer on bottom of pot. Put beef on top of onion rounds in single layer. Cover and cook until meat is thoroughly browned and soft, 2½ to three hours.

2. Using slotted spoon, move beef to big container and cover. Strain liquid through fine mesh strainer into 2 cup liquid measuring cup (do not wash pot). Discard onion rounds and bay leaves, then move remaining solids to blender. Allow strained liquid to settle for five minutes, then skim any fat off surface and put in water as required to equal 1 cup. Put in liquid to blender with solids and pulse until smooth, approximately 2 minutes; move to now empty pot.

3. Using 2 forks, shred beef into bite size pieces. Bring sauce to simmer on moderate heat. Mix in shredded beef and sprinkle with salt to taste. Serve with warm tortillas, queso fresco, slaw, and lime wedges.

SHREDDED PORK AND TOMATO FILLING FOR TACOS (PUERCO EN SALSA DE JITOMATE)

Yield: enough filling for twelve to fifteen small tacos, 1½ cups (375 ml)

Ingredients:

- ⅓ cup (85 ml) finely chopped white onion
- 1 garlic clove, roughly chopped
- 1⅓ cups (335 ml) cooked and shredded pork (approximately 12 ounces/340 g)
- 12 ounces (340 g) tomatoes, broiled
- 2 fresh jalapeño chiles, with seeds, thinly cut into thin strips
- 2 tablespoons lard or vegetable oil
- Salt to taste

Directions:

1. Combine the tomatoes with the garlic until almost smooth. Set aside.

2. Heat the lard in a big frying pan and cook the onion and chiles, without browning, until translucent. Put in the tomato mixture and cook on moderate heat for approximately five minutes; put in salt.

3. Put in the meat and carry on cooking the mixture for eight minutes, or until it is all well seasoned and the sauce moist but not juicy.

SOPES

Yield: 12 sopes; serves four to 6

Ingredients:

- 1 cup refried beans
- 1 recipe filling, warmed
- 1 teaspoon salt
- 1¾ cups hot tap water
- 2 cups (8 ounces) masa harina
- 2 cups vegetable oil

Directions:

1. Mix masa harina and salt in medium container, then fold in water using a rubber spatula. Use your hands to knead mixture in container until tender dough forms, one to two minutes. Cover dough using a damp dish towel and allow it to sit for five minutes.

2. Coat baking sheet using parchment paper. Cut sides of 1 quart zipper lock bag, leaving bottom seam undamaged. Knead dough for a short period of time, then split into 12 equivalent portions, roll into balls, and place on prepared sheet. Cover dough using a damp dish towel.

3. Working with 1 piece dough at a time, place on 1 side of zipper lock bag and fold other side over top. Push dough flat into 3½ inch wide disk with the help of a pie plate. Take the plastic off from top and pinch dough around edges as required to create ¾ inch tall sides. Take the plastic off from bottom of sope, return sope to baking sheet, and cover using a damp dish towel.

4. Adjust oven rack to middle position and heat oven to 200 degrees. Heat 1an inch straight sided sauté pan on moderate heat until hot, two to three minutes. Cautiously

place 6 sopes in hot, dry pan. Using paper towels, press lightly in center of each sope to make sure contact with pan. Cook until bottoms start to brown, four to five minutes; return to baking sheet (do not cover). Repeat with remaining sopes. (Sopes can be wrapped firmly using plastic wrap and frozen for maximum three months; thaw completely before continuing.)

5. Coat baking sheet using paper towels. Cautiously add oil to now empty pan and heat over moderate high heat to 375 degrees. Put in 6 sopes, browned side down, and fry until bottom is crisp and golden, two to three minutes, adjusting heat as required to maintain oil temperature of 325 to 350 degrees. Lightly flip sopes and fry until sides are crisp and golden (center of sopes will not brown), two to three minutes.

6. Move sopes upright to prepared sheet and dab using paper towels to remove surplus oil; keep warm in oven. Repeat with remaining sopes. Spread refried beans uniformly into center of sopes, then top with filling before you serve.

SPONGY TAMALES FILLED WITH CHILE STRIPS AND CHEESE (TAMALES CERNIDOS DE RAJAS Y QUESO)

Yield: about 30 3-inch (8-cm) tamales

Ingredients:

The masa

- 1 pound (450 g) tamale flour
- 36 (to be safe) corn husks, soaked to tenderize and shaken dry
- 8 ounces (225 g) pork lard (approximately 1 cup/250 ml)
- About 1 cup (250 ml) warm chicken broth
- Salt to taste

The filling

- 12 ounces (340 g) chihuahua, mexican manchego, or muenster cheese, cut into strips about ½ inch (1.5 cm) wide
- 2 cups (500 ml) rajas of poblano chiles, approximately eight chiles
- 2 cups (500 ml) salsa de tomate verde

Directions:

1. Using an electric mixer, beat the lard until light and fluffy—about five minutes. Slowly beat in the flour alternately with the broth, beating meticulously after each addition. Put in salt. If beaten adequately, a small piece of dough should float on the surface of a glass of water.
2. Place a prepared tamale steamer using low heat.
3. Spread 1 heaped tablespoon of the masa finely over the upper part, and about 3 inches (8 cm) down the leaf. Put 2 strips of the chile, a strip of the cheese, and a tablespoon of the sauce over them. Fold the husk so that the filling is mostly covered by the masa and turn the spare part of the husk up the back of the tamale.
4. Set the tamales vertically in the top part of the steamer, cover well, and steam for approximately 1¼ hours. To test, open up a tamale; the masa should separate cleanly from the husk. Leave the tamales in the steamer until they are cool; they will become slightly firmer and less likely to break as you serve them.

SWEET FRESH CORN TAMALES (TAMALES DULCES DE ELOTE)

Yield: about 24 tamales

Ingredients:

- ¼ teaspoon salt
- ½ teaspoon baking powder
- 1 cup (250 ml) grated piloncillo or dark brown sugar
- 1 small tablespoon anise seeds
- 30 (to be safe) fresh corn husks, washed and shaken dry
- 4 cups (1 l) field or white starchy corn kernels
- 4 ounces (115 g) pork lard (½ cup/125 ml), melted and cooled
- 4 ounces (115 g) unsalted butter (½ cup/125 ml), melted and cooled
- 8-inch (20-cm) piece of cinnamon stick
- About ½ cup (125 ml) water

Directions:

1. Ready a tamale steamer and line the top part with fresh corn husks.
2. Use a food processor/blender to blend the corn with the water, in two batches, to a rough-textured consistency—you will have to keep stopping the machine and loosening the mixture using a spatula, but do not put in more liquid.
3. Grind the spices to a powder and put in with the sugar and salt to the corn, mixing meticulously. Slowly mix in the fats and lastly the baking powder. Again mix meticulously. The consistency must be that of a loose, textured paste.
4. Put approximately 1½ tablespoons of the corn mixture down the center of each husk to extend about 3 inches (8 cm) long. Curl one side of the leaf over the mixture, ensuring there is a good overlap and the mixture cannot ooze out. Push the leaf tightly where the mixture ends and fold the empty part, and pointed end, to the back of the tamale.
5. Ensure that the water is boiling in the steamer, then lay the tamales in horizontal layers in the top of the steamer. It is best to put one layer in first and allow it to firm up a little—about ten minutes—before stacking the other layers on top. Steam for approximately 1½ hours until, when tested, the dough separates cleanly from the husk.
6. Eat accompanied by a cup of atole or hot chocolate. Reheat this type of tamale, with the husk removed, on a comal or griddle on moderate heat.

SWEET TAMALES (TAMALES DE DULCE)

Yield: about 24 3-inch (8-cm) tamales

Ingredients:

- ⅓ cup (85 ml) chicken broth or water
- ½ cup (125 ml) sugar
- ½ teaspoon salt
- ⅔ cup (165 ml) roughly chopped pecans
- ¾ cup (185 ml) raisins
- 1 tablespoon ground cinnamon
- 1¼ pounds (570 g) tamale dough (about 2½ cups/625 ml)
- 7 ounces (200 g) pork lard
- About 24 corn husks (always do a few extra) soaked to tenderize and shaken dry

Directions:

Place a prepared tamale steamer using low heat.

1. Place the lard into a container and beat with an electric beater until the lard is very white and opaque—about five minutes. Slowly beat in the masa, broth, and salt, beating well after each addition. Continue beating for another five minutes, progressively putting in the cinnamon and sugar. Mix in the chopped pecans.
2. Spread a slim layer of the dough over the inside of the husk and place a teaspoon of raisins down the middle of the dough. Fold the husk over so that it covers the dough and turn the pointed end up to the back of the tamale.
3. When the water is boiling stack the tamales vertically in the top part, cover, and steam approximately 1 hour or until the pale pink dough comes cleanly away from the husk.

TACOS AL PASTOR

Yield: Servings 6

Ingredients:

- ⅛ teaspoon ground cloves
- ½ cup chopped fresh cilantro
- ½ pineapple, peeled, cored and slice into ½ inch thick rings
- ½ teaspoon ground cumin
- ¾ teaspoon sugar
- 1 lime, cut into 8 wedges
- 1¼ pounds plum tomatoes, cored and quartered
- 1½ cups water
- 12 dried guajillo chiles, stemmed, seeded and torn into ½ inch pieces (1½ cups)
- 18 (6 inch) corn tortillas
- 3 pounds boneless pork butt roast, fat cap trimmed to ¼ inch thick and cut against grain into ½ inch thick slabs
- 4 bay leaves
- 8 garlic cloves, peeled
- Salt and pepper
- Vegetable oil

Directions:

1. Toast guajillos in Dutch oven on moderate heat, stirring regularly, until aromatic, 2 to six minutes. Mix in water, tomatoes, garlic, bay leaves, 2 teaspoons salt, ½ teaspoon pepper, sugar, cumin, and cloves. Increase heat to moderate high and bring to simmer. Cover, decrease the heat to low, and simmer while stirring once in a while, until guajillos become tender and tomatoes purée easily, approximately twenty minutes.

2. Move mixture to blender and pulse until smooth, approximately one minute. Strain puree through fine mesh strainer, pushing on solids to extract as much liquid as you can; discard solids and return puree to pot.

3. Put in pork to pot, immerse in sauce, and bring to simmer on moderate heat. Partly cover, reduce heat, and gently simmer until pork is soft but still holds together, 1½ to 1¾ hours, turning and rearranging pork midway through cooking. (Pork and sauce can be placed in your fridge for maximum 2 days.)

4. Move pork to big plate, season both sides with salt, and cover firmly with aluminium foil. Whisk sauce to blend. Move ½ cup to container for grilling. Pour off all but ½ cup sauce left in pot (reserve surplus sauce for future use). Squeeze 2 lime wedges into sauce in pot and put in spent lime wedges; sprinkle with salt to taste. Brush pineapple with oil and sprinkle with salt.

5. **For a Charcoal Grill:** Open bottom vent fully. Light big chimney starter filled with charcoal briquettes (6 quarts). When top coals are partly covered with ash, pour uniformly over grill. Set cooking grate in place, cover, and open lid vent fully. Heat grill until hot, approximately five minutes. **For a Gas Grill:** Set all burners to high, cover, and heat grill until hot, approximately fifteen minutes. Turn all burners to moderate.

6. Clean and oil cooking grate. Put pineapple on grill and cook, turning as required, until tender and caramelized, ten to fifteen minutes; move to cutting board. In the meantime, brush 1 side of pork with ¼ cup reserved sauce, then place on grill, sauce side down. Cook until thoroughly browned and crunchy, five to seven minutes. Repeat with second side using remaining ¼ cup reserved sauce; move to cutting board and tent using foil.

7. Working in batches, grill tortillas, turning as required, until warm and soft, approximately half a minute; wrap firmly in foil to keep tender.

8. Chop pineapple and move to serving container. Using tongs to stable pork, slice each piece crosswise into ⅛ inch pieces. Bring sauce left in pot to simmer on moderate

heat. Remove the heat, put in cut pork and toss to coat with sauce. Serve with tortillas, cilantro, pineapple, and remaining 6 lime wedges.

TACOS OF CHILE STRIPS (TACOS DE RAJAS DE ZACATECAS)

Yield: 12 tacos

Ingredients:

The filling

- 2 tablespoons vegetable oil
- 3 big eggs
- 3 poblano chiles, charred, peeled, cleaned, and slice into thin strips
- 3 tablespoons roughly chopped white onion
- 8 ounces (225 g) tomatoes, broiled
- Salt to taste

To serve

- 1⅓ cups (335 ml) prepared sour cream
- twelve tortillas
- Vegetable oil for frying

Directions:

1. Heat the oil in a big frying pan. Put in the chile strips and cook using low heat for approximately 3 minutes.
2. Combine the tomatoes with the onion until the desired smoothness is achieved, then put in the puree to the chiles in the pan. Sprinkle with salt and cook on moderate heat for approximately five minutes, stirring and scraping the bottom of the pan occasionally.
3. Beat the eggs lightly and mix them into the mixture. Continue stirring until they are just set, then take out of the heat and keep warm.
4. Heat the oil in a frying pan and fry the tortillas on both sides. Fry slightly more than you would for enchiladas, but not allowing them to get so crisp that you cannot easily

fold them over. Drain thoroughly, then fill each one with a little of the chile-egg filling. Double the tortillas over and set on the serving dish.

5. Pour the sour cream over the tacos and serve instantly.

TAMALES

Yield: 18

A tamale is a classic Mesoamerican dish, made of masa or dough, which is steamed in a corn husk or banana leaf. The wrapping can either be discarded before eating, or used as a plate.

Ingredients:

- ¾ teaspoon salt
- 1 cup (4 ounces) plus 2 tablespoons masa harina
- 1 cup plus 2 tablespoons quick grits
- 1 recipe filling
- 1 tablespoon sugar
- 1½ cups boiling water
- 1½ cups frozen corn, thawed
- 20 big dried corn husks
- 2¼ teaspoons baking powder
- 6 tablespoons lard, softened
- 6 tablespoons unsalted butter, cut into ½ inch cubes and softened

Directions:

1. Put grits in medium container, whisk in boiling water, and allow it to stand until water is mostly absorbed, approximately ten minutes. Mix in masa harina, cover, and let cool completely, approximately twenty minutes. In the meantime, place husks in big container, cover with hot water, and allow to soak until flexible, approximately 30 minutes.
2. Process masa dough, corn, butter, lard, sugar, baking powder, and salt together inside a food processor until mixture is light, sticky, and super smooth, approximately 1 minute, scraping down sides as required. Remove husks from water and pat dry using a dish towel.

3. Working with 1 husk at a time, lay on counter, cupped side up, with long side facing you and wide end on right side. Spread ¼ cup tamale dough into 4 inch square over bottom right hand corner, pushing it flush to bottom edge but leaving ¼ inch border at wide edge. Mound 2 small tablespoons filling in line across center of dough, parallel to bottom edge. Roll husk away from you and over filling, so that dough surrounds filling and makes a cylinder. Fold up the tapered end, leaving top open, and move seam side down to platter.

4. Fit big pot or Dutch oven with steamer basket, removing feet from steamer basket if pot is short. Fill pot with water until it just touches bottom of basket and bring to boiling point. Lightly lay tamales in basket with open ends facing up and seam sides facing out. Cover and steam, checking water level frequently and putting in extra water as required, until tamales easily come free from husks, approximately 1 hour. Move tamales to big platter. Reheat remaining sauce from filling in covered container in microwave, approximately half a minute, and serve with tamales.

TAMALE FILLINGS

Each filling makes enough for 18 tamales.

CHIPOTLE BEEF FILLING

- ⅛ teaspoon ground cloves
- ½ teaspoon ground cinnamon
- ¾ teaspoon ground cumin
- 1 big onion, chopped
- 1 teaspoon dried oregano
- 1 teaspoon sugar, plus extra as required
- 1½ tablespoons minced canned chipotle chile in adobo sauce
- 1½ tablespoons red wine vinegar
- 1¾ pounds top blade steaks, trimmed
- 3 cups beef broth
- 3 tablespoons vegetable oil
- 4 dried ancho chiles, stemmed, seeded, and torn into ½ inch pieces (1 cup)
- 6 garlic cloves, minced
- Salt and pepper

Directions:

1. Toast anchos in 12 inch frying pan on moderate heat, stirring regularly, until aromatic, 2 to six minutes; move to container.
2. Heat oil in now empty frying pan on moderate heat until it starts to shimmer Put in onion and cook until tender, five to seven minutes. Mix in garlic, chipotle, oregano, sugar, cumin, cinnamon, cloves, 1 teaspoon salt, and toasted chiles and cook for half a minute. Mix in broth and simmer until slightly reduced, approximately ten minutes. Move mixture to blender and pulse until smooth, approximately twenty seconds; return to frying pan.
3. Season beef with salt and pepper, nestle into frying pan, and bring to simmer on moderate heat. Cover, decrease the heat to low, and cook until beef is super soft, approximately 1½ hours.
4. Move beef to carving board and allow to cool slightly. Using 2 forks, shred beef into little pieces. Stir vinegar into sauce and sprinkle with salt, pepper, and sugar to taste. Toss shredded beef with 1 cup sauce. Reheat remaining sauce and serve with tamales.

RED CHILE CHICKEN FILLING

- ¾ teaspoon dried oregano
- ¾ teaspoon ground cumin
- 1 big onion, chopped
- 1¼ pounds boneless, skinless chicken thighs, trimmed
- 1½ tablespoons cider vinegar
- 3 cups chicken broth
- 3 tablespoons vegetable oil
- 4 dried ancho chiles, stemmed, seeded, and torn into ½ inch pieces (1 cup)
- 4 dried New Mexican chiles, stemmed, seeded, and torn into ½ inch pieces (1 cup)
- 6 garlic cloves, minced
- Salt and pepper
- Sugar

Directions:

1. Toast anchos and New Mexican chiles in 12 inch frying pan on moderate heat, stirring regularly, until aromatic, 2 to six minutes; move to container.
2. Heat oil in now empty frying pan on moderate heat until it starts to shimmer Put in onion and cook until tender, five to seven minutes. Mix in garlic, cumin, oregano, ½

teaspoon salt, and toasted chiles and cook for half a minute. Mix in broth and simmer until slightly reduced, approximately ten minutes. Move mixture to blender and pulse until smooth, approximately twenty seconds; return to frying pan.

3. Season chicken with salt and pepper, nestle into frying pan, and bring to simmer on moderate heat. Cover, decrease the heat to low, and cook until chicken records 160 degrees, twenty to twenty-five minutes.

4. Move chicken to carving board and allow to cool slightly. Using 2 forks, shred chicken into little pieces. Stir vinegar into sauce and sprinkle with salt, pepper, and sugar to taste. Toss shredded chicken with 1 cup sauce. Reheat remaining sauce and serve with tamales.

TORTILLA "SANDWICH" (TORTILLAS COMO SANDWICH)

Yield: 6 tortilla sandwiches

Ingredients:

- ½ cup (125 ml) finely chopped white onion
- ¾ cup (185 ml) prepared sour cream
- ¾ cup (185 ml) salsa de tomate verde, guacamole, or salsa ranchera
- 1½ cups (375 ml) finely shredded lettuce
- 6 ounces (180 g) chihuahua cheese or cheddar, finely cut
- 6 ounces (180 g) cooked ham, thinly cut
- 6 radishes, cut into flowers or cut
- twelve tortillas
- Vegetable oil for frying

Directions:

1. Lay 6 of the tortillas out flat; spread each one with some of the ham and cheese. Cover each with another tortilla to make a sandwich, then secure each pair of tortillas with 2 toothpicks, one on each side.

2. Heat the oil and fry each sandwich on either side until just starting to get crunchy, not hard. Drain thoroughly, then top with the sour cream, sauce, and chopped onion. Garnish each plate with the lettuce and radishes. Serve instantly.

TORTILLAS STACKED WITH GUACAMOLE AND TOMATO SAUCE (TORTILLAS PILADAS CON GUACAMOLE Y SALSA DE JITOMATE)

Yield: Servings four to 6

Ingredients:

The sauce

- 1 pound (450 g) tomatoes, roughly chopped (about 3 cups/750 ml)
- 2 garlic cloves
- 2 tablespoons vegetable oil
- 5 scallions, finely chopped
- Salt to taste

To serve

- ¾ cup (185 ml) prepared sour cream
- 1½ cups (375 ml) guacamole
- 4 ounces (115 g) chihuahua cheese or mild cheddar cheese, grated
- twelve tortillas, freshly made, if possible, and not too thin
- Vegetable oil for frying

Directions:

1. Heat the oil in a big frying pan and cook the scallions gently until they are tender but not browned.
2. Combine the tomatoes with the garlic. Put into the pan with the salt and fry the sauce over quite high heat while stirring and scraping the bottom of the pan almost continuously, until it has reduced and seasoned—about five minutes. Set aside and keep warm.
3. Heat the oil in a different frying pan and fry the tortillas for a short period of time on both sides. Drain thoroughly.
4. Make 3 piles. Immerse 3 of the tortillas into the sauce and lay them flat onto the serving dish. Spread them with approximately 2 tablespoons each of the guacamole, a little cheese, and some sour cream.

5. Immerse 3 more tortillas into the sauce and cover the filling. Repeat with an additional layer of tortillas on top of the first "sandwich," then repeat a layer of guacamole, cheese, and sour cream, ending with a layer of the rest of the tortillas.
6. Pour the remaining sauce over the stacks of tortillas and drizzle the rest of the cheese over the top. Cut into wedges and serve instantly.

TOSTADAS

Yield: twelve tostadas; serves four to 6

Ingredients:

- ¾ cup peanut oil
- 1 recipe topping, warmed
- 12 (6 inch) corn tortillas
- Kosher salt

Directions:

1. Using fork, poke center of each tortilla three to four times (to stop puffing and allow for even cooking). Heat oil in 8 inch frying pan on moderate heat to 350 degrees. Coat baking sheet with several layers of paper towels.
2. Working with one tortilla at a time, put in to hot oil and place metal potato masher on top to keep tortilla flat and submerged in oil. Fry until crunchy and mildly browned, 45 to 60 seconds (no flipping is necessary). Move fried tortilla to readied baking sheet. Repeat with remaining tortillas. Drizzle with salt. (Tostadas can be stored at room temperature for maximum 1 day.)
3. Ladle filling onto center of each tostada before you serve.

BAKED TOSTADAS

Spray tortillas meticulously with vegetable oil spray and spread out over 2 rimmed baking sheets. Bake on upper middle and lower middle racks in 450 degree oven until mildly browned and crisp, approximately ten minutes, switching and rotating sheets midway through baking. Drizzle lightly with salt.

TOSTADA FILLINGS

SPICY ZUCCHINI WITH SCALLIONS AND COTIJA CHEESE

Ingredients:

- ½ teaspoon dried oregano
- 1 cup vegetable broth
- 1 pound zucchini, cut into ½ inch pieces
- 1 serrano chile, stemmed, seeded, and minced
- 1 small onion, chopped fine
- 1 tablespoon chopped fresh cilantro
- 1 tablespoon vegetable oil
- 2 scallions, cut thin
- 2 tablespoons tomato paste
- 3 garlic cloves, minced
- 4 ounces Cotija cheese, crumbled (1 cup)
- Salt and pepper

Directions:

1. Heat oil in 12 inch nonstick frying pan on moderate heat until it starts to shimmer Put in onion and serrano and cook until mildly browned, approximately eight minutes. Mix in tomato paste, garlic, and oregano and cook until aromatic, approximately one minute. Mix in broth, 1 teaspoon salt, and ½ teaspoon pepper and simmer until slightly thickened, approximately 6 minutes.
2. Mix in zucchini, cover, and cook until zucchini is slightly softened, five to seven minutes. Remove the cover, increase heat to moderate high, and cook, stirring frequently, until sauce has thickened and coats zucchini, approximately 4 minutes. Remove the heat, mix in cilantro and sprinkle with salt and pepper to taste. Decorate using scallions and Cotija.

CHICKEN WITH PICKLED ONION AND CABBAGE

Ingredients:

- ½ cup chicken broth
- ½ teaspoon dried oregano

- ½ teaspoon grated lime zest plus 1 tablespoon juice
- 1 avocado, halved, pitted, and cut thin
- 1 pound boneless, skinless chicken breasts, trimmed
- 1 recipe Pickled Onion and Cabbage
- 1 small onion, chopped fine
- 1 tablespoon ancho chile powder
- 1 tablespoon chopped fresh cilantro
- 2 garlic cloves, minced
- 2 ounces queso fresco, crumbled (½ cup)
- 2 tablespoons vegetable oil
- Salt and pepper

Directions:

1. Heat oil in medium deep cooking pan on moderate heat until it starts to shimmer Put in onion and cook until tender, approximately 4 minutes. Mix in chile powder, garlic, oregano, lime zest, and pinch salt and cook for half a minute. Mix in broth and bring to simmer. Nestle chicken into sauce. Cover, decrease the heat to moderate low, and cook until chicken records 160 degrees, ten to fifteen minutes, turning midway through cooking.

2. Move chicken to carving board and allow to cool slightly. Using 2 forks, shred chicken into little pieces. Return sauce to high heat and simmer until it becomes thick, approximately five minutes. Remove the heat, mix in shredded chicken, lime juice, and cilantro and sprinkle with salt and pepper to taste. Decorate using avocado, Pickled Onion and Cabbage, and queso fresco.

TOMATILLO CHICKEN WITH RADISHES AND QUESO FRESCO

Ingredients:

- ¼ cup chicken broth
- ½ small onion, chopped
- ¾ cup fresh cilantro leaves plus ¼ cup chopped
- 1 garlic clove, peeled
- 1 jalapeño chile, stemmed, halved, and seeded
- 1 pound boneless, skinless chicken breasts, trimmed
- 1 pound fresh tomatillos, husks and stems removed, washed well and dried

- 1 tablespoon lime juice
- 1 teaspoon vegetable oil
- 4 ounces queso fresco, crumbled (1 cup)
- 4 radishes, cut thin
- Salt and pepper

Directions:

1. Adjust oven rack 6 inches from broiler element and heat broiler. Coat rimmed baking sheet with aluminium foil. Toss tomatillos, onion, jalapeño, and garlic with oil and spread over prepared sheet. Broil, shaking sheet once in a while, until vegetables are well charred, ten to twelve minutes.

2. Move broiled vegetables to food processor and allow to cool slightly. Put in cilantro, broth, lime juice, and ¼ teaspoon salt and pulse until crudely chopped, approximately 7 pulses. Move to 10 inch nonstick frying pan, sprinkle with salt to taste, and bring to simmer.

3. Nestle chicken into sauce. Cover, decrease the heat to moderate low, and cook until chicken records 160 degrees, ten to fifteen minutes, turning midway through cooking. Move chicken to carving board and allow to cool slightly. Using 2 forks, shred chicken into little pieces. Toss chicken with sauce left in pan and sprinkle with salt and pepper to taste. Decorate using radishes, queso fresco, and cilantro.

PORK TINGA WITH AVOCADO AND QUESO FRESCO

- ¼ cup fresh cilantro leaves
- ½ teaspoon dried oregano
- 1 (fifteen ounce) can tomato sauce
- 1 avocado, halved, pitted, and diced
- 1 tablespoon minced canned chipotle chile in adobo sauce
- 2 bay leaves
- 2 onions (1 quartered, 1 chopped fine)
- 2 ounces queso fresco, crumbled (½ cup)
- 2 pounds boneless pork butt roast, trimmed and slice into an inch pieces
- 2 tablespoons olive oil
- 4 sprigs fresh thyme
- 5 garlic cloves (3 peeled and smashed, 2 minced)

- Lime wedges
- Salt

Directions:

1. Bring pork, quartered onion, smashed garlic, thyme sprigs, 1 teaspoon salt, and 6 cups water to simmer in big deep cooking pan over moderate high heat, skimming off any foam that rises to surface. Decrease the heat to moderate low, partly cover, and cook until pork is soft, 1¼ to 1½ hours.

2. Drain pork, saving for later 1 cup cooking liquid. Discard onion, garlic, and thyme. Return pork to now empty deep cooking pan and purée into rough ½ inch pieces using potato masher. (Pork can be placed in your fridge for maximum 2 days.)

3. Heat oil in 12 inch nonstick frying pan over moderate high heat until it starts to shimmer Put in oregano, shredded pork, and chopped onion and cook, stirring frequently, until pork is thoroughly browned and crunchy, 7 to ten minutes. Mix in minced garlic and cook until aromatic, approximately half a minute. Mix in tomato sauce, chipotle, bay leaves, and reserved pork cooking liquid and simmer until almost all liquid has vaporized, five to seven minutes. Discard bay leaves and sprinkle with salt to taste. Decorate using avocado, queso fresco, cilantro, and lime wedges.

VERACRUZ RANCH TAMALES (TAMALES VERACRUZANOS TIPO RANCHERO)

Yield: approximately twenty tamales

Ingredients:

The meat for the filling

- ¼ white onion, roughly chopped
- 1 garlic clove
- 1 pound (450 g) pork shoulder with some fat, cut into ¼-inch (.75-cm) cubes
- Salt to taste

The sauce for the filling

- 1 chipotle chile, dried or canned

- 1 cup (250 ml) reserved pork broth
- 1 garlic clove, roughly chopped
- 1 tablespoon roughly chopped white onion
- 1½ tablespoons pork lard or vegetable oil
- 4 ancho chiles, seeds and veins removed
- 6 ounces (180 g) tomatoes, broiled
- Salt to taste

The masa

- 1¼ pounds (565 g) tamale or tortilla dough (about 2½ cups/625 ml)
- 5 ounces (140 g) pork lard (approximately 1 heaped cup/265 ml)
- About ½ cup (125 ml) of the reserved broth, warm
- Salt to taste

Assembling the tamales

- 20 pieces of banana leaves, approximately 9 by 7 inches (23 by 18 cm)
- 5 big hoja santa leaves, cut into four equivalent portions

Directions:

1. Place the pork, onion, garlic, and salt into a big deep cooking pan. Barely cover with water and bring to its boiling point. Reduce the heat and simmer the pork for approximately thirty-five minutes. Allow the pork to cool off in the broth, then strain the meat, saving for later the broth, and set both aside. There must be approximately 1½ cups (375 ml) of broth; if not, make up to that amount with water.
2. Heat the comal and toast the chiles lightly, turning them occasionally so they do not burn.
3. Cover the chiles with hot water and allow them to soak for approximately ten minutes, then remove using a slotted spoon and put into a blender jar. Put in ½ cup of broth, the onion, garlic, and tomatoes and blend to a smooth sauce.
4. Heat the lard in a big frying pan, put in the chile sauce, and cook for approximately five minutes, stirring occasionally to prevent sticking. Put in salt to taste.
5. Put in the pork and ½ cup of broth to the sauce and allow the mixture to cook for approximately five minutes on moderate heat until it is all well seasoned and the liquid has reduced a little. Put in salt to taste. Set aside.

6. To prepare the dough, beat the lard until white and well aerated—about five minutes.

7. Beat the rest of the broth and dough alternately into the lard, putting in the salt. Continue beating for approximately five minutes more. (do not try to float a piece of the dough; it will be a much softer and damper consistency than that for ordinary tamales.)

8. Pass the leaves over a bare flame to make them slightly more flexible. Spread 1 big tablespoon of the dough over an area approximately four by 3 inches (10 by 8 cm) and ¼ inch (.75 cm) thick. Put two cubes of the meat and a little of the sauce into the center of the dough and cover with a piece of the hoja santa. Fold the edges of the banana leaf over until they completely cover the dough and filling. Stack the tamales horizontally in overlapping layers in the top of the steamer. Cover them with more leaves and then cover the top of the steamer with a thick cloth or piece of toweling and the steamer lid. Steam in the normal way for an hour.

YUCATECAN CHICKEN AND PORK TAMALE PIE (MUK-BIL POLLO)

Yield: Servings 6

Ingredients:

The fat for the dough

- 8 ounces (225 g) pork fat, cut into little cubes

The filling

- ¼ teaspoon dried mexican oregano, yucatecan if possible
- ¼ teaspoon peppercorns and 1 tablespoon achiote seeds (or 2 teaspoons recado rojo)
- ⅓ cup (85 ml) finely chopped white onion
- ½ medium green pepper, seeded and diced
- 1 big sprig epazote
- 1 habanero chile, whole
- 1 tablespoon mild white vinegar
- 1½ cups (375 ml) reserved meat broth
- 1½ teaspoons salt

- 2 garlic cloves, crushed
- 2 tablespoons tortilla masa
- 3 tablespoons of the rendered pork fat
- 4 garlic cloves, toasted
- 8 ounces (225 g) pork shoulder
- 8 ounces (225 g) tomatoes, finely chopped (approximately 1⅓ cups/333 ml)
- A 3-pound (1.35-kg) chicken
- Salt to taste

The dough

- ¼ teaspoon yucatecan chile seco or hot paprika
- 2 pounds (900 g) tortilla dough (approximately four cups/1 l)
- 2 teaspoons salt
- banana leaves to line the pan
- the rest of the rendered pork fat

Directions:

1. Lay two pieces of string—each 30 inches (76 cm) long—parallel across the length of a metal baking pan approximately eight by 8 by 2½ inches (20 by 20 by 6.5 cm) and two other pieces of string of the same length across the width—there will be a big overlap for tying.
2. Swiftly pass the banana leaves over a flame to make them more flexible, and line the dish with them, smooth, glossy side up, so that they overlap the pan by about 5 inches (13 cm) all the way around. Cut one leaf slightly bigger than the size of the pan.
3. Heat the fat in a frying pan on moderate heat, or in your oven, until the lard renders out of it. Turn the pieces occasionally so that they do not burn but become uniformly crisp and brown. Ladle out 3 tablespoons fat for frying the filling and reserve the rest for the dough.
4. Chop the chicken into serving pieces and the pork into 1-inch (2.5-cm) cubes. Place them into a pan with the garlic, oregano, and salt and barely cover with water. Bring up to a simmer and cook using low heat until the meat is just soft—the chicken should take about 30 minutes; the pork a little longer.

5. Strain the meat, saving for later the broth. Take away the bones from the chicken. Set the meat aside. Return the broth to a clean pan; there must be minimum 1½ cups (375 ml).
6. Mix the masa progressively into the broth. Bring to its boiling point, reduce the heat, and stir the mixture until it thickens a little. Set the thickened broth aside.
7. Grind the peppercorns, achiote, and salt and mix with the crushed garlic and vinegar.
8. Heat the 3 tablespoons of rendered fat in a big pan and fry the onion, chile, green pepper, epazote, and tomatoes until tender and still slightly juicy—approximately eight minutes.
9. Put in the ground seasoning and carry on cooking the mixture for approximately 3 minutes.
10. Put in the cooked meats and carry on cooking the mixture for five minutes on moderate heat. Set aside.
11. Preheat your oven to 350° f (180° c).
12. To the dough put in the salt, chile seco or paprika, and remaining rendered fat and browned pieces and mix meticulously.
13. Push about two thirds of the dough into the readied baking pan to make a crust about ¼ inch (1 cm) thick on the bottom and sides of the pan. Put in the filling and pour the thickened broth over it.
14. Push the rest of the dough onto the smooth, glossy side of the reserved banana leaf. This will be the cover for the pie. Cautiously turn the leaf upside down so that the dough completely covers the pan, with enough of an overlap to secure the pie with the dough around the sides of the pan.
15. Fold the leaves over the top of the pie and tie them down tightly with the string.
16. Bake the muk-bil pollo for about ninety minutes and serve it instantly.

Tortillas and tortilla dishes

Tortilla is easily one of the most versatile breads that exist on this planet. These are eaten all over the world, and are called by different names depending on the regions. Indians, for example, call it a "Roti" or a chapatti.

It is popular all over the world because of how easy and inexpensive it is to make. All you really need is flour, water, and griddle or another surface to cook it on.

Use the recipes in this section as a base, and feel free to experiment and invent your own recipes once you get a hang of it. Only then, will you truly master the tortilla.

FLOUR TORTILLAS

Yield: 12 (8 inch) tortillas

The best tortillas are those made at home. Considering how easy and inexpensive these are to make once you get a hang of it, there really is no reason to buy these at a store. Allowing the dough to rest in the refrigerator for a while will make it easier to work with, else it might be a little sticky.

Ingredients:

- ¾ cup plus 2 tablespoons water, heated to 110 degrees
- 1 teaspoon vegetable oil
- 1½ teaspoons salt
- 2¾ cups (13¾ ounces) all purpose flour
- 6 tablespoons vegetable shortening, cut into 6 pieces

Directions:

1. Mix flour and salt in big container. Use your hands to rub shortening into flour until mixture looks like coarse meal. Mix in water with wooden spoon until blended and dough forms. Turn dough out onto counter and knead for a short period of time to make smooth, consistent ball. Split dough into 12 pieces (2½ tablespoons each), roll into balls, and move to plate. Cover using plastic wrap and place in your fridge until dough is firm, minimum 30 minutes or maximum 3 days.

2. Working with 1 piece dough at a time and two 12 inch squares greased parchment paper, roll dough into 8 inch tortilla using a rolling pin. Take off the top piece of the parchment and softly reshape edges as required.

3. Heat oil in 12 inch nonstick frying pan over moderate high heat until it starts to shimmer Use a paper towel to wipe out frying pan, leaving thin film of oil on bottom. Flip tortilla onto your palm, take off parchment on bottom, and lay tortilla in frying pan. Cook tortilla until surface starts to bubble and it moves freely when pan is shaken, approximately one minute.

4. Turn the tortilla over and cook until puffed and bottom is spotty brown, approximately one minute. Move to plate and cover using a dish towel. Repeat with the rest of the tortillas and serve. (Tortillas can be layered between clean parchment paper, wrapped using plastic wrap, and placed in the fridge for maximum 3 days.)

CORN TORTILLAS

Mix the corn flour with warm water, in accordance with the directions on the package. Different brands recommend different proportions. Mix and allow the mixture to sit for approximately 5 minutes. For the rest, follow the directions for four tortillas.

BURRITOS, CHIMICHANGAS, AND QUESADILLAS

Flour tortillas filled and rolled up become burritos. They can be filled with whatever you want! We will give you a few suggestions for the fillings in this section, but don't be limited to these. Play around and experiment with your favourite ingredients!

ANCHO ORANGE PORK BURRITOS

Yield: Servings 8

Ingredients:

- ¼ cup minced fresh cilantro
- ½ cup distilled white vinegar
- ¾ cup orange juice (2 oranges)
- 1½ cups long grain white rice, washed

- 2 bay leaves
- 2 cups water
- 2 scallions, cut thin
- 2 tablespoon minced canned chipotle chile in adobo sauce
- 2 tablespoons tomato paste
- 2 teaspoons dried oregano
- 2 teaspoons ground cumin
- 4 dried ancho chiles, stemmed, seeded, and torn into ½ inch pieces (1 cup)
- 4 pounds boneless pork butt roast, trimmed and slice into 2 inch pieces
- 5 garlic cloves, lightly crushed and peeled
- 8 (10 inch) flour tortillas
- Salt and pepper

Directions:

1. Adjust oven rack to lower middle position and heat oven to 300 degrees. Whisk orange juice, vinegar, anchos, tomato paste, chipotle, garlic, bay leaves, cumin, oregano and 1 teaspoon salt together in Dutch oven. Sprinkle the pork with salt and pepper, mix into pot, and position in single layer. Cover and cook in oven until pork is super soft, approximately 2 hours.

2. Move pork to big container using slotted spoon and allow to cool slightly. Use two forks to shred pork into bite size pieces. Strain braising liquid into fat separator, saving for later solids, and let settle for five minutes. Discard bay leaves and move solids to blender. Put in 1½ cups defatted liquid to blender and pulse until smooth, approximately one minute. Mix sauce and pork in now empty Dutch oven; before making burritos, reheat mixture on moderate heat until hot. (Pork can placed in the fridge for maximum three days or frozen for maximum 1 month.)

3. In the meantime, bring water, rice, and 1 teaspoon salt to boil in medium deep cooking pan over moderate high heat. Cover, decrease the heat to low, and cook until rice is soft and water is absorbed, approximately twenty minutes. Take the rice off the heat and allow it to sit, covered, for about ten minutes. Put in cilantro and scallions and fluff with fork to blend; cover to keep warm.

4. Cover tortillas in damp dish towel and microwave until warm and flexible, approximately one minute. Place warm tortillas on counter. Mound warm rice and pork across center of tortillas, close to bottom edge. Working with one tortilla at a

time, fold sides then bottom of tortilla over filling, pulling back on it tightly to tighten it around filling, then carry on rolling firmly into burrito and serve.

BAKED BEEF AND BEAN BURRITOS

Yield: Servings 6

Ingredients:

- ¼ cup minced fresh cilantro
- ¾ cup long grain white rice, washed
- 1 (fifteen ounce) can pinto beans, washed
- 1 onion, chopped fine
- 1 tablespoon ground cumin
- 1 tablespoon lime juice
- 1 tablespoon vegetable oil
- 1 teaspoon chipotle chile powder
- 1 teaspoon dried oregano
- 10 ounces sharp cheddar cheese, shredded (2½ cups)
- 1¾ cups chicken broth
- 12 ounces 90 percent lean ground beef
- 3 garlic cloves, minced
- 3 tablespoons tomato paste
- 6 (10 inch) flour tortillas
- 6 tablespoons sour cream
- Salt

Directions:

1. Bring 1¼ cups broth, rice, garlic, and ½ teaspoon salt to boil in small deep cooking pan over moderate high heat. Cover, decrease the heat to low, and cook until rice is soft and broth is absorbed, approximately twenty minutes. Take the rice off the heat and allow it to sit, covered, for about ten minutes. Put in cilantro and fluff with fork to blend; cover to keep warm.

2. In the meantime, heat oil in 12 inch nonstick frying pan on moderate heat until it starts to shimmer Put in onion and cook until tender, approximately five minutes. Mix

in tomato paste, garlic, cumin, oregano, and chile powder and cook until aromatic, approximately one minute. Put in beef, breaking up pieces with wooden spoon, and cook until no longer pink, about eight to ten minutes.

3. Using potato masher, crudely purée half of beans with remaining ½ cup broth in container, then mix into frying pan. Cook while stirring continuously, until nearly all liquid has vaporized, approximately 3 minutes. Remove the heat, mix in remaining whole beans, lime juice, and ¾ teaspoon salt; cover to keep warm.

4. Adjust oven rack 6 inches from broiler element and heat broiler. Coat baking sheet with aluminium foil. Cover tortillas in damp dish towel and microwave until warm and flexible, approximately one minute. Place warm tortillas on counter. Mound warm rice, beef mixture, and 1½ cups cheddar across center of tortillas, close to bottom edge, then top with sour cream. Working with one tortilla at a time, fold sides then bottom of tortilla over filling, pulling back on it tightly to tighten it around filling, then carry on rolling firmly into burrito.

5. Put burritos, seam side down, on readied sheet and drizzle remaining 1 cup cheddar over top. Broil until cheese is melted and beginning to brown, three to five minutes and serve.

CHICKEN BURRITOS MOJADOS

Yield: Servings 6

Ingredients:

- ½ cup Mexican crema
- ¾ cup long grain white rice, washed
- 1 (fifteen ounce) can pinto beans, washed
- 1½ cups tomatillo salsa Water, as required
- 1½ pounds boneless, skinless chicken breasts, trimmed
- 2 (8 ounce) cans tomato sauce
- 2 avocados, halved, pitted, and slice into ½ inch pieces
- 2 scallions, cut thin
- 2 tablespoons vegetable oil
- 2¼ cups chicken broth
- 3 garlic cloves, minced

- 3½ tablespoons chili powder
- 6 (10 inch) flour tortillas
- 6 tablespoons minced fresh cilantro
- 8 ounces Monterey Jack cheese, shredded (2 cups)
- Salt and pepper

Directions:

1. Bring 1¼ cups broth, rice, beans, 1½ teaspoons chili powder, and ½ teaspoon salt to boil in medium deep cooking pan oven over moderate high heat. Cover, decrease the heat to low, and cook until rice is soft and broth is absorbed, approximately twenty minutes. Take the rice off the heat and allow it to sit, covered, for about ten minutes. Put in scallions and fluff with fork to blend; cover to keep warm.

2. In the meantime, cook oil, garlic, and remaining 3 tablespoons chili powder in big deep cooking pan over moderate high heat until aromatic, one to two minutes. Mix in tomato sauce and remaining 1 cup broth and bring to simmer. Nestle chicken into sauce. Cover, decrease the heat to moderate low, and cook until chicken records 160 degrees, ten to fifteen minutes, turning midway through cooking.

3. Move chicken to cutting board and allow to cool slightly. Use two forks to shred chicken into bite size pieces. Toss chicken with ¼ cup sauce and 2 tablespoons cilantro in container. Set rest of the sauce aside.

4. Adjust oven rack to middle position and heat oven to 450 degrees. Coat baking sheet with aluminium foil. Cover tortillas in damp dish towel and microwave until warm and flexible, approximately one minute. Place warm tortillas on counter. Mound rice in center of tortillas, close to bottom edge, then top with chicken, avocado, and Monterey Jack. Working with one tortilla at a time, fold sides then bottom of tortilla over filling, pulling back on it tightly to tighten it around filling, then carry on rolling firmly into burrito. (Burritos can be held at room temperature for maximum 1 hour before you bake.) Put burritos seam side down on readied sheet, cover firmly using foil, and bake until hot throughout, twenty minutes to half an hour.

5. Before you serve, whisk salsa and 2 tablespoons cilantro together in container, cover, and microwave until hot, approximately one minute. Reheat red sauce in deep cooking pan on moderate heat until hot, approximately 3 minutes, putting in water as required to loosen consistency

6. Position burritos on separate plates. Pour tomatillo sauce over half of each burrito and pour red sauce over other half of burrito. Sprinkle with crema, drizzle with remaining 2 tablespoons cilantro, before you serve.

CHICKEN CHIMICHANGAS

Yield: Servings 4

Ingredients:

- ½ cup long grain white rice, washed
- ½ teaspoon ground cumin
- 1 (fifteen ounce) can pinto beans, washed
- 1 cup chicken broth
- 1 cup plus 2 tablespoons water
- 1 onion, chopped fine
- 1 pound boneless, skinless chicken breasts, trimmed
- 1 scallion, cut thin
- 1 tablespoon minced canned chipotle chile in adobo sauce
- 1 tablespoon plus 3 cups vegetable oil
- 2 garlic cloves, minced
- 2 tablespoons all purpose flour
- 2 tablespoons ancho chile powder
- 2 tablespoons minced fresh cilantro
- 4 (10 inch) flour tortillas
- 4 ounces sharp cheddar cheese, shredded (1 cup)
- Salt and pepper

Directions:

1. Bring 1 cup water, rice, and ¼ teaspoon salt to boil in small deep cooking pan over moderate high heat. Decrease the heat to low, cover, and cook until rice is soft and water is absorbed, approximately twenty minutes. Take the rice off the heat and allow it to sit, covered, for about ten minutes. Put in cilantro and scallion and fluff with fork to blend; cover to keep warm.

2. In the meantime, heat 1 tablespoon oil in 12 inch nonstick frying pan on moderate heat until it starts to shimmer Put in onion and cook until tender, approximately five minutes. Mix in chile powder, chipotle, garlic, and cumin and cook until aromatic, approximately one minute. Mix in broth and bring to simmer. Nestle chicken into sauce. Cover, decrease the heat to moderate low, and cook until chicken records 160 degrees, ten to fifteen minutes, turning midway through cooking.

3. Move chicken to cutting board, allow to cool slightly, then cut crosswise into super slim pieces. Continue to simmer sauce until it becomes thick and measures ½ cup, approximately ten minutes; turn off the heat. Coarsely purée half of beans in container using potato masher, then put in to sauce with the rest of the beans and cut chicken.

4. Whisk flour and remaining 2 tablespoons water together in container. Cover tortillas in damp dish towel and microwave until warm and flexible, approximately one minute. Place warm tortillas on counter. Mound rice, chicken bean mixture, and cheddar across center of tortillas. Working with one tortilla at a time, brush edges of tortilla with flour paste, then wrap top and bottom of tortilla firmly over filling and press tightly to secure. Brush ends of tortilla meticulously with paste, fold into center, and press tightly to secure.

5. Adjust oven rack to middle position and heat oven to 200 degrees. Coat plate with multiple layers of paper towels. Set wire rack in rimmed baking sheet. Heat remaining 3 cups oil in Dutch oven over moderate high heat to 325 degrees. Put 2 chimichangas, seam side down, in oil. Fry, turning as required, until thoroughly browned on both sides, approximately 4 minutes, adjusting burner as required to maintain oil temperature between 300 and 325 degrees. Allow to drain for a short period of time using paper towels, then move to wire rack and keep warm in oven while frying remaining 2 chimichangas and serve.

CHICKEN QUESADILLAS

Yield: Servings 4

Ingredients:

- ¼ cup minced fresh cilantro
- ½ cup jarred roasted red peppers, patted dry and chopped

- 1 pound boneless, skinless chicken breasts, trimmed
- 1 teaspoon ground cumin
- 1 teaspoon hot sauce
- 2 garlic cloves, minced
- 3 scallions, white and green parts separated, cut thin
- 3 tablespoons plus 1 teaspoon vegetable oil
- 4 (10 inch) flour tortillas
- 8 ounces Monterey Jack cheese, shredded (2 cups)
- Salt and pepper

Directions:

1. Adjust oven rack to middle position and heat oven to 450 degrees. Coat rimmed baking sheet with aluminium foil and brush with 1 tablespoon oil.
2. Pat chicken dry using paper towels and sprinkle with salt and pepper. Heat 1 tablespoon oil in 12 inch nonstick frying pan over moderate high heat until just smoking. Lightly lay chicken in frying pan and cook, turning as required, until lightly golden on both sides and records 160 degrees, approximately twelve minutes. Move chicken to cutting board and allow to cool slightly. Use two forks to shred into bite size pieces.
3. Put in 1 teaspoon oil, scallion whites, garlic, cumin, and ¼ teaspoon salt to now empty frying pan and cook on moderate heat until tender, approximately 2 minutes. Move to moderate container, put in shredded chicken, peppers, cilantro, scallion greens, hot sauce, and cheese, and toss to blend.
4. Place tortillas on counter. Spread chicken filling over half of each tortilla, leaving ½ inch border around edge. Fold other half of tortilla over top and press tightly to compact. Position quesadillas in single layer on readied sheet with rounded edges facing center of sheet. Brush with remaining 1 tablespoon oil.
5. Bake until quesadillas start to brown, approximately ten minutes. Flip quesadillas over and push softly with spatula to compact. Carry on baking until crunchy and golden brown on second side, approximately five minutes. Allow quesadillas to cool on wire rack for five minutes, then slice each into 4 wedges before you serve.

CHORIZO AND BLACK BEAN CHIMICHANGAS

Yield: Servings 4

Ingredients:

- ½ cup long grain white rice, washed
- ½ teaspoon ground cumin
- 1 (fifteen ounce) can black beans, washed
- 1 onion, chopped fine
- 1 scallion, cut thin
- 1 tablespoon minced canned chipotle chile in adobo sauce
- 1 tablespoon plus 3 cups vegetable oil
- 1 teaspoon chili powder
- 1½ cups plus 2 tablespoons water
- 12 ounces Mexican style chorizo sausage, casings removed
- 2 garlic cloves, minced
- 2 tablespoons all purpose flour
- 2 tablespoons minced fresh cilantro
- 4 (10 inch) flour tortillas
- 4 ounces sharp cheddar cheese, shredded (1 cup)
- Salt

Directions:

1. Bring 1 cup water, rice, and ½ teaspoon salt to boil in small deep cooking pan over moderate high heat. Decrease the heat to low, cover, and cook until rice is soft and water is absorbed, approximately twenty minutes. Take the rice off the heat and allow it to sit, covered, for about ten minutes. Put in cilantro and scallion and fluff with fork to blend; cover to keep warm.

2. In the meantime, heat 1 tablespoon oil in 12 inch nonstick frying pan oven on moderate heat until it starts to shimmer Put in onion and cook until tender, approximately five minutes. Mix in chipotle, garlic, chili powder, and cumin and cook until aromatic, approximately half a minute. Put in chorizo and cook, breaking up pieces with wooden spoon, until no longer pink, approximately five minutes. Coarsely purée half of beans with ½ cup water in container using potato masher, then put in to frying pan with the rest of the beans. Simmer until beans are warmed through, approximately five minutes; turn off the heat.

3. Whisk flour and remaining 2 tablespoons water together in container. Cover tortillas in damp dish towel and microwave until warm and flexible, approximately one minute. Place warm tortillas on counter. Mound rice, chorizo bean mixture, and cheddar across center of tortillas. Working with one tortilla at a time, brush edges of tortilla with flour paste, then wrap top and bottom of tortilla firmly over filling and press tightly to secure. Brush ends of tortilla meticulously with paste, fold into center, and press tightly to secure.

4. Adjust oven rack to middle position and heat oven to 200 degrees. Coat plate with multiple layers of paper towels. Set wire rack in rimmed baking sheet. Heat remaining 3 cups oil in Dutch oven over moderate high heat to 325 degrees. Put 2 chimichangas, seam side down, in oil. Fry, turning as required, until thoroughly browned on both sides, approximately 4 minutes, adjusting burner as required to maintain oil temperature between 300 and 325 degrees. Allow to drain for a short period of time using paper towels, then move to wire rack and keep warm in oven while frying remaining 2 chimichangas and serve.

MUSHROOM AND SWISS CHARD QUESADILLAS

Yield: Servings 4

Ingredients:

- ¼ cup vegetable oil
- ¼ teaspoon red pepper flakes
- 1 onion, chopped fine
- 1 pound Swiss chard, stemmed, leaves cut into ½ inch wide strips
- 1 pound white mushrooms, trimmed and cut thin
- 1 teaspoon cider vinegar
- 2 garlic cloves, minced
- 2 tablespoons minced fresh cilantro
- 2 teaspoons ground coriander
- 4 (10 inch) flour tortillas
- 8 ounces Monterey Jack cheese, shredded (2 cups)
- Salt and pepper

Directions:

1. Adjust oven rack to middle position and heat oven to 450 degrees. Coat rimmed baking sheet with aluminium foil and brush with 1 tablespoon oil.
2. Heat 2 tablespoons oil in 12 inch nonstick frying pan over moderate high heat until it starts to shimmer Put in onion and mushrooms and sprinkle with salt and pepper. Cover and cook, stirring once in a while, until mushrooms have released their moisture, about eight to ten minutes. Remove the cover and cook, stirring once in a while, until liquid has vaporized and mushrooms are thoroughly browned, about eight to ten minutes.
3. Mix in garlic, coriander, and pepper flakes and cook until aromatic, approximately half a minute. Put in chard, cover, and cook until wilted but still bright green, one to two minutes. Remove the cover and cook, stirring frequently, until liquid evaporates, four to six minutes. Remove the heat, mix in vinegar. Allow the mixture to cool slightly, then mix in Monterey Jack and cilantro.
4. Place tortillas on counter. Spread vegetable filling over half of each tortilla, leaving ½ inch border around edge. Fold other half of tortilla over top and press tightly to compact. Position quesadillas in single layer on readied sheet with rounded edges facing center of sheet. Brush with remaining 1 tablespoon oil.
5. Bake until quesadillas start to brown, approximately ten minutes. Flip quesadillas over and push softly with spatula to compact. Carry on baking until crunchy and golden brown on second side, approximately five minutes. Allow quesadillas to cool on wire rack for five minutes, then slice each into 4 wedges before you serve.

SPICY CHICKEN FLAUTAS

Yield: 4-6 Servings

Ingredients:

- ⅛ teaspoon cayenne pepper
- ¼ teaspoon dried oregano
- 1 (8 ounce) can tomato sauce
- 1 onion, chopped fine
- 1 recipe Avocado Sauce (recipe follows)
- 1 tablespoon chili powder
- 1 tablespoon plus 1 cup vegetable oil
- 12 (8 inch) flour tortillas
- 2 garlic cloves, minced
- 2 jalapeño chiles, stemmed, seeded, and minced
- 2 pounds boneless, skinless chicken breasts, trimmed
- 2 tablespoons all purpose flour
- 2 tablespoons lime juice
- 2 tablespoons minced fresh cilantro
- 2 tablespoons water
- Salt and pepper

Directions:

1. Heat 1 tablespoon oil in 12 inch nonstick frying pan on moderate heat until it starts to shimmer Put in onion and cook until tender, approximately five minutes. Mix in jalapeños, chili powder, garlic, oregano, and cayenne and cook until aromatic, approximately half a minute. Mix in tomato sauce and bring to simmer.
2. Sprinkle the chicken with salt and pepper and nestle into sauce. Cover, decrease the heat to moderate low, and cook until chicken records 160 degrees, ten to fifteen minutes, turning midway through cooking. Move chicken to cutting board and allow to cool slightly. Use two forks to shred chicken fine. Stir shredded chicken, cilantro, and lime juice into sauce.
3. Coat rimmed baking sheet using parchment paper. Whisk flour and water together in container. Cut off bottom third of each tortilla (discard or reserve for future use).

Cover tortillas in damp dish towel and microwave until warm and flexible, approximately one minute.

4. Place six warm tortillas on counter with trimmed edge facing you. Mound half of chicken filling alongside trimmed edges. Roll trimmed edge of one tortilla up over filling, then pull back on tortilla to tighten it around filling. Working with one tortilla at a time, brush remaining uncovered tortilla with flour paste, then roll it up firmly around filling. Push on edges tightly to secure; move to readied baking sheet. Repeat with the rest of the six tortillas and rest of the filling. (Flautas can be covered with damp towel, wrapped firmly using plastic wrap, and placed in the fridge for maximum one day.)

5. Adjust oven rack to middle position and heat oven to 200 degrees. Coat plate with multiple layers of paper towels. Set wire rack in second rimmed baking sheet. Heat remaining 1 cup oil in clean 12 inch nonstick frying pan over moderate high heat until 325 degrees. Put 6 flautas, seam side down, in oil. Fry, turning as required, until a golden-brown colour is achieved on all sides, three to five minutes, adjusting burner as required to maintain oil temperature between 300 and 325 degrees. Allow to drain for a short period of time using paper towels, then move to wire rack and keep warm in oven while frying remaining 6 flautas. Serve with Avocado Sauce.

AVOCADO SAUCE

Yield: 2½ CUPS

Make sure you use very ripe avocados when making this sauce.

Ingredients:

- ¼ cup water
- ½ cup sour cream
- 2 avocados, halved, pitted, and chopped coarse
- 2 tablespoons minced fresh cilantro
- 3 tablespoons lime juice (2 limes)
- Salt and pepper

Directions:

Mash all ingredients together in container with potato masher (or fork) until the desired smoothness is achieved. Sprinkle with salt and pepper to taste and serve.

SWISS CHARD AND PINTO BEAN BURRITOS

Yield: Servings 6

Ingredients:

- ¼ cup minced fresh cilantro
- ¾ cup long grain white rice, washed
- 1 (fifteen ounce) can pinto beans, washed
- 1 onion, chopped fine
- 1 pound Swiss chard, stemmed, leaves cut into an inch wide strips
- 1 tablespoon ground cumin
- 1 tablespoon lime juice
- 1 tablespoon vegetable oil
- 1 teaspoon dried oregano
- 1 teaspoon minced canned chipotle chile in adobo sauce
- 10 ounces Monterey jack, shredded (2½ cups)
- 2¼ cups vegetable broth
- 3 tablespoons tomato paste
- 6 (10 inch) flour tortillas
- 6 garlic cloves, minced
- Salt

Directions:

1. Bring 1¼ cups broth, rice, half of garlic, and ½ teaspoon salt to boil in small deep cooking pan over moderate high heat. Cover, decrease the heat to low, and cook until rice is soft and broth is absorbed, approximately twenty minutes. Take the rice off the heat and allow it to sit, covered, for about ten minutes. Put in cilantro and fluff with fork to blend; cover to keep warm.
2. In the meantime, heat oil in Dutch oven on moderate heat until it starts to shimmer Put in onion and cook until just starting to brown, approximately five minutes. Mix in tomato paste, chipotle, cumin, oregano, remaining garlic, and ½ teaspoon salt and cook until aromatic, approximately one minute. Put in chard and ½ cup broth, cover, and simmer until chard is soft, approximately fifteen minutes.

3. Using potato masher, crudely purée half of beans with remaining ½ cup broth in container, then mix into pot. Cook while stirring continuously, until liquid is nearly vaporized, approximately 3 minutes. Remove the heat, mix in lime juice and remaining whole beans; cover to keep warm.

4. Adjust oven rack 6 inches from broiler element and heat broiler. Coat baking sheet with aluminium foil. Cover tortillas in damp dish towel and microwave until warm and flexible, approximately one minute. Place warm tortillas on counter. Mound warm rice, chard bean mixture, and 1½ cups Monterey Jack across center of tortillas, close to bottom edge. Working with one tortilla at a time, fold sides then bottom of tortilla over filling, pulling back on it tightly to tighten it around filling, then carry on rolling firmly into burrito.

5. Put burritos, seam side down, on readied sheet and drizzle remaining 1 cup Monterey Jack over top. Broil until cheese is melted and beginning to brown, three to five minutes and serve.

TEQUILA LIME SHRIMP QUESADILLAS

Yield: Servings 4

Ingredients:

- ¼ cup minced fresh cilantro
- ⅓ cup tequila
- 1 teaspoon grated lime zest
- 1 teaspoon minced canned chipotle chile in adobo sauce
- 1½ pounds medium big shrimp (31 to 40 per pound), peeled, deveined, tails removed, and halved along the length
- 12 ounces Monterey Jack cheese, shredded (3 cups)
- 2 garlic cloves, minced
- 2 scallions, white and green parts separated, cut thin
- 3 tablespoons vegetable oil
- 4 (10 inch) flour tortillas
- Salt and pepper

Directions:

1. Adjust oven rack to middle position and heat oven to 450 degrees. Coat rimmed baking sheet with aluminium foil and brush with 1 tablespoon oil. Toss Monterey Jack with cilantro and scallion greens.

2. Pat dry shrimp using paper towels and sprinkle with salt and pepper. Heat 1 tablespoon oil in 12 inch nonstick frying pan on moderate heat until it starts to shimmer Put in scallion whites, garlic, chipotle, and ¼ teaspoon salt and cook until tender, approximately 2 minutes. Put in tequila amd simmer until tequila has vaporized and pan is dry, approximately five minutes.

3. Put in shrimp and cook, stirring frequently, until thoroughly cooked and opaque throughout, approximately 3 minutes. Move to container, mix in zest, and allow to cool for five minutes; drain thoroughly.

4. Place tortillas on counter. Drizzle half of cheese mixture over half of each tortilla, leaving ½ inch border around edge. Position shrimp on top in single layer, then drizzle with rest of the cheese mixture. Fold other half of each tortilla over top and press tightly to compact.

5. Position quesadillas in single layer on readied sheet with rounded edges facing center of sheet. Brush with remaining 1 tablespoon oil. Bake until quesadillas start to brown, approximately ten minutes. Flip quesadillas over and push softly with spatula to compact. Carry on baking until crunchy and golden brown on second side, approximately five minutes. Allow quesadillas to cool on wire rack for five minutes, then slice each into 4 wedges before you serve.

ENCHILADAS AND CASSEROLES

BEEF ENCHILADA CASSEROLE

Yield: Servings 8 to 10

Ingredients:

- ½ cup chopped fresh cilantro
- 1 (10 ounce) can Ro Tel tomatoes
- 1 pound Colby Jack cheese, shredded (4 cups)
- 1 tablespoon hot sauce
- 1 teaspoon ground cumin

- 1½ cups beef broth
- 2 onions, chopped fine
- 2 pounds 85 percent lean ground beef
- 2 tablespoons chili powder
- 2 tablespoons vegetable oil
- 20 (6 inch) corn tortillas
- 3 (fifteen ounce) cans tomato sauce
- 3 jalapeño chiles, stemmed, seeded, and minced
- 8 garlic cloves, minced
- Salt and pepper

Directions:

1. Adjust oven rack to middle position and heat oven to 450 degrees. Toast tortillas, one by one, in 12 inch nonstick frying pan over moderate high heat until mildly browned, approximately twenty seconds per side; move to plate and cover using a dish towel.
2. Tear 8 toasted tortillas into rough pieces and move to food processor. Put in tomatoes and their juice and ¾ cup broth and pulse until smooth; move to big container. Put in beef to now empty frying pan and cook over moderate high heat, breaking up meat with wooden spoon, until no longer pink, approximately five minutes. Drain beef in colander, then mix into processed tortilla mixture.
3. Put in oil and onions to now empty frying pan and cook on moderate heat until tender, approximately five minutes. Mix in garlic, chili powder, and cumin and cook until aromatic, approximately half a minute. Mix in tomato sauce and remaining ¾ cup broth and simmer until slightly thickened, five to seven minutes; move to container.
4. Stir half of tomato sauce mixture, 1½ cups Colby Jack, half of jalapeños, cilantro, and hot sauce into beef mixture. Sprinkle with salt and pepper.
5. Position 6 toasted tortillas in bottom of greased 13 by 9 inch baking dish, overlapping them slightly. Spread beef mixture uniformly into dish, then top with remaining 6 tortillas followed by rest of the tomato sauce mixture. Bake until filling is bubbling around edges, approximately 30 minutes. Drizzle with remaining 2½ cups Colby Jack and remaining jalapeños and carry on baking until cheese is browned, fifteen to twenty minutes. Allow the casserole to cool for about twenty minutes before you serve.

BEEF ENCHILADAS

Yield: Servings four to 6

Ingredients:

- ¼ cup red wine
- ¼ teaspoon cayenne pepper
- 12 (6 inch) corn tortillas
- 2 (fifteen ounce) cans tomato sauce
- 2 onions, chopped fine
- 2 pounds boneless beef chuck eye roast, trimmed and slice into 1½ inch cubes
- 2 teaspoons ground coriander
- 2 teaspoons ground cumin
- 3 tablespoons chili powder
- 3 tablespoons vegetable oil
- 4 garlic cloves, minced
- 8 ounces cheddar cheese, shredded (2 cups)
- Salt and pepper

Directions:

1. Adjust oven rack to lower middle position and heat oven to 300 degrees. Pat beef dry using paper towels and sprinkle with salt and pepper. Heat 1 tablespoon oil in Dutch oven over moderate high heat until just smoking. Brown half of beef well on all sides, 7 to ten minutes; move to container. Repeat with rest of the beef using fat left in pot.
2. Pour off all but 1 tablespoon fat from pot. Put in onions and ½ teaspoon salt and cook on moderate heat until tender, approximately eight minutes. Mix in chili powder, cumin, coriander, cayenne, and ¼ teaspoon pepper and cook until spices darken, approximately 2 minutes. Mix in garlic and cook until aromatic, approximately half a minute. Mix in tomato sauce, wine, and browned beef and any collected juices and bring to simmer. Cover, move to oven, and cook until meat is fork soft, 2 to 2½ hours.
3. Move beef to big container and allow to cool slightly. Use two forks to shred into bite size pieces; place in your fridge for about twenty minutes. Strain sauce through fine mesh strainer, discarding solids. Mix chilled beef, 1 cup cheddar, and ¼ cup reserved sauce in container.

4. Adjust oven rack to middle position and raise oven temperature to 450 degrees. Spread ¾ cup sauce over bottom of 13 by 9 inch baking dish. Brush both sides of tortillas with remaining 2 tablespoons oil. Stack tortillas, wrap in damp dish towel, and place on plate; microwave until warm and flexible, approximately one minute.
5. Working with 1 warm tortilla at a time, spread ⅓ cup beef filling across center of tortilla. Roll tortilla firmly around filling and place seam side down in baking dish; position enchiladas in 2 columns across width of dish.
6. Pour rest of the sauce over top to cover completely and drizzle remaining 1 cup cheddar over enchiladas. Cover dish firmly with greased aluminium foil. Bake until enchiladas are thoroughly heated and cheese is melted, fifteen to twenty minutes. Allow to cool for five minutes before you serve.

CASSEROLE OF TORTILLAS IN CHILE SAUCE (CASEROLA DE TORTILLAS EN CHILES GUAJILLO)

Yield: Servings 6

Ingredients:

The sauce

- ⅛ teaspoon cumin seeds, crushed
- ½ cup (125 ml) roughly chopped white onion
- 1 cup (250 ml) chicken broth or water
- 12 guajillo chiles, seeds and veins removed
- 2 garlic cloves, roughly chopped
- 2 tablespoons vegetable oil
- Salt to taste

The chilaquiles

- 2 big sprigs epazote
- 2 cups (500 ml) chicken broth, roughly
- 8 ounces (225 g) queso fresco, crumbled, or substitute mild cheddar, grated (approximately 1⅓ cups/335 ml), or muenster (1¼ cups/315 ml)
- eighteen tortillas, cut into strips or triangles and dried

- Vegetable oil for frying

To serve

- ¾ cup (185 ml) thinly cut white onion rings
- 1 cup (250 ml) prepared thin sour cream
- 2 chorizos (about 5 ounces/140 g), crumbled and fried
- 2 limes, cut into wedges

Directions:

1. Prepare a flameproof dish approximately 10 inches (25 cm) in diameter and 4 inches (10 cm) deep.
2. Heat the griddle and toast the chiles lightly on both sides. Be careful—they burn very swiftly.
3. Cover the chiles with hot water and VVVVVVVVVVVVVVVVVVVVVVVV soak for approximately ten minutes, then move using a slotted spoon to a blender jar. Put in the onion, garlic, and cumin seeds and blend to a smooth sauce with ½ cup (125 ml) of the broth.
4. Heat the oil in a pan and put in the sauce through a fine strainer, pushing down to extract as much of the substance and juice as you can.
5. Put in the other ½ cup broth and allow the sauce to cook using high heat for a few minutes longer. Put in salt to taste. Set aside.
6. Heat the oil in a frying pan and fry the tortilla strips until they are a pale gold, but not too crunchy. Remove and drain using paper towels.
7. Cover the bottom of the dish with a third of the tortilla pieces, then one third of the cheese and one third of the sauce. Repeat the layers two more times.
8. Put in the 2 cups broth and bring to its boiling point. Reduce the heat and carry on cooking the chilaquiles at a brisk simmer, until most of the broth has been absorbed— about fifteen minutes. Put in the epazote one minute or so before the chilaquiles are done cooking.
9. Pour the sour cream around the edge of the dish, then top with the chorizos and the onion rings. Serve in small deep bowls with lime wedges on the side.

CHEESE ENCHILADAS

Yield: Servings four to 6

Ingredients:

- 1 onion, chopped fine
- 1 tablespoon cumin seeds
- 1 tablespoon garlic powder
- 12 (6 inch) corn tortillas
- 2 cups chicken broth
- 2 dried ancho chiles, stemmed, seeded, and torn into ½ inch pieces (½ cup)
- 2 teaspoons distilled white vinegar
- 2 teaspoons dried oregano
- 3 tablespoons all purpose flour
- 5 tablespoons vegetable oil
- 6 ounces sharp cheddar cheese, shredded (1½ cups)
- 8 ounces Monterey Jack cheese, shredded (2 cups)
- Salt and pepper

Directions:

1. Toast anchos and cumin in 12 inch frying pan on moderate heat, stirring regularly, until aromatic, 2 to six minutes. Move to spice grinder and allow to cool slightly. Put in garlic powder and oregano and grind to fine powder.

2. Heat 3 tablespoons oil in now empty frying pan over moderate high heat until it starts to shimmer Whisk in flour, ½ teaspoon salt, ½ teaspoon pepper, and ground spices and cook until aromatic and slightly deepened in color, approximately one minute. Slowly whisk in broth and bring to simmer. Decrease the heat to moderate low and cook, whisking frequently, until sauce has thickened and measures 1½ cups, approximately five minutes. Whisk in vinegar and sprinkle with salt and pepper to taste. Turn off the heat, cover, and keep warm.

3. Adjust oven rack to middle position and heat oven to 450 degrees. Spread ½ cup sauce over bottom of 13 by 9 inch baking dish. Mix Monterey Jack and cheddar in container; set ½ cup cheese mixture aside for topping. Brush both sides of tortillas with remaining 2 tablespoons oil. Stack tortillas, wrap in damp dish towel, and place on plate; microwave until warm and flexible, approximately one minute.

4. Working with 1 warm tortilla at a time, spread ¼ cup cheese mixture across center of tortilla and drizzle with 1 tablespoon onion. Roll tortilla firmly around filling and place seam side down in baking dish; position enchiladas in 2 columns across width of dish.

5. Pour rest of the sauce over top to cover completely and drizzle reserved cheese over enchiladas. Cover dish firmly with greased aluminium foil. Bake until enchiladas are thoroughly heated and cheese is melted, fifteen to twenty minutes. Allow to cool for five minutes and drizzle with remaining onion and serve.

CHICKEN CHILAQUILES

Yield: Servings 4

Ingredients:

- ¼ cup olive oil
- 1 (28 ounce) can whole peeled tomatoes
- 1 avocado, halved, pitted, and slice into ½ inch pieces
- 1 cup finely chopped onion
- 1 jalapeño chile, stemmed, seeded, and chopped
- 1 poblano chile, stemmed, seeded, and chopped
- 1½ cups chicken broth
- 1½ pounds boneless, skinless chicken breasts, trimmed
- 16 (6 inch) corn tortillas, cut into 8 wedges
- 2 radishes, trimmed and cut thin
- 3 garlic cloves, peeled and chopped
- 4 ounces queso fresco, crumbled (1 cup)
- 5 dried guajillo chiles, stemmed, seeded, and torn into ½ inch pieces (⅔ cup)
- 8 sprigs fresh cilantro plus 2 tablespoons minced
- Salt

Directions:

1. Adjust oven racks to upper middle and lower middle positions and heat oven to 425 degrees. Spread tortillas uniformly over 2 rimmed baking sheets. Sprinkle each sheet with 2 tablespoons oil and ¼ teaspoon salt and toss until uniformly coated. Bake,

stirring once in a while, until tortillas are golden brown and crunchy, fifteen to twenty minutes, switching sheets midway through baking.

2. Toast guajillos in Dutch oven on moderate heat, stirring regularly, until aromatic, 2 to six minutes. Move toasted guajillos to blender and pulse until thoroughly ground, 60 to 90 seconds. Put in tomatoes and their juice, ¾ cup onion, poblano, jalapeño, garlic, cilantro sprigs, and ¾ teaspoon salt to blender and pulse until super smooth, 60 to 90 seconds.

3. Mix guajillo tomato mixture and broth in now empty Dutch oven and bring to boiling point over moderate high heat. Nestle chicken into sauce. Cover, decrease the heat to moderate low, and cook until chicken records 160 degrees, ten to fifteen minutes, turning midway through cooking.

4. Move chicken to plate and allow to cool slightly. Use two forks to shred chicken into bite size pieces. In the meantime, increase heat to moderate and simmer sauce until it becomes thick and measures 4½ cups, approximately five minutes.

5. Mix in shredded chicken and cook until warmed through, approximately 2 minutes. Remove the heat, mix in tortillas, cover, and allow it to sit until tortillas have become tender slightly, 2 to five minutes. Move tortilla mixture to serving dish and drizzle with queso fresco, avocado, radishes, remaining ¼ cup onion, and minced cilantro. Serve instantly.

CHICKEN ENCHILADAS VERDES

Yield: Servings four to 6

Ingredients:

- ½ cup chopped fresh cilantro
- ½ teaspoon ground cumin
- 1 onion, chopped fine
- 1 pound boneless, skinless chicken breasts, trimmed
- 1 teaspoon sugar, plus extra as required
- 1½ cups chicken broth
- 1½ pounds tomatillos, husks and stems removed, washed well, dried, and halved
- 12 (6 inch) corn tortillas
- 2 scallions, cut thin

- 3 garlic cloves, minced
- 3 poblano chiles, halved along the length, stemmed, and seeded
- 3 tablespoons vegetable oil
- 8 ounces pepper Jack or Monterey Jack cheese, shredded (2 cups)
- Salt and pepper

Directions:

1. Heat 2 teaspoons oil in medium deep cooking pan on moderate heat until it starts to shimmer Put in onion and cook until golden, six to eight minutes. Mix in cumin and two thirds of garlic and cook until aromatic, approximately half a minute. Mix in broth and bring to simmer.
2. Nestle chicken into sauce. Cover, decrease the heat to moderate low, and cook until chicken records 160 degrees, ten to fifteen minutes, turning chicken midway through cooking. Move chicken to plate and allow to cool slightly. Use two forks to shred chicken into bite size pieces; place in your fridge for about twenty minutes to chill. Reserve ¼ cup cooking liquid for sauce, discarding extra.
3. In the meantime, adjust oven rack 6 inches from broiler element and heat broiler. Coat rimmed baking sheet with aluminium foil. Toss tomatillos and poblanos with 1 teaspoon oil. Position tomatillos cut side down and poblanos skin side up on readied sheet. Broil until vegetables are blackened and starting to tenderize, 5 to ten minutes. Move poblanos to container, cover using aluminium foil, and allow to steam until skins peel off easily, approximately ten minutes. Using back of spoon, scrape loosened skins from poblanos.
4. Process broiled tomatillos with any collected juices, peeled poblanos, ¼ cup reserved cooking liquid, sugar, 1 teaspoon salt, and remaining garlic inside a food processor until sauce is fairly lumpy, approximately eight pulses. Sprinkle with salt, pepper, and extra sugar to taste. Mix chilled chicken, cilantro, and 1½ cups cheese in container and sprinkle with salt and pepper to taste.
5. Adjust oven rack to middle position and heat oven to 450 degrees. Spread ¾ cup tomatillo sauce over bottom of 13 by 9 inch baking dish. Brush both sides of tortillas with remaining 2 tablespoons oil. Stack tortillas, wrap in damp dish towel, and place on plate; microwave until warm and flexible, approximately one minute.
6. Working with 1 warm tortilla at a time, spread ⅓ cup chicken filling across center of tortilla. Roll tortilla firmly around filling and place seam side down in baking dish; position enchiladas in 2 columns across width of dish.

7. Pour rest of the sauce over top to cover completely and drizzle remaining ½ cup cheese over enchiladas. Cover dish firmly with greased aluminium foil. Bake until enchiladas are thoroughly heated and cheese is melted, fifteen to twenty minutes. Allow to cool for five minutes, drizzle with scallions, before you serve.

CHICKEN ENCHILADAS WITH RED CHILE SAUCE

Yield: Servings four to 6

Ingredients:

- ¼ cup jarred jalapeños, chopped
- ¼ cup vegetable oil
- ½ cup chopped fresh cilantro
- ½ teaspoon salt
- 1 cup water
- 1 onion, chopped fine
- 1 pound boneless, skinless chicken thighs, trimmed and slice into ¼ inch wide strips
- 12 (6 inch) corn tortillas
- 12 ounces sharp cheddar cheese, shredded (3 cups)
- 2 (8 ounce) cans tomato sauce
- 2 teaspoons ground coriander
- 2 teaspoons ground cumin
- 2 teaspoons sugar
- 3 garlic cloves, minced
- 3 tablespoons chili powder

Directions:

1. Heat 2 tablespoons oil in medium deep cooking pan over moderate high heat until it starts to shimmer Put in onion and cook until tender, five to seven minutes. Mix in chili powder, garlic, coriander, cumin, sugar, and salt and cook until aromatic, approximately half a minute. Mix in chicken and coat completely with spices. Mix in tomato sauce and water, bring to simmer, and cook until chicken is thoroughly cooked, approximately eight minutes.

2. Drain mixture in fine mesh strainer set over container, pushing on chicken and onion to extract as much sauce as you can; set sauce aside. Move chicken mixture to separate container, place in your fridge for about twenty minutes to chill, then mix in cilantro, jalapeños, and 2½ cups cheese.

3. Adjust oven rack middle position and heat oven to 450 degrees. Spread ¾ cup sauce over bottom of 13 by 9 inch baking dish. Brush both sides of tortillas with remaining 2 tablespoons oil. Stack tortillas, wrap in damp dish towel, and place on plate; microwave until warm and flexible, approximately one minute.

4. Working with 1 warm tortilla at a time, spread ⅓ cup chicken filling across center of tortilla. Roll tortilla firmly around filling and place seam side down in baking dish; position enchiladas in 2 columns across width of dish.

5. Pour rest of the sauce over top to cover completely and drizzle remaining ½ cup cheese over enchiladas. Cover dish firmly with greased aluminium foil. Bake until enchiladas are thoroughly heated and cheese is melted, fifteen to twenty minutes. Allow to cool for five minutes before you serve.

CHILES RELLENOS CASSEROLE

Yield: Servings 6 to 8

Ingredients:

- ¼ teaspoon cayenne pepper
- ½ cup all purpose flour
- ¾ cup skim milk
- 1 (10 ounce) can Ro Tel tomatoes, drained
- 1 onion, chopped fine
- 1 tablespoon vegetable oil
- 1 teaspoon dried oregano
- 10 ounces Monterey Jack cheese, shredded (2½ cups)
- 2 big egg whites
- 2 garlic cloves, minced
- 2 pounds 90 percent lean ground beef
- 2 teaspoons ground cumin
- 4 poblano chiles, stemmed, seeded, and chopped

- Salt and pepper

Directions:

1. Adjust oven rack to upper middle position and heat oven to 450 degrees. Heat oil in 12 inch nonstick frying pan on moderate heat until it starts to shimmer Put in onion and cook until tender, approximately five minutes. Mix in beef, breaking up meat with wooden spoon, and cook until no longer pink, about eight to ten minutes. Using slotted spoon, move beef mixture to paper towel–lined plate. Pour off all but 2 tablespoons fat from frying pan.

2. Put in poblanos to fat left in frying pan and cook over moderate high heat until browned, about eight to ten minutes. Mix in garlic, cumin, oregano, cayenne, ¾ teaspoon salt, ½ teaspoon pepper, and beef mixture and cook until aromatic, approximately half a minute. Mix in tomatoes and cook until mixture is dry, approximately one minute. Remove the heat, mix in 2 cups Monterey Jack. Scrape mixture into 13 by 9 inch baking dish and press into even layer.

3. Mix flour, ½ teaspoon salt, and ¼ teaspoon pepper in container. Slowly whisk in milk until the desired smoothness is achieved. Using stand mixer fitted with whisk, whip egg whites on medium low speed until foamy, approximately one minute. Increase speed to moderate high and whip until stiff peaks form, approximately 3 minutes. Whisk one third whipped egg whites into milk flour batter to lighten. Lightly fold in remaining whites, 1 scoop at a time, until blended.

4. Pour batter uniformly over beef mixture. Bake until topping is light golden and puffed, approximately fifteen minutes. Drizzle with remaining ½ cup Monterey Jack and bake until a golden-brown colour is achieved, approximately ten minutes. Allow to cool on wire rack for about ten minutes and serve.

ENCHILADAS DE FRESNILLO

Yield: 12 enchiladas

Ingredients:

The sauce

- ⅛ teaspoon dried mexican oregano
- ¼ cup (65 ml) shelled peanuts, toasted and crushed

- ¼-inch (.75-cm) piece of cinnamon stick, crushed
- 1 tablespoon sesame seeds, toasted and crushed
- 1 whole clove, crushed
- 1½ cups (375 ml) cold water
- 2 tablespoons vegetable oil
- 3 ancho chiles, seeds and veins removed, mildly toasted
- 3 peppercorns, crushed
- 3 sprigs fresh marjoram or ⅛ teaspoon dried
- 3 sprigs fresh thyme or ⅛ teaspoon dried
- Salt to taste

The filling

- 1 medium white onion, finely chopped
- 8 ounces (225 g) queso fresco, crumbled (approximately 1½ cups/375 ml)
- twelve tortillas
- Vegetable oil for frying

To serve

- ¾ cup (185 ml) prepared sour cream
- 1 avocado, thinly cut
- 2 chorizos, crumbled and fried
- 6 big radishes, thinly cut

Directions:

1. Cover the chiles with hot water and VVVVVVVVVVVVVVVVVVVVVVVVV soak for approximately five minutes. Drain, then move the chiles to a blender jar, put in the rest of the sauce ingredients, and blend until the desired smoothness is achieved.
2. Heat the oil in a frying pan and cook the sauce over moderate heat for approximately 8 minutes, stirring and scraping the bottom of the pan almost continuously. Turn off the heat and keep warm.
3. One at a time, fry the tortillas lightly on both sides, drain thoroughly, and keep them warm while you do the rest.
4. Immerse the tortillas into the sauce, then fill each one with some of the cheese and onion. Roll up loosely and place side by side in the serving dish. Put in a little water to

the rest of the sauce, then bring to its boiling point and pour over the enchiladas. Top with the avocado slices, cut radishes, sour cream, and chorizos and serve instantly.

ENCHILADAS DE JALISCO

Yield: Servings 6

Ingredients:

The filling (or picadillo)

- ⅓ cup (85 ml) reserved meat broth
- ½ cup (125 ml) finely chopped white onion
- 1 pound (450 g) tomatoes
- 1 tablespoon finely chopped parsley
- 1 zucchini squash (approximately four ounces/115 g)
- 2 small carrots (approximately four ounces/115 g)
- 2 teaspoons salt, or to taste
- 3 small red bliss or waxy new potatoes (approximately eight ounces/225 g)
- 3 tablespoons lard
- 8 ounces (225 g) ground beef
- 8 ounces (225 g) ground pork
- Salt to taste

The chile sauce

- ¼-inch (.75-cm) piece of cinnamon stick, crushed
- 1 cup (250 ml) reserved meat broth
- 10 guajillo chiles (about 2 ounces/60 g), veins and seeds removed
- 2 tablespoons lard
- 2 whole cloves, crushed
- Salt to taste

The enchiladas

- ¼ cup (65 ml) lard
- 24 4-inch (10-cm) tortillas

To serve

- ¼ cup (65 ml) grated queso añejo, or substitute romano or sardo
- ½ cup (125 ml) finely chopped white onion
- Shredded lettuce
- Strips of jalapeño chiles en escabeche
- Thinly cut radishes

Directions:

1. Trim the squash and leave whole. Trim and scrape the carrots and slice into quarters along the length. Peel the potatoes and slice into halves. Cover the vegetables with boiling water in a big deep cooking pan, put in the salt, and allow them to cook for five minutes.
2. Combine the meat with salt to taste. Push firmly into two big balls and put in them, with the whole tomatoes, to the vegetables in the pan. Cover and cook all together using low heat until the vegetables are just soft—do not overcook—and the meat balls are almost thoroughly cooked—about ten minutes. Drain and reserve the broth.
3. When the vegetables are sufficiently cool to handle, cut them into little cubes and save for later.
4. Combine the tomatoes for a few seconds. Set aside.
5. Melt the lard in a big frying pan and cook the onion until translucent.
6. Crush the cooked meat balls into the pan, put in the parsley, and fry for approximately five minutes over moderate heat. Put in the mixed tomato puree and cook over brisk heat until some of the juice has vaporized. Put in the broth and vegetables and carry on cooking the mixture until it is well seasoned—about ten minutes. Put in salt as required. Set aside.
7. Heat a comal and toast the chiles lightly, turning them continuously, since they burn very swiftly. Cover the chiles with hot water in a container and let soak for approximately ten minutes. Move using a slotted spoon to a blender jar. Put in the broth, blend, and strain to remove any traces of the tough skin, return to the blender, put in the spices and salt, and blend until the desired smoothness is achieved.
8. Melt the lard and cook the sauce until it is well seasoned and a rich, dark-red color—approximately eight minutes.
9. Preheat your oven to 350° f (180° c).

10. Heat a little of the lard in a frying pan, and fry the tortillas on both sides, putting in more lard as required—they should just tenderize and heat through in the hot fat. Pile one on top of the other between sheets of toweling and keep warm.

11. Immerse the tortillas into the sauce, which should lightly cover them (if it is too thick, then put in slightly more broth). Put some of the picadillo across each tortilla and roll up. Put one layer of the enchiladas on the bottom of an ovenproof dish approximately four inches (10 cm) deep. Pour a little of the rest of the sauce over them. Then place another enchilada layer on top and pour over the remaining sauce.

12. Cover the dish and heat the enchiladas through in your oven for approximately fifteen minutes, then serve instantly, topped with the lettuce, radishes, and canned chiles, and sprinkled with the cheese and chopped onion.

ENCHILADAS PLACERAS O POLLO DE PLAZA

Yield: Servings 6

Ingredients:

The topping

- ⅓ cup (85 ml) mild vinegar
- 1 teaspoon salt
- 8 ounces (225 g) carrots (3 medium)
- 8 ounces (225 g) red bliss or waxy new potatoes (3 small ones), unpeeled

The sauce

- ¼ teaspoon dried mexican oregano
- 1 slice white onion
- 2 garlic cloves, roughly chopped
- 3 ancho chiles, seeds and veins removed
- 3 guajillo chiles, seeds and veins removed
- About 1½ cups (375 ml) water
- Salt to taste

The enchiladas

- ½ cup (125 ml) finely chopped white onion
- 12 freshly made tortillas
- 8 ounces (225 g) queso fresco, crumbled and lightly salted (approximately 1⅓ cups/333 ml)
- A 3-pound (1.35-kg) chicken, poached and slice into serving pieces
- Lard or vegetable oil for frying

To serve

- ¼ cup (65 ml) grated queso añejo, or substitute romano or sardo
- ⅔ cup (165 ml) prepared sour cream
- 1 cup (250 ml) finely shredded lettuce or raw cabbage
- Strips of canned jalapeño chiles en escabeche

Directions:

1. Wash the potatoes and cut them into little cubes; scrape the carrots and cut them into smaller cubes. Cover the carrots with boiling water, put in the salt, and cook them for approximately five minutes using high heat. Put in the potatoes and cook them for approximately 8 minutes—they should still be firm to the bite—then drain.
2. Cover the vegetables with cold water and put in the vinegar. Stir and save for later.
3. Heat a griddle and toast the chiles lightly, turning continuously so they do not burn.
4. Cover the chiles with hot water and VVVVVVVVVVVVVVVVVVVVVVVVVV soak for ten minutes.
5. Put ½ cup (125 ml) of the water into a blender jar, put in the guajillos, and blend until the desired smoothness is achieved. Strain. Put in the remaining 1 cup (250 ml) water, the anchos, garlic, and onion and blend until the desired smoothness is achieved. Put in the guajillo puree, the oregano, and salt to taste.
6. Melt a little of the lard, and when it is sizzling, dip each tortilla into the raw sauce—it should just lightly cover it (if the sauce is too thick dilute it with slightly more water) and fry it swiftly on both sides.
7. Take out of the frying pan and put approximately 1 small tablespoon of the cheese and ½ tablespoon of the onion across each tortilla. Roll them up loosely and set them side by side on the serving dish. Keep warm.
8. In the same fat, fry the pieces of chicken until they become golden brown. Drain and place them around the enchiladas.

9. In the same fat, fry the vegetables until just starting to brown, and drain thoroughly. In the same fat, cook the rest of the sauce for a little time and pour it over the enchiladas. Cover with the fried vegetables.
10. Top with the chile strips and on each serving put in a spoonful of sour cream and a drizzling of cheese, with lettuce on the side.

GREEN ENCHILADAS (ENCHILADAS VERDES DE AGUASCALIENTES)

Yield: 12 enchiladas

Ingredients:

The sauce

- ½ cup (125 ml) sour cream, commercial or homemade
- 1 cup (250 ml) chicken broth
- 1 whole clove, crushed
- 2 big romaine lettuce leaves
- 2 tablespoons vegetable oil
- 3 poblano chiles, charred, peeled, and seeds removed (not veins;)
- Salt to taste

The filling

- 1½ to 2 cups (375 to 500 ml) cooked, shredded, and well-salted chicken
- twelve tortillas
- Vegetable oil for frying

To serve

- ½ cup (125 ml) pitted, halved green olives
- 1½ cups (375 ml) finely shredded lettuce
- 6 big radishes, thinly cut

Directions:

1. Combine the chiles with the lettuce, clove, and ½ cup (125 ml) of the chicken broth until super smooth.
2. Heat the 2 tablespoons of oil in a big frying pan, put in the sauce, and cook over quite high heat for approximately five minutes, stirring and scraping the bottom of the pan to prevent sticking. Put in the salt, sour cream, and the rest of the ½ cup chicken broth and just heat through, then take out of the heat and keep warm.
3. Heat the oil in a different frying pan and fry the tortillas, one by one, for a short period of time on both sides. Drain thoroughly and keep warm.
4. Immerse the tortillas, one at a time, into the sauce, then fill each one with some of the chicken. Roll up and place side by side on a warmed dish. Pour the rest of the sauce over the enchiladas, top with the lettuce, cut radishes, and olives, and serve instantly.

GREEN ENCHILADAS (ENCHILADAS VERDES DE SAN LUIS POTOSÍ)

Yield: 12 enchiladas

Ingredients:

The sauce

- ⅓ cup (85 ml) milk
- 1 garlic clove
- 2 cups (500 ml) cooked tomate verde, drained
- 2 tablespoons sour cream, commercial or homemade
- 2 tablespoons vegetable oil
- 3 sprigs cilantro
- 4 serrano chiles
- Salt to taste

The tortillas

- twelve tortillas
- Vegetable oil for frying

The filling

- 1½ to 2 cups (375 to 500 ml) shredded cooked chicken

To serve

- ½ cup (125 ml) prepared sour cream
- ¾ cup (190 ml) finely chopped white onion
- 3 ounces (85 g) queso fresco, crumbled (about ½ cup/125 ml)

Directions:

1. Combine the tomate verde with the chiles, cilantro, milk, garlic, and salt until the desired smoothness is achieved.
2. Heat the oil in a big frying pan and cook the sauce over quite high heat until reduced and seasoned—about five minutes. Turn off the heat, put in the sour cream, and save for later. Keep warm.
3. Heat the oil in a second frying pan and fry the tortillas, one at a time, for a short period of time on each side. Drain thoroughly and keep warm.
4. One at a time, immerse the tortillas into the sauce. Fill each one with some of the chicken, then roll and place side by side in the warmed dish. Dilute the remaining sauce, if required, and pour it over the enchiladas. Top lavishly with the onion, cheese, and sour cream and serve instantly.

GREEN ENCHILADAS (ENCHILADAS VERDES)

Yield: 12 enchiladas

Ingredients:

The sauce

- ⅓ cup (85 ml) plus ½ cup (125 ml) chicken broth
- ½ cup (125 ml) toasted (shelled), unsalted peanuts, crushed
- 1 cup (250 ml) cooked tomate verde, drained
- 2 sprigs cilantro, thick stems removed
- 2 tablespoons vegetable oil
- 3 poblano chiles, charred, peeled, and cleaned
- Salt to taste

The tortillas

- 12 freshly made tortillas

The filling

- 1½ to 2 cups (375 to 500 ml) shredded, cooked chicken
- 2 poblano chiles, prepared in rajas and fried with a little onion

To serve

- ⅓ cup (85 ml) crumbled queso fresco (about 2 ounces/60 g)
- ½ cup (125 ml) prepared sour cream
- ⅔ cup (165 ml) finely chopped white onion

Directions:

1. Combine the tomate verde with the remaining sauce ingredients, apart from the oil and ½ cup (125 ml) chicken broth, until the desired smoothness is achieved.
2. Heat the oil in a big frying pan and fry the sauce over quite high heat for five minutes, stirring and scraping the bottom of the pan occasionally to prevent sticking. Put in the remaining ½ cup (125 ml) broth and bring to its boiling point, then take out of the heat and keep warm.
3. If the tortillas are not freshly made and still warm, heat them for a short period of time in a steamer. Immerse them, one at a time, into the sauce, fill each one with a little of the chicken and a few rajas, roll loosely, and set side by side in the serving dish. Reheat the rest of the sauce, diluting it if required with a little broth or water. Pour it over the enchiladas and top with the cheese, onion, and sour cream before you serve.

GREEN ENCHILADAS FROM VERACRUZ (ENCHILADAS VERDES VERACRUZANAS)

Based on a recipe by señora josefina velázquez de león

Yield: 12 enchiladas

Ingredients:

The sauce

- ½ cup (125 ml) cooking liquid from the tomatoes
- ½ cup (125 ml) roughly chopped white onion
- ½ cup (125 ml) sour cream, commercial or homemade
- 1 cup (250 ml) cooked tomate verde, drained
- 2 tablespoons vegetable oil
- 4 poblano chiles, charred, peeled, and cleaned
- Salt to taste

The tortillas

- 12 freshly made tortillas

The filling

- 2 cups (500 ml) guacamole

To serve

- ¼ cup (65 ml) roughly chopped flat-leaf parsley
- 3 ounces (85 g) queso fresco, crumbled (about ½ cup/125 ml)

Directions:

1. Combine the tomate verde with the cooking liquid, chilies, onion, and salt until the desired smoothness is achieved.
2. Heat the oil in a frying pan and cook the sauce over quite high heat for approximately five minutes, stirring and scraping the bottom of the pan occasionally to prevent sticking. Turn off the heat and put in the sour cream, then set the sauce over a very low heat just to heat it through. Set aside and keep warm.
3. If the tortillas are not freshly made and still warm, heat them for a short period of time in a steamer. Immerse them, one at a time, into the sauce, put approximately 1½ tablespoons of the guacamole across the face of each, roll up loosely, and place side by side in the serving dish. Dilute the rest of the sauce with a little water or milk and pour over the enchiladas. Drizzle with the parsley and cheese and serve instantly.

GREEN ENCHILADAS WITH CARNITAS (ENCHILADAS VERDES CON CARNITAS)

Yield: Servings 6

Ingredients:

- 2 garlic cloves, crushed
- 3 pounds (1.35 kg) country-style spareribs
- Salt to taste

The sauce

- ¼ cup (65 ml) broth or water
- ⅓ cup (85 ml) finely chopped white onion
- 1 cup (250 ml) cooked tomate verde, drained
- 2 big romaine lettuce leaves
- 2 garlic cloves
- 2 poblano chiles, charred, peeled, seeds and veins removed
- 2 sprigs epazote
- 2 tablespoons vegetable oil
- 6 sprigs cilantro
- Salt to taste

The filling

- ¼ medium white onion, finely chopped
- 3 tablespoons vegetable oil
- 4 serrano chiles, finely chopped
- 5 big eggs
- 6 ounces (180 g) tomatoes, finely chopped (approximately 1 cup/250 ml)
- Salt to taste

The tortillas

- 2 cups (500 ml) finely shredded lettuce
- 6 big radish flowers

- **To serve**

- twelve tortillas
- Vegetable oil for frying

Directions:

1. Place the meat into a wide pan just big enough to accommodate it in no more than two layers. Barely cover the meat with water, put in the garlic and salt, and bring to its boiling point. Reduce the heat to moderate and allow the meat to cook until it is soft, the water evaporates, and the fat is rendered out. Allow the meat fry in its fat, turning it occasionally until thoroughly browned—approximately 1 hour. Set aside and keep warm.
2. Heat the oil in a frying pan and fry the onion until translucent.
3. Combine the rest of the ingredients for the sauce until the desired smoothness is achieved. Put into the onion in the pan and fry over quite high heat while stirring and scraping the bottom of the pan until it has reduced a little and is well seasoned— about five minutes. Turn off the heat and keep warm.
4. Heat the oil in a second frying pan.
5. In the meantime, beat the eggs together well, then mix in the salt, onion, tomatoes, and chiles. Pour into the hot oil and scramble them using super low heat; they must be just set and soft. Turn off the heat and keep warm.
6. Heat the oil in a frying pan and fry the tortillas, one at a time, lightly on both sides. Drain and keep warm.
7. Immerse the tortillas into the green sauce, fill each one with some of the egg mixture, then roll up and put them on the serving dish. Dilute the rest of the sauce, if required, and pour over the enchiladas. Put the pork, lettuce, and radish flowers around the dish, and serve instantly.

MOCTEZUMA PIE (BUDÍN AZTECA)

Yield: Servings 6

Ingredients:

The green tomato sauce

- 2 small garlic cloves, roughly chopped
- 2 tablespoons finely chopped white onion
- 2 tablespoons vegetable oil
- 3 cups (750 ml) cooked <u>tomate verde</u> (approximately 1½ pounds/680 g), drained, saving for later ½ cup (125 ml) of the liquid
- 3 serrano chiles, cooked with the <u>tomate verde</u>

The rajas

- ⅓ cup (85 ml) thinly cut white onion
- 3 tablespoons vegetable oil
- 7 poblano chiles, prepared in rajas
- Salt to taste

The budín

- ⅓ cup (85 ml) vegetable oil
- 1½ cups (375 ml) thick sour cream
- 1¾ cups (440 ml) grated chihuahua cheese or cheddar (approximately eight ounces/225 g)
- 18 freshly made tortillas, approximately 5 inches (13 cm) across, cut into halves
- 2 cups (500 ml) shredded, poached chicken, well salted

Directions:

1. Prepare an ovenproof dish approximately 10 inches (25 cm) in diameter and 4 inches (10 cm) deep.
2. Preheat your oven to 350° f (180° c).
3. In a blender, blend the <u>tomate verde</u> with the ½ cup (125 ml) reserved liquid and the chiles, garlic, and onion to a smooth sauce.
4. Heat the oil in a frying pan, put in the sauce, and cook using high heat for approximately five minutes, stirring occasionally to prevent sticking, by which time it will have thickened a little and will be well seasoned. Set aside.
5. Chop the chiles into thin strips and save for later.
6. Heat the 3 tablespoons of oil in a different frying pan, then put in the onion and fry until translucent—about one minute. Put in the chile strips and salt, cover the pan,

and cook over gentle heat until the chiles are soft but not too soft—about five minutes.

7. Heat the oil in a different frying pan and fry each tortilla for a few seconds—they should not get crisp or hard. Blot off surplus oil on the next unfried tortilla.

8. Spread one third of the tortillas over the bottom of the dish. Then spread, in layers on top of them, half the chicken, half the rajas, and a third each of the sauce, sour cream, and cheese. Repeat the layers and finish off with a layer of tortillas, sprinkled with the remaining sauce, sour cream, and cheese.

9. Bake the budín for approximately twenty-five minutes, or until it is well thoroughly heated and the cheese has melted.

MUSHROOM PUDDING (BUDÍN DE HONGOS)

Yield: Servings 4

Ingredients:

The filling

- ½ cup (125 ml) thinly cut white onion
- 1 big sprig epazote or parsley, leaves only, roughly chopped
- 1 pound (450 g) mushrooms, washed and thinly cut, or roughly chopped cuitlacoche
- 2 garlic cloves, peeled and finely chopped
- 2 tablespoons vegetable oil
- 3 serrano chiles, finely chopped
- Salt to taste

The sauce

- ¼ cup (65 ml) roughly chopped white onion
- 1 garlic clove, roughly chopped
- 1 pound (450 g) tomatoes, roughly chopped (about 3 cups/750 ml)
- 1 tablespoon vegetable oil
- Salt to taste

The tortillas

- 12 5- to 6-inch (12.5- to fifteen-cm) tortillas, cut into four and dried
- 4 ounces (115 g) chihuahua cheese (see substitutes), grated (approximately 1 heaped cup/265 ml)
- Vegetable oil for frying

Directions:

1. Prepare a mildly greased ovenproof dish about 9 by 6 by 3 inches (23 by fifteen by 8 cm).
2. Heat the oil in a big frying pan and fry the onion and garlic for a couple of minutes, stirring occasionally to prevent sticking—they should not brown. Put in the mushrooms, chiles, and salt, then cover the pan and cook over moderate heat until the mushrooms are soft—about twenty minutes; they must be juicy. Put in the epazote and cook for a minute more. Set aside in a container.
3. Combine the tomatoes, onion, and garlic together until the desired smoothness is achieved.
4. Heat the oil in a frying pan and cook the sauce over quite high heat while stirring it occasionally, for approximately 4 minutes to reduce. Put in salt.
5. Heat the oil in a second frying pan and fry the tortillas, approximately one third at a time so they fry uniformly, until they are just becoming stiff but do not harden and brown. Drain using paper towels.
6. Preheat your oven to 375° f (190° c).
7. Put one third of the tortilla pieces at the bottom of the dish, then put in half of the mushroom mixture, one third of the cheese, and ⅓ cup (85 ml) sauce. Repeat the layers and top off with the remaining cheese, sauce, and any mushroom juice left in the pan. Bake until well thoroughly heated and bubbling—twenty to twenty-five minutes.

PASTEL AZTECA

Yield: Servings 6 to 8

Ingredients:

2 dried ancho chiles, stemmed, seeded, and torn into ½ inch pieces (½ cup)

- ⅓ cup chopped fresh cilantro

- 1 onion, chopped
- 1 tablespoon lime juice
- 1 tablespoon tomato paste
- 1 tablespoon vegetable oil
- 1 teaspoon ground coriander
- 1 teaspoon ground cumin
- 18 (6 inch) corn tortillas
- 2 teaspoons dried oregano
- 2 tomatoes, cored and chopped
- 2½ pounds boneless, skinless chicken breasts, trimmed
- 3 cups chicken broth
- 3 garlic cloves, minced
- 3 tablespoons all purpose flour
- 5 scallions, cut thin
- 8 ounces Monterey Jack cheese, shredded (2 cups)
- 8 ounces queso fresco, crumbled (2 cups)
- Salt and pepper

Directions:

1. Adjust oven rack to middle position and heat oven to 425 degrees. Toast anchos in 12 inch frying pan on moderate heat, stirring regularly, until aromatic, 2 to six minutes; move to blender.

2. Heat oil in Dutch oven over moderate high heat until it starts to shimmer Put in onion and cook until tender, approximately five minutes. Mix in tomato paste, garlic, oregano, cumin, coriander, 1 teaspoon salt, and ½ teaspoon pepper and cook until aromatic, approximately one minute. Mix in flour and cook until slightly deepened in color, approximately one minute. Slowly whisk in broth and bring to simmer. Decrease the heat to moderate low and cook, whisking frequently, until sauce is slightly thickened, approximately 3 minutes.

3. Put in sauce to blender and pulse until smooth, approximately half a minute; return to now empty pot. Nestle chicken into sauce, cover, and cook over moderate low heat until chicken records 160 degrees, approximately fifteen minutes. Move chicken to cutting board, allow to cool slightly, then shred into bite size pieces with the help of

two forks; move to container. Put in 1½ cups sauce, two thirds of scallions, ¼ cup cilantro, and lime juice and toss to blend.

4. In the meantime, toast tortillas, one by one, in 8 inch frying pan over moderate high heat until mildly browned, approximately twenty seconds per side; move to plate and cover using a dish towel. Mix Monterey Jack and queso fresco in container.

5. Spread ½ cup rest of the sauce over bottom of 13 by 9 inch baking dish. Lay 6 tortillas into dish, overlapping them slightly. Spread ½ cup sauce over tortillas and top with half of chicken mixture and one third of cheese mixture. Repeat with 6 more tortillas, ½ cup sauce, remaining chicken mixture, and half of rest of the cheese mixture. Top with remaining 6 tortillas, rest of the sauce, and rest of the cheese.

6. Cover dish with aluminium foil and bake until sauce is bubbling and cheese is melted, fifteen to twenty minutes. Allow the casserole to cool for about ten minutes. Drizzle with tomatoes, remaining scallions, and remaining cilantro and serve.

RED ENCHILADAS (ENCHILADAS ROJAS DE AGUASCALIENTES)

Yield: 12 enchiladas

Ingredients:

The sauce

- 1 garlic clove
- 1 hard-cooked egg yolk
- 1½ cups (375 ml) hot milk
- 2 tablespoons vegetable oil
- 4 ancho chiles, wiped clean, seeds and veins removed, mildly toasted
- Salt to taste

The filling

- 1 cup (250 ml) finely chopped white onion
- 8 ounces (225 g) queso fresco, crumbled (approximately 1½ cups/375 ml)
- twelve tortillas
- Vegetable oil for frying

To serve

- 1 hard-cooked egg white, finely chopped
- 1½ cups (375 ml) finely shredded lettuce
- 6 radishes, thinly cut
- Strips of jalapeño chiles en escabeche

Directions:

1. Tear the chiles into pieces and put in to a blender jar with the milk and let soak for approximately ten minutes. Put in the salt, garlic, and egg yolk and blend until the desired smoothness is achieved. (you will have about 2 cups/500 ml of sauce; put in water if required to make up that quantity.)
2. Heat the oil in a moderate-sized frying pan, put in the sauce, and cook for approximately five minutes over moderate heat, stirring and scraping the sides and bottom of the pan occasionally. Turn off the heat and keep warm.
3. Heat the oil in a different frying pan and fry the tortillas, one at a time, for a short period of time on both sides. Drain thoroughly and keep warm.
4. Immerse the tortillas, one at a time, into the sauce. Fill each one with some of the cheese and onion, then roll and place side by side in a serving dish. Dilute the rest of the sauce, if required, and pour it over the enchiladas. Top with the chopped egg white, the lettuce, cut radishes, and chile strips and serve instantly.

ROASTED POBLANO AND BLACK BEAN ENCHILADAS

Yield: Servings four to 6

Ingredients:

- ¼ cup heavy cream
- ⅓ cup vegetable broth
- ½ teaspoon ground coriander
- ½ teaspoon ground cumin
- 1 (fifteen ounce) can black beans, washed, half of beans mashed smooth
- 1 cup fresh cilantro leaves
- 1 pound tomatillos, husks and stems removed, washed well, dried, and halved
- 1 tablespoon lime juice

- 1 teaspoon chili powder
- 1 teaspoon plus ¼ cup vegetable oil
- 1 teaspoon sugar
- 12 (6 inch) corn tortillas
- 2 onions, chopped fine
- 4 garlic cloves, minced
- 4 poblano chiles, halved along the length, stemmed, and seeded
- 8 ounces Monterey Jack cheese, shredded (2 cups)
- Salt and pepper

Directions:

1. Adjust oven rack 6 inches from broiler element and heat broiler. Coat rimmed baking sheet with aluminium foil. Toss tomatillos and poblanos with 1 teaspoon oil. Position tomatillos cut side down and poblanos skin side up on readied sheet. Broil until vegetables are blackened and starting to tenderize, 5 to ten minutes. Move poblanos to container, cover using aluminium foil, and allow to steam until skins peel off easily, approximately ten minutes. Using back of spoon, scrape loosened skins from poblanos. Chop tomatillos and poblanos into ½ inch pieces.
2. Process broiled tomatillos, 1 cup onion, ½ cup cilantro, broth, cream, 1 tablespoon oil, half of garlic, lime juice, sugar, and 1 teaspoon salt inside a food processor until sauce is smooth, approximately 2 minutes. Sprinkle with salt and pepper to taste.
3. Heat 1 tablespoon oil in 12 inch frying pan on moderate heat until it starts to shimmer Put in remaining onion and cook until tender, five to seven minutes. Mix in chili powder, coriander, cumin, and remaining garlic and cook until aromatic, approximately half a minute. Mix in mashed and whole beans and chopped poblanos and cook until warmed through, approximately 2 minutes. Move mixture to big container and allow to cool slightly. Mix in 1 cup Monterey Jack, ½ cup tomatillo sauce, and remaining ½ cup cilantro. Sprinkle with salt and pepper to taste.
4. Adjust oven rack to middle position and heat oven to 400 degrees. Spread ½ cup tomatillo sauce over bottom of 13 by 9 inch baking dish. Brush both sides of tortillas with remaining 2 tablespoons oil. Stack tortillas, wrap in damp dish towel, and place on plate; microwave until warm and flexible, approximately one minute.
5. Working with 1 warm tortilla at a time, spread ¼ cup bean cheese filling across center of tortilla. Roll tortilla firmly around filling and place seam side down in baking dish; position enchiladas in 2 columns across width of dish.

6. Pour rest of the sauce over top to cover completely and drizzle remaining 1 cup cheese down center of enchiladas. Cover dish firmly with greased aluminium foil. Bake until enchiladas are thoroughly heated and cheese is melted, fifteen to twenty minutes. Allow to cool for five minutes before you serve.

SIMPLE ENCHILADAS (ENCHILADAS SENCILLAS)

Yield: 12 enchiladas

Ingredients:

The tomato sauce

- ½ cup (125 ml) thick sour cream, at room temperature
- 1 garlic clove
- 1 pound (450 g) tomatoes, broiled
- 2 fresh serrano chiles, toasted
- 2 tablespoons vegetable oil
- Salt to taste

The enchiladas

- 1 cup (250 ml) finely chopped white onion
- 12 freshly made tortillas
- 7 big eggs, scrambled with sufficient salt, or 1½ cups (375 ml) cooked and shredded chicken, well salted
- Vegetable oil for frying

To serve

- 1 cup (250 ml) grated chihuahua cheese or cheddar

Directions:

1. In a blender, puree the tomatoes, garlic, and chiles until the desired smoothness is achieved—you'll have about 2 cups (500 ml).
2. Heat the oil in a big frying pan and fry the sauce for approximately five minutes, or until it has reduced and thickened. Put in the salt. Set aside to cool a little.

3. Mix the sour cream thoroughly into the sauce and just heat it through lightly. Do not let the sauce come to a boil after the cream has been added or it will curdle.

4. Heat the oil in a different frying pan and fry the tortillas swiftly, one at a time, without letting them become crisp around the edges.

5. Preheat your oven to 350° f (180° c).

6. Immerse the tortillas into the warm sauce—they must be just lightly covered—then put about 2 tablespoons of the scrambled egg or shredded chicken across each tortilla and drizzle it with a little of the onion. Roll the filled tortillas up loosely and set them side by side in an ovenproof dish.

7. Cover the enchiladas with the rest of the sauce and drizzle with the cheese and remaining onion. Place the dish into the oven and just heat them through for a very short time, no more than ten minutes. Serve instantly.

SIMPLE TORTILLA CASSEROLE (CASEROLA DE TORTILLAS SENCILLA)

Yield: Servings 4

Ingredients:

The sauce

- ¼ cup (65 ml) roughly chopped white onion
- 1 big garlic clove, roughly chopped
- 1 pound (450 g) tomatoes, roughly chopped (about 3 cups/750 ml)
- 2 tablespoons vegetable oil
- Salt to taste

The filling

- ⅓ cup (85 ml) broth or hot water
- 4 ounces (115 g) chihuahua cheese (about ¾ cup/185 ml), or queso fresco (about ⅔ cup/165 ml)
- twelve tortillas cut into strips and dried
- Vegetable oil for frying

To serve

- 1 cup (250 ml) prepared sour cream
- 2 tablespoons finely chopped parsley (not necessary)

Directions:

1. Prepare a mildly greased ovenproof dish about 9 by 6 by 3 inches (23 by fifteen by 8 cm).
2. Combine the tomatoes with the remaining sauce ingredients apart from the oil until the desired smoothness is achieved.
3. Heat the oil in a moderate-sized frying pan and fry the sauce over a quite high heat to reduce and season—approximately four minutes. Turn off the heat and set in a warm place.
4. Heat the oil in a second frying pan and fry the tortilla pieces, approximately one third at a time so they will cook uniformly, until they are just stiffening but not brown. Drain thoroughly.
5. Preheat your oven to 375° f (190° c).
6. Put one third of the tortilla pieces at the bottom of the dish; drizzle with ⅓ cup (85 ml) of the sauce and one third of the cheese. Repeat with half of the rest of the tortillas, sauce, and cheese, then top off with the rest of the ingredients. Moisten the top cover with the broth. Set in the top level of the oven, uncovered, and bake for fifteen to twenty minutes, or until thoroughly heated and bubbling. (the liquid should have been absorbed and the tortilla pieces just soft, not falling apart, at the bottom and still a little chewy on top. Slight adjustments may be needed to suit the tortillas that are available to you.)
7. Serve, sprinkled with parsley, if you prefer it. Pass the sour cream separately.

TAMALE PIE

Yield: Servings 6 to 8

Ingredients:

- ¾ cup coarse cornmeal
- 1 (14.5 ounce) can diced tomatoes
- 1 (fifteen ounce) can black beans, washed

- 1 cup fresh or frozen corn
- 1 jalapeño chile, stemmed, seeded, and minced
- 1 onion, chopped fine
- 1 pound 90 percent lean ground beef
- 1 tablespoon minced fresh oregano or 1 teaspoon dried
- 2 garlic cloves, minced
- 2 tablespoons chili powder
- 2½ cups water
- 3 tablespoons vegetable oil
- 4 ounces Monterey Jack cheese, shredded (1 cup)
- Salt and pepper

Directions:

1. Adjust oven rack to lower middle position and heat oven to 375 degrees. Heat 1 tablespoon oil in 12 inch frying pan over moderate high heat until just smoking. Put in beef and cook, breaking up meat with wooden spoon, until just starting to brown, approximately five minutes.

2. Mix in onion, jalapeño, and ¼ teaspoon salt and cook until vegetables become tender, approximately five minutes. Mix in chili powder, oregano, and garlic and cook until aromatic, approximately half a minute. Mix in beans, tomatoes and their juice, and corn and simmer until most of liquid has vaporized, approximately 3 minutes. Remove the heat, sprinkle with salt and pepper to taste.

3. Bring water to boil in big deep cooking pan. Put in ¼ teaspoon salt and then slowly pour in cornmeal while whisking vigorously to stop clumping. Turn heat to moderate and cook, whisking continuously, until cornmeal thickens, approximately 3 minutes. Mix in remaining 2 tablespoons oil.

4. Stir Monterey Jack into beef mixture, then scrape into deep dish pie plate (or other 3 quart baking dish). Spread cornmeal mixture over top and seal against edge of dish. Cover with aluminium foil and bake until crust has set and filling is hot throughout, approximately 30 minutes. Allow the casserole to cool for about ten minutes and serve.

TORTILLA AND VEGETABLE CASSEROLE (CASEROLA DE TORTILLAS Y LEGUMBRES)

Yield: Servings 4

Ingredients:

The sauce

- ⅓ cup (85 ml) thinly cut white onion
- ⅔ cup (165 ml) chicken broth or vegetable broth for vegetarians
- 1½ tablespoons vegetable oil
- 12 ounces (340 g) tomatoes, broiled
- Salt to taste

The filling

- 1 cup (250 ml) cooked fresh peas, or defrosted uncooked
- 1 cup (250 ml) cooked green beans, cut into little pieces
- 1 cup (250 ml) cooked, diced carrot
- 12 5- to 6-inch (12.5- to fifteen-cm) tortillas, cut into strips and dried
- Vegetable oil for frying

To serve

- 4 ounces (115 g) chihuahua cheese or substitute grated (approximately 1 heaped cup/265 ml)

Directions:

1. Prepare a mildly greased ovenproof dish about 9 by 6 by 3 inches (23 by fifteen by 8 cm).
2. Heat the oil in a big frying pan and cook the onion gently until soft, approximately 3 minutes; do not brown.
3. Combine the unskinned tomatoes for a short period of time, then add, with the salt, to the onion in the pan. Cook over quite high heat while stirring occasionally, until it reduces—about three minutes. Put in the broth or vegetable water and cook for one minute or so longer, then set aside.

4. Heat the oil in a different frying pan and fry the tortilla pieces, approximately one third at a time so they fry uniformly, until just starting to stiffen, not brown. Drain thoroughly.

5. Preheat your oven to 375° f (190° c).

6. Spread half of the tortilla pieces over the bottom of the dish. Drizzle with approximately one third of the sauce, then cover with the vegetables, the remaining tortillas, and finally the remaining sauce. Cover the dish using foil and bake for approximately twenty minutes, or until the bottom tortillas are tender but not falling apart and the top ones are still slightly chewy. Take away the foil.

7. Drizzle the cheese over the top of the casserole and return the dish to the oven just until the cheese melts. Once this casserole is assembled it must be cooked and served, or it will become rather soggy.

CHILAQUILES

Fried tortillas immersed in a chile sauce and topped with delicious stuff. Who doesn't want that?

GREEN CHILAQUILES (CHILAQUILES VERDES TAMPIQUEÑOS)

Yield: Servings 6

Ingredients:

The sauce

- ⅓ medium white onion, roughly chopped
- 1 cup (250 ml) chicken broth
- 1 tablespoon vegetable oil
- 2 sprigs epazote
- 3 poblano chiles, charred, peeled, seeds and veins removed
- 3 sprigs cilantro
- 8 ounces (225 g) tomate verde, cooked and drained (approximately 1 cup/250 ml;)
- Salt to taste

The tortillas

- twelve tortillas, each cut into 6 triangular pieces and left to dry
- Vegetable oil for frying

To serve

- ½ cup (125 ml) roughly chopped white onion
- 2 hard-cooked eggs, cut
- 2 tablespoons roughly chopped cilantro
- 4 ounces (115 g) queso fresco, crumbled (about ⅔ cup/165 ml)
- 6 big radishes, thinly cut

Directions:

1. Combine the tomate verde with the chiles, epazote, cilantro, onion, and salt until the desired smoothness is achieved.
2. Heat the oil in a big frying pan and fry the sauce over moderate heat, stirring occasionally to prevent sticking, for five minutes. Put in the broth and carry on cooking for a minute more, then take out of the heat and save for later.
3. In a second frying pan, heat the oil and fry the tortilla pieces, approximately one third at a time so they will be uniformly cooked, until they barely start to stiffen but do not brown. Drain thoroughly.
4. Return the sauce to the heat and bring to its boiling point; mix in the tortilla pieces and cook them over moderate heat, scraping the bottom of the pan almost continuously, until most of the liquid has been absorbed and the tortillas are just tenderizing—5 to 8 minutes. Drizzle the cheese, onion, eggs, radishes, and cilantro over the top and serve instantly.

CHILAQUILES DE AGUASCALIENTES

Yield: Servings 4

Ingredients:

The sauce

- ⅛ teaspoon dried mexican oregano

- ¼ cup (65 ml) roughly chopped white onion
- ⅔ cup (165 ml) cooked and drained <u>tomate verde</u>
- 1½ tablespoons sesame seeds, toasted and crushed
- 2 garlic cloves, crushed
- 2 plum tomatoes (about 6 ounces/180 g), broiled
- 2 sprigs cilantro
- 2 tablespoons vegetable oil
- 4 canned chipotle chiles en adobo
- Salt to taste

The tortillas

- 12 stale tortillas, each cut into 6 triangular pieces
- Vegetable oil for frying

To serve

- ¾ cup (190 ml) thinly cut white onion
- 1 tablespoon roughly chopped cilantro (not necessary)
- 3 chorizos (approximately eight ounces/225 g), skinned, crumbled, and fried
- 8 ounces (225 g) queso fresco, crumbled (approximately 1⅓ cups/335 ml)

Directions:

1. In a blender, blend all the sauce ingredients apart from the oil until the desired smoothness is achieved.
2. Heat the oil in a frying pan and cook the sauce over a quite high heat while stirring and scraping the bottom of the pan for approximately five minutes. Turn off the heat and save for later. Preheat your oven to 350° f (180° c).
3. Heat the oil in a different frying pan and fry the tortilla pieces, approximately one third at a time so they are uniformly cooked, until they barely start to stiffen but do not brown. Drain thoroughly.
4. Put one third of the tortillas at the bottom of the dish, then put in half the chorizos and cheese and ⅓ cup (85 ml) of the sauce. Repeat the layers and top off with the remaining tortillas and sauce. Cover the dish using foil and bake for fifteen to twenty minutes, or until it is well thoroughly heated and the tortillas are just tender. Drizzle with the onion and cilantro and serve instantly.

CHILAQUILES VERACRUZANOS

Yield: Servings 4

Ingredients:

The chicken

- ¼ cup (65 ml) roughly cut white onion
- 1 big garlic clove
- 1 whole chicken breast, or 2 big legs, if you want
- 2 cups (500 ml) water
- 2 sprigs cilantro
- 2 sprigs fresh mint, or 1 small tablespoon dried
- Salt to taste

The sauce

- ¼ cup (65 ml) water
- 1 ancho chile, seeds and veins removed
- 1 big garlic clove
- 1 cup (250 ml) chicken broth
- 2 tablespoons vegetable oil
- 8 ounces (225 g) roughly chopped tomatoes (approximately 1½ cups/375 ml)
- Salt to taste

The tortillas

- 12 5-inch (12.5-cm) tortillas, each cut into 6 pieces and dried
- Vegetable oil for frying

To serve

- 1 cup (250 ml) prepared sour cream
- 1 cup (250 ml) thinly cut white onion
- 1 small avocado, peeled, cut into little squares, and dressed with a simple vinaigrette
- 3 ounces (85 g) queso fresco, crumbled (about ⅓ cup/85 ml)

Directions:

1. Place the chicken, salt, garlic, onion, cilantro, and mint with the water into a big deep cooking pan. Heat to a simmer, then reduce the heat and simmer until the chicken is just soft—about twenty minutes for breast, 25 or more for legs. Let the chicken cool off in the broth. When the meat is sufficiently cool to handle, remove from bones and shred. Strain and reserve the broth.

2. Heat the oil in a frying pan. Fry the chile for approximately one minute on each side, flattening it down in the pan using a spatula. Take away the chile, cover with hot water, and let soak for five to ten minutes. Leave the oil in the pan.

3. Move the drained chile to a blender jar, put in the rest of the sauce ingredients apart from the broth, and blend until the desired smoothness is achieved.

4. Reheat the oil and fry the sauce over quite high heat for approximately three minutes, scraping the bottom of the pan to prevent sticking. Put in the broth and cook for a minute more. Adjust the seasoning, take out of the heat, and save for later.

5. In a separate frying pan, heat the oil and fry the tortilla pieces, approximately one third at a time so they cook uniformly, until they barely start to stiffen but do not brown. Drain thoroughly.

6. Return the sauce to the heat. As it starts to boil, mix in the tortillas and cook over moderate heat for five to 8 minutes, or until most of the sauce has been absorbed and the tortilla pieces are just starting to become tender. Stir almost continuously or the sauce and tortillas will stick and burn.

7. Place the chilaquiles into the dish, then top with the sour cream, chicken, avocado, onion, and cheese. Serve instantly.

CHILAQUILES DE GUANAJUATO

Yield: Servings 4

Ingredients:

The sauce

- ¼ cup (65 ml) roughly chopped white onion
- 12 ounces (340 g) tomate verde, cooked and partly drained (approximately 1½ cups/375 ml;)
- 2 garlic cloves, crushed
- 2 tablespoons vegetable oil

- 6 guajillo chiles, seeds and veins removed, mildly toasted and soaked
- Salt to taste

The tortillas

- 12 stale tortillas, each cut into 6 triangular pieces
- Vegetable oil for frying

To serve

- ½ cup (125 ml) finely chopped white onion
- 6 ounces (180 g) grated chihuahua cheese or muenster (approximately 1¼ cups/315 ml)

Directions:

1. Place the chiles into a blender jar. Put in the rest of the sauce ingredients apart from the oil and blend until fairly smooth.
2. Heat the oil in a frying pan, put in the sauce, and fry over moderate heat for approximately five minutes, scraping the bottom of the pan occasionally. Turn off the heat and save for later.
3. Heat the oil in a different frying pan and fry the tortillas, approximately one third at a time so they are cooked uniformly, until they barely start to stiffen but do not brown. Drain thoroughly.
4. Preheat your broiler or oven.
5. Heat the sauce, mix in the tortilla pieces, and cook over moderate heat, stirring occasionally to prevent sticking, for approximately five minutes, or until they are just starting to tenderize and some of the sauce has been absorbed. (take care, as the sauce sticks and burns easily.) Move the chilaquiles to the serving dish. Cover with the cheese, then run the dish under a hot broiler or into the oven until the cheese just starts to melt. Top with the onion and serve instantly.

POULTRY RECIPES

ALMOND CHICKEN (POLLO ALMENDRADO)

Yield: Servings 6

Ingredients:

- ¼ cup (65 ml) cold water, roughly
- 1 cup (250 ml) peeled almonds, roughly chopped
- 1 pound (450 g) tomatoes, broiled
- 2 mexican bay leaves
- 2 thick rounds of stale french bread or hard roll
- 2 whole cloves, crushed
- 2½ teaspoons salt, or to taste
- 3 tablespoons fresh lime juice
- 4 to 6 tablespoons pork lard
- 4½ pounds (2 kg) chicken parts
- 6 peppercorns, crushed
- Freshly ground black pepper

Directions:

1. Flavour the chicken with 2 teaspoons of the salt, pepper, and the lime juice and set aside for minimum 1 hour.
2. Preheat your oven to 350° f (180° c).
3. Place the peppercorns, cloves, bay leaves, ¼ cup (65 ml) of water, and ½ teaspoon salt into a blender jar and blend meticulously, then progressively put in the tomatoes and blend once more. Melt about half of the lard in a small frying pan and fry the almonds to a deep golden color, crush, and move to the blender jar. Adding slightly more lard, fry the bread, break up roughly, and put in to the blender, then blend all the ingredients to a slightly textured paste, putting in slightly more water only if required to release the blades.
4. Pick a shallow, ovenproof dish into which the pieces of chicken will just fit in a single layer. Pour some of the melted lard from the frying pan into the dish and spread the

bottom of it with slightly more than one third of the almond sauce. Put the chicken pieces over the sauce and then cover them with the rest of the sauce. Bake, uncovered, coating occasionally with the remaining lard until the chicken is soft and the sauce slightly crusty on top—about forty-five minutes.

BARBECUED CHICKEN COMITÁN (POLLO EN BARBACOA COMITECA)

Yield: Servings 6

Ingredients:

- ¼ cup (65 ml) raisins
- ¼ cup (65 ml) slivered almonds
- ½ cup (125 ml) roughly chopped flat-leaf parsley
- 1 cup (250 ml) roughly chopped white onion
- 1 mexican bay leaf, broken up
- 1 teaspoon mexican dried oregano
- 12 pitted green olives, halved
- 2 ancho chiles, seeds and veins removed
- 2 garlic cloves, roughly chopped
- 2 whole cloves, crushed
- 3 sprigs fresh thyme, or ¼ teaspoon dried
- 4 ounces (115 g) tomate verde, husks removed and roughly chopped (approximately 1 cup/250 ml)
- 4 peppercorns, crushed
- 6 big portions of chicken
- 6 ounces (180 g) tomatoes, roughly chopped (approximately 1¼ cups/315 ml)
- Banana leaves or parchment to cover the dish
- Salt to taste

Directions:

1. Put the chicken pieces in a single layer in an ovenproof dish minimum 3 inches (8 cm) deep and set aside while preparing the seasoning paste.

2. Cover the ancho chiles with hot water and let soak for five minutes.
3. Place the tomatoes into a blender jar and blend thoroughly. Slowly put in the drained anchos, tomate verde, onion, garlic, crushed spices, and salt and blend until quite smooth. Pour over the chicken, cover, and place in your fridge overnight.
4. Preheat your oven to 325° f (165° c).
5. The next day, flip the chicken pieces over to meticulously coat with the sauce. Spread the herbs, almonds, raisins, and olives over the surface, cover with 2 layers of banana leaf, and bake for approximately thirty-five minutes. Flip the chicken pieces over and coat well with the sauce. Cover the dish and carry on baking until the chicken is soft and the sauce thickened—about thirty-five minutes more.

CHICKEN ADOBO

Yield: Servings 4

Ingredients:

- 1 (14.5 ounce) can diced tomatoes, drained
- 1 onion, chopped
- 1 tablespoon minced fresh cilantro or parsley
- 1½ pounds boneless, skinless chicken thighs, trimmed and slice into 2 inch pieces
- 1½ teaspoons instant espresso powder
- 2 tablespoons vegetable oil
- 2 teaspoons dried oregano
- 3 garlic cloves, minced
- 3 tablespoons minced canned chipotle chile in adobo sauce
- 3 tablespoons molasses
- Salt and pepper

Directions:

1. Process tomatoes inside a food processor until the desired smoothness is achieved; set aside. Mix chipotle, garlic, oregano, espresso powder, ½ teaspoon salt, and ¼ teaspoon pepper in container. Pat chicken dry using paper towels, then coat thoroughly with chipotle mixture.

2. Heat 1 tablespoon oil in 12 inch nonstick frying pan over moderate high heat until just smoking. Cook chicken until a golden-brown colour is achieved on both sides, approximately 6 minutes; move to plate.

3. Heat remaining 1 tablespoon oil in now empty frying pan on moderate heat until it starts to shimmer Put in onion and cook until tender and mildly browned, six to eight minutes. Mix in molasses, processed tomatoes, and chicken with any collected juices. Cover and simmer until chicken records 175 degrees and sauce has become thick, approximately ten minutes.

4. Move chicken to platter, tent with aluminium foil, and allow to rest for five to ten minutes. Season sauce with salt and pepper to taste, then spoon over chicken. Drizzle with cilantro before you serve.

CHICKEN AND FRUIT CASSEROLE (TAPADO DE POLLO)

Yield: Servings 6

Ingredients:

- ⅛ teaspoon dried mexican oregano
- ¼ cup (65 ml) dry sherry
- ¼ cup (65 ml) mild vinegar
- ½-inch (1.5-cm) piece of cinnamon stick
- 1 small apple, peeled, cored, and slice into thick slices
- 1 small pear, peeled, cored, and slice into thick slices
- 1 tablespoon granulated sugar
- 1 whole clove
- 12 ounces (340 g) tomatoes, cut (about 2 cups/500 ml)
- 2 cups (500 ml) thinly cut white onion
- 2 mexican bay leaves
- 3 garlic cloves, finely chopped
- 4½ pounds (2 kg) big chicken parts
- 6 peppercorns
- 6 sprigs fresh thyme or ¼ teaspoon dried
- Salt

To serve

- ¼ cup (65 ml) vegetable oil
- 1 large, very ripe plantain (approximately 12 ounces/340 g), peeled and slice into along the length slices
- 2 tablespoons big capers, drained
- fifteen green olives, pitted and halved

Directions:

1. Preheat your oven to 375° f (190° c). Drizzle the chicken pieces with salt. Crush the peppercorns, clove, and cinnamon together and mix with the sugar, sherry, garlic, vinegar, and approximately 1½ teaspoons salt.
2. Spread one third of the onion on the bottom of a deep ovenproof casserole; cover with a third of the tomato slices and the fruits. Put in the bay leaves and drizzle with a little of the herbs, then put half of the chicken pieces on top of the fruits and vegetables and pour on half the vinegar–spice mixture. Repeat the layers, finishing up with a topping of onion, tomatoes, and fruit.
3. Cover the casserole and bake for approximately 1 hour, then uncover the casserole for thirty minutes longer, or until the chicken is soft and some of the juices have been reduced.
4. In the meantime, heat the oil and fry the plantain pieces until a deep golden brown. Remove and drain. To serve, cover the top of the stew with the capers, olives, and fried plantain.

CHICKEN AND PORK STEWED WITH FRUIT (MANCHAMANTELES)

Yield: Servings 6

Ingredients:

- ¼ cup (65 ml) vegetable oil or pork lard
- 1 big chicken (about 3½ pounds/1.5 kg), cut into serving pieces
- 1 plantain (approximately 12 ounces/340 g), peeled and slice into thick rounds

- 1 small jicama (approximately 12 ounces/340 g), peeled and slice into ¼-inch (.5-cm) slices
- 1½ tablespoons sesame seeds
- 1½-inch (4-cm) piece of cinnamon stick
- 12 ounces (340 g) boneless stewing pork, cut into 1-inch (2.5-cm) cubes
- 12 ounces (340 g) tomatoes, broiled
- 2 thick slices fresh pineapple, peeled and slice into ½-inch (1.5-cm) cubes
- 25 almonds, unskinned
- 5 ancho chiles, wiped clean
- Salt to taste

Directions:

1. Place the pork cubes into a deep cooking pan, put in water to cover and 1 teaspoon of the salt, and bring to a simmer. Cover and cook for about twenty-five minutes, then drain, saving for later the broth. Strain the broth and skim off the fat, putting in enough water to make 4 cups (1 l), and save for later.
2. In a heavy, flameproof casserole, heat the oil and fry the chicken pieces lightly, a few at a time. Remove and save for later. In the same oil, separately fry the almonds, cinnamon stick, and sesame seeds, draining each of surplus oil. Crush the almonds and move the fried ingredients to the blender jar.
3. In the same oil, fry the chiles lightly on both sides, then drain and move to the blender jar. Put in the broiled tomatoes and 1 cup (250 ml) of the broth to the blender jar and blend until the desired smoothness is achieved. (be careful to put in only enough broth to release the blades of the blender; the sauce must not be too watery.)
4. Pour off all but 3 tablespoons of the oil remaining in the casserole and fry the chile sauce for approximately 4 minutes, stirring and scraping the bottom continuously. Put in 3 cups (750 ml) of the reserved broth and bring to a simmer. Put in the chicken pieces, pork cubes, fruit, jicama, and salt to taste, then cover and cook using low heat for one to 1¼ hours, or until the meat and fruit are soft, stirring occasionally.
5. Serve hot, with freshly made tortillas.

CHICKEN BREASTS WITH POBLANO CHILES AND CREAM (PECHUGAS DE POLLO CON RAJAS)

Yield: Servings 6

Ingredients:

- ¼ cup (65 ml) butter
- ¼ cup (65 ml) vegetable oil
- ½ cup (125 ml) milk
- 2 cups (500 ml) crème fraîche or thick sour cream
- 2 cups (500 ml) thinly cut white onion
- 2¼ pounds (1 kg) poblano chiles, charred, peeled, seeds and veins removed, and slice into thin strips
- 4 ounces (115 g) chihuahua (or cheddar) cheese, grated (approximately 1 cup/250 ml)
- 6 small chicken breasts
- Salt and freshly ground pepper
- Salt to taste

Directions:

1. Take away the bones from the breasts and cut each of them into 4 parts. Flavour them well with salt and pepper.
2. Heat the butter and the oil together in a big frying pan and fry the chicken for a little time on both sides until mildly browned. Drain and set them aside.
3. In the same fat, fry the onion until translucent. Put in all but ⅔ cup (165 ml) of the chile strips to the onion with salt. Cover the pan and cook on moderate heat for approximately five minutes, shaking the pan occasionally to prevent sticking.
4. Combine the reserved chile strips with the milk until the desired smoothness is achieved. Put in the sour cream and blend for a few seconds longer. Put in the salt at the final moment since it tends to curdle the sauce.
5. Preheat your oven to 350° f (180° c).
6. Position half of the chicken pieces in an ovenproof dish. Cover them with half of the chile strips and half of the sauce. Repeat the layers.
7. Bake until the chicken is cooked—about thirty minutes. Drizzle with the cheese and put back into the oven until melted.

CHICKEN GUANAJUATO (POLLO ESTILO GUANAJUATO)

Yield: Servings 6

Ingredients:

- ¾-inch (2-cm) piece of cinnamon stick, broken up
- 1 cup (250 ml) thickly cut white onion
- 1 pound (450 g) tomatoes, broiled
- 1¼ cups (315 ml) fresh orange juice
- 12 minuscule new potatoes, unpeeled (approximately 12 ounces/340 g)
- 3 garlic cloves, finely chopped
- 3 tablespoons vegetable oil or melted chicken fat
- 4½ pounds (2 kg) big chicken pieces
- 5 medium carrots (approximately 12 ounces/340 g), scraped and slice into quarters along the length
- 6 sprigs fresh marjoram or ¼ heaped teaspoon dried
- 6 sprigs fresh thyme or ¼ heaped teaspoon dried
- Salt and freshly ground pepper
- Zest of ½ orange

Directions:

1. Preheat your oven to 350° f (180° c). Flavour the chicken with salt and pepper.
2. Heat the oil in a flameproof casserole in which the chicken pieces will just fit tightly and fry them to a deep golden color. Remove from the casserole and drizzle with more salt and pepper, then set aside.
3. Take out all except 2 tablespoons of the oil from the casserole. Fry the onion and garlic gently, without browning, until translucent.
4. Combine the unskinned tomatoes until the desired smoothness is achieved. Put into the pan, with the thyme, marjoram, and cinnamon stick, and fry using high heat for approximately 3 minutes, stirring and scraping the bottom of the pan occasionally. Put in the chicken pieces, orange juice, orange zest, potatoes, and carrots. Cover the casserole and bake for approximately 30 minutes, then flip the chicken pieces over and bake until soft—another twenty to twenty-five minutes, roughly.
5. Serve with sufficient the sauce and vegetables.

CHICKEN IN AN ONION AND CHILE SOUSE (POLLO EN ESCABECHE ORIENTAL)

Yield: Servings 6 to 8

Ingredients:

- 4 medium white onions, thinly cut (about 6 cups/1.5 l), left to soak in mild vinegar for an hour

The seasoning paste

- 1 tablespoon peppercorns, crushed
- 1 teaspoon cumin seeds, crushed
- 1 teaspoon dried mexican oregano, yucatecan if possible, toasted
- 10 garlic cloves
- 10 whole cloves, crushed
- 3 tablespoons mild white vinegar or seville orange juice
- 8 whole allspice, crushed
- Salt to taste

Cooking the chicken

- ⅛ teaspoon dried mexican oregano, yucatecan if possible, toasted
- 1 teaspoon salt
- 3 cups (750 ml) water, roughly
- 4 garlic cloves, unpeeled and charred
- 6 x-cat-ik or güero whole chiles, charred, but not skinned
- A big chicken or small turkey (about 5 pounds/2.25 kg), cut into serving pieces
- A little melted lard for brushing over the chicken

Directions:

1. Prepare the onions.
2. Grind the spices together to a powder. Crush the garlic and mix in the salt, vinegar, and powdered spices. The mixture must be like a rather thick paste.
3. Using one third only of the paste, coat each piece of the chicken very lightly. Set the pieces aside to season for minimum 30 minutes.

4. Pour sufficient water into a deep pan to barely cover the chicken. Put in the garlic, oregano, and salt and bring to a simmer, then put in the chicken pieces and carry on cooking using low heat until the chicken is nearly soft—take care not to overcook— about twenty-five minutes.

5. Drain the chicken and set it on a rack, saving for later the broth and keeping it warm. Once the chicken is sufficiently cool to handle, spread each piece lightly with the rest of the paste.

6. Brush the chicken pieces with the lard and broil until the skin is just crisp and a pale golden color.

7. Place the prepared onion and mildly charred chiles (unskinned) into the broth and heat it to a simmer. Put the chicken pieces on a warmed serving dish and pour the broth with the onions and chiles over them.

CHICKEN IN CUICLACOCHE (POLLO EN CUITLACOCHE)

Yield: Servings 6

Ingredients:

- ¼ cup (65 ml) melted chicken fat or vegetable oil
- ⅓ cup (85 ml) tightly packed, roughly chopped epazote leaves
- 1 cup (250 ml) light chicken broth or water
- 1 cup (250 ml) water or light chicken broth
- 1½ pounds (675 g) cuitlacoche, roughly chopped (about 6¼ cups/1.563 l)
- 12 big chicken pieces, approximately 3 pounds (1.35 kg)
- 2 cups (500 ml) thinly cut white onion
- 2 garlic cloves, finely chopped
- 4 poblano chiles, charred, peeled, seeds and veins removed, and slice into strips
- Salt to taste

Directions:

1. Heat the fat in a deep flameproof casserole or frying pan and fry the chicken pieces, a few at a time, until a golden-brown colour is achieved. Drain and save for later.

2. Remove all but ¼ cup (65 ml) fat from the pan. Put in the onion and garlic and fry gently without browning until translucent—about two minutes. Put in the cuitlacoche,

drizzle well with salt, and carry on cooking, scraping the bottom of the pan to prevent sticking, for approximately ten minutes.

3. Put in the chicken pieces and broth, cover the pan, and carry on cooking using low heat for approximately 30 minutes.

4. Put in the chile strips and epazote and carry on cooking covered using low heat until the chicken is nearly soft—twenty additional minutes. Set aside to season.

CHICKEN IN PEANUT SAUCE (POLLO EN SALSA DE CACAHUATE)

Yield: Servings 6

Ingredients:

- 1 medium white onion, cut into 4 pieces
- 1 pound (450 g) tomatoes, broiled
- 1 teaspoon salt, or to taste
- 1¼ cups (315 ml) raw (unroasted, unsalted) peanuts, measured shelled and with papery husks removed
- 1-inch (2.5-cm) piece of cinnamon stick
- 2 cups (500 ml) water
- 2 garlic cloves, unpeeled
- 3 tablespoons vegetable oil or rendered chicken fat
- 4 chipotle chiles en vinagre or adobo, or to taste
- 4 to 5 tablespoons fresh lime juice
- 4½ pounds (2 kg) chicken parts
- 6 peppercorns
- 6 whole cloves
- Freshly ground black pepper
- The sauce is not very picante. There should just be a pleasant "afterglow" from the chiles.

Directions:

1. Drizzle the chicken with salt, pepper, and the lime juice and set aside to season while preparing the sauce.
2. Heat a small, ungreased frying pan or comal and toast the onion and garlic until tender. Peel the garlic. Toss the spices in the hot pan to toast them lightly, then toast the peanuts until they are golden (a toaster oven works even better).
3. Place the unskinned tomatoes, chiles, and the toasted ingredients, apart from the peanuts, into a blender jar and blend until fairly smooth. Put in the peanuts slowly and gradually and blend until almost smooth. Put in a little water only if required to release the blades of the blender.
4. Heat the oil or chicken fat in a heavy casserole and fry the chicken pieces, a few at a time, until a golden-brown colour is achieved. Take away the chicken from the pan and save for later. There must be about ¼ cup (65 ml) oil in the pan. Remove, or make up to that amount. Reheat the oil and fry the mixed ingredients on moderate heat for about three minutes, continuously stirring and scraping the bottom of the pan. Reduce the heat and allow the sauce to cook for approximately fifteen minutes longer, continuing to scrape the bottom of the pan occasionally.
5. Put in the chicken pieces and the 2 cups (500 ml) of water. Adjust the seasoning and cook using low heat until the chicken is soft—thirty-five to forty minutes. The sauce will thicken—it should lightly cover the back of a wooden spoon—and pools of oil will form on the surface.
6. Serve the chicken with sufficient the sauce, accompanied by small boiled potatoes.

CHICKEN IN RED SESAME SEED SAUCE (POLLO EN PIPIÑN ROJO)

Yield: Servings 6

Ingredients:

The chicken

- ½ white onion, cut
- 1 mexican bay leaf
- 1 sprig flat-leaf parsley
- 1 sprig fresh thyme, or a big pinch of dried

- 2 garlic cloves
- A 3½- to 4-pound (1.5- to 1.8-kg) chicken, cut into serving pieces
- Salt to taste
- The chicken giblets

The sauce

- ½-inch (1.5-cm) piece of cinnamon stick, broken up
- ¾ cup (185 ml) sesame seeds
- 1 big avocado leaf, fresh or dried
- 1 garlic clove, roughly chopped
- 3 tablespoons lard
- 3 whole cloves
- 5 peppercorns
- 6 ancho chiles, seeds and veins reserved (reserving 1 tablespoon of the seeds)
- Salt to taste

Directions:

1. Place the giblets, onion, garlic, herbs, and salt into a pan, cover with water, and bring to a fast simmer. Continue simmering for approximately 30 minutes. Put in the chicken pieces and cook using low heat until just soft—about twenty-five minutes. Strain, saving for later the broth.
2. Toast the chiles lightly, cover with hot water, and let soak for about ten minutes.
3. Meanwhile, put the reserved chile seeds into an ungreased frying pan and shake on moderate heat until they turn a deep golden brown—take care not to burn. Set aside to cool a little. Move the toasted seeds with the spices and grind to a powder.
4. Toast the sesame seeds to a deep gold color in the ungreased pan and set them aside to cool off a little. Put in the toasted, cooled seeds to the spice grinder and grind them very fine.
5. Melt the lard in a frying pan and fry the ground chile, sesame seeds, and spices using low heat for approximately 3 minutes, stirring continuously.
6. Move the chiles using a slotted spoon to the blender jar. Put in ½ cup (125 ml) of the reserved broth and the garlic and blend to a smooth puree.
7. Put in the mixed chiles to the fried spice and seed mixture and allow it to cook fast for approximately five minutes, stirring it continuously. Put in 3 cups (750 ml) of the

reserved broth and allow the sauce to carry on cooking using low heat for approximately twenty minutes, or until it thickens and is well seasoned. Put in the cooked chicken and salt, and let the chicken heat through.

8. Toast the avocado leaf for a short period of time on a warm comal and then grind it finely. Put in it to the sauce.

CHICKEN MOLE POBLANO

Yield: Servings four to 6

Ingredients:

- ⅛ teaspoon ground cloves
- ¼ cup almond butter
- ¼ cup raisins
- ½ dried chipotle chile, stemmed, seeded, and torn into ½ inch pieces (small tablespoon)
- ½ teaspoon ground cinnamon
- 1 (14.5 ounce) can diced tomatoes, drained
- 1 onion, chopped fine
- 1 ounce bittersweet, semisweet, or Mexican chocolate, chopped coarse
- 2 cups chicken broth
- 2 dried ancho chiles, stemmed, seeded, and torn into ½ inch pieces (½ cup)
- 2 garlic cloves, minced
- 2 tablespoons sesame seeds, plus extra for decoration, toasted
- 3 tablespoons vegetable oil
- 3½ pounds bone in chicken pieces (split breasts, legs, and/or thighs), skin removed, trimmed
- Salt and pepper
- Sugar

Directions:

1. Toast anchos and chipotle in 12 inch frying pan on moderate heat, stirring regularly, until aromatic, 2 to six minutes; move to plate. Put in oil and onion to now empty frying pan and cook over moderate high heat until tender, five to seven minutes.

2. Mix in cinnamon, cloves, chocolate, and toasted chiles and cook until chocolate is melted and bubbly, approximately 2 minutes. Mix in garlic and cook until aromatic, approximately half a minute. Mix in broth, tomatoes, raisins, almond butter, and sesame seeds and bring to simmer. Decrease the heat to moderate and simmer gently, stirring once in a while, until slightly thickened and measures about 2½ cups, approximately ten minutes.

3. Move mixture to blender and pulse until smooth, approximately twenty seconds. Sprinkle with salt, pepper, and sugar to taste. (Sauce can be placed in your fridge for maximum 3 days; loosen with water as required before continuing.)

4. Adjust oven rack to middle position and heat oven to 400 degrees. Pat chicken dry using paper towels and sprinkle with salt and pepper. Position chicken in single layer in shallow baking dish and cover with mole sauce, flipping to coat chicken uniformly. Bake, uncovered, until breasts register 160 degrees, and thighs or drumsticks register 175 degrees, thirty-five to forty-five minutes.

5. Remove chicken from oven, tent with aluminium foil, and allow to rest for five to ten minutes. Drizzle with sesame seeds before you serve.

CHICKEN SEASONED WITH GARLIC AND CUMIN (POLLO EN AJO-COMINO)

Yield: Servings 6

Ingredients:

- 1 tablespoon salt, or to taste
- 1 teaspoon cumin seeds, crushed
- 1 whole clove, crushed
- 12 peppercorns, crushed
- 3 tablespoons vegetable oil
- 3½ cups (875 ml) water, roughly
- 4 ancho chiles, veins and seeds removed
- 4 garlic cloves
- 4½ pounds (2 kg) big chicken pieces

Directions:

1. Cover the chiles with water and simmer for approximately five minutes, then let soak for five minutes. Drain. In a molcajete or mortar, grind the cumin, peppercorns, salt, and clove, then purée in the garlic progressively, putting in ¼ cup (65 ml) of the water to dilute the mixture. Set aside.

2. Move the drained ancho chiles to a blender jar with ¾ cup (185 ml) of the water. Blend until the desired smoothness is achieved and save for later.

3. Heat the oil and fry the chicken pieces (a few at a time so as not to touch in the pan) to a pale gold. Put in the spice mixture and fry on moderate heat for approximately 3 minutes, stirring continuously. Put in the mixed chiles and fry for another three minutes, scraping the bottom of the pan continuously. Put in the remaining water, then tweak the seasoning and cook slowly, uncovered, until the chicken is soft—about forty minutes flipping the pieces over occasionally. (the sauce should not be thick; put in more water if required.)

4. Serve hot, with freshly made tortillas.

CHICKEN WITH ANCHO PEANUT SAUCE

Yield: Servings 4

Ingredients:

- ⅛ teaspoon ground cloves
- ½ teaspoon ground cinnamon
- 1 cup whole unsalted dry roasted peanuts, plus ¼ cup chopped
- 1 onion, chopped fine
- 1 teaspoon minced canned chipotle chile in adobo sauce
- 1 teaspoon sugar, plus extra as required
- 1½ cups chicken broth
- 2 garlic cloves, minced
- 2 tablespoons chopped fresh cilantro
- 2 tablespoons sesame seeds, toasted
- 2 teaspoons cider vinegar
- 2 tomatoes, cored and chopped coarse
- 3 dried ancho chiles, stemmed, seeded, and torn into ½ inch pieces (¾ cup)
- 3 tablespoons vegetable oil

- 4 (6 to 8 ounce) boneless, skinless chicken breasts, trimmed
- Salt and pepper

Directions:

1. Toast anchos in 12 inch frying pan on moderate heat, stirring regularly, until aromatic, 2 to six minutes; move to blender. Put in onion, tomatoes, whole peanuts, ¼ cup broth, sesame seeds, garlic, vinegar, sugar, chipotle, ½ teaspoon salt, cinnamon, and cloves to blender and pulse until smooth, approximately one minute.
2. Heat oil in now empty frying pan over moderate high heat until it starts to shimmer Put in pureed chile mixture and cook, stirring frequently, until mixture has become thick and darkened in color, approximately eight minutes.
3. Mix in remaining 1¼ cups broth, scraping up any browned bits, and bring to simmer. Sprinkle the chicken with salt and pepper and nestle into sauce. Cover, decrease the heat to moderate low, and cook until chicken records 160 degrees, ten to fifteen minutes, turning midway through cooking.
4. Move chicken to platter, tent with aluminium foil, and allow to rest for five to ten minutes. Season sauce with sugar, salt, and pepper to taste, and spoon over chicken. Drizzle with cilantro and chopped peanuts before you serve.

CHICKEN WITH FRIED BREAD CRUMBS (POLLO EN RELLENO DE PAN)

Yield: Servings 6

Ingredients:

- ¼ cup (65 ml) thinly cut white onion
- ⅓ cup (85 ml) vegetable oil
- ½ small white onion
- 1 chorizo, crumbled and fried
- 1 pound (450 g) tomatoes, broiled
- 1½ cups (375 ml) dried but not toasted bread crumbs
- 2 garlic cloves, thinly cut
- 2 tablespoons slivered almonds

- 2 teaspoons juice from the chile can
- 3 jalapeño chiles en escabeche
- 3 medium carrots, scraped and slice into ½-inch (1.5-cm) cubes
- 3 medium zucchini (12 ounces/340 g), cut into ½-inch (1.5-cm) cubes
- 3 tablespoons raisins
- 3 tablespoons vegetable oil
- 5 peppercorns
- A 4-pound (1.8-kg) chicken, cut into several pieces
- Salt to taste
- Water or chicken broth to cover

Directions:

1. Place the chicken into a big pan with the onion, 1 garlic clove, the peppercorns, and salt, cover with cold water, and bring to a simmer. Continue simmering for approximately fifteen minutes, put in the carrots, and cook for ten more minutes. Put in the zucchini and carry on cooking using low heat until the chicken is just soft and the vegetables still a little firm to the bite, approximately ten minutes. Strain, saving for later the stock.
2. Heat the oil in a flameproof casserole and lightly fry the onion and remaining garlic until translucent.
3. Combine the tomatoes to a quite smooth sauce and put in to the onion with ½ cup (125 ml) of the reserved stock. Allow the sauce reduce on moderate heat for approximately five minutes.
4. Put in the chicken pieces and vegetables, the raisins, almonds, chorizo, chiles, and chile juice and cook slowly for eight minutes more, stirring the mixture occasionally to prevent sticking. The sauce by then must be reduced.
5. Heat the oil in a frying pan, put in the bread crumbs, and fry them, stirring them all the time until they are a uniform gold color, approximately eight minutes. Then drizzle the bread crumbs over the chicken and vegetables and serve instantly.

CHICKEN WITH GRAPES (POLLO A LA UVA)

Yield: Servings 8

Ingredients:

- ⅔ cup (165 ml) dry white wine
- 1 cup (250 ml) thinly cut white onion
- 1 pound (450 g) seedless white grapes
- 2 big chickens, approximately 3 pounds (1.35 kg) each
- 2 celery ribs, chopped
- 2 garlic cloves
- 2 pounds (900 g) tomatoes, roughly chopped (about 4¼ cups/1.65 l)
- 2 tablespoons butter
- 2 tablespoons vegetable oil
- 6 sprigs fresh marjoram or ½ teaspoon dried
- 6 sprigs fresh thyme or ½ teaspoon dried
- Salt and freshly ground pepper

Directions:

1. Preheat your oven to 350° f (180° c).
2. Truss the chickens. Heat the butter and oil together in a deep flameproof casserole and brown the chickens well all over. Flavour them with salt and pepper, remove, and set them aside.
3. In the same fat, fry the onion, garlic, and celery using low heat for approximately five minutes. Put in the tomatoes and herbs to the pan. Put the chickens on their sides in the tomato mixture. Cover the pan and bake for approximately twenty minutes.
4. Turn the chickens over and carry on baking them until they become soft—twenty to twenty-five minutes. Turn off the oven. Move them to a warmed serving dish and return to a warm oven.
5. Combine the vegetables and juices in the pan to a smooth sauce. Return to the pan and cook it on moderate heat until it has reduced and thickened—about ten minutes. Put in the wine and carry on cooking the sauce for approximately 3 minutes, stirring it occasionally. Put in the grapes and carry on cooking the sauce over brisk heat for about three minutes more.

CHICKEN WITH PUMPKIN SEED SAUCE

Yield: Servings 4

Ingredients:

- ¼ cup sesame seeds
- ⅓ cup pepitas
- 1 cup fresh cilantro leaves
- 1 jalapeño chile, stemmed, seeded, and chopped
- 1 onion, chopped fine
- 1 tablespoon lime juice
- 1 teaspoon fresh minced thyme or ¼ teaspoon dried
- 1½ cups chicken broth
- 2 tablespoons vegetable oil
- 3 garlic cloves, minced
- 4 (6 to 8 ounce) boneless, skinless chicken breasts, trimmed
- 6 ounces fresh tomatillos, husks and stems removed, washed well and dried, chopped
- Pinch sugar
- Salt and pepper

Directions:

1. Toast pepitas and sesame seeds in 12 inch nonstick frying pan on moderate heat until seeds are golden and aromatic, approximately fifteen minutes; move to container. Reserve 1 tablespoon toasted seeds separately for decoration.
2. Put in oil, onion, and ½ teaspoon salt to now empty frying pan and cook over moderate high heat until tender, five to seven minutes. Mix in jalapeño, garlic, and thyme and cook until aromatic, approximately half a minute. Mix in tomatillos, broth, and toasted seeds, cover, and cook until tomatillos start to tenderize, approximately ten minutes.
3. Sprinkle the chicken with salt and pepper, then nestle into frying pan. Cover, decrease the heat to moderate low, and cook until chicken records 160 degrees, ten to fifteen minutes, turning midway through cooking. Move chicken to platter, tent with aluminium foil, and allow to rest for five to ten minutes.
4. Cautiously move mixture left in frying pan to blender. Put in cilantro, lime juice, and sugar and pulse until mostly smooth, approximately one minute. Sprinkle with salt and pepper to taste. Ladle some of sauce over chicken and drizzle with reserved seeds. Serve with rest of the sauce.

CHILE RUBBED ROAST CHICKEN

Yield: Servings 4

Ingredients:

- ⅛ teaspoon cayenne pepper
- ¼ cup vegetable oil
- ¼ teaspoon ground cinnamon
- ¼ teaspoon ground cloves
- ½ teaspoon garlic powder
- ½ teaspoon onion powder
- ½ teaspoon pepper
- 1 (3 to 4 pound) whole chicken, giblets discarded
- 1 dried chipotle chile, stemmed, seeded, and torn into ½ inch pieces (1½ tablespoons)
- 1 tablespoon coriander seeds
- 1 tablespoon cumin seeds
- 1 tablespoon kosher salt
- 2 teaspoons sugar
- 4 dried New Mexican chiles, stemmed, seeded, and torn into ½ inch pieces (1 cup)
- Lime wedges

Directions:

1. Toast New Mexican and chipotle chiles, cumin seeds, and coriander seeds in 12 inch ovensafe frying pan on moderate heat, stirring regularly, until aromatic, 2 to six minutes. Move mixture to spice grinder and allow to cool slightly. Put in pepper, onion powder, garlic powder, cloves, cinnamon, and cayenne to grinder and pulse until crudely ground, 5 to 10 seconds. Move spice mixture to container and mix in oil, salt, and sugar.

2. Wipe out now empty frying pan, place on middle rack of oven, and heat oven to 450 degrees. Pat chicken dry using paper towels, then gently separate skin from meat. Rub 3 tablespoons spice paste underneath skin over breast, thighs, and legs. Rub remaining spice paste over top and sides of chicken (do not rub bottom of chicken). Tuck wings behind back and tie legs together loosely using a kitchen twine.

3. Move chicken, breast side up, to preheated frying pan in oven. Roast chicken until breast records 120 degrees and thighs register 135 degrees, twenty-five minutes to thirty-five minutes. Turn off oven and leave chicken in oven until breast records 160 degrees and thighs register 175 degrees, twenty-five minutes to thirty-five minutes.

4. Move chicken to carving board and allow to rest, uncovered, for fifteen minutes. Carve and serve with lime wedges.

CLASSIC ARROZ CON POLLO

Yield: Servings four to 6

Ingredients:

- ¼ cup minced fresh cilantro
- ¼ cup water, plus extra as required
- ¼ teaspoon red pepper flakes
- ½ cup green Manzanilla olives, pitted and halved
- ½ cup jarred whole pimentos, cut into 2 by ¼ inch strips
- ½ teaspoon dried oregano
- 1 (8 ounce) can tomato sauce
- 1 onion, chopped fine
- 1 small green bell pepper, stemmed, seeded, and chopped fine
- 1 tablespoon capers, washed
- 1¾ cups chicken broth
- 2 tablespoons olive oil
- 3 cups medium grain white rice
- 4 pounds bone in chicken thighs, trimmed
- 5 teaspoons distilled white vinegar
- 6 garlic cloves, minced
- Lemon wedges
- Salt and pepper

Directions:

1. Adjust oven rack to middle position and heat oven to 350 degrees. Mix garlic, 1 tablespoon vinegar, 1 teaspoon salt, ½ teaspoon pepper, and oregano in big container. Put in chicken, toss to coat, and marinate for fifteen minutes.

2. Heat 1 tablespoon oil in Dutch oven on moderate heat until it starts to shimmer Put in onion, bell pepper, and pepper flakes and cook until starting to tenderize, approximately five minutes. Mix in 2 tablespoons cilantro.

3. Clear center of pot and increase heat to moderate high. Put in chicken, skin side down, to center of pot and cook until outer layer of meat becomes opaque, 2 to 4 minutes per side, reducing heat if chicken starts to brown. Mix in broth, tomato sauce, and water. Bring to simmer, cover, decrease the heat to moderate low, and simmer for about twenty minutes.

4. Mix in rice, olives, capers, and ¾ teaspoon salt and bring to simmer. Cover pot, move to oven, and cook, stirring every ten minutes, until chicken register 175 degrees, approximately 30 minutes. (If, after twenty minutes of cooking, rice appears dry and bottom of pot starts to scorch, mix in additional ¼ cup water.)

5. Move chicken to cutting board; cover pot and save for later. Using 2 spoons, pull chicken into big chunks, discarding skin and bones. Put chicken in big container, toss with pimentos, remaining 2 teaspoons vinegar, remaining 1 tablespoon oil, and remaining 2 tablespoons cilantro and sprinkle with salt and pepper to taste. Put chicken on top of rice, cover, and allow it to stand until warmed through, approximately five minutes. Serve with lemon wedges.

DUCK IN A GREEN PUMPKIN SEED MOLE (PATO EN MOLE VERDE DE PEPITA)

Yield: Servings 6

Ingredients:

Cooking the duck

- 1 garlic clove
- 1 small carrot, scraped and cut
- 1 small white onion, cut
- 5- to 6-pound (2.25- to 2.75-kg) duck

- 6 peppercorns
- Pepper to taste
- Salt to taste
- The duck giblets

The sauce

- ⅛ teaspoon cumin seeds, crushed
- 1 cup (250 ml) duck broth
- 1 cup (250 ml) tomate verde, cooked and drained
- 1 small bunch radish leaves
- 2 big romaine lettuce leaves, torn into pieces
- 2 cups (500 ml) reserved duck broth
- 2 small garlic cloves, roughly chopped
- 3 sprigs epazote
- 3 tablespoons reserved duck drippings
- 3 tablespoons roughly chopped white onion
- 3½ ounces (100 g) hulled raw pumpkin seeds (about ¾ cup/188 ml;)
- 5 sprigs cilantro
- 6 black peppercorns, crushed
- 6 serrano chiles, roughly chopped
- Salt as required

Directions:

1. Preheat your oven to 325° f (165° c).
2. Place the giblets with the vegetables and seasonings into a big pan, submerge them in water, and bring to its boiling point. Reduce the heat and simmer, covered, for approximately 1½ hours.
3. Heat a casserole well and brown the duck all over, pricking the skin (not the flesh) to render out the fat from the layer underneath it. Drain off the surplus fat occasionally and save for later. Cover the casserole with a firmly fitting lid and braise the duck, approximately forty minutes, depending on how soft the duck is.
4. Set the duck aside to cool a little, then cut into serving pieces. Skim the fat from the juices in the casserole and reserve and put in the juices to the giblet broth. There must be about 5 cups (1.25 l); if not, put in water to make up to that amount.

5. In an ungreased frying pan, toast the pumpkin seeds about five minutes, stirring them occasionally until they swell—but do not allow them to brown. Set aside to cool, then grind them in a coffee/spice grinder with the peppercorns and cumin.

6. Place the ground ingredients into a container and mix in the 1 cup (250 ml) broth until you have a smooth sauce. Set it aside.

7. Combine the tomate verde with the chiles, onion, and garlic until the desired smoothness is achieved. Put in the greens and blend a little at a time until almost smooth, and save for later.

8. Heat 3 tablespoons of the reserved duck fat in a casserole and fry the ground ingredients over low heat while stirring and scraping the bottom of the pan to prevent sticking (it will swiftly scorch), approximately five minutes.

9. Slowly mix in the mixed ingredients and cook over low heat while stirring occasionally for approximately ten minutes. Dilute with 2 cups (500 ml) of broth and carry on cooking using super low heat for ten more minutes. Adjust salt to taste.

10. Slowly put in the remaining broth. Allow the sauce heat through, still using super low heat. When it is cooked, the mole should cover rather thickly the back of a wooden spoon. Put in the duck pieces and just warm them through.

11. Serve instantly.

GRILLED CHICKEN FAJITAS

Yield: Servings 4

Ingredients:

- ⅓ cup lime juice (3 limes)
- 1 big red onion, peeled and slice into ½ inch thick rounds (do not separate rings)
- 1 jalapeño chile, stemmed, seeded, and minced
- 1 tablespoon Worcestershire sauce
- 1½ pounds boneless, skinless chicken breasts, trimmed and pounded to ½ inch thickness
- 1½ tablespoons minced fresh cilantro
- 1½ teaspoons packed brown sugar
- 12 (6 inch) flour tortillas
- 2 big bell peppers, quartered, stemmed, and seeded

- 3 garlic cloves, minced
- 6 tablespoons vegetable oil
- Salt and pepper

Directions:

1. Whisk ¼ cup oil, lime juice, jalapeño, cilantro, garlic, Worcestershire, sugar, 1 teaspoon salt, and ¾ teaspoon pepper together in container. Measure out and reserve ¼ cup marinade separately for serving. Whisk 1 teaspoon salt into remaining marinade and move to 1 gallon zipper lock bag. Put in chicken to bag and toss to coat. Push out as much air as you can, seal bag, and place in your fridge for fifteen minutes, turning bag once in a while.

2. Brush bell peppers and onion with remaining 2 tablespoons oil and sprinkle with salt and pepper. Remove chicken from marinade, let surplus marinade drip off, and move to plate.

3. FOR A CHARCOAL GRILL: Open bottom vent fully. Light big chimney starter filled with charcoal briquettes (6 quarts). When top coals are partly covered with ash, pour coals over two thirds of grill, leaving remaining one third empty. Set cooking grate in place, cover, and open lid vent fully. Heat grill until hot, approximately five minutes. FOR A GAS GRILL: Set all burners to high, cover, and heat grill until hot, approximately fifteen minutes. Leave primary burner on high and turn other burner(s) to moderate.

4. Clean and oil cooking grate. Put chicken on hotter side of grill and vegetables on cooler side of grill. Cook (covered if using gas), turning chicken and vegetables as required, until chicken is thoroughly browned and records 160 degrees and vegetables are soft and mildly charred, about eight to twelve minutes. Move chicken and vegetables to cutting board and tent with aluminium foil.

5. Working in batches, grill tortillas, turning as required, until warm and mildly browned, approximately 40 seconds; move to plate and cover using foil.

6. Slice bell peppers into ¼ inch strips, separate onion into rings, and toss with 2 tablespoons reserved marinade. Slice chicken on bias into ¼ inch thick slices and toss with remaining 2 tablespoons marinade in separate container. Move chicken and vegetables to platter and serve with warmed tortillas.

GRILLED CHIPOTLE CHICKEN KEBABS WITH CILANTRO DIPPING SAUCE

Yield: Servings 4

Ingredients:

- ¼ cup chopped fresh cilantro
- ½ teaspoon dried oregano
- ½ teaspoon garlic powder
- 1 scallion, minced
- 1 teaspoon cumin seeds
- 1½ teaspoons sugar
- 2 dried guajillo chiles, stemmed, seeded, and torn into ½ inch pieces (¼ cup)
- 2 dried New Mexican chiles, stemmed, seeded, and torn into ½ inch pieces (½ cup)
- 2 pounds boneless, skinless chicken breasts, trimmed and slice into an inch pieces
- 2 tablespoons lime juice, plus extra as required
- 2 tablespoons mayonnaise
- 3 tablespoons vegetable oil
- 4 dried chipotle chiles, stemmed, seeded, and torn into ½ inch pieces (6 tablespoons)
- 6 tablespoons sour cream
- Salt and pepper

Directions:

1. Dissolve 2 tablespoons salt in 1 quart cold water. Submerge chicken in brine, cover, and place in your fridge for half an hour
2. In the meantime, toast New Mexican, chipotle, and guajillo chiles and cumin seeds in 10 inch frying pan, stirring regularly, until aromatic, 2 to six minutes. Move mixture to spice grinder and allow to cool slightly. Put in oregano and garlic powder to grinder and pulse until thoroughly ground, approximately twenty seconds. Move spice mixture to container and mix in oil and sugar.
3. Remove chicken from brine and pat dry using paper towels. Toss chicken with spice mixture and thread onto four 12 inch metal skewers.
4. FOR A CHARCOAL GRILL: Open bottom vent fully. Light big chimney starter filled with charcoal briquettes (6 quarts). When top coals are partly covered with ash, pour

uniformly over grill. Set cooking grate in place, cover, and open lid vent fully. Heat grill until hot, approximately five minutes. FOR A GAS GRILL: Set all burners to high, cover, and heat grill until hot, approximately fifteen minutes. Leave all burners on high.

5. Clean and oil cooking grate. Put chicken skewers on grill. Cook (covered if using gas), turning as required, until chicken is mildly charred on all sides and records 160 degrees, approximately eight minutes. Move skewers to platter, tent with aluminium foil, and allow to rest for five to ten minutes.

6. Mix sour cream, cilantro, mayonnaise, lime juice, scallion, and ⅛ teaspoon pepper together in container and flavor with extra lime juice, salt, and pepper to taste. Using tongs, remove chicken from skewers and serve with cilantro dipping sauce.

GRILLED TEQUILA CHICKEN WITH ORANGE, AVOCADO, AND PEPITA SALAD

Yield: Servings 4

Ingredients:

- ¼ teaspoon cayenne pepper
- ⅓ cup pepitas, toasted
- ½ cup tequila
- ½ cup water
- 1 shallot, cut thin
- 1 tablespoon honey
- 2 ripe but firm avocados, halved and pitted
- 3 oranges, peeled and slice into ½ inch pieces
- 4 (6 to 8 ounce) boneless, skinless chicken breasts, trimmed
- 4 garlic cloves, minced
- 5 tablespoons extra virgin olive oil
- 6 ounces (6 cups) watercress, chopped coarse
- 6 tablespoons lime juice (3 limes)
- Salt and pepper

Directions:

1. Whisk tequila, water, 3 tablespoons lime juice, garlic, and 2 teaspoons salt together in container until salt is dissolved. Move ½ cup marinade to small deep cooking pan. Pour remaining marinade into 1 gallon zipper lock bag, put in chicken, and toss to coat. Push out as much air as you can, seal bag, and place in your fridge for thirty minutes to an hour, turning bag once in a while.

2. Let oranges drain in colander set over big container, saving for later juice. In big container, whisk ¼ cup oil, honey, cayenne, ¼ teaspoon salt, ¼ pepper, and remaining 3 tablespoons lime juice together; set aside for salad.

3. Before grilling, brush avocado halves with remaining 1 tablespoon oil and sprinkle with salt and pepper. Remove chicken from marinade, let surplus marinade drip off, and move to plate.

4. 4A. FOR A CHARCOAL GRILL: Open bottom vent fully. Light big chimney starter filled with charcoal briquettes (6 quarts). When top coals are partly covered with ash, pour two thirds uniformly over half of grill, then pour remaining coals over other half of grill. Set cooking grate in place, cover, and open lid vent fully. Heat grill until hot, approximately five minutes. FOR A GAS GRILL: Set all burners to high, cover, and heat grill until hot, approximately fifteen minutes. Leave primary burner on high and turn other burner(s) to moderate.

5. Clean and oil cooking grate. Put chicken on hotter side of grill. Cook (covered if using gas), turning as required, until chicken is nicely charred and records 160 degrees, about eight to twelve minutes. In the meantime, place avocados cut side down on cooler side of grill and cook until mildly charred, three to five minutes. Move chicken and avocados to cutting board and tent with aluminium foil.

6. Put in drained orange juice to reserved marinade in deep cooking pan, bring to simmer over moderate high heat, and cook until reduced to ¼ cup, three to five minutes. Whisk dressing to recombine, then put in watercress, pepitas, shallots, and drained oranges and toss lightly to coat; move to platter. Peel grilled avocado, slice thin, and lay on top of salad. Slice chicken on bias into ½ inch thick pieces, lay on top of salad, and sprinkle with reduced marinade and serve.

ORANGE ANNATTO GLAZED CHICKEN

Yield: Servings 4

Ingredients:

- ¼ cup lime juice (2 limes)
- ½ teaspoon cornstarch
- ¾ teaspoon dried oregano
- 1 teaspoon ground coriander
- 1½ cups orange juice (3 oranges)
- 1½ teaspoons ground annatto
- 2 tablespoons sugar, plus extra as required
- 2 teaspoons minced canned chipotle chile in adobo sauce
- 2 teaspoons vegetable oil
- 4 garlic cloves, minced
- 8 (5 to 7 ounce) bone in chicken thighs, trimmed
- Salt and pepper

Directions:

1. Put several heavy cans inside Dutch oven. Pat chicken dry using paper towels and sprinkle with salt and pepper. Heat oil in 12 inch nonstick frying pan over moderate high heat until just smoking. Put chicken skin side down in frying pan. Put weighted Dutch oven on top of chicken and cook until skin is deep brown and very crunchy, 16 to twenty minutes, checking browning after ten minutes and adjusting heat as required.
2. Remove pot and flip chicken. Decrease the heat to moderate and carry on cooking (using splatter screen if required) until second side is thoroughly browned and chicken records 175 degrees, three to five minutes. Move chicken to serving platter.
3. Whisk orange juice, lime juice, sugar, and cornstarch together in container. Pour off all but 2 teaspoons fat left in frying pan. Put in garlic, chipotle, annatto, coriander, and oregano and cook on moderate heat until aromatic, approximately half a minute. Whisk in orange juice mixture. Increase heat to high and simmer, whisking frequently, until it becomes thick, about eight to ten minutes.
4. Return chicken and any collected juices to frying pan and turn to coat with sauce. Return chicken to platter. Move sauce to container and sprinkle with salt, pepper, and sugar to taste and serve.

SAUTÉED CHICKEN WITH CHERRY TOMATO AND ROASTED CORN SALSA

Yield: Servings 4

Ingredients:

- ¼ cup minced fresh cilantro
- ½ cup all purpose flour
- 1 shallot, minced
- 1 teaspoon chili powder
- 12 ounces cherry tomatoes, halved
- 2 garlic cloves, minced
- 2 tablespoons lime juice
- 3 cups fresh or thawed frozen corn
- 3 tablespoons vegetable oil
- 4 (6 to 8 ounce) boneless, skinless chicken breasts, trimmed and pounded to ½ inch thickness
- Salt and pepper

Directions:

1. Spread flour into shallow dish. Pat chicken dry using paper towels and flavor with chili powder, salt, and pepper. Working with 1 chicken breast at time, dredge in flour, shaking off surplus.
2. Heat 2 tablespoons oil in 12 inch nonstick frying pan over moderate high heat until just smoking. Lay chicken in frying pan and cook until thoroughly browned on first side, six to eight minutes.
3. Flip chicken over, decrease the heat to moderate, and carry on cooking until chicken records 160 degrees, six to eight minutes. Move chicken to plate and tent with aluminium foil.
4. Put in remaining 1 tablespoon oil to now empty frying pan and place over moderate high heat until it starts to shimmer Put in corn and cook, without stirring, until thoroughly browned and roasted, about eight to ten minutes. Mix in shallot and garlic and cook until aromatic, approximately half a minute. Mix in tomatoes, scraping up any browned bits, and cook until just softened, approximately 2 minutes.

5. Remove the heat, mix in cilantro and lime juice and sprinkle with salt and pepper to taste. Move vegetables to platter and serve with chicken.

SINALOA STYLE GRILL ROASTED CHICKENS

Yield: Servings 4

Ingredients:

- ¼ cup extra virgin olive oil
- 1 (12 ounce) can frozen orange juice concentrate, thawed
- 1 tablespoon chopped fresh oregano
- 1 tablespoon minced fresh thyme
- 1½ cups wood chips
- 2 (3½ to 4 pound) whole chickens, giblets discarded
- 2 garlic heads, cloves separated and peeled (20 cloves)
- 2 onions, chopped
- 2 teaspoons minced canned chipotle chile in adobo sauce
- Lime wedges
- Salt and pepper

Directions:

1. With chickens breast side down, use kitchen shears to cut out backbone and butterfly chicken. Flip chickens over and split chickens in half along the length through breastbones using chef's knife. Cut ½ inch deep slits across breasts, thighs, and legs, approximately ½ inch apart. Tuck wingtips behind backs.
2. Blend onions, orange juice concentrate, oil, garlic, and 2 tablespoons salt in blender until the desired smoothness is achieved, approximately one minute. Move ¾ cup mixture to container and mix in oregano, thyme, and chipotle; set aside for grilling. Split remaining marinade among two 1 gallon zipper lock bags. Put in chickens to bags and toss to coat. Push out as much air as you can, seal bags, and place in your fridge for minimum 2 hours or maximum one day, turning once in a while.
3. Immediately before grilling, soak wood chips in water for fifteen minutes, then drain. Using big piece of heavy duty aluminium foil, wrap soaked chips in foil packet and cut several vent holes in top. Remove chickens from marinade and pat dry using paper

towels; discard marinade. Insert 1 skewer along the length through thickest part of breast down through thigh of each chicken half.

4. FOR A CHARCOAL GRILL: Open bottom vent midway. Light big chimney starter filled with charcoal briquettes (6 quarts). When top coals are partly covered with ash, pour into steeply banked pile against side of grill. Put wood chip packet on coals. Set cooking grate in place, cover, and open lid vent midway. Heat grill until hot and wood chips are smoking, approximately five minutes. FOR A GAS GRILL: Remove cooking grate and place wood chip packet directly on primary burner. Set grate in place, turn all burners to high, cover, and heat grill until hot and wood chips are smoking, approximately fifteen minutes. Leave primary burner on high and turn off other burner(s). (Adjust primary burner as required to maintain grill temperature between 350 to 375 degrees.)

5. Clean and oil cooking grate. Put chicken halves skin side up on cooler side of grill with legs pointing toward fire. Cover and cook for about forty-five minutes, coating every fifteen minutes with reserved marinade.

6. Switch placement of chickens, with legs still pointing toward fire, and carry on cooking, covered, until breasts register 160 degrees and thighs register 175 degrees, 30 to forty-five minutes longer. Move chicken to carving board, tent using foil, and allow to rest for about twenty minutes. Carve and serve with lime wedges.

SKILLET CHICKEN FAJITAS

Yield: Servings 4

Ingredients:

CHICKEN

- ¼ cup vegetable oil
- ¼ teaspoon cayenne pepper
- ½ teaspoon ground cumin
- ½ teaspoon pepper
- 1 teaspoon salt
- 1 teaspoon sugar
- 1½ pounds boneless, skinless chicken breasts, trimmed and pounded to ½ inch thickness

- 1½ teaspoons smoked paprika
- 2 tablespoons lime juice
- 4 garlic cloves, peeled and smashed

RAJAS CON CREMA

- ¼ cup minced fresh cilantro
- ¼ teaspoon dried oregano
- ¼ teaspoon dried thyme
- ¼ teaspoon pepper
- ½ cup heavy cream
- ½ teaspoon salt
- 1 onion, halved and cut ¼ inch thick
- 1 pound poblano chiles, stemmed, halved, and seeded
- 1 tablespoon lime juice
- 1 tablespoon vegetable oil
- 12 (6 inch) flour tortillas, warmed
- 2 garlic cloves, minced
- Lime wedges

Directions:

1. FOR THE CHICKEN: Whisk 3 tablespoons oil, lime juice, garlic, paprika, sugar, salt, cumin, pepper, and cayenne together in container. Put in chicken, toss to coat, cover, and place in your fridge for minimum 30 minutes or maximum 1 hour.
2. FOR THE RAJAS CON CREMA: In the meantime, adjust oven rack 6 inches from broiler element and heat broiler. Position poblanos skin side up on aluminium foil–lined rimmed baking sheet and broil until blackened and starting to tenderize, four to ten minutes, rotating baking sheet midway through cooking.
3. Move poblanos to container, cover, and allow to steam for about ten minutes. Remove majority of skin from poblanos (preserving some skin for flavor) and slice peppers into ¼ inch thick strips.
4. Adjust oven racks to middle and lowest positions and heat oven to 200 degrees. Heat oil in 12 inch ovensafe nonstick frying pan using high heat until just smoking. Put in onion and cook until just softened, approximately 3 minutes. Mix in garlic, thyme, and oregano and cook until aromatic, approximately fifteen seconds. Mix in cream and

cook, stirring frequently, until reduced and cream lightly coats onion, one to two minutes. Mix in lime juice, salt, pepper, and poblanos. Move vegetables to container, cover, and place on upper oven rack.

5. Wipe out now empty frying pan. Remove chicken from marinade and wipe off surplus. Heat remaining 1 tablespoon oil in frying pan using high heat until just smoking. Put in chicken and cook without moving until well charred on bottom, approximately 4 minutes. Flip chicken, move frying pan to lower oven rack, and cook until chicken records 160 degrees, 7 to ten minutes.

6. Move chicken to cutting board, allow to rest for five minutes, then slice crosswise into ¼ inch thick strips; return chicken to frying pan and toss with pan juices. Serve with warmed tortillas, rajas con crema, cilantro, and lime wedges.

SPICY PICKLED RADISHES

Yield: About 1¾ CUPS

These easy to make spicy pickled radishes are the perfect decorate for numerous Mexican dishes including stews, tacos, tostadas, sopes, braised beans, and more.

Ingredients:

- ¼ teaspoon salt
- ½ cup lime juice (4 limes)
- ½ jalapeño chile, stemmed and cut thin
- 1 teaspoon sugar
- 10 radishes, trimmed and cut thin

Directions:

Mix all ingredients in container, cover, and allow it to stand at room temperature for half an hour (Mixture can be placed in your fridge for maximum one day).

TEKANTÓ CHICKEN (POLLO TEKANTÓ)

Yield: Servings 6

Ingredients:

- ½ teaspoon dried mexican oregano, yucatecan if possible

- ½ teaspoon peppercorns, crushed
- ¾ cup (185 ml) whole almonds, unskinned
- 1 head garlic, unpeeled, plus 2 garlic cloves peeled
- 1½ tablespoons all-purpose flour
- 12 ounces (340 g) white onions (about 2 medium)
- 2 tablespoons mild vinegar
- 3 x-cat-ik or güero chiles, or fresh, hot italian peppers
- 3½ cups (875 ml) water, roughly
- 4 to 5 tablespoons vegetable oil or melted chicken fat
- 4½ pounds (2 kg) big chicken or small turkey parts
- Salt to taste

To serve

- ½ cup (125 ml) vegetable oil, roughly
- 1 big plantain (approximately 12 ounces/340 g), peeled and cut on the diagonal into ½-inch rounds
- 12 thick rounds of stale french bread
- 6 radish "roses"
- Lettuce leaves, if possible green leaf or romaine

Directions:

1. Place the whole onions, chiles, and unpeeled head of garlic straight onto the flame of a gas stove or charcoal (with an electric stove use a super hot griddle or comal) and allow them to char all over. The chiles must be mildly charred; the onion and garlic should have well-charred crusts and the inside flesh must be transparent but not too tender. Chop the outside crust off the onion and roughly cut the flesh. Set the head of garlic aside; do not peel. Leave the chiles whole; do not peel.
2. In the meantime, cover the almonds with hot water, bring to its boiling point, and simmer for five minutes. Set aside to cool in the water. When the almonds are sufficiently cool to handle, slip off the skins, crush lightly, and move to a blender jar (the object of boiling them is to tenderize them for the sauce). Put in the salt, oregano, the two peeled (uncooked) garlic cloves, the cooked onion, peppercorns, ½ teaspoon of the vinegar, and about ½ cup (125 ml) of the water and blend until the desired smoothness is achieved. (you may need to put in slightly more water to

release the blades of the blender, but do not put in too much, as the consistency must be that of a loose paste.)

3. Spread one-fourth of the almond mixture over the chicken pieces—it will be a very light coating—and set aside to season for a minimum of 2 hours or overnight.

4. In a heavy pan, heat 3 tablespoons of the oil to a medium temperature—if it is too hot the almond paste will burn. Put in the chicken pieces, a few at a time, and fry very lightly until just changing color—you may need to use slightly more oil.

5. Drain any remaining oil from the pan. Break up the head of cooked garlic and put the garlic cloves over the bottom of the pan, together with the chiles. Place the chicken pieces on top: put in the remaining 3 cups (750 ml) of water—it should nearly cover the chicken—cover the pan, and simmer until the chicken is just soft—anywhere from thirty-five to 50 minutes. Change the position of the pieces occasionally so they cook uniformly.

6. In the meantime, prepare the toppings. Heat the oil and fry the bread until crunchy and golden, then remove and drain. Fry the plantain rounds in the same oil until golden. Remove and drain.

7. When the chicken is nearly soft, mix in the rest of the almond paste and vinegar and simmer, uncovered, for approximately ten minutes.

8. Place the flour into a small container. Put in a little of the hot sauce and stir until the desired smoothness is achieved. Put into the chicken, stirring it in well, and cook for a few minutes longer, or until the sauce becomes thick.

9. Coat the edges of a serving platter with the lettuce leaves. Position the chicken pieces, coated with some of the sauce, on the lettuce and garnish with the radish roses and rounds of plantain. Position the fried bread around the edges of the platter and sprinkle the charred chiles and garlic over.

10. Serve the chicken hot, passing the remaining sauce separately.

TEPEHUAN CHICKEN (POLLO TEPEHUANO)

Yield: Servings 6

Ingredients:

- ¼ teaspoon cumin seeds, crushed
- 10 ounces (285 g) tomatoes, finely chopped (approximately 1⅔ cups/415 ml)

- 10 sprigs cilantro, roughly chopped
- 1½ cups (375 ml) long-grain unconverted white rice
- 12 scallions (3 cebollas de rabo in mexico)
- 2 serrano chiles or any fresh, hot green chiles, finely chopped (not necessary)
- 2 tablespoons vegetable oil
- 4½ pounds (2 kg) big chicken pieces
- 8 cups (2 l) strong chicken broth
- Salt to taste

Directions:

1. Cut four of the scallions into four equivalent portions along the length, using the soft part of the green, and put, together with the chicken pieces and broth, into a big deep cooking pan. Bring slowly to a simmer and carry on simmering covered for approximately ten minutes.
2. In the meantime, wash the rice twice in cold water and leave to drain in a strainer. Shake it meticulously and stir it progressively into the simmering broth, then put in salt. Carry on cooking until the chicken and rice are just soft—anywhere from 25 to forty minutes (the time varies tremendously with the kind of cookware used, the kind of rice, and the quality of the chicken).
3. In the meantime, cut the rest of the scallions finely. Heat the oil in a frying pan and fry the scallions for approximately 2 minutes, without browning, then put in the tomatoes, chiles, and cilantro and carry on cooking for approximately five minutes (the ingredients must be reduced to a textured sauce). Cautiously stir the tomato mixture and cumin into the pan with the chicken and rice and carry on cooking for five minutes longer. The dish should have a soupy consistency.
4. Serve hot, with freshly made tortillas.

TURKEY BREAST EN COCOTTE WITH MOLE

Yield: Servings 6 to 8

Ingredients:

- ⅛ teaspoon ground cloves
- ¼ cup raisins

- ½ teaspoon ground cinnamon
- 1 (14.5 ounce) can diced tomatoes, drained
- 1 (6 to 7 pound) whole bone in turkey breast
- 1 bay leaf
- 1 onion, chopped
- 2 sprigs fresh thyme
- 2 tablespoons chili powder
- 2 tablespoons creamy peanut butter
- 2 tablespoons unsweetened cocoa powder
- 5 tablespoons vegetable oil
- 9 garlic cloves, peeled (6 crushed, 3 minced)
- Salt and pepper

Directions:

1. Adjust oven rack to lowest position and heat oven to 250 degrees. Using kitchen shears, trim rib bones and surplus fat from edges of turkey breast. Pat turkey dry using paper towels and sprinkle with salt and pepper.
2. Heat 2 tablespoons oil in Dutch oven over moderate high heat until just smoking. Put in turkey, breast side down, to pot. Spread onion, crushed garlic, thyme, and bay leaf around turkey. Cook, turning turkey on its sides and stirring vegetables as required, until turkey and vegetables are thoroughly browned, twelve to 16 minutes, reducing heat if pot starts to scorch.
3. Remove the heat, place big piece aluminium foil over pot and press to secure, then cover firmly with lid. Move pot to oven and cook until turkey records 160 degrees, 1½ to 1¾ hours.
4. Take the pot out of the oven. Move turkey to cutting board, tent using foil, and allow to rest while making sauce. Strain juices from pot into fat separator, saving for later strained vegetables. Let juices settle for approximately five minutes, then defat juices; set aside.
5. Put in remaining 3 tablespoons oil, minced garlic, chili powder, cocoa powder, cinnamon, and cloves to now empty pot and cook on moderate heat until aromatic, approximately one minute. Mix in defatted juices, strained vegetables, any collected juices from turkey, tomatoes, raisins, and peanut butter and simmer over moderate

high heat while stirring once in a while, until slightly thickened, about eight to ten minutes.

6. Discard thyme and bay leaf, then puree sauce in blender until the desired smoothness is achieved, approximately twenty seconds. Season sauce with salt and pepper to taste. Remove and discard turkey skin, carve turkey, and serve with sauce.

TURKEY IN MOLE POBLANO (GUAJOLOTE EN MOLE POBLANO)

Yield: Servings approximately 10

Ingredients:

Step 1—the chiles

- 5 ancho chiles, seeds and veins removed
- 6 pasilla chiles, seeds and veins removed
- 8 mulato chiles, seeds and veins removed
- Approximately ½ cup (125 ml) lard
- reserve 1 tablespoon chile seeds for step 4)

Step 2—the giblet broth

- 1 medium white onion, roughly chopped
- 1 small carrot, trimmed and cut
- 6 peppercorns
- Salt to taste
- The turkey giblets

Step 3—the turkey

- 1 small turkey, approximately eight pounds (3.6 kg), cut into serving pieces
- Approximately ⅓ cup (85 ml) lard
- Salt to taste

Step 4—the extra sauce ingredients

- ⅛ teaspoon anise seeds, toasted and crushed

- ⅛ teaspoon coriander seeds, toasted
- ½ cup (125 ml) tomate verde, cooked and drained
- ½-inch (1.5-cm) piece of cinnamon stick, toasted, broken up
- 1 small dried tortilla
- 1 tablespoon reserved chile seeds, toasted separately
- 10 peppercorns, crushed
- 1½ ounces (45 g) mexican drinking chocolate
- 2 cups (500 ml) turkey broth
- 2 ounces (60 g) raw, hulled pumpkin seeds (just over ⅓ cup/85 ml)
- 2 tablespoons raisins
- 20 unskinned almonds
- 3 garlic cloves, charred and peeled
- 3 small slices dry french bread
- 4 whole cloves, crushed
- 7 tablespoons sesame seeds, toasted separately
- About 6 cups (1.5 l) turkey broth
- Approximately ¼ cup (65 ml) lard
- Salt to taste

Directions:

1. Heat the lard in a frying pan and for a short period of time fry the chiles on both sides—the inside flesh should turn a tobacco color—ensuring not to allow them to burn. Reserve the lard. Drain the chiles and move to a container of cold water and allow them to soak for approximately 1 hour. Drain but do not attempt to skin.
2. Preheat your oven to 325° f (165° c).
3. Place the giblets into a deep cooking pan, cover well with water, put in the carrot, onion, peppercorns, and salt, and bring to a simmer. Continue simmering for approximately 1½ hours, putting in more water as required. Strain the broth and save for later.
4. Meanwhile, heat the lard in a dutch oven, put in the turkey pieces a few at a time, and fry until the skin turns a gold brown. Drain off the surplus fat and reserve to fry the remaining ingredients. Return all the pieces to the dutch oven, drizzle well with salt, cover, and braise in your oven until the meat is nearly soft—about forty minutes. Pour

off the pan juices and put in them to the giblet broth, then put in water to make up to approximately eight cups (2 l) liquid.

5. Put 1 cup (250 ml) water into your blender jar and blend the drained chiles, a few at a time, to a slightly textured puree, putting in only enough extra water to release the blender blades. In a heavy flameproof casserole heat the reserved lard and fry the chile puree on moderate heat (because it will splatter ferociously) for approximately ten minutes, scraping the bottom of the pan almost continuously to prevent sticking. Set aside.

6. Put 1 cup (250 ml) of the broth into your blender jar, put in the tomate verde and peeled garlic, and blend until the desired smoothness is achieved. Slowly put in the remaining ingredients in small quantities at a time as they are fried or toasted:

7. First, grind the spices with the chile seeds in an electric coffee/spice grinder to a finely textured powder. Then grind all but 4 tablespoons of the sesame seeds again to a textured powder. Put into the blender jar.

8. Melt the ¼ cup lard in a frying pan and separately fry the raisins, almonds, pumpkin seeds, tortilla, and bread, draining each ingredient in a colander before you put in to the blender jar. (it is easier if the almonds, bread, and tortilla are crushed a little before blending.) Put in another cup (250 ml) of the broth, or enough to release the blades of the blender, until you have a thick, slightly textured paste.

9. Put in the paste to the chiles in the casserole and carry on cooking, again scraping the bottom of the pan well, for approximately five minutes. Break the chocolate into little pieces and put in it to the mole with another cup (250 ml) of the broth and carry on cooking for five minutes more. Dilute the mole with another 4 cups (1 l) of the broth, test for salt, and carry on cooking on moderate heat until well seasoned and pools of oil form on the surface—about forty minutes. Put in the turkey pieces and cook for twenty additional minutes.

10. Serve each portion sprinkled with a little of the reserved sesame seeds.

YUCATECAN BARBECUED CHICKEN (POLLO PIBIL)

Yield: Servings 1

Ingredients:

- ¼ big chicken

- ½ teaspoon achiote paste
- 1 tablespoon achiote paste
- 1 tablespoon water
- 2 tablespoons lard or vegetable oil
- 4 thick slices tomato
- 4 thin slices white onion
- A piece of banana leaf, approximately 12 by 12 inches (30 by 30 cm;)
- Salt to taste

Directions:

1. Prick the chicken all over using a fork. Dilute the seasoning paste with the water and set ½ teaspoon aside. Thoroughly rub the rest, together with the salt, into the chicken.
2. Sear the leaf swiftly over an open flame to make it more flexible, and wrap it around the chicken to make a small package. Set it aside to season, placed in the fridge, if possible overnight.
3. Preheat your oven to 375° f (190° c).
4. Melt the lard in a frying pan and fry the onion until translucent. Put in the tomato and the ½ teaspoon seasoning paste and fry it gently on both sides.
5. Unwrap the chicken. Put half the onion and tomato under the chicken and the other half on top. Cover it up again in the leaf.
6. Put the "package" into the dish and cover it firmly. Cook for about twenty minutes. Turn it over, coat with the juices, and cook for twenty additional minutes, or until just soft. Do not overcook.
7. Turn the oven up to 450° f (230° c). Take away the cover, open up the leaf, and let the chicken brown on top.
8. Serve still wrapped in the banana leaf.

YUCATECAN CHICKEN WITH ORANGE (POLLO EN NARANJA DE CHINA)

Yield: Servings 6

Ingredients:

- ⅓ cup (85 ml) raisins

- ½ cup (125 ml) water
- 1 big chile dulce or red bell pepper, seeds and veins removed and slice into thin strips
- 1 big head of garlic, charred
- 1 big white onion, quartered and charred
- 1 cup (250 ml) orange juice (normal, not bitter)
- 1 tablespoon recado de toda clase
- 1 whole orange, thinly cut (not peeled)
- 12 ounces (340 g) tomatoes, cut
- 2 garlic cloves
- 2 heaped tablespoons big capers, drained or washed of salt
- 2 tablespoons bitter orange juice or substitute
- 2 x-cat-ik chiles, or yellow peppers, charred, seeds removed, and torn into strips unskinned
- 20 pitted green olives, halved
- 3 tablespoons vegetable or olive oil
- 4½ pounds (2 kg) big chicken pieces
- Salt to taste
- Salt to taste

Directions:

1. Prepare an ovenproof dish minimum 3 inches (8 cm) deep, into which the chicken pieces and vegetables will just fit in a single layer.
2. In a small container, crush the garlic and salt with the bitter orange juice and mix in the recado. Spread the chicken very lightly with this paste and set aside to season for minimum 2 hours or overnight.
3. Heat the oven to 350° f (180° c).
4. Heat the oil in a big frying pan, put in the bell pepper and a drizzle of salt, and fry gently without browning for a minute. Put in the tomato slices and cook using high heat to reduce for approximately 3 minutes. Put in the raisins, capers, and olives and cook for another three minutes. Spread half of this mixture over the bottom of the dish, put the chicken in a single layer on top, and cover with the rest of the tomato mixture.
5. Put the onion and chiles over the surface. Chop the head of garlic in half horizontally and place cut side down into the dish. Pour over the orange juice and water, cover,

and bake for approximately ½ hour. Take away the cover and coat with the juices, re-cover, and bake for around thirty minutes more or until the chicken is soft. Serve with the slices of orange.

BEEF AND PORK

Ayocote Beans With Pork (Ayocotes Con Carne De Puerco Estilo Querétaro)

Yield: Servings 6

Ingredients:

The beans

- 2 teaspoons salt, or to taste
- 3 cups (750 ml) dried ayocotes, big navy beans, or haricot beans (approximately 18 ounces, 510 g)
- 8 cups (2 l) cold water

The meat

- 1½ pounds (675 g) country-style spareribs, cut into 1½-inch (4-cm) cubes (half carne maciza and half costillitas in mexico)
- Pork lard, if required
- Salt to taste

The sauce

- ¾ teaspoon cumin seeds, crushed
- 2 garlic cloves, crushed
- 2 mexican bay leaves
- 2½ cups (625 ml) hot water
- 3 whole cloves, crushed
- 5 peppercorns, roughly crushed
- 9 guajillo chiles, seeds and veins removed
- 9 pasilla chiles, seeds and veins removed

Directions:

1. Wash the beans well, then put in a bean pot or slow cooker. Cover with the water and let soak for half an hour In the same water, bring the beans to its boiling point, reduce the heat, and simmer until soft—two to three hours, depending on how dry they are. Put in salt.

2. Meanwhile, cook the pork. Place the cubes into a wide, heavy pan, barely cover with water, put in salt, and cook, uncovered, on moderate heat until all the water is consumed and the meat soft. Carry on cooking, turning occasionally, so that the fat renders out and the meat browns well. If the pork is very lean you may have to put in some lard, say ¼ cup (65 ml). Take away the meat and all but ¼ cup (65 ml) of the fat.

3. Heat a griddle or comal and toast the chiles meticulously, ensuring not to burn them or the sauce will have a bitter taste. Cover the chiles with hot water separately and allow them to soak for approximately five minutes; drain.

4. Put in the crushed spices and garlic with ½ cup (125 ml) water to the blender jar and blend meticulously. Put in another cup of water (250 ml) and the drained pasillas and blend until nearly smooth. Reheat the lard in the pan, then put in the mixed ingredients and fry on moderate heat. In 1 cup (250 ml) of water, blend the guajillo chiles meticulously and put in to the pan, pushing the mixture through a fine strainer to eliminate any tough pieces of skin. Carry on cooking the sauce on moderate heat, stirring once in a while.

5. Put in the beans with their broth and the bay leaves, tweak the seasoning, and cook using low heat for twenty additional minutes.

Beans With Pork (Frijol Con Puerco)

Yield: Servings 6

Ingredients:

THE BEANS

- ⅓ cup (85 ml) roughly cut white onion
- 1 pound (450 g) black beans (about 2¼ cups/565 ml)
- 1 sprig epazote
- 1 tablespoon pork lard
- 14 cups (3.5 l) cold water, roughly
- Salt to taste

Directions:

1. Run the beans through your fingers and pick out any small stones or little pieces of earth that may be among them.
2. Wash the beans and put into a very large, flameproof bean pot with the lard, onion, and water. Heat to a simmer and carry on cooking slowly until the skins start breaking, approximately 1½ hours.
3. Put in the salt and epazote and carry on cooking until the beans are just soft but not soft, approximately ½ hour.

The pork

Ingredients:

- 1 green bell pepper, seeds and veins removed and cut into little squares
- 1 pig's ear, cut into little pieces (not necessary)
- 1 pound (450 g) country-style spareribs (costillitas in mexico), cut into two-inch (5-cm) cubes
- 1 pound (450 g) pork hocks (chamberete de puerco in mexico), cut into ½-inch (1.5-cm) slices
- 1 tablespoon salt, or to taste
- 2 big sprigs epazote
- 2 tablespoons roughly chopped white onion
- 8 ounces (225 g) boneless stewing pork (carne maciza in mexico), cut into big cubes

Directions:

1. Put in the pork and rest of the ingredients to the beans, then cover and carry on cooking over low heat while stirring well occasionally. (there must be sufficient broth, bearing in mind that 3 cups/750 ml of it have to go into the rice. If it appears to have reduced too much, put in a cup or so of water.) Cook until the beans are fairly soft and the meat soft—1 hour fifteen minutes, depending on the meat.
2. During the cooking time, start preparations for the rice.

The rice

Ingredients:

- ¼ small white onion, roughly chopped (approximately 1 tablespoon)

- ⅓ cup (85 ml) vegetable oil
- 1 garlic clove, roughly chopped
- 1½ cups (375 ml) long-grain unconverted white rice
- 3 cups (750 ml) bean broth
- Salt to taste

Directions:

1. Cover the rice with hot water and allow it to stand for approximately five minutes, then wash in cold water twice and drain thoroughly. Heat the oil in a very heavy pan (the bean broth tends to stick rather badly) and stir the rice into it until the grains are uniformly coated. Put in the onion and garlic and fry the rice, flipping it over occasionally so that it becomes a uniform, pale gold color. Tip the pan and drain off the surplus oil.
2. Put in the broth from the beans and salt, then cover the pot and cook the rice gently until all the liquid has been absorbed, approximately fifteen minutes. Turn off the heat. Cover the rice with a piece of terry cloth and set aside for approximately twenty-five minutes, to let the rice carry on cooking and expanding in the steam it generates.

Assembling the dish

Ingredients:

- ½ cup (125 ml) very finely chopped cilantro
- 1 cup (250 ml) very finely chopped radishes
- 2 avocados, cut
- 2 cups (500 ml) salsa de jitomate yucateca
- 4 small limes, quartered

Directions:

1. Take away the meat from the beans and serve on a warmed platter.
2. Serve the rice in the casserole in which it was cooked. Serve the beans and their broth in individual small bowls and pass the remaining ingredients separately so each person can serve himself, al gusto.

Beef Taco Salad

Yield: Servings 4

Ingredients:

TACO MEAT

- ½ cup chicken broth
- 1 (8 ounce) can tomato sauce
- 1 onion, chopped fine
- 1 pound 90 percent lean ground beef
- 1 tablespoon vegetable oil
- 1 teaspoon packed light brown sugar
- 2 tablespoons chili powder
- 2 teaspoons cider vinegar
- 3 garlic cloves, minced
- Salt and pepper

SALAD

- ¼ cup chopped fresh cilantro
- 1 (fifteen ounce) can black beans, washed
- 2 ounces shredded Mexican cheese blend (½ cup)
- 2 romaine lettuce hearts (12 ounces), shredded
- 2 scallions, cut thin
- 2 tablespoons lime juice
- 4 (10 inch) flour tortillas
- 8 ounces cherry or grape tomatoes, quartered
- Salt and pepper
- Vegetable oil spray

Directions:

1. FOR THE TACO MEAT: Heat oil in 12 inch nonstick frying pan over moderate high heat until it starts to shimmer Put in onion and cook until tender, approximately five minutes. Mix in chili powder and garlic and cook until aromatic, approximately half a minute. Put in ground beef and cook, breaking up meat with wooden spoon, until almost thoroughly cooked but still slightly pink, approximately 2 minutes. Mix in tomato sauce, broth, vinegar, and sugar and simmer until slightly thickened,

approximately five minutes; mixture will be saucy. Remove the heat, sprinkle with salt and pepper to taste.

2. FOR THE SALAD: Adjust oven racks to upper middle and lower middle positions and heat oven to 425 degrees. Position 4 ovensafe soup bowls (or 4 slightly flattened 3 inch aluminium foil balls) upside down on 2 rimmed baking sheets. Put tortillas on plate, cover with damp paper towel, and microwave until warm and flexible, approximately half a minute.

3. Generously spray both sides of warm tortillas with oil spray. Drape tortillas over soup bowls, pushing top flat and pinching sides to create 4 sided container. Bake until tortillas are golden and crunchy, ten to fifteen minutes, switching and rotating sheets midway through baking. Allow to cool upside down.

4. Mix lettuce, beans, tomatoes, scallions, and 2 tablespoons cilantro in big container; toss with lime juice and sprinkle with salt and pepper to taste. Put tortilla bowls on separate plates. Split salad among bowls, top with taco meat, and drizzle with cheese and remaining 2 tablespoons cilantro and serve.

Beef With Green Chile (Carne Con Chile Verde)

Yield: Servings 6

Ingredients:

- 1¼ cups (315 ml) finely chopped white onion
- 1½ tablespoons all-purpose flour
- 12 anaheim chiles, charred, peeled, seeds removed, and slice into squares
- 2 cups (500 ml) water, roughly
- 2¼ pounds (1 kg) stewing beef, with some fat, cut into ½-inch (1.5-cm) cubes
- 3 garlic cloves, finely chopped
- 8 ounces (225 g) tomatoes, broiled and mashed
- Salt to taste
- two to three tablespoons vegetable oil, roughly

Directions:

1. Place the meat—in two layers, no more—into a large, heavy pan. Put in the salt, garlic, and ½ cup (125 ml) of the water, then cover the pan and cook using super low heat

until the meat is nearly soft, the liquid vaporized, and the fat rendering out—about forty-five minutes, depending on the cut and quality of the meat. (it may be necessary to put in slightly more water to stop the meat from adhering. On the other hand, if there is too much liquid as the meat approaches the correct point of tenderness, remove the cover, raise the heat, and reduce quickly.) Shake the pan and flip the meat over occasionally.

2. Put in sufficient oil to the fat in the pan to make about 3 tablespoons. Turn the heat to moderate, then put in the onion, and brown the meat lightly. Drizzle the flour into the pan and allow it to brown lightly, stirring continuously. Put in the chiles, tomatoes, and remaining 1½ cups (375 ml) water, then cover the pan and cook using low heat for twenty additional minutes. (at the end of the cooking time there must be some liquid in the pan, but it should not be soupy; it may be necessary to put in slightly more water during the cooking time.)

3. Adjust the seasoning and serve hot, with flour tortillas.

Braised Pork Loin With Black Mole Sauce

Yield: Servings 6

Ingredients:

- ⅛ teaspoon ground cinnamon
- ⅛ teaspoon ground cloves
- ¼ cup unsalted dry roasted peanuts
- 1 (2½ to 3 pound) boneless pork loin roast, fat trimmed to ¼ inch, tied at 1½ inch gaps
- 1 onion, chopped
- 1 tomato, cored and slice into an inch pieces
- 2 cups chicken broth
- 2 garlic cloves, peeled
- 2 tablespoons raisins
- 2 tablespoons vegetable oil
- 2 teaspoons minced fresh oregano or ½ teaspoon dried
- 2 tomatillos, husks and stems removed, washed well, dried, and slice into an inch pieces
- 3 tablespoons black or Dutch processed cocoa powder

- 3 tablespoons sesame seeds, toasted
- 4 pasilla chiles, stemmed, seeded, and torn into ½ inch pieces (1 cup)
- Salt and pepper

Directions:

1. Adjust oven rack to lowest position and heat oven to 250 degrees. Toast pasilla chiles in Dutch oven over moderate high heat, stirring regularly, until aromatic, 2 to six minutes; move to container.

2. Pat roast dry using paper towels and sprinkle with salt and pepper. Heat oil in now empty pot over moderate high heat until just smoking. Brown roast well on all sides, 7 to ten minutes; move to plate.

3. Put in onion to fat left in pot and cook on moderate heat until tender and thoroughly browned, approximately five minutes. Mix in garlic, oregano, cloves, and cinnamon and cook until aromatic, approximately half a minute. Mix in tomatillos and tomato and cook until tender, approximately five minutes. Mix in broth, scraping up any browned bits. Mix in peanuts, cocoa, 2 tablespoons sesame seeds, raisins, toasted pasillas, 1 teaspoon salt, and ½ teaspoon pepper and bring to simmer.

4. Nestle browned pork fat side up into pot together with any collected juices. Cover, move pot to oven, and cook until pork records 140 degrees, forty minutes to an hour.

5. Move pork to carving board, tent with aluminium foil, and allow to rest for fifteen to twenty minutes. In the meantime, process cooking liquid in blender until the desired smoothness is achieved, one to two minutes. Season sauce with salt and pepper to taste.

6. Remove twine from roast, slice into ¼ inch thick slices, and move to serving platter. Ladle 1 cup sauce over pork, drizzle with remaining 1 tablespoon sesame seeds, and serve with rest of the sauce.

Braised Short Ribs With Peppers And Onions

Yield: Servings 4

Ingredients:

- ½ teaspoon ground coriander
- 1 (14.5 ounce) can diced tomatoes

- 1 jalapeño chile, stemmed and cut thin
- 1 teaspoon ancho chile powder
- 1 teaspoon ground cumin
- 1½ tablespoons minced fresh oregano or 1½ teaspoons dried
- 2 onions, halved and cut thin
- 2 pounds boneless beef short ribs, trimmed
- 2 red bell peppers, stemmed, seeded, and slice into ½ inch wide strips
- 2 tablespoons chopped fresh cilantro
- 2 tablespoons vegetable oil
- 2 teaspoons lime juice
- 4 garlic cloves, minced
- Pinch ground cloves
- Salt and pepper

Directions:

1. Adjust oven rack to lower middle position and heat oven to 325 degrees. Pat beef dry using paper towels and sprinkle with salt and pepper. Heat 1 tablespoon oil in 12 inch ovensafe frying pan over moderate high heat until just smoking. Brown beef well, four to five minutes per side; move to plate.

2. Put in onions, bell peppers and ¼ teaspoon salt to fat left in frying pan and cook over moderate high heat until tender, about eight to ten minutes. Mix in jalapeño, oregano, garlic, cumin, chile powder, coriander, and cloves and cook until aromatic, approximately half a minute. Mix in tomatoes and their juice, scraping up any browned bits. Nestle browned beef into frying pan together with any collected juices. Cover, move frying pan to oven, and cook until fork slips easily in and out of meat, approximately 2 hours.

3. Remove frying pan from oven. Move beef to serving platter and tent with aluminium foil. Let vegetable mixture settle for five minutes, then skim any fat off surface. Mix in cilantro and lime juice and sprinkle with salt and pepper to taste. Ladle vegetable mixture over beef before you serve.

Carne Asada

Yield: Servings four to 6

Ingredients:

- ¾ teaspoon ground cumin
- 1 (13 by 9 inch) disposable aluminum roasting pan (if using charcoal)
- 1 (2 pound) skirt steak, trimmed, cut with grain into 4 equal steaks, and pounded ¼ inch thick
- 1 garlic clove, peeled and smashed
- 2 teaspoons kosher salt
- Lime wedges

Directions:

1. Mix salt and cumin and drizzle uniformly over both sides of steaks. Move steaks to wire rack set in rimmed baking sheet and refrigerate, uncovered, for minimum 45 minutes or maximum one day. In the meantime, if using charcoal, use kitchen shears to remove and discard bottom of roasting pan; reserve pan collar.
2. 2A. FOR A CHARCOAL GRILL: Open bottom vent fully. Light big chimney starter filled with charcoal briquettes (6 quarts). When top coals are partly covered with ash, place roasting pan collar in center of grill, oriented over bottom vents, and pour coals into even layer in collar. Set cooking grate in place, cover, and open lid vent fully. Heat grill until hot, approximately five minutes. FOR A GAS GRILL: Set all burners to high, cover, and heat grill until hot, approximately fifteen minutes. Leave all burners on high.
3. Clean and oil cooking grate. Put steaks on grill (over coals if using charcoal). Cook, uncovered, until thoroughly browned on both sides and meat records 130 to 135 degrees (for medium), 2 to 4 minutes per side. Move steaks to carving board, tent with aluminium foil, and allow to rest for five minutes.
4. Rub garlic clove meticulously over 1 side of steaks. Slice steaks against grain into ¼ inch thick slices and serve with lime wedges.

Chiapas Roast Pork (Cochito Al Horno)

Yield: Servings 6 to 8

Ingredients:

- ⅔ cup (165 ml) mild vinegar, roughly
- 1 cup (250 ml) warm water

- 10 peppercorns, crushed
- 1½ tablespoons salt
- 20 whole allspice, crushed
- 2-inch (5-cm) piece of cinnamon stick, crushed
- 4 ancho chiles, seeds and veins removed
- 4 garlic cloves, crushed
- 4 mexican bay leaves
- 5 pounds (2.5 kg) pork roast, with rind, if possible
- 6 sprigs fresh thyme or ½ teaspoon dried
- 6 whole cloves, crushed

To serve

- 2 cups (500 ml) shredded romaine lettuce
- 2 cups (500 ml) thinly cut white onion

Directions:

1. Cover the chiles with boiling water in a container and let soak for approximately fifteen minutes, or until tender. Place the herbs, spices, garlic, salt, and vinegar into a blender jar and blend meticulously. Slowly put in the soaked and drained chiles and blend until the desired smoothness is achieved, stopping once in a while to release the blades of the blender—you may need to put in a little water, but the mixture should have the consistency of a loose paste.
2. Pierce the meat all over with the point of a sharp knife. Smear the meat liberally with the seasoning paste and set aside for a minimum of 4 hours, but if possible overnight.
3. Preheat your oven to 350° f (180° c).
4. Place the meat into a casserole, cover, and cook for an hour. Flip the meat and cook for an hour more, still covered. At this point, scrape up the paste that is clinging to the bottom of the pan and dilute it with the warm water. Flip the meat again and cook for one more hour, or until the meat is super soft, coating occasionally with the pan juices. When the meat is cooked, there must be sufficient sauce in the casserole.
5. Serve the meat cut, with some of the sauce from the pan and topped with sufficient onion rings and shredded lettuce. Eat with freshly made tortillas.

Chiles Rellenos With Pork

Yield: Servings 4

Ingredients:

FILLING

- ⅛ teaspoon ground cloves
- ¼ cup raisins
- ¼ cup slivered almonds, toasted and chopped
- ½ teaspoon ground cinnamon
- ½ teaspoon minced canned chipotle chile in adobo sauce
- 1 (8 ounce) can tomato sauce
- 1 pound ground pork
- 1 tablespoon cider vinegar
- 1 tablespoon vegetable oil
- 1 teaspoon minced fresh oregano or ¼ teaspoon dried
- 2 garlic cloves, minced
- 2 ounces Monterey Jack cheese, shredded (½ cup)
- Salt and pepper

POBLANOS

- ⅔ cup all purpose flour
- 1 cup seltzer
- 1 teaspoon baking powder
- 1 teaspoon salt
- 1⅓ cups cornstarch
- 5 cups vegetable oil
- 8 poblano chiles (4 ounces each)

Directions:

1. FOR THE FILLING: Cook oil, garlic, oregano, chipotle, cinnamon, and cloves in 12 inch nonstick frying pan on moderate heat until aromatic, approximately one minute. Mix in ground pork and cook, breaking up meat with wooden spoon, until no longer pink,

approximately five minutes. Mix in tomato sauce, raisins, vinegar, and ¼ teaspoon salt and simmer until most of liquid has vaporized, three to five minutes.

2. Move meat mixture to container and purée into fine pieces with potato masher. Let meat cool slightly, then mix in Monterey Jack and almonds. Sprinkle with salt and pepper to taste.

3. FOR THE POBLANOS: Arrange oven rack 4 inches from broiler element and heat broiler. Coat rimmed baking sheet with aluminium foil. Lay poblanos on sheet and broil until skin is charred and puffed but flesh is still firm, approximately eight minutes, turning after five minutes. Move poblanos to container, cover, and steam for about ten minutes. Lightly remove any loosened pieces of poblano skin, cut off stem end, and remove seeds; you do not need to remove all of skin or seeds.

4. Set wire rack in rimmed baking sheet. Stuff poblanos with meat mixture, leaving ½ inch room at top. Seal open end by weaving toothpick through top of chile. Put ⅔ cup cornstarch in shallow container; coat stuffed poblanos meticulously with cornstarch and place on readied wire rack.

5. Put in oil to big Dutch oven and bring to 375 degrees over moderate high heat. Whisk flour, baking powder, salt, and remaining ⅔ cup cornstarch together in big container. Slowly whisk in seltzer until just blended (some lumps will remain). Coat 1 poblano with batter and put in to hot oil; repeat with 3 more poblanos. Fry chiles, turning as required, until golden and crisp, approximately 6 minutes, adjusting burner as required to maintain oil temperature of 325 degrees.

6. Move fried chiles to prepared rack and remove toothpicks. Repeat with remaining chiles. (Chiles can be held in 200 dgree oven for half an hour)

CHILES RELLENOS WITH CHEESE

Omit filling and skip steps 1 and 2. Toss 8 ounces shredded Monterey Jack cheese with 3 thinly cut scallions and 3 tablespoons minced fresh cilantro; substitute cheese mixture for meat filling when stuffing poblanos.

Durango Pork Stew (Caldillo De Puerco Duranguense)

Yield: Servings 6

Ingredients:

- ¼ teaspoon dried mexican oregano

- ⅔ cup (165 ml) finely chopped white onion
- 1 cup (250 ml) tomate verde, cooked and partly drained
- 2 garlic cloves, finely chopped
- 2 teaspoons all-purpose flour
- 2¼ pounds (1 kg) boneless pork, with some fat, cut into ½-inch (1.5-cm) cubes
- 3 tablespoons vegetable oil or pork lard
- 5½ cups (1.375 l) water, roughly
- 8 ancho chiles
- Salt to taste

Directions:

1. Cover the whole chiles with water and simmer until soft—about ten minutes, depending on how dry the chiles are—then drain and move to a blender jar. Put in 2 cups (500 ml) of the water and the tomate verde and blend until the desired smoothness is achieved. Set aside.
2. Heat the oil or lard in a wide pan and fry the meat, with the garlic, onion, and salt, until golden, stirring continuously, approximately five minutes. Drizzle the flour into the pan and fry, stirring until it is mildly browned. Put in the mixed chiles to the pan and cook, over quite high heat, for approximately ten minutes, scraping the bottom of the pan to prevent sticking.
3. Put in the oregano and roughly 3 cups (750 ml) of the water—the meat must be covered with the sauce—then cover the pan and simmer until the meat is soft—about thirty minutes. (when cooked, the sauce must be fairly soupy like a thin gravy; put in more water if required.)
4. Serve in bowls, with lots of sauce and flour tortillas.

Grilled Ancho Rubbed Pork Chops

Yield: Servings 4

Ingredients:

- ¼ teaspoon garlic powder
- ½ dried ancho chile, stemmed, seeded, and torn into ½ inch pieces (2 tablespoons)
- 1 dried chipotle chile, stemmed, seeded, and torn into ½ inch pieces (1½ tablespoons)

- 1 teaspoon dried oregano
- 2 teaspoons packed brown sugar
- 3 tablespoons granulated sugar
- 4 (12 ounce) bone in pork rib or center cut chops, 1½ inches thick, trimmed
- Salt

Directions:

1. Dissolve 3 tablespoons salt and granulated sugar in 1½ quarts cold water in big container. Submerge chops in brine, cover, and place in your fridge for minimum 30 minutes or maximum 1 hour.

2. In the meantime, toast chipotle and ancho chiles in 8 inch frying pan on moderate heat, stirring regularly, until aromatic, 2 to six minutes. Move chiles to spice grinder and allow to cool slightly. Put in oregano and garlic powder and pulse until thoroughly ground, approximately 10 seconds. Move mixture to container and mix in brown sugar and ¼ teaspoon salt.

3. Immediately before grilling, remove chops from brine, pat dry using paper towels, and rub with spice rub.

4. 4A. FOR A CHARCOAL GRILL: Open bottom vent fully. Light big chimney starter filled with charcoal briquettes (6 quarts). When top coals are partly covered with ash, pour two thirds uniformly over grill, then pour remaining coals over half of grill. Set cooking grate in place, cover, and open lid vent fully. Heat grill until hot, approximately five minutes. FOR A GAS GRILL: Set all burners to high, cover, and heat grill until hot, approximately fifteen minutes. Leave primary burner on high and turn off other burner(s).

5. Clean and oil cooking grate. Put chops on hotter side of grill and cook (covered if using gas) until thoroughly browned on both sides, 2 to 4 minutes per side. Move chops to cooler side of grill, cover, and carry on cooking until pork records 145 degrees, 7 to 9 minutes, turning chops midway through cooking. Move chops to serving platter, tent with aluminium foil, and allow to rest for five to ten minutes and serve.

Grilled Citrus Marinated Pork Cutlets

Yield: Servings four to 6

Ingredients:

- ⅓ cup extra virgin olive oil
- ⅓ cup lime juice (3 limes)
- ½ teaspoon ground coriander
- ¾ teaspoon brown sugar
- 1 (13 by 9 inch) disposable aluminum roasting pan (if using charcoal)
- 1 avocado, halved, pitted, and slice into ½ inch pieces
- 1 tablespoon annatto powder
- 1 tomato, cored and slice into ½ inch pieces
- 1½ pounds boneless country style pork ribs, trimmed
- 2 radishes, trimmed and cut thin
- 2 tablespoons chopped fresh cilantro
- 3 garlic cloves, minced
- Salt and pepper

Directions:

1. Cut each rib along the length to create 2 or 3 cutlets about ⅜ inch wide. Put cutlets cut side down between 2 sheets of plastic wrap and gently pound to even ¼ inch thickness.
2. Mix lime juice, oil, garlic, annatto powder, sugar, ¾ teaspoon salt, ½ teaspoon pepper, and coriander in 1 gallon zipper lock bag. Put in pork to bag and toss to coat. Push out as much air as you can, seal bag, and place in your fridge for minimum 30 minutes or maximum 2 hours, turning bag once in a while.
3. Immediately before grilling, remove cutlets from bag and pat dry using paper towels; discard marinade. If using charcoal, use kitchen shears to remove and discard bottom of roasting pan; reserve pan collar.
4. 4A. FOR A CHARCOAL GRILL: Open bottom vent fully. Light big chimney starter filled with charcoal briquettes (6 quarts). When top coals are partly covered with ash, place roasting pan collar in center of grill, oriented over bottom vents, and pour coals into even layer in collar. Set cooking grate in place, cover, and open lid vent fully. Heat grill until hot, approximately five minutes. FOR A GAS GRILL: Set all burners to high, cover, and heat grill until hot, approximately fifteen minutes. Leave all burners on high.
5. Clean and oil cooking grate. Put cutlets on grill (over coals if using charcoal), Cook, uncovered, until mildly browned on first side, approximately 2 minutes. Flip cutlets and carry on cooking until just thoroughly cooked, approximately half a minute. Move

cutlets to serving platter, top with avocado, tomato, radishes, and cilantro, and serve instantly.

Grilled Steak Fajitas

Yield: Servings 4

Ingredients:

- ¼ cup vegetable oil
- ½ cup lime juice (4 limes)
- 1 (1½ pound) flank steak, trimmed
- 1 jalapeño chile, stemmed, seeded, and minced
- 1 onion, cut into ½ inch thick rounds (do not separate rings)
- 1 tablespoon chopped fresh cilantro
- 12 (6 inch) flour tortillas
- 2 bell peppers, stemmed, seeded, and quartered
- 2 tablespoons soy sauce
- 2 teaspoons ground cumin
- 2 teaspoons packed brown sugar
- 3 garlic cloves, minced
- Salt and pepper

Directions:

1. Mix lime juice, 2 tablespoons oil, jalapeño, soy sauce, garlic, cumin, and sugar in container. Move ¼ cup of marinade to separate container and mix in cilantro; set aside for serving. Poke each side of steak about 25 times with fork. Pour remaining marinade into 1 gallon zipper lock bag, put in steak, and toss to coat. Push out as much air as you can, seal bag, and place in your fridge for minimum 30 minutes or maximum 2 hours, turning bag once in a while.
2. Immediately before grilling, remove steak from bag and pat dry using paper towels. Brush bell peppers and onion rounds with remaining 2 tablespoons oil and sprinkle with salt and pepper.
3. 3A. FOR A CHARCOAL GRILL: Open bottom vent fully. Light big chimney starter filled with charcoal briquettes (6 quarts). When top coals are partly covered with ash, pour

two thirds uniformly over half of grill, then pour remaining coals over other half of grill. Set cooking grate in place, cover, and open lid vent fully. Heat grill until hot, approximately five minutes. FOR A GAS GRILL: Set all burners to high, cover, and heat grill until hot, approximately fifteen minutes. Leave primary burner on high and turn other burner(s) to moderate.

4. Clean and oil cooking grate. Put steak on hotter side of grill and place bell peppers and onion rounds on cooler side of grill. Cook (covered if using gas), turning as required, until vegetables are nicely charred on both sides and meat records 120 to 125 degrees (for medium rare), about eight to twelve minutes. As they finish cooking, move steak and vegetables to carving board and tent loosely with aluminium foil. Let steak rest for five to ten minutes.

5. Working in batches, grill tortillas over cooler part of grill, turning as required, until warmed and mildly browned, approximately 40 seconds. As tortillas finish cooking, wrap in dish towel or big sheet of foil.

6. Separate onion rings and slice bell peppers into ¼ inch wide strips; toss together in container with half of reserved marinade. Slice steak against grain into ¼ inch thick slices and toss with remaining reserved marinade in separate container. Position steak and vegetables on serving platter and serve with tortillas.

Ground Beef With Cabbage (Carne De Res Con Col)

Yield: about 4¼ cups (1.63 l) for tostadas serves 4 as a main course

It is a good idea to prepare this dish a little ahead so that the flavors intensify.

Ingredients:

- ¼ cup (65 ml) finely chopped white onion
- ½ cup (125 ml) tightly packed, roughly chopped cilantro
- ⅔ cup (165 ml) water
- 1 chile verde criollo or jalapeño, finely chopped
- 1 pound (450 g) ground sirloin with a little fat
- 3 garlic cloves, roughly chopped
- 3 tablespoons vegetable oil
- 4 cups (1 l) finely shredded cabbage
- 6 ounces (180 g) tomatoes, finely chopped (approximately 1 rounded cup/265 ml)

- 6 peppercorns
- Salt to taste

Directions:

1. Crush the garlic, peppercorns, and salt together and mix thoroughly into the beef (hands are best). Set aside for a few minutes to season.
2. Heat the oil in a large, heavy frying pan, put in the onion, chile, and a drizzle of salt, and cook on moderate heat until the onion is translucent—about one minute. Put in the tomatoes and carry on cooking until most of the juice has been absorbed—about three minutes.
3. Mix the meat into the pan and cook over quite high heat while stirring occasionally—about seven minutes. Put in the cabbage, water, and cilantro and carry on cooking on moderate heat, stirring occasionally until the mixture is well seasoned and moist but not juicy—about fifteen minutes. Serve.

Indoor Steak Fajitas

Yield: Servings 4

Ingredients:

- ½ teaspoon ground cumin
- 1 (1½ pound) flank steak, trimmed
- 1 big red onion, halved and cut thin
- 1 teaspoon chili powder
- 1 teaspoon hot sauce
- 2 red bell peppers, stemmed, seeded, and cut thin
- 2 tablespoons lime juice
- 2 tablespoons vegetable oil
- 2 tablespoons water
- 8–12 (6 inch) flour tortillas, warmed
- Salt and pepper

Directions:

1. Pat steak dry using paper towels and sprinkle with salt and pepper. Heat 1 tablespoon oil in 12 inch frying pan over moderate high heat until just smoking. Cook steak until thoroughly browned on both sides and meat records 120 to 125 degrees (for medium rare), four to six minutes per side. Move steak to carving board, sprinkle with lime juice, and tent with aluminium foil.

2. While steak rests, heat remaining 1 tablespoon oil in now empty frying pan over moderate high heat until it starts to shimmer Put in bell peppers, onion, water, chili powder, hot sauce, cumin, and ½ teaspoon salt. Cook, scraping up any browned bits, until peppers become tender and onion is browned, approximately eight minutes. Move vegetables to serving platter and sprinkle with salt and pepper to taste.

3. Slice steak against grain into ¼ inch thick slices and move to serving platter with vegetables. Serve with warm tortillas.

Meat And Vegetables With Tomato Sauce Sinaloa (Asado Placero Sinaloense)

Yield: Servings 6

The meat and vegetables

Ingredients:

- ¼ cup (65 ml) vegetable oil
- ½ cup (125 ml) cubed, cooked beets (not necessary)
- ½ cup (125 ml) mild vinegar
- ½ medium white onion, roughly cut
- 1 cup (250 ml) finely shredded cabbage, blanched in boiling water
- 1 pound (450 g) red bliss or other waxy potatoes, cut into ½-inch (1.5-cm) cubes
- 2 cups (500 ml) shredded lettuce
- 2 cups (500 ml) thinly cut white onion
- 2¼ pounds (1 kg) beef brisket, cut into ½-inch (1.5-cm) cubes
- 3 garlic cloves
- Salt

Directions:

1. Place the meat, roughly cut onion, garlic, and approximately 1 tablespoon salt into a big deep cooking pan and cover with water. Heat to a simmer and cook the beef until soft, approximately 45 minutes—time will differ tremendously, depending on the thickness of the piece of meat. Allow the meat cool off in the broth.
2. Cover the potatoes in a deep cooking pan with water, put in salt to taste, and boil until still slightly crunchy. Drain and cool slightly, then peel.
3. Place the thinly cut onion into the vinegar in a nonreactive container with the beets, if used, put in salt to taste, and leave to macerate.
4. Heat the oil and fry the meat and potatoes together until mildly browned, then tweak the seasoning and serve topped with the onion, cabbage, and lettuce. Pass the sauce separately.

The sauce

Ingredients:

- ½ teaspoon dried mexican oregano
- 1 garlic clove
- 1 serrano chile or any fresh, hot green chile
- 1¼ pounds (500 g) tomatoes
- Salt to taste

Directions:

Cover the tomatoes with boiling water and simmer until soft—about fifteen minutes. Drain, then blend with the garlic, chile, and salt until the desired smoothness is achieved. Put in the oregano and set aside, but keep warm.

Meatballs In Chipotle Sauce

Yield: Servings four to 6

Ingredients:

- ¼ teaspoon ground cumin
- ½ cup long grain white rice
- ½ cup whole milk
- 1 (14.5 ounce) can crushed fire roasted tomatoes

- 1 bay leaf
- 1 cup chicken broth
- 1 onion, chopped fine
- 1 tablespoon minced canned chipotle chile in adobo sauce
- 1 tablespoon minced fresh oregano or 1 teaspoon dried
- 1 tablespoon packed brown sugar
- 12 ounces 90 percent lean ground beef
- 12 ounces Mexican style chorizo sausage, casings removed
- 2 slices hearty white sandwich bread, torn into an inch pieces
- 2 tablespoons chopped fresh cilantro
- 2 tablespoons extra virgin olive oil
- 2 tablespoons red wine vinegar
- 3 garlic cloves, minced
- Salt and pepper

Directions:

1. Adjust oven rack to middle position and heat oven to 350 degrees. Bring 4 cups water to boil in medium deep cooking pan. Put in rice and 1 teaspoon salt and cook, stirring once in a while, for eight minutes. Drain rice in fine mesh strainer, wash with cold water, and drain again; set aside.

2. Heat oil in now empty deep cooking pan on moderate heat until it starts to shimmer Put in onion and cook until tender, approximately five minutes. Mix in garlic, oregano, and cumin and cook until aromatic, approximately half a minute. Mix in tomatoes, broth, vinegar, chipotle, sugar, and bay leaf and bring to simmer; move sauce to 13 by 9 inch baking dish.

3. Mash bread and milk to paste with fork in big container. Put in chorizo, ground beef, parcooked rice, 1 teaspoon pepper, and ½ teaspoon salt and mix with your hands until meticulously blended.

4. Pinch off and roll mixture into 16 meatballs (¼ cup each) and nestle into sauce. Ladle some sauce over meatballs, cover firmly with aluminium foil, and bake until meatballs are thoroughly cooked, approximately 1 hour.

5. Remove dish from oven and let meatballs rest in sauce, covered, for fifteen minutes. Move meatballs to serving platter. Discard bay leaf, skim any fat off surface of sauce,

and sprinkle with salt and pepper to taste. Pour sauce over meatballs, drizzle with cilantro, before you serve.

Mexican Style Picadillo

Yield: Servings four to 6

Ingredients:

- ¼ cup chopped fresh cilantro
- 1 jalapeño chile, stemmed, halved, and seeded
- 1 onion, cut into an inch pieces
- 1 pound 85 percent lean ground beef
- 1 red bell pepper, stemmed, seeded, and slice into an inch pieces
- 1 tablespoon vegetable oil
- 1½ pounds tomatoes, cored and quartered
- 1½ tablespoons chili powder
- 2 carrots, peeled and slice into an inch pieces
- 3 (6 inch) corn tortillas, torn into an inch pieces
- 3 garlic cloves, minced
- 6 ounces red potatoes, unpeeled, cut into an inch pieces
- Salt and pepper

Directions:

1. Pulse onion and bell pepper inside a food processor until broken down into rough ¼ inch pieces, approximately 12 pulses, scraping down sides of container as required; move mixture to container. Pulse potatoes and carrots in now empty food processor until broken down into rough ¼ inch pieces, approximately 12 pulses; move mixture to separate container. Process tomatoes, tortillas, jalapeño, and 1½ teaspoons salt in now empty food processor until the desired smoothness is achieved, approximately one minute.

2. Heat oil in 12 inch frying pan on moderate heat until it starts to shimmer Put in onion mixture and cook until tender, approximately five minutes. Mix in chili powder and garlic and cook until aromatic, approximately half a minute. Mix in ground beef and

cook, breaking up meat with wooden spoon, until no longer pink, approximately five minutes.

3. Mix in potato mixture and tomato mixture and bring to simmer. Cover, decrease the heat to low, and simmer gently, stirring once in a while, until potatoes and carrots are soft, approximately 30 minutes. Mix in cilantro and sprinkle with salt and pepper to taste and serve.

Oaxacan Style Beef Brisket

Yield: Servings 6

Ingredients:

- ¼ teaspoon ground cloves
- 1 (28 ounce) can diced tomatoes
- 1 (3½ pound) beef brisket, flat cut, fat trimmed to ¼ inch
- 1 cup chicken broth
- 1 tablespoon dried oregano
- 1 tablespoon vegetable oil
- 1 teaspoon ground coriander
- 2 onions, chopped
- 2 teaspoons dried thyme
- 2 teaspoons ground cumin
- 4 pasilla chiles, stemmed, seeded, and torn into ½ inch pieces (1 cup)
- 8 garlic cloves, peeled and smashed
- Salt and pepper

Directions:

1. Poke holes all over brisket with fork and rub with 1 tablespoon salt. Cover brisket using plastic wrap and place in your fridge for minimum 6 or maximum one day.
2. Adjust oven rack to lower middle position and heat oven to 325 degrees. Pat brisket dry using paper towels and flavor with pepper. Toast pasillas in 12 inch frying pan on moderate heat, stirring regularly, until aromatic, 2 to six minutes; move to container.

3. Heat oil in now empty frying pan over moderate high heat until just smoking. Lay brisket in frying pan, place heavy Dutch oven on top, and cook until thoroughly browned on both sides, approximately 4 minutes per side; move to platter.

4. Pour off all but 1 tablespoon fat from frying pan. Put in onions and cook on moderate heat until tender, about eight to ten minutes. Mix in garlic, oregano, cumin, thyme, coriander, cloves, and 1 teaspoon pepper and cook until aromatic, approximately one minute. Mix in broth, tomatoes and their juice, and toasted chiles, scraping up any browned bits, and bring to simmer. Move to 13 by 9 inch baking dish.

5. Nestle browned brisket, fat side up, into dish and spoon some sauce over top. Cover dish firmly with aluminium foil and bake until soft and fork easily slips in and out of meat, 3½ to 4 hours. Remove dish from oven and let brisket rest, covered, for an hour.

6. Move brisket to carving board and tent loosely using foil. Strain cooking liquid through fine mesh strainer into container; move solids to blender. Let liquid settle for five minutes, then skim fat from surface. Put in defatted liquid to blender and puree until the desired smoothness is achieved, approximately 2 minutes. Season sauce with salt and pepper to taste.

7. Slice brisket against grain into ¼ inch thick slices and return to baking dish. Pour sauce over top before you serve. (Brisket can be placed in your fridge for maximum 2 days; reheat, covered, in 350 degree oven for about forty-five minutes before you serve.)

Pork Chops Seasoned With Adobo Paste (Chuletas De Puerco Adobados)

Yield: Servings 6

Ingredients:

Seasoning

- ⅛ teaspoon cumin seeds, crushed
- ⅛ teaspoon dried mexican oregano
- ½ cup (125 ml) mild white vinegar or seville orange juice
- 1 tablespoon salt
- 2 garlic cloves
- 3 sprigs fresh thyme or ⅛ teaspoon dried

- 4 big ancho chiles, seeds and veins removed
- 6 thick shoulder pork chops
- Melted lard or pork fat for frying (barely sufficient to cover the bottom of the pan)

To serve

- 1½ cups (375 ml) thinly cut white onions
- Shredded lettuce
- Sliced radishes

Directions:

1. One day before you serve, toast the chiles lightly, turning them occasionally so that they do not burn.
2. Place the chiles into a container and cover them with hot water. Allow them to soak for approximately ten minutes, then remove using a slotted spoon and move to a blender jar. Put in the rest of the seasoning ingredients and blend into a quite smooth paste.
3. Have the butcher pound the chops to the thickness required. Spread them with the paste on both sides and set aside to season, placed in the fridge, overnight.
4. The next day, heat the fat and fry the chops very slowly on both sides until they are well cooked—about twenty minutes depending on the thickness of the meat. When they have thoroughly cooked, raise the heat and brown them swiftly.
5. Serve the chops instantly, topped with the cut onion, and garnish the plate with the radishes and lettuces.
6. Note: you can actually flavor the pork and keep it for quite a few days in your fridge. The meat tends to dry out, but the flavor improves daily.

Pork Chops With Chile Peanut Rice

Yield: Servings 4

Ingredients:

- ¼ cup chopped fresh cilantro
- ¼ teaspoon ground coriander
- ⅓ cup unsalted dry roasted peanuts, chopped

- 1 cup long grain white rice, washed
- 1 onion, chopped fine
- 1 tablespoon honey
- 1 tablespoon minced fresh oregano or 1 teaspoon dried
- 1 tablespoon tomato paste
- 1 teaspoon ancho chile powder
- 2 teaspoons grated lime zest plus 3 tablespoons juice (2 limes)
- 2½ cups chicken broth
- 3 garlic cloves, minced
- 3 tablespoons extra virgin olive oil
- 4 (6 to 8 ounce) boneless pork chops, ¾ to an inch thick, trimmed
- Pinch cayenne pepper
- Salt and pepper

Directions:

1. Mix 1¼ cups broth and rice in container, cover, and microwave until liquid is absorbed, approximately twelve minutes. Fluff rice with fork.
2. In the meantime, cut 2 slits, approximately 2 inches apart, through fat on edges of each chop. Pat chops dry using paper towels and sprinkle with salt and pepper. Heat 1 tablespoon oil in 12 inch frying pan over moderate high heat until just smoking. Brown chops until thoroughly browned on 1 side, approximately five minutes; move to plate.
3. Pour off all but 1 tablespoon fat from frying pan. Put in onion and cook until tender, approximately five minutes. Mix in garlic, tomato paste, oregano, chile powder, coriander, and cayenne and cook until aromatic, approximately half a minute. Mix in remaining 1¼ cups broth and microwaved rice, scraping up any browned bits, and bring to simmer.
4. Nestle chops browned side up into rice together with any collected juices. Cover, decrease the heat to moderate low, and simmer gently until pork records 145 degrees, rice is soft, and liquid is absorbed, six to eight minutes.
5. Move chops to carving board, tent with aluminium foil, and allow to rest for five to ten minutes. Lightly fold peanuts and 2 tablespoons cilantro into rice and sprinkle with salt and pepper to taste; cover to keep warm.
6. Whisk honey, lime zest and juice, remaining 2 tablespoons oil, remaining 2 tablespoons cilantro, and ⅛ teaspoon salt together in container. Slice chops into ½

inch thick slices. Move rice to platter, position pork over top, and spoon vinaigrette over pork and serve.

Pork Cooked In Orange Juice (Puerco En Naranja)

Yield: Servings 6 to 8

Ingredients:

- 12 peppercorns
- 2 teaspoons dried mexican oregano
- 3 oranges
- 5 garlic cloves
- 5 pounds (2.5 kg) rib-end pork loin (in two pieces, if required, to make up this weight)
- Salt to taste

Directions:

1. Pierce the meat all over with the point of a sharp knife. Crush the garlic, with the salt, oregano, and peppercorns, and moisten with the juice of 1 orange. Rub this mixture into the pork and set aside to season for an hour.
2. Preheat your oven to 350° f (180° c).
3. Put the pork in a heavy casserole into which it will just fit easily and moisten it with the juice of a second orange. Put in the skin of the orange to the casserole, then cover and bake for about two hours.
4. Drain off all but about 3 tablespoons of the pan juices and save for later. Flip the meat over and bake for one more hour, uncovered, coating the meat occasionally.
5. Drain off the pan juices again and save for later. Turn the oven up to 400° f (205° c) and brown the top of the meat, then flip it over and brown the other side.
6. In the meantime, skim the reserved pan juices of most of their fat. Put in the pan juices and the juice of the third orange and reduce swiftly over a high heat. Cut the meat and either pass the sauce separately or spoon it over the cut meat at the moment of serving.

Pork In Adobo Sauce (Puerco En Adobo)

Yield: Servings 6 to 8

Ingredients:

- ½ white onion, cut
- 1 pound (450 g) pork neck bones
- 1 tablespoon salt
- 2 garlic cloves
- 3½ to 4 pounds (1.5 to 1.8 kg) stewing pork with some fat, cut into 1½-inch (4-cm) cubes
- 8 peppercorns

The adobo

- ¼ teaspoon cumin seeds, crushed
- 10 pasilla chiles, seeds and veins removed
- 1-inch (2.5-cm) piece of cinnamon stick, crushed
- 2 tablespoons mild white vinegar
- 5 whole cloves, crushed
- 6 ancho chiles, seeds and veins removed
- 6 garlic cloves, roughly chopped
- 6 peppercorns, crushed
- 6 sprigs fresh marjoram or ¼ teaspoon dried
- 6 sprigs fresh thyme or ¼ teaspoon dried

The final stage

- ¼ cup (65 ml) lard
- 2 cups (500 ml) thinly cut white onion
- 2 mexican bay leaves
- 2 tablespoons granulated sugar
- 3 cups (750 ml) reserved meat broth
- Salt to taste

Directions:

1. Place the meat, bones, onion, garlic, peppercorns, and salt into a big deep cooking pan and barely cover with water. Bring the meat to its boiling point, then reduce the heat

and simmer it until it is just soft—about thirty-five minutes. Allow the meat cool in the broth.

2. Drain the meat, saving for later the broth. Set them aside.

3. Toast the chiles lightly, turning them occasionally so that they do not burn. Cover them with hot water and allow them to soak about ten minutes. Move the chiles to the blender with 1 cup (250 ml) of water. Put in the rest of the adobo ingredients and blend to a quite smooth texture.

4. Melt the lard in a big casserole. Put in the adobo sauce, bay leaves, and sugar to the dish and cook for approximately fifteen minutes, stirring most of the time to prevent sticking. Keep a splatterproof lid handy. When the sauce becomes a very dark red and thickens so that it will barely slide off a wooden spoon, it is cooked.

5. Slowly mix in the broth and put in salt as required. Put in the meat and carry on cooking the adobo using low heat for another ten minutes.

6. Serve topped with the onion rings.

Pork In Chatino Mole (Puerco En Mole Chatino)

Yield: Servings approximately 10

Ingredients:

The meat

- ½ medium white onion, roughly cut
- 1 big tomato, roughly cut
- 3½ pounds (1.575 kg) country-style pork ribs, cut into two-inch (5-cm) pieces
- 6 unpeeled garlic cloves
- Salt to taste

The sauce

- ¼ teaspoon cumin seeds, crushed
- ½ cup (125 ml) melted lard or vegetable oil
- 1 small white onion, cut into 6 pieces and toasted
- 1 tablespoon dried mexican oregano, or 2 tablespoons dried oaxacan oregano
- 2 cloves, crushed
- 2 ounces (60 g) pecan pieces (about ⅔ cup/165 ml), toasted

- 2 ounces (60 g) sesame seeds (about ½ cup/125 ml), toasted
- 2 ounces (60 g) whole unpeeled almonds (about 40), toasted
- 25 guajillo chiles, veins and seeds removed and toasted
- 28 chiles de árbol, toasted whole
- 3 sprigs fresh thyme or ¼ teaspoon dried
- 4 peppercorns, crushed
- 4½ ounces (125 g) hulled, raw pumpkin seeds (approximately 1 cup/250 ml), toasted
- 4½ ounces (125 g) raw, skinned peanuts (approximately 1 scant cup/225 ml), toasted
- 8 unpeeled garlic cloves, toasted
- 9 ounces (250 g) plum tomatoes, broiled
- Salt to taste

Directions:

1. Place the meat into a big deep cooking pan, then put in the tomato, onion, garlic, and salt. Cover well with water and set over moderate heat to come to a simmer. Continue simmering covered until the meat is just soft, then allow to cool in the broth. Drain the meat and save for later. You will require approximately 10 cups (2.5 l) of broth; make up to that amount with water if required.
2. Grind all the sauce ingredients, apart from the lard and tomatoes, to a crumbly paste consistency.
3. Heat the lard in a heavy, flameproof casserole, put in the ground ingredients, and fry on moderate heat, stirring all the time to prevent sticking, for approximately ten minutes. Combine the tomatoes, mix into the fried mixture in the pan, and cook for an extra five minutes. Slowly mix in the reserved broth and cook on moderate heat until it is well blended and the mole starts to thicken—it will splatter alarmingly at this stage. Examine for salt, then put in the meat and cook again for approximately ten minutes. The mole will be fairly thick and make a slim layer on the back of a wooden spoon.

Pork In Green Peanut Sauce (Puerco En Mole Verde De Cacahuate)

Yield: Servings 6

Ingredients:

The meat

- ⅓ cup (85 ml) roughly chopped white onion
- 2 garlic cloves, roughly chopped
- 2 teaspoons salt, or to taste
- 2¼ pounds (1 kg) pork, with some fat, cut into 1-inch (2.5-cm) cubes, or 3½ pounds (1.58 kg) country-style spareribs, in small pieces

The sauce

- ½ cup (125 ml) thinly cut white onion
- 1 cup (250 ml) raw peanuts (about 5 ounces/140 g shelled weight)
- 1 small bunch cilantro
- 2 garlic cloves
- 3 to 4 serrano chiles, or any fresh, hot green chile, roughly chopped, with seeds
- 4 tablespoons vegetable oil or pork lard
- 6 peppercorns, crushed
- 9 ounces (250 g) tomate verde, roughly chopped (about 2 cups/500 ml)

Directions:

1. Place the pork, chopped onion, garlic, and salt into a deep cooking pan, cover with water, bring to a simmer, and cook—about thirty minutes (much depending on quality and cut of meat). Drain the meat, saving for later the broth. There must be about 3¼ cups (815 ml) of broth. Reduce or make up to that amount with water.
2. Meanwhile, heat 1 tablespoon of the oil and fry the peanuts (or toast in a toaster oven), turning them continuously, until they are a golden brown. Crush and move to a blender jar. Put in the tomate verde, cilantro, peppercorns, chiles, garlic, and ¾ cup (185 ml) of the meat broth and blend until the desired smoothness is achieved (you may need slightly more broth, but make sure you don't make the sauce too watery).
3. Heat the rest of the 3 tablespoons of oil in a heavy pan and fry the pork and cut onion together until golden flipping the pieces continuously. Put in the mixed sauce and cook for a few minutes longer, stirring and scraping the bottom of the pan all the time. Put in roughly 2½ cups (625 ml) of the broth, then tweak the seasoning and simmer the stew for approximately twenty minutes, or until well seasoned. (you may need to

dilute the sauce further—it must be of a medium consistency, like thin cream—and it will become thick considerably as it cooks.)

4. Serve with sufficient the sauce and fresh, hot tortillas.

Pork In Red Chile (Carne De Puerco En Chile Colorado)

Yield: Servings 6

Ingredients:

- ⅛ teaspoon cumin seeds
- ¼ teaspoon dried mexican oregano
- 2 garlic cloves
- 2 tablespoons vegetable oil, roughly
- 2 teaspoons all-purpose flour
- 2 teaspoons salt, or to taste
- 2¼ pounds (1 kg) boneless pork, with some fat, cut into ½-inch (1.5-cm) cubes
- 3½ cups (875 ml) water, roughly
- 8 chiles de la tierra, or new mexican or californian chiles, including their seeds

Directions:

1. Place the meat, salt, and ¼ cup (65 ml) of the water into a large, heavy pan in which the meat will just fit in two layers. Cover the pan and cook using low heat, shaking the pan occasionally to stop sticking, until the meat is just soft, all the liquid absorbed, and the fat rendering out—about forty-five minutes, depending on the cut of meat and how soft it is. If it becomes too dry during the cooking time, then put in slightly more water.

2. Crush the garlic, cumin, and oregano in a molcajete or mortar. Cover the chiles with water in a small deep cooking pan, and simmer uncovered for approximately ten minutes, or until the skin is tender. Drain and move to a blender jar, together with 1 cup (250 ml) of the water and the crushed ingredients, and blend until the desired smoothness is achieved. Set aside.

3. Put in oil as required to the fat in the pan to make up to 3 tablespoons, roughly. Heat the oil and fry the meat lightly, flipping it over occasionally. Drizzle the flour over the meat and keep turning and frying until it browns slightly. Pass the chile sauce through

a strainer into the pan and fry for a few minutes longer, stirring and scraping the bottom of the pan. Put in the remaining 2 cups (500 ml) of water—the sauce must be rather thin—and cook for fifteen to twenty minutes more.

4. Serve in bowls, with lots of sauce and flour tortillas.

Pork In Veracruz Green Mole (Puerco En Mole Verde Veracruzano)

Yield: Servings 6

Ingredients:

The meat

- 4 pounds (1.8 kg) pork, if possible country-style spareribs

The vegetables

- ½ white onion, roughly cut
- 1 pound (450 g) chayote
- 1 pound (450 g) zucchini (about 3 medium)
- 1 tablespoon salt
- 10 soft shoots of chayote vine, cut into little lengths
- 2 garlic cloves
- 8 ounces (225 g) fava or lima beans
- 8 ounces (225 g) green beans
- 8 peppercorns

The sauce

- ¼ cup (65 ml) lard or vegetable oil
- 1 big sprig parsley
- 2 cups (500 ml) reserved broth
- 2 garlic cloves, roughly chopped
- 3 big romaine lettuce leaves
- 3 cups (750 ml) roughly chopped raw tomate verde
- 3 hoja santa leaves

- 4 sprigs fresh cilantro
- 6 serrano chiles, roughly chopped
- Salt to taste

Directions:

1. Have the meat cut up into serving pieces. Place them into a big deep cooking pan with the onion, garlic, peppercorns, and salt, cover with water, and bring to its boiling point. Reduce the heat and simmer for about twenty-five minutes.
2. Clean and trim the zucchini and cut them into four equivalent portions. Peel the chayote and remove the core, then cut into wedges about ½ inch (1.5 cm) thick. Trim the green beans and slice into halves. Put in the vegetables (except the limas) to the meat in the pan and cook for fifteen more minutes, or until both meat and vegetables are just soft. Do not overcook. Drain the meat and vegetables and set them aside. Cool and skim the broth and save for later.
3. Cook the lima beans separately and set them aside.
4. Combine the tomate verde, garlic, and chiles to a smooth sauce. Heat the lard in a deep pan and cook the sauce using high heat until it has reduced and thickened a little—about ten minutes. Put in the broth and carry on cooking the sauce a few minutes more.
5. Put in the meat and vegetables to the sauce and heat them through using low heat. Combine the parsley, cilantro, lettuce, and hoja santa until the desired smoothness is achieved and strain them into the mole at the final minute. Bring the mole just to its boiling point, put in salt as required, and serve instantly.
6. This mole is conventionally served with tortillas only.

Pork Stew (Guiso De Puerco)

Yield: Servings 6

Ingredients:

The meat

- 1 tablespoon salt
- 1½ cups (375 ml) thinly cut white onion
- 2 garlic cloves

- 4 pounds (1.8 kg) country-style spareribs, cut into 12 portions
- 6 peppercorns

The sauce

- ¼ cup (65 ml) lard
- ½-inch (1.5-cm) piece of cinnamon stick
- 1 big ripe plantain, peeled
- 1 heaped tablespoon slivered almonds
- 1 medium white onion, thinly cut
- 1 teaspoon salt
- 10 pitted green olives
- 1½ thick slices fresh pineapple, peeled
- 2 sprigs parsley
- 2 tablespoons raisins
- 2 teaspoons granulated sugar (not necessary)
- 2 to 3 cups (500 to 750 ml) reserved meat broth, roughly
- 2½ pounds (1.125 kg) tomatoes, roughly chopped (approximately seven cups/1.75 l)
- 3 garlic cloves, cut
- 4 whole cloves
- 4 whole serrano or güero chiles
- Salt as required
- Scant ¼ teaspoon dried mexican oregano, or ½ teaspoon dried oaxacan oregano

Directions:

1. Place the meat, with the salt, peppercorns, garlic, and onion, into a big pan, cover with cold water, and bring to its boiling point. Reduce the heat and simmer the meat covered until it is just soft—about thirty-five minutes. Set aside to cool in the broth.
2. Melt the lard in a cazuela or flameproof casserole and cook the onion and garlic until translucent.
3. Combine the tomatoes for a few seconds only and put in them to the onion and garlic in the pan. Cook using high heat until it has reduced and thickened—about ten minutes.
4. Chop the pineapple into little wedges. Chop the plantain into thick rounds. Put in them with the remaining ingredients to the sauce and cook over quite high heat for

fifteen minutes. By that time the sauce will have thickened considerably and be very well seasoned.

5. Strain the meat and put in it with the broth to the sauce and cook for an extra fifteen minutes using low heat. Put in salt as required. The sauce must be neither too watery nor too dry—you may need to put in a little extra broth.

Pork Tenderloin With Garlic Sauce

Yield: Servings 4

Ingredients:

- ¼ cup chopped fresh cilantro
- ¼ teaspoon red pepper flakes
- 1 tablespoon chopped fresh chives
- 10 garlic cloves, minced to paste
- 2 (twelve to 16 ounce) pork tenderloins, trimmed
- 2 tablespoons vegetable oil
- 2 tablespoons water
- 2 teaspoons packed light brown sugar
- 3 tablespoons lime juice (2 limes)
- 4 tablespoons unsalted butter, cut into 4 pieces and chilled
- Salt and pepper

Directions:

1. Adjust oven rack to middle position and heat oven to 400 degrees. Pat tenderloins dry using paper towels and sprinkle with salt and pepper. Heat 1 tablespoon oil in 12 inch frying pan over moderate high heat until just smoking. Brown tenderloins well on all sides, approximately ten minutes. Move tenderloins to rimmed baking sheet and roast in oven until pork records 145 degrees, ten to 16 minutes, turning pork midway through roasting.

2. In the meantime, mix garlic and water in container. Put in remaining 1 tablespoon oil and garlic mixture to now empty frying pan. Cook using frying pan's residual heat, scraping up any browned bits, until sizzling subsides, approximately 2 minutes. Put

frying pan using low heat and cook, stirring frequently, until garlic is sticky, about eight to ten minutes; turn off the heat and save for later.

3. Move tenderloins to carving board, tent with aluminium foil, and allow to rest for five to ten minutes. Stir sugar and pepper flakes into frying pan and cook on moderate heat until sticky and sugar is dissolved, approximately one minute. Mix in cilantro, lime juice, and chives and simmer until flavors meld, one to two minutes. Mix in any collected pork juices and simmer for a minute. Remove the heat, whisk in butter, 1 piece at a time. Sprinkle with salt and pepper to taste.

4. Slice tenderloins into ½ inch thick slices, position on serving platter or separate plates, and spoon sauce over top and serve.

Pork With Fresh Corn Tamales (Carne De Puerco Con Uchepos)

Yield: Servings 6

Ingredients:

The meat

- 2 teaspoons salt
- 4½ pounds (2 kg) country-style spareribs

The sauce

- 2 big garlic cloves
- 3 pounds (1.35 kg) tomatoes, broiled
- 4 serrano chiles, charred
- Salt to taste

To serve

- 1 cup (250 ml) thick sour cream
- 18 small uchepos
- 3 big chilacas or poblano chiles, charred, peeled, and slice into strips
- 8 ounces (225 g) queso fresco

Directions:

1. In a flameproof casserole, barely cover the meat with water, put in the salt, and bring to its boiling point. Carry on cooking the meat uncovered on moderate heat for approximately 30 minutes. Remove about 2 cups (500 ml) of the broth and save for later. Then carry on cooking the meat until it is just soft—about fifteen minutes more. Allow the fat render out of the meat and fry it until it is mildly browned (as for carnitas). Take away the meat and all but approximately four tablespoons of the fat.

2. In the meantime, prepare the tomato sauce. Combine the tomatoes with the chiles, garlic, and salt, to a smooth consistency. Put in the tomato sauce to the fat in the casserole and cook it using high heat for approximately 8 minutes, until it has reduced and thickened a little. Reduce the heat, put in the meat, and heat through gently.

3. Serve each portion of meat with two or three uchepos, or corundas, and sufficient sauce, some sour cream, strips of cheese, and finely shredded peeled chile.

Pork With Purslane (Puerco Con Verdolagas)

Yield: Servings 6

Ingredients:

- ¼ teaspoon dried mexican oregano
- ½ teaspoon cumin seeds
- 1 medium white onion, roughly cut
- 2 cups (500 ml) boiling water, roughly
- 2 cups (500 ml) thinly cut white onion
- 2 ounces (60 g) pork lard
- 2 pounds (900 g) purslane (approximately 16 cups/4 l)
- 4 cups (1 l) tomate verde, cooked and drained, saving for later 1 cup (250 ml) of the cooking water
- 4 to 6 jalapeño chiles or any fresh, hot green chiles, boiled with the tomate verde
- 4½ pounds (2 kg) country-style spareribs, cut into 1½-inch (4-cm) pieces
- 8 garlic cloves
- Salt to taste

Directions:

1. Place the meat into a big deep cooking pan and barely cover with water. Put in the roughly cut onion, 2 garlic cloves, and salt and bring to its boiling point. Reduce the heat and simmer until the meat is just soft—about forty minutes; do not overcook. Drain the meat, straining and reserving the broth. There must be minimum 3 cups (750 ml). Put in water if required or reduce to make up that amount.

2. Rinse the purslane. Take away the roots and very thick stems and cut the leaves and more soft stems roughly. Put roughly 2 cups (500 ml) of boiling water into a pan and put in the purslane and 1 teaspoon salt. Cover the pan, bring to its boiling point using high heat, and cook the purslane for approximately 3 minutes, flipping it over occasionally. Drain, discarding the cooking water, and save for later.

3. Combine the tomate verde and chiles with 1 cup (250 ml) of water in which they were cooked. Set aside.

4. In a big flameproof pan, melt the lard and fry the meat and thinly cut white onion together until the meat is mildly browned and the onion is soft flipping the pieces continuously.

5. Crush the rest of the garlic, cumin, and oregano together in a molcajete or mortar and put in to the meat frying in the pan. Take a little of the tomate verde puree to "wipe out" the seasoning in the mortar. Put in this and the rest of the tomate verde puree to the pan and fry a few minutes more, stirring occasionally to prevent sticking.

6. Put in the purslane to the pan with 3 cups (750 ml) of the reserved pork broth and simmer for about ten minutes longer. Adjust the seasoning before you serve with freshly made tortillas.

Pot Roast Leonor (Aguayón Estilo Leonor)

Yield: Servings 6

Ingredients:

- ¾ cup (185 ml) sesame seeds, toasted
- 12 ounces (340 g) tomatoes, roughly chopped (about 2 cups/500 ml)
- 2 garlic cloves, roughly chopped
- 2 teaspoons salt, or to taste
- 2½ cups (625 ml) water, roughly
- 2½ to 3 pounds (1.125 to 1.35 kg) beef pot roast, in one piece

- 3 pasilla chiles, wiped clean, seeds and veins removed
- 3 tablespoons vegetable oil
- 3 thick, crisply toasted rounds of french bread, crushed
- Freshly ground pepper

To serve

- 4 pasilla chiles, wiped clean and fried crisp
- Small, unskinned waxy potatoes, boiled

Directions:

1. Flavour the meat with salt and pepper. Heat the oil in a heavy dutch oven and brown the meat lightly all over. Remove from the oil and save for later.
2. Toast the chiles on a medium-hot griddle or comal; when they are cool they must be rather crunchy, but take care not to burn them or the sauce will have a bitter taste. Put 1 cup (250 ml) of the water into your blender and put in the tomatoes, the toasted chiles, sesame seeds, bread, and the garlic and blend until the desired smoothness is achieved. (you may need a little extra water but use only enough to loosen the blades of the blender.)
3. Fry the sauce over quite high heat while stirring and scraping the bottom of the pot, for approximately five minutes. Put in the meat and 1½ cups (375 ml) of water. Adjust the seasoning, then cover and cook over slow heat approximately four hours or until soft.
4. To serve, slice the meat rather thick, pour the sauce over, top with the fried pasilla chiles, and surround with the boiled potatoes.

Pot Roast Studded With Almonds And Bacon (Carne Claveteada)

Yield: Servings 6

Ingredients:

- ¼ teaspoon dried mexican oregano, or ½ teaspoon dried oaxacan oregano
- ½-inch (1.5-cm) piece of cinnamon stick, crushed
- ¾ cup (185 ml) water

- 1½ pounds (675 g) red bliss or new potatoes
- 1½ tablespoons mild vinegar
- 1½ tablespoons slivered almonds
- 3 big ancho chiles, seeds and veins removed
- 3 garlic cloves, roughly chopped
- 3 pounds (1.35 kg) brisket in one piece, trimmed of some of the fat
- 3 tablespoons lard or vegetable oil
- 3 whole cloves, crushed
- 4 peppercorns, crushed
- 6 sprigs fresh marjoram or ½ teaspoon dried
- 6 sprigs fresh thyme or ½ teaspoon dried
- 8 ounces (225 g) bacon or ham, cut into little pieces
- Salt to taste

Directions:

1. Preheat your oven to 325° f (165° c).
2. Pierce the meat all over using a knife point and insert the almonds and bacon. Set it aside while the sauce is prepared.
3. Toast the chiles lightly, turning them frequently so they won't burn. Place the chiles into a container, cover with hot water, and allow them to soak for approximately ten minutes.
4. Place the vinegar and water into your blender jar, put in the spices, herbs, and garlic, and blend as smoothly as you can. Put in the chiles and blend to a quite smooth consistency.
5. Heat the lard in a dutch oven and when it is super hot sear the meat well all over. Take away the meat and set it aside. Drain off the fat, leaving only 2 tablespoons in the pan. Put in the sauce to the pan and allow it to cook fast for approximately five minutes, stirring it all the time. Put in salt to taste.
6. Return the meat to the pan and coat it with the sauce. Cover the casserole with a firmly fitting lid and cook the meat in your oven for approximately 2 hours.
7. Place the potatoes, unskinned, into a deep cooking pan, cover them with boiling water, and let boil fast for five minutes. Drain them and set them aside to cool. When the potatoes are sufficiently cool to handle, skin.

8. Take away the casserole from the oven, flip the meat over, and coat it well with the sauce. Scrape the sauce from the sides and bottom of the pan and put in a little water if it has become thick excessively.

9. Place the potatoes into the sauce around the meat, replace the lid, and allow the meat to cook until it is super soft but not falling apart—test after 1 hour and ten minutes.

10. Cut the meat quite thick and place it on a serving dish with the potatoes around it. Pour the sauce over it.

Pumpkin Cooked With Pork (Calabaza Guisada Con Puerco)

Yield: Servings 6

Ingredients:

The meat

- ¼ small white onion, roughly chopped
- 2 garlic cloves, roughly chopped
- 2 teaspoons salt
- 2½ pounds (1 kg) country-style spareribs, cut into 1½-inch (4-cm) cubes

The sauce

- ⅛ teaspoon cumin seeds, crushed
- 1 ancho chile
- 1 medium-size, very ripe plantain (approximately eight ounces/225 g), skinned and slice into ½-inch (1.5-cm) rounds
- 1 pound (450 g) small green pumpkin or zucchini, trimmed and slice into ½-inch (1.5-cm) cubes
- 1 thick slice fresh pineapple, peeled and cut into little pieces
- 1½ cups (375 ml) fresh corn kernels
- 1½ tablespoons vegetable oil
- 2 small garlic cloves, finely chopped
- 2 tablespoons finely chopped white onion

- 6 ounces (180 g) tomatoes, finely chopped (approximately 1 cup/250 ml)
- Salt to taste

Directions:

1. Place the pork into a big deep cooking pan, with the salt, onion, and garlic, and barely cover with water. Bring to its boiling point, then reduce the heat and simmer uncovered until just soft—about forty-five minutes. Drain the meat, saving for later the broth. You will require 2 cups.

2. Heat the oil in a large, heavy pan and fry the onion and garlic until translucent. Put in the tomatoes and carry on frying using high heat, stirring to stop sticking, until mixture is slightly reduced, approximately 4 minutes. Put in the pumpkin, corn kernels, pineapple, and 2 cups (500 ml) of the pork broth. Cover the pan and cook on moderate heat, stirring occasionally, for approximately ten minutes—the zucchini, if you're using it, and corn must be just soft.

3. Slit open the ancho chile, remove the seeds and veins, cover with hot water, and cook for five minutes. Move the chile to a blender jar, together with ⅓ cup (85 ml) of water and the cumin. Blend until the desired smoothness is achieved.

4. Put in the plantain, the mixed chile, and the meat to the sauce, adjust the salt, and simmer for approximately fifteen minutes longer.

5. Serve with fresh hot tortillas.

Shredded Savory Pork (Tinga Poblana Con Carne De Puerco)

Yield: enough for approximately twelve tostadas

Ingredients:

- ⅛ teaspoon dried mexican oregano
- ⅓ cup (85 ml) roughly cut white onion
- ½ teaspoon salt, or to taste
- 1 pound (450 g) boneless stewing pork, cut into 1-inch (2.5-cm) cubes
- 1 pound (450 g) tomatoes, finely chopped (about 2⅔ cups/665 ml)
- 2 mexican bay leaves
- 2 tablespoons liquid or sauce from the canned chiles

- 3 canned chipotle chiles en vinagre, or en adobo, cut into strips
- 3 sprigs fresh thyme or ⅛ teaspoon dried
- 8 ounces (225 g) chorizos

To serve

- 1 avocado, thinly cut
- 1 cup (250 ml) shredded lettuce

Directions:

1. Cover the pork cubes with water, put in salt, and bring to its boiling point, then reduce the heat and simmer until soft—about forty minutes. Allow the pork cool in the broth for a short period, then drain, saving for later the broth, and shred the meat fine.
2. Skin the chorizos, crumble the meat into a frying pan, and cook using low heat until the fat has rendered out. Take away the chorizo pieces from the pan and save for later.
3. Take out all except 2 tablespoons of the fat in the pan. Put in the tomatoes and onion to the pan and fry over quite high heat for approximately five minutes, stirring the mixture well and scraping the bottom of the pan occasionally. Put in the shredded pork, fried chorizo, thyme, oregano, bay leaves, chiles, liquid or sauce from the chile can, and ½ cup (125 ml) of the reserved broth to the tomato sauce. Adjust the seasoning and allow the mixture to cook and season for approximately ten minutes, stirring it well occasionally. It must be moist, not juicy.
4. Use as a topping for tostadas, topping with the avocado and shredded lettuce.

Sonoran Country Steaks (Bisteces Rancheros Sonorenses)

Yield: Servings 6

Ingredients:

- ¼ cup (65 ml) vegetable oil
- 1 big garlic clove, crushed
- 1 pound (450 g) red bliss or waxy new potatoes
- 2 cups (500 ml) thinly cut white onion
- 2 pounds (900 g) tomatoes

- 3 anaheim chiles, charred, peeled, seeds and veins removed
- 6 shoulder or chuck steaks, approximately ¼ inch/.75 cm thick (about 2 pounds/ 900 g)
- 8 whole sprigs cilantro
- Salt and pepper to taste
- Salt to taste

Directions:

1. Flavour the steaks on both sides with garlic, salt, and pepper and set aside for approximately 1 hour.
2. Preheat your oven to 350° f (180° c).
3. Heat 2 tablespoons of the oil in a frying pan. Swiftly brown the steaks on both sides, putting in more oil as required. Put them in a single layer on a shallow ovenproof dish, set aside, and keep warm.
4. Allow the oil to cool a little, then put in the onion and cook it gently, without browning, until it is translucent.
5. Cut a slice off the top of each tomato. Grate the flesh on a coarse grater until only the flattened skin is left in your hand. Do not forget to grate the flesh from the top slices.
6. Put in the tomato pulp, cilantro, and salt to the onion in the pan and allow the sauce to cook fast over quite high heat for five minutes. Stir occasionally to stop sticking.
7. Peel and slice the potatoes about ¼ inch (.75 cm) thick. Put the slices on top of the steaks. Pour the sauce over the meat and potatoes.
8. Chop the chiles into thin strips, put the strips on top of the sauce, cover the dish, and bake for a little more than half an hour. Bake, uncovered, for another thirty-five minutes, by which time the sauce must be reduced and the potatoes just starting to brown.

Spicy Grilled Beef And Chorizo Kebabs

Yield: Servings four to 6

Ingredients:

- ¼ teaspoon ground cumin
- ½ teaspoon garlic powder
- 1 big red onion, cut into an inch pieces, 3 layers thick

- 1 pound Mexican style chorizo sausage, cut into 2 inch lengths
- 1 pound sirloin steak tips, trimmed and slice into 2 inch pieces
- 1 tablespoon minced fresh oregano or 1 teaspoon dried
- 2 tablespoons chopped fresh cilantro
- 3 tablespoons extra virgin olive oil
- 4 jalapeño chiles, stemmed, halved, seeded, and slice into an inch pieces
- Lime wedges
- Salt and pepper

Directions:

1. Lightly toss onion and jalapeños with 1 tablespoon oil in container. Cover vegetables and microwave until just soft, three to five minutes. In big container, mix oregano, garlic powder, ½ teaspoon salt, ¼ teaspoon pepper, cumin, and remaining 2 tablespoons oil. Put in steak and toss to coat. Thread steak, chorizo, onion, and jalapeños firmly onto four 12 inch metal skewers in alternating pattern.
2. 2A. FOR A CHARCOAL GRILL: Open bottom vent fully. Light big chimney starter filled with charcoal briquettes (6 quarts). When top coals are partly covered with ash, pour uniformly over grill. Set cooking grate in place, cover, and open lid vent fully. Heat grill until hot, approximately five minutes. FOR A GAS GRILL: Set all burners to high, cover, and heat grill until hot, approximately fifteen minutes. Leave all burners on high.
3. Clean and oil cooking grate. Put kebabs on grill and cook (covered if using gas), turning as required, until thoroughly browned and meat records 130 to 135 (for medium), ten to fifteen minutes. Move kebabs to serving platter, tent loosely with aluminium foil, and allow to rest for five to ten minutes. Drizzle with cilantro and serve with lime wedges.

The Devil's Pants (Calzones Del Diablo)

Yield: Servings four to 6

Ingredients:

- 1 allspice
- 1 ancho chile, veins and seeds removed
- 1 bay leaf, mexican if possible

- 1 big scallion with some of the green top, or 1 small white onion cut into thick slices
- 1 garlic clove
- 1 whole clove
- 2 ounces (60 g) sesame seeds (about ⅔ cup/165 ml)
- 2 peppercorns
- 2 slices french bread approximately 1 inch (2.5 cm) thick
- 2 sprigs fresh marjoram or ⅛ teaspoon dried
- 2 sprigs fresh thyme or ⅛ teaspoon dried
- 2¼ pounds (1 kg) country-style ribs, cut into two-inch (5-cm) cubes
- 3 tablespoons pork lard or vegetable oil
- 4 chiles serranos en escabeche (should not be too hot)
- 4 plum tomatoes
- Salt to taste

Directions:

1. In a deep pan, cover the pork with water, put in salt, and cook covered on moderate heat until soft but not soft—about forty minutes. Drain, saving for later the broth. Cool and skim, saving for later the fat.
2. In an ungreased frying pan, toast the sesame seeds until a deep gold color, ensuring not to burn them. Cool and then grind to a textured powder in an electric coffee/spice grinder.
3. Melt 2 tablespoons of the lard in a frying pan, flatten out the ancho chile, and fry for a few seconds until the inside turns a light brown. Drain, tear into pieces, and put into your blender jar. In the same fat fry the scallion, garlic, chiles, and whole tomatoes for approximately 1 minute or until the scallion is translucent. Move to the blender jar. Put in the remaining lard to the pan and fry the bread until crunchy on the outside; crumble into your blender jar. Put in 1 cup (250 ml) of the reserved broth and blend until quite smooth.
4. Put 2 tablespoons of the fat from the broth into a flameproof casserole, put in the mixed ingredients and the ground seeds, and fry on moderate heat, stirring and scraping the bottom of the pan to prevent sticking, for approximately five minutes. Put in the meat and the remaining ingredients (whole), together with the rest of the broth and cook using low heat for ten more minutes. Adjust seasoning. The sauce must be of medium consistency and thinly cover the back of a wooden spoon.

Tongue In Oaxacan Sauce (Estofado De Lengua)

Yield: Servings 6 to 8

Ingredients:

- 1 small white onion, roughly chopped
- 3 garlic cloves, roughly chopped
- 8 peppercorns
- A 5-pound (2.25-kg) fresh beef tongue
- Salt to taste

The sauce

- ⅛ teaspoon dried mexican oregano, or ¼ teaspoon dried oaxacan oregano
- ½ cup (125 ml) pitted green olives
- ½ cup (125 ml) tongue broth or water
- ½-inch (1.5-cm) piece of cinnamon stick, crushed
- 1 small dry tortilla, broken into pieces
- 2 ancho chiles, wiped clean, seeds and veins removed
- 2 ounces (60 g) unskinned almonds—a good ⅓ cup (85 ml)
- 2 pounds (900 g) tomatoes, finely chopped (about 5⅓ cups/1.3 l)
- 2 tablespoons sesame seeds
- 6 sprigs fresh marjoram or ½ teaspoon dried
- 6 sprigs fresh thyme or ½ teaspoon dried
- 6 tablespoons lard or vegetable oil
- Salt to taste

Directions:

1. Place the tongue into a deep cooking pan with the onion, garlic, peppercorns, and salt. Cover with water and bring to its boiling point. Reduce the heat and simmer until the tongue is soft—about three hours. Allow the tongue cool in the broth, and the moment it is sufficiently cool to handle, remove and discard the skin. Strain the broth and return the tongue to the broth. Keep warm.

2. Toast the sesame seeds in a frying pan over low heat while stirring them and shaking the pan occasionally until they are a deep golden color—take care not to allow them to burn—about five minutes.

3. Heat 3 tablespoons of the lard in a small frying pan and fry the chiles on moderate heat for approximately ½ minute on each side—the inside flesh should turn the color of tobacco. Drain and save for later.

4. In the same lard, fry the almonds on moderate heat, turning them and shaking the pan until they turn a darker color. Drain and crush them well (so as not to strain the blender).

5. In the same lard, fry the tortilla pieces for a few minutes until crunchy. Drain and save for later.

6. Place the ½ cup (125 ml) tongue broth or water into your blender jar, put in the dried herbs and spices, and blend as smooth as you can. Slowly put in the chiles, tomatoes, sesame seeds, almonds, and tortillas, blending meticulously after each addition.

7. Heat the rest of the 3 tablespoons lard in a heavy pan, put in the sauce, and cook on moderate heat for approximately ten minutes, stirring and scraping the bottom of the pan occasionally to prevent sticking. Mix in salt to taste. The sauce must be of medium consistency and lightly cover the back of a wooden spoon. Put in broth to dilute if required.

8. Drain the tongue and slice into thick slices. Position on a big platter in one slightly overlapping layer and cover with most of the sauce. Drizzle the top with the olives and serve instantly. Pass the remaining sauce separately.

Veracruz Pork Roast (Asado De Puerco A La Veracruzana)

Yield: Servings 6 to 8

Ingredients:

- ½ cup (250 ml) water, roughly
- 1 tablespoon salt
- 3 tablespoons fresh lime juice
- 4 morita chiles, or 1 chipotle or 1 mora
- 4 whole allspice, crushed
- 5 pounds (2.5 kg) pork roast on the bone, if possible butt

- 6 ancho chiles, seeds and veins removed
- 6 garlic cloves
- banana leaves sufficient to wrap the roast in a twofold layer (optional;)

Directions:

1. Pierce the meat all over with the point of a sharp knife. Mash the garlic with the salt and moisten with the lime juice. Rub this mixture meticulously into the roast and set aside to season while preparing the chile mixture.
2. Lightly toast the ancho chiles on a hot griddle or comal. Cover them with hot water, put in the whole, untoasted morita chiles, and simmer for five minutes. Remove the heat and leave the chiles to soak for five minutes longer. Drain the chiles.
3. Move the chiles to a blender jar with the water. Put in the allspice and blend until the desired smoothness is achieved. Put in slightly more water only if required to release the blades of the blender.
4. Coat the meat liberally with the chile paste. Hold the banana leaf over a hot heat until it softens and wrap it around the meat. Allow the meat season overnight in your fridge. (if you are not using the banana leaf, simply leave the meat unwrapped.)
5. Preheat your oven to 325° f (165° c).
6. Put the meat in a dutch oven or casserole with a firmly fitting lid and bake for about two hours, by the end of which time there must be sufficient juices at the bottom of the casserole. Take away the lid and carry on cooking the meat, coating it occasionally, for approximately 1 hour longer, or until tender.
7. Serve hot, with fresh corn tortillas.

Yucatán Style Barbecued Pork

Yield: Servings 8

Ingredients:

- ¼ cup orange juice
- ¼ teaspoon ground cloves
- ½ cup plus 2 tablespoons lime juice (5 limes)
- 1 (4 to 5 pound) boneless pork butt roast, trimmed and quartered
- 1 tablespoon dried oregano

- 1 tablespoon minced canned chipotle chile in adobo sauce
- 1 teaspoon ground cumin
- 2 cups wood chips
- 2 tablespoons annatto powder
- 2 teaspoons ground cinnamon
- 3 garlic cloves, minced
- Salt and pepper

Directions:

1. Mix ½ cup lime juice, orange juice, annatto powder, chipotle, garlic, oregano, 1 tablespoon salt, 2 teaspoons pepper, cinnamon, cumin, and cloves in 1 gallon zipper lock bag. Put pork in bag, press out as much air as you can, and seal. Turn bag to spread marinade, then place in your fridge pork for minimum 1 hour or maximum 2 hours, turning once in a while.

2. Immediately before grilling, soak wood chips in water for fifteen minutes, then drain. Using big piece of heavy duty aluminium foil, wrap soaked chips in foil packet and cut several vent holes in top.

3. 3A. FOR A CHARCOAL GRILL: Open bottom vent midway. Light big chimney starter three quarters filled with charcoal briquettes (4½ quarts). When top coals are partly covered with ash, pour into steeply banked pile against side of grill. Put wood chip packet on coals. Set cooking grate in place, cover, and open lid vent midway. Heat grill until hot and wood chips are smoking, approximately five minutes. A GAS GRILL: Remove cooking grate and place wood chip packet directly on primary burner. Set grate in place, turn all burners to high, cover, and heat grill until hot and wood chips are smoking, approximately fifteen minutes. Turn primary burner to moderate high and turn off other burner(s). (Adjust primary burner as required to maintain grill temperature around 325 degrees.)

4. Clean and oil cooking grate. Remove pork from marinade and pat dry using paper towels; discard marinade. Put pork on cooler side of grill, cover (position lid vent over meat if using charcoal), and cook for an hour. During final twenty minutes of grilling, adjust oven racks to upper middle (at least 6 inches below broiler) and lower middle positions and heat oven to 325 degrees. Coat rimmed baking sheet using foil.

5. Move pork to readied sheet, cover using foil, and crimp edges firmly to secure. Roast pork on lower rack in oven until fork slips easily in and out of meat, one to 2 hours.

6. Remove top layer of foil and place sheet on upper rack. Turn on broiler and broil pork until thoroughly browned and crunchy in spots, 5 to ten minutes. Move pork to cutting board and allow to cool slightly. Use two forks to shred into bite size pieces; discard surplus fat. Toss shredded pork with remaining 2 tablespoons lime juice in container. Sprinkle with salt and pepper to taste and serve.

PICKLED ONIONS AND JALAPEÑOS

Yield: 2 CUPS

- ¼ cup distilled white vinegar
- ¼ cup lime juice (2 limes)
- 1 teaspoon salt
- 2 red onions, halved and cut thin
- 2 teaspoons sugar
- 4 jalapeño chiles, stemmed and cut thin

Directions:

1. Mix onions and jalapeños in big container. Bring lime juice, vinegar, sugar, and salt to boil in small deep cooking pan.
2. Pour vinegar mixture over onion mixture and allow it to sit for minimum 30 minutes, or place in your fridge for maximum 2 days.

Yucatecan Pit-Barbecued Pig (Cochinita Pibil)

Yield: Servings 6

Ingredients:

One day ahead

- ⅛ teaspoon powdered chile seco yucateco (optional;) or hot paprika
- ¼ teaspoon cumin seeds
- ¼ teaspoon dried mexican oregano, yucatecan if possible
- ½ cup (125 ml) cold water
- 1 heaped tablespoon achiote seeds
- 12 peppercorns

- 2 big pieces of banana leaf
- 2 tablespoons seville orange juice or substitute
- 3 tablespoons seville orange juice or substitute, or mild white vinegar
- 3 teaspoons salt
- 3 whole allspice
- 3½ to 4½ pounds (1.5 to 2 kg) pork, if possible rib end of loin, with fat
- 4 garlic cloves

Directions:

1. The day before you serve, pierce the pork all over and rub in 2 teaspoons of the salt and the juice. Set aside while preparing the seasoning paste.
2. In an electric spice grinder, grind the achiote seeds, cumin, oregano, peppercorns, and allspice together until thoroughly powdered. Pass through a fine strainer and grind the debris one more time.
3. Crush the garlic with the chile seco, remaining 1 teaspoon salt, and seville orange juice and mix in the other powdered spices. The mixture should resemble a thick paste. Smear the paste all over the pork.
4. Lightly sear the banana leaves over a bare flame to make them more flexible. Cover the meat up in them and leave to season in your fridge for minimum 6 hours or overnight.
5. Preheat your oven to 325° f (165° c).
6. Put a rack at the bottom of the dutch oven and set the wrapped meat on it. Put in the water and cover the dish with a firmly fitting lid. Cook for 2½ hours. Flip the meat and coat it well with the juices at the bottom of the dish. Cook for an extra 2½ hours, or until the meat is tender and falling off the bone.

THE SAUCE

- ½ cup (125 ml) very finely chopped purple onion
- ½ teaspoon salt
- ⅔ cup (165 ml) seville orange juice or substitute
- 3 habanero chiles, very finely chopped
- *Directions:*

1. In the meantime, make the sauce. Mix all the ingredients together. Set aside to season for approximately 2 hours.

2. To serve, shred the meat roughly. Pour the fat and juices from the pan over it. Serve hot, with tortillas and the sauce in a separate dish so that each person can make his own tacos.

Yucatecan Pork Pieces (Lomitos)

Yield: Servings 6

Ingredients:

- ½ green bell pepper, finely chopped
- ⅔ cup (165 ml) finely chopped white onion
- 1 small head of garlic, unpeeled
- 1 tablespoon simple recado rojo
- 1 whole habanero chile or any fresh, hot green chile
- 12 ounces (340 g) tomatoes, finely chopped (approximately 1¾ cups/435 ml)
- 2 pounds (900 g) boneless pork, cut into ½-inch (1.5-cm) cubes
- 2 tablespoons seville orange juice or substitute
- 2 tablespoons vegetable oil or pork lard
- 2 teaspoons salt
- 2 to 2½ cups (500 to 625 ml) cold water, roughly

Directions:

1. Dilute the recado rojo with the orange juice and rub it into the pieces of meat. Set aside for approximately 30 minutes to season.
2. Heat the oil in a frying pan and fry the tomatoes, pepper, and onion together over quite high heat while stirring well and scraping the bottom of the pan occasionally, for approximately ten minutes. Put in the salt and save for later.
3. Toast the whole head of garlic on a griddle or comal, turning it occasionally, until it is browned on the outside and the cloves inside are quite tender. Toast the habanero chile.
4. Place the meat into a large, heavy deep cooking pan with the water, which should barely cover the meat. Put in the tomato mixture and the toasted, unpeeled garlic and chile and bring to its boiling point. Reduce the heat and simmer the meat, uncovered,

until it is soft—approximately 1 hour. (the sauce must be of a medium consistency; if it appears to be too watery, turn the heat higher and reduce swiftly.) Serve hot.

Seafood

Mexico has a huge coastline, and is home to some the best seafood on this planet. Below are a few of my personaly favourites that you should probably try out!

ARROZ CON CAMARONES

Yield: Servings four to 6

Ingredients:

- 1 (14.5 ounce) can diced tomatoes
- 1 green bell pepper, stemmed, seeded, and chopped
- 1 tablespoon black peppercorns
- 1 tablespoon minced fresh oregano or ¾ teaspoon dried
- 1½ pounds extra big shrimp (21 to 25 per pound), peeled and deveined, shells reserved
- 2 bay leaves
- 2 cups long grain white rice
- 2 onions, chopped
- 4 cups water
- 4 guajillo chiles, stemmed, seeded, and torn into ½ inch pieces (½ cup)
- 5 garlic cloves, minced
- 5 sprigs fresh cilantro plus 2 tablespoons minced
- 6 tablespoons extra virgin olive oil
- Lime wedges
- Pinch cayenne pepper
- Salt and pepper

Directions:

1. Heat 1 tablespoon oil in big deep cooking pan on moderate heat. Put in shrimp shells, 1 cup onion, guajillos, and 1 teaspoon salt and cook, stirring once in a while, until shells are spotty brown, approximately ten minutes. Put in water, peppercorns, cilantro sprigs, and bay leaves, increase heat to high, and bring to boiling point.

Decrease the heat to low, cover, and simmer for half an hour Strain shrimp stock through fine mesh strainer into big liquid measuring cup; you should have 3 cups stock. (If you have extra, reserve for future use.)

2. In the meantime, whisk 2 tablespoons oil, half of garlic, cayenne, and ½ teaspoon pepper together in big container. Put in shrimp and toss to coat. Cover and place in your fridge for half an hour

3. Heat remaining 3 tablespoons oil in Dutch oven on moderate heat until it starts to shimmer Put in bell pepper, remaining onion, and ½ teaspoon salt and cook until vegetables start to tenderize, five to seven minutes. Mix in rice, remaining garlic, and oregano and cook until aromatic and rice is translucent, approximately 2 minutes. Mix in tomatoes and their juice and 3 cups shrimp stock. Bring to boil, then decrease the heat to low, cover, and cook for about twenty minutes.

4. Nestle shrimp attractively into rice, in concentric circles, with tails sticking up out of rice. Cover and cook until shrimp are opaque, about eight to ten minutes. Remove pot from heat and allow it to sit, covered, until shrimp are thoroughly cooked, approximately five minutes. Drizzle with minced cilantro and serve with lime wedges.

BROILED FISH SEASONED WITH ACHIOTE (PESCADO EN TIKIN XIK)

Yield: Servings 6

Ingredients:

- ¼ cup (65 ml) olive oil
- 2 groupers or red snappers, approximately 2½ pounds (1.125 kg) each

The seasoning paste

- ¼ cup (65 ml) seville orange juice or mild white vinegar
- ¼ teaspoon dried mexican oregano, yucatecan if possible, toasted
- ¼ teaspoon peppercorns, crushed
- ¼ teaspoon powdered chile seco or árbol
- 1 tablespoon achiote seeds, crushed
- 3 garlic cloves, roughly chopped

- Salt to taste

To serve

- Habanero chiles, chopped
- Pickled Onions, chopped
- Sliced avocado
- Sliced seville oranges
- Sliced tomatoes
- Toasted mexican oregano

Directions:

1. *Do not have the scales removed from the fish.* Have the heads and tails removed and the fish opened out flat in one piece. Take away the backbone.
2. Grind and blend all the ingredients for the seasoning paste to a smooth consistency. Spread the paste, not too thickly, over the flesh (opened side of the fish) and set aside to season for approximately 2 hours.
3. Brush the seasoned side of the fish with the oil and cook it, seasoned side down, over the charcoal or under the broiler for five to 8 minutes. Turn the fish over and cook it on the skin side for a slightly longer period or until flesh is just thoroughly cooked—about fifteen minutes, depending on the thickness of the fish.
4. Serve hot with fresh tortillas.

BROILED FISH SEASONED WITH CHILE PASTE (PESCADO ENCHILADO)

Yield: Servings 6

Ingredients:

- ⅓ to ½ cup (85 to 125 ml) mild vinegar
- 1 4-pound (1.8-kg) red snapper or grouper, gutted but scales, head, and tail left on
- 2 teaspoons salt, or to taste
- 3 garlic cloves
- 3 tablespoons vegetable oil

- 4 ancho chiles, seeds and veins removed
- 4 piquín chiles, left whole

Directions:

1. Cover the ancho chiles with boiling water and allow them to soak until soft—about five minutes. Drain the chiles, then move to a blender jar. Put in the piquín chiles (whole), garlic, salt, and vinegar and blend until the desired smoothness is achieved. (the mixture must be like a thick paste. If any more liquid is needed to release the blades of the blender, use a minimum amount of water.)
2. Broil the fish for a short period of time on both sides, unseasoned, and strip off the skin. Spread the outside of the fish with the chile paste, then coat with the oil and broil until thoroughly cooked—ten to fifteen minutes on each side depending on the thickness of the fish.
3. Serve instantly, with hot, freshly made tortillas.

CRABS IN A CHILE AND TOMATO BROTH (JAIBAS EN CHILPACHOLE)

Yield: Servings 6

Ingredients:

- ½ big white onion, thickly cut and broiled
- 1 ancho chile, seeds and veins removed
- 1 pound (450 g) tomatoes, broiled
- 1½ quarts (1.5 l) boiling, salted water
- 12 live female crabs
- 2 jalapeño chiles, broiled
- 3 big sprigs epazote
- 3 tablespoons olive oil
- 6 garlic cloves, broiled and peeled

Directions:

1. If you dare, scrub the crabs well in cold water, and drop them into the pan with the boiling water. Allow them to cook for no more than three minutes. Remove all but 2 of the crabs and allow to cool. Boil the rest of the crabs for about ten minutes, then discard them.

2. When sufficiently cool to handle, remove the bell-shaped piece of the shell, and pry off the back shell. Scrape out the orange eggs, if any, and pry out any fat lurking in the extreme points of the shell and reserve in a small container. Take away the spongy gills and grind them until a paste is achieved with the eggs and fat in a molcajete or blender. Reserve.

3. Cut each crab in half and crack the claws. Reserve. Return the shells and debris to the pan and allow them to simmer for approximately ten minutes.

4. Strain the broth through a twofold thickness of cheesecloth and return to the pan, discarding all the debris. There must be about 5½ cups (1.375 l) broth. If not, put in water to make up to that amount.

5. Put 1 cup (250 ml) of the reserved crab broth into your blender jar, put in the ancho chile pieces, onion, garlic, tomatoes, and chiles, and blend to a slightly textured consistency.

6. Heat the oil in a frying pan and fry the sauce using high heat, stirring occasionally to prevent sticking, until reduced and seasoned—about five minutes. Put into the broth in the pan and simmer for approximately five minutes. Put in the paste of fat and eggs and simmer for a few minutes more. Then put in the crabs, including the claws, and epazote and simmer again for yet another five minutes.

7. Serve in deep bowls with french bread or rolls.

FISH AND SHRIMP SAUSAGE (RELLENO DE GUAVINO)

Yield: 4 feet (1.25 m) sausage

Ingredients:

- 1 pound (450 g) fish, cut in ½-inch (1.5-cm) slices, skin and bone removed and reserved
- 8 ounces (225 g) raw shrimps, cleaned and deveined, shells reserved

The broth

- 1 celery rib, roughly chopped
- 1 tablespoon fresh lime juice
- 2 bay leaves, mexican if possible
- 2 small carrots, scraped and cut
- 2 sprigs flat-leaf parsley
- 2 teaspoons salt, or to taste
- 3 sprigs fresh thyme, or ⅛ teaspoon dried
- 4 cups (1 l) water
- 6 peppercorns

The sausage

- ¼ cup (65 ml) finely chopped white onion
- ⅔ cup (165 ml) peas
- 1 jalapeño chile or any fresh, hot green chile, finely chopped
- 1 medium carrot, scraped, diced small, and partly cooked
- 1 medium waxy potato, peeled, diced small, and partly cooked
- 1 tablespoon fresh lime juice
- 1 teaspoon salt, or to taste
- 1½ tablespoons finely chopped fresh parsley
- 4½ feet (1.35 m) sausage casings (not plastic), roughly
- 6 ounces (180 g) tomatoes, finely chopped (1 scant cup/250 ml)
- 6 tablespoons olive oil, roughly
- Freshly ground black pepper

To serve

- ¼ cup (65 ml) drained, chopped big capers
- ¼ cup (65 ml) pitted, chopped green olives

Directions:

1. Place the fish and shrimps into the freezer and leave for approximately 2 hours or until half frozen. Prepare the broth. Place the debris from the fish and shrimps into a wide deep cooking pan, with the remaining broth ingredients. Bring to its boiling point

and simmer for approximately forty minutes. Strain the broth and return to the deep cooking pan.

2. Place the fish and shrimps, a small quantity at a time to stop the blades from clogging, into a blender jar or food processor and grind until fine. Combine the fish paste with the remaining sausage ingredients, using only 2 tablespoons of the oil. Fry one spoonful of the mixture now for taste, then tweak the seasoning if required and stuff into the casing, using any standard stuffing method; make two lengths approximately 1 inch (2.5 cm) thick, then prick all over with a very sharp pointed fork.

3. Reheat the broth, and when it begins to simmer, put in the sausages in flat coils. The broth should completely cover the sausages; if it does not, then put in more hot water. Heat to a simmer and cook for approximately fifteen to twenty minutes, then remove and drain. Let ripen in your fridge for a few days—this will improve the flavor—then proceed.

4. Chop the sausage into slices about ½ inch (1.5 cm) thick. Heat the rest of the 4 tablespoons oil, then reduce the heat and fry the sausage slices until a golden-brown colour is achieved. Serve hot, sprinkled with the capers and olives.

FISH COOKED IN CILANTRO (PESCADO EN CILANTRO)

Yield: Servings 6 as a first course

Ingredients:

- ⅓ cup (85 ml) fresh lime juice
- ⅓ cup (85 ml) olive oil
- 1 scant teaspoon salt
- 1½ cups (375 ml) thinly cut white onions
- 2 cups (500 ml) roughly chopped cilantro
- 3 jalapeño chiles en escabeche
- 3 tablespoons juice from the chile can
- A 3- to 3½-pound (1.35- to 1.575-kg) red snapper
- Freshly ground pepper

Directions:

1. Have the fish cleaned, leaving the head and tail on.

2. Prick the fish well on both sides with a coarse-tined fork, and rub it with the salt and pepper. Put the fish onto a baking dish with half the onions underneath and the rest on top. Pour the lime juice over it and set it aside for approximately 1 hour, flipping it over once during that time.
3. Preheat your oven to 350° f (180° c).
4. Cover the dish and bake the fish for approximately fifteen minutes on each side.
5. Put in the remaining ingredients and carry on cooking the fish, covered, until it is just cooked, coating it occasionally with the juices in the dish—about twenty minutes.

FISH IN CAPER SAUCE (PESCADO ALCAPARRADO)

Yield: Servings 6

Ingredients:

The fish broth

- ⅓ cup (85 ml) thinly cut white onion
- 12 peppercorns
- 2 mexican bay leaves
- 2 tablespoons fresh lime juice
- 4 cups (1 l) water, or enough to just cover the fish
- 8 ounces (225 g) carrots, scraped and thinly cut
- 8 ounces (225 g) turnips, peeled and thinly cut
- A 3-pound (1.35-kg) striped bass or snook
- Salt to taste

The sauce

- ¼ cup (65 ml) roughly cut white onion
- ½ cup (125 ml) fresh bread crumbs
- ½ cup (125 ml) olive oil
- 1 sprig flat-leaf parsley
- 1 tablespoon big capers, washed
- 1½ cups (375 ml) reserved fish broth
- 3 ounces (85 g) blanched almonds, roughly chopped (about ¾ cup/170 ml)

- 4 big lettuce leaves, torn into pieces
- 4 garlic cloves
- Salt to taste

The topping

- ¾ cup (185 ml) thinly cut white onion
- 1 tablespoon big capers, washed
- 12 pitted green olives
- 6 ounces (180 g) tomatoes, thinly cut (approximately 1 cup/250 ml)
- The heart of a romaine lettuce

Directions:

1. Put all the ingredients for the broth in a big deep cooking pan and simmer for approximately 30 minutes. Strain and set aside but keep warm.
2. Clean the fish, leaving the head and tail on, and put in a shallow flameproof baking dish. Cover the fish with the warm broth and poach on top of the stove using low heat until just cooked—about twenty minutes. Pour off the broth and save for later.
3. Preheat your oven to 350° f (180° c).
4. In a coffee/spice grinder, grind the almonds as fine as you can—this should make about ½ cup (125 ml). Put 1 cup (250 ml) of the reserved broth into a blender jar, put in the ground almonds, bread crumbs, lettuce leaves, capers, parsley, 2 garlic cloves, and the onion, and blend to a slightly textured sauce. Set aside.
5. Heat the oil gently, put in the remaining 2 garlic cloves, and the moment they start to brown, remove using a slotted spoon and discard. Mix in the mixed sauce, put in ½ cup reserved broth, and cook using low heat until well seasoned—approximately eight minutes.
6. Pour the sauce over the fish and put into the oven until thoroughly heated—about fifteen minutes.
7. Place the lettuce leaves around the dish and top with the remaining ingredients.

FISH VERACRUZ

Yield: Servings 4

Ingredients:

- ½ cup dry white wine
- ½ teaspoon ground cumin
- 1 (14.5 ounce) can diced tomatoes, drained
- 1 onion, halved and cut thin
- 1 teaspoon chili powder
- 1 teaspoon minced fresh thyme or ¼ teaspoon dried
- 2 tablespoons extra virgin olive oil, plus extra for serving
- 2 tablespoons minced fresh cilantro
- 4 (6 to 8 ounce) skinless cod fillets, one to 1½ inches thick
- 4 garlic cloves, minced
- Salt and pepper

Directions:

1. Heat oil in 12 inch nonstick frying pan over moderate high heat until it starts to shimmer Put in onion and ½ teaspoon salt and cook until tender, approximately five minutes. Mix in garlic, chili powder, and cumin and cook until aromatic, approximately half a minute. Mix in tomatoes, wine, and thyme and bring to simmer.
2. Season cod with salt and pepper. If using any tail end fillets, tuck tail under. Nestle cod into frying pan and spoon some sauce over fish. Cover, decrease the heat to moderate low, and cook until fish flakes apart when gently prodded with paring knife and records 140 degrees, approximately ten minutes.
3. Move fish to separate plates. Stir cilantro into sauce and sprinkle with salt and pepper to taste. Ladle sauce over fish and sprinkle with extra oil before you serve.

FISH WITH CHARRED GARLIC (PESCADO EN AJO QUEMADO)

Yield: Servings 6

Ingredients:

- ⅓ cup (85 ml) plus 2 tablespoons olive oil
- 1 big green bell pepper, seeds and veins removed, thinly cut

- 1 heaped tablespoon dried mexican oregano, yucatecan if possible, toasted and crumbled
- 1 heaped tablespoon recado de toda clase (or any other tastemaker of choice)
- 1 small bunch flat-leaf parsley, roughly chopped
- 1½ cups (375 ml) thickly cut white onions
- 1½ tablespoons bitter orange juice or fruity vinegar
- 12 ounces (340 g) tomatoes, thinly cut
- 2 garlic cloves, roughly chopped
- 2 small heads garlic, well charred and cut in half horizontally
- 3 tablespoons fresh lime juice
- 6 fish steaks about ¾ inch (2 cm) thick, approximately 2½ pounds (1.125 kg)
- 6 x-cat-ik or güero chiles, charred and left whole, without peeling
- A fish head, approximately 12 ounces (340 g)
- Salt to taste

Directions:

1. Flavour the fish, including the head, with the lime juice and salt and set aside for approximately fifteen minutes.
2. In a small container crush the garlic with the recado (or any other tastemaker of choice) and dilute with the orange juice. Spread a thin coating over the fish (and head) and set aside to season for minimum 1 hour.
3. Preheat your oven to 350° f (180° c).
4. Heat the ⅓ cup (85 ml) olive oil in a frying pan, put in the onions and bell pepper with a drizzling of salt, and fry using low heat until wilted, approximately 2 minutes. Put in the tomato slices and carry on frying until some of the juice has vaporized—about three minutes.
5. Put one half of the tomato mixture in an ovenproof dish into which the fish and head will fit in a single layer, drizzle with half of the parsley, and cover with the remaining tomato mixture. Put the garlic halves and chiles on the surface and drizzle with the oregano and the rest of the 2 tablespoons olive oil.
6. Cover the dish and bake for approximately twenty minutes. Take out of the oven and coat well with the juices, then cover and bake for 20 more minutes or until barely cooked. Set aside to season for approximately ½ hour before you serve and then reheat gently to avoid overcooking the fish.

GARLICKY SHELL ON SHRIMP WITH CILANTRO AND LIME

Yield: Servings four to 6

Ingredients:

- ¼ cup minced fresh cilantro
- ¼ cup salt
- ½ cup vegetable oil
- ½ teaspoon red pepper flakes
- 1 teaspoon annatto powder
- 2 pounds shell on jumbo shrimp (16 to 20 per pound)
- 2 teaspoons coriander seeds, lightly crushed
- 2 teaspoons grated lime zest, plus lime wedges for serving
- 6 garlic cloves, minced

Directions:

1. Dissolve salt in 1 quart cold water in big container. Using kitchen shears or sharp paring knife, cut through shells of shrimp and devein but do not remove shells. Use a paring knife to continue to cut shrimp ½ inch deep, ensuring not to cut in half completely. Submerge shrimp in brine, cover, and place in your fridge for fifteen minutes.
2. Adjust oven rack 4 inches from broiler element and heat broiler. Set wire rack in rimmed baking sheet. Mix oil, cilantro, garlic, coriander seeds, lime zest, annatto, and pepper flakes in big container. Remove shrimp from brine, pat dry using paper towels, and put in to oil mixture. Toss thoroughly, ensuring mixture gets into interior of shrimp. Position shrimp in single layer on prepared rack.
3. Broil shrimp until opaque and shells are starting to brown, 2 to 4 minutes, rotating sheet midway through broiling. Flip shrimp and continue to broil until second side appears opaque and shells are starting to brown, 2 to 4 minutes, rotating sheet midway through broiling. Move shrimp to serving platter and serve with lime wedges.

GRILLED SALMON STEAKS WITH LIME CILANTRO SAUCE

Yield: Servings 4

Ingredients:

- ½ teaspoon ground cumin
- 1 (13 by 9 inch) disposable aluminum roasting pan
- 1 teaspoon grated lime zest plus 6 tablespoons juice (3 limes)
- 2 garlic cloves, minced
- 2 tablespoons chopped fresh cilantro
- 2 tablespoons vegetable oil
- 3 tablespoons unsalted butter
- 4 (10 ounce) skin on salmon steaks, one to 1½ inches thick
- Salt and pepper

Directions:

1. Pat salmon steaks dry using paper towels. Working with 1 steak at a time, cautiously trim 1½ inches of skin from 1 tail. Firmly wrap other tail around skinned portion and tie steaks using a kitchen twine. Season salmon with salt and pepper and brush both sides with oil. Mix lime zest and juice, butter, garlic, cumin, and ⅛ teaspoon salt in disposable pan.
2. FOR A CHARCOAL GRILL: Open bottom vent fully. Light big chimney starter filled with charcoal briquettes (6 quarts). When top coals are partly covered with ash, pour uniformly over half of grill. Set cooking grate in place, cover, and open lid vent fully. Heat grill until hot, approximately five minutes. A GAS GRILL: Set all burners to high, cover, and heat grill until hot, approximately fifteen minutes. Leave primary burner on high and turn off other burner(s).
3. Clean cooking grate, then constantly brush grate with well oiled paper towels until black and shiny, five to ten times. Put salmon on hotter part of grill. Cook until browned on both sides, two to three minutes per side. In the meantime, set disposable pan on cooler part of grill and cook until butter has melted, approximately 2 minutes.
4. Move salmon to pan and gently turn to coat. Cook salmon (covered if using gas) until center is still translucent when checked with tip of paring knife and records 125 degrees (for medium rare), six to fourteen minutes, turning salmon and rotating pan midway through grilling.
5. Move salmon to platter; remove twine. Whisk cilantro into sauce left in pan. Sprinkle sauce over salmon before you serve.

GRILLED SWORDFISH, LIME, AND RED ONION SKEWERS

Yield: Servings 4

Ingredients:

- 1 (1½ pound) skinless swordfish steak, cut into 1¼ inch pieces
- 1 big red onion, cut into an inch pieces, 3 layers thick
- 1 tablespoon ground coriander
- 1 teaspoon ground cumin
- 1 teaspoon sugar
- 1½ teaspoons minced shallot
- 2 tablespoons chopped fresh cilantro
- 3 limes, halved, then each half quartered
- 5 tablespoons extra virgin olive oil
- Salt and pepper

Directions:

1. Lightly toss onion with 1 tablespoon oil in container, cover, and microwave until just soft, approximately 2 minutes. Mix 2 tablespoons oil, coriander, cumin, sugar, ½ teaspoon salt, and ½ teaspoon pepper in big container. Pat fish dry using paper towels, put in to spice mixture, and toss lightly to coat. Thread fish, limes, and onion uniformly onto four 12 inch metal skewers, in alternating pattern.
2. FOR A CHARCOAL GRILL: Open bottom vent fully. Light big chimney starter filled with charcoal briquettes (6 quarts). When top coals are partly covered with ash, pour uniformly over grill. Set cooking grate in place, cover, and open lid vent fully. Heat grill until hot, approximately five minutes. FOR A GAS GRILL: Set all burners to high, cover, and heat grill until hot, approximately fifteen minutes. Turn all burners to moderate high.
3. Clean cooking grate, then constantly brush grate with well oiled paper towels until black and shiny, five to ten times. Put skewers on grill. Cook (covered if using gas), turning as required, until fish appears opaque and flakes apart when gently prodded with paring knife, 5 to 8 minutes.
4. Move skewers to platter, tent loosely with aluminium foil, and allow to rest for five minutes. Mix remaining 2 tablespoons oil, cilantro, and shallot in container and

sprinkle with salt and pepper to taste. Brush skewers with oil mixture before you serve.

GRILLED WHOLE RED SNAPPER WITH ORANGE, LIME, AND CILANTRO VINAIGRETTE

Yield: Servings 4

Ingredients:

- ¼ cup orange juice
- ½ cup plus 1 tablespoon extra virgin olive oil
- 1 garlic clove, minced
- 1 tablespoon chopped fresh cilantro
- 1 tablespoon lime juice, plus lime wedges for serving
- 2 (1½ pound) whole red snapper, scaled and gutted
- 2 teaspoons sugar
- Salt and pepper

Directions:

1. Whisk orange juice, lime juice, sugar, garlic, ½ teaspoon salt, and ¼ teaspoon pepper together in medium container, then whisk in 6 tablespoons oil. Whisk in cilantro and sprinkle with salt and pepper to taste. Pat snapper dry using paper towels. Using sharp knife, make shallow diagonal slashes an inch apart through skin on both sides of fish, being cautious not to cut into flesh. Rub fish with remaining 3 tablespoons oil, then season meticulously (including cavities) with salt and pepper.
2. 2A. FOR A CHARCOAL GRILL: Open bottom vent fully. Light big chimney starter filled with charcoal briquettes (6 quarts). When top coals are partly covered with ash, pour uniformly over grill. Set cooking grate in place, cover, and open lid vent fully. Heat grill until hot, approximately five minutes. FOR A GAS GRILL: Set all burners to high, cover, and heat grill until hot, approximately fifteen minutes. Leave all burners on high.
3. Clean cooking grate, then constantly brush grate with well oiled paper towels until black and shiny, five to ten times. Put fish on grill. Cook (covered if using gas) until both sides are browned and crisp and flesh is no longer translucent in center, twelve

to 16 minutes, softly turning fish over using 2 spatulas midway through grilling. Move to carving board.

4. Working with 1 fish at a time, softly cut through skin and flesh down back of fish, from head to tail, without cutting through bones. Lightly cut through skin and flesh just behind head, from top to bottom, without cutting through bones. Beginning at head and working toward tail, slowly run metal spatula between bones and flesh to separate, then softly lift whole fillet from skeleton in single piece. Repeat on second side of fish. Sprinkle fish with vinaigrette and serve with lime wedges.

PAN ROASTED COD WITH AMARILLO SAUCE

Yield: Servings 4

Ingredients:

- ⅛ teaspoon ground allspice
- ⅛ teaspoon ground cloves
- ¼ teaspoon whole cumin seeds
- ½ teaspoon dried oregano
- ½ teaspoon sugar
- 1 (8 ounce) bottle clam broth
- 1 onion, chopped
- 2 tablespoons vegetable oil
- 3 guajillo chiles, stemmed, seeded, and torn into ½ inch pieces (6 tablespoons)
- 3 tablespoons masa harina
- 4 (6 to 8 ounce) skinless cod fillets, one to 1½ inches thick
- 4 garlic cloves, peeled
- 6 sprigs cilantro
- 8 ounces tomatillos, husks and stems removed, washed well, dried, and slice into ½ inch pieces
- Salt and pepper

Directions:

1. Toast guajillos in medium deep cooking pan on moderate heat, stirring regularly, until aromatic, 2 to six minutes; move to container. Heat 1 tablespoon oil in now empty pot

on moderate heat until it starts to shimmer Put in onion and cook until tender, approximately five minutes. Mix in garlic, oregano, cumin seeds, cloves, and allspice, and cook until aromatic, approximately half a minute. Mix in masa harina and cook for a minute. Slowly whisk in clam broth, scraping up any browned bits and smoothing out any lumps.

2. Mix in tomatillos, cilantro sprigs, toasted chiles, ½ teaspoon salt, and ¼ teaspoon pepper, bring to simmer, and cook until tomatillos start to tenderize, approximately 3 minutes. Cautiously move mixture to blender and pulse until smooth, one to two minutes. Return to pot and cover to keep warm.

3. Adjust oven rack to middle position and heat oven to 425 degrees. Pat fish dry using paper towels and season both sides with salt and pepper. If using any tail end fillets, tuck tail under. Drizzle sugar uniformly over 1 side of fish.

4. Heat remaining 1 tablespoon oil in 12 inch ovensafe nonstick frying pan using high heat until just smoking. Put fillets in frying pan, sugar side down, and press lightly to make sure even contact with pan. Cook until browned, approximately 2 minutes. Using 2 spatulas, flip fillets. Move frying pan to oven and roast fish until centers are just opaque and register 140 degrees, 5 to ten minutes.

5. Using potholders (frying pan handle will be hot), remove frying pan from oven. Move fish to serving platter or individual dishes. Serve with sauce.

PAN SEARED TROUT WITH SALSA BORRACHA

Yield: Servings 4

Ingredients:

- ⅓ cup orange juice
- ½ teaspoon ground coriander
- 1 garlic clove
- 1 tablespoon plus ½ teaspoon sugar
- 2 tablespoons lime juice, plus lime wedges for serving
- 3 dried pasilla chiles, stemmed, seeded, and torn into ½ inch pieces (¾ cup)
- 3 scallions, white parts chopped, green parts cut thin
- 3 tablespoons tequila
- 4 (6 to 8 ounce) trout fillets, ¼ to ½ inch thick

- 6 tablespoons extra virgin olive oil
- Salt and pepper

Directions:

1. Toast pasillas in small deep cooking pan on moderate heat, stirring regularly, until aromatic, 2 to six minutes; move to blender. Put in orange juice, tequila, scallion whites, 3 tablespoons oil, 1 tablespoon sugar, garlic, coriander, and ¼ teaspoon salt to blender and pulse until smooth, approximately one minute. Return sauce to now empty pot and simmer on moderate heat, stirring frequently, until slightly thickened, 2 to 4 minutes. Turn off the heat; cover to keep warm.
2. In the meantime, pat fish dry using paper towels and season both sides with salt and pepper. Drizzle remaining ½ teaspoon sugar uniformly over 1 side of fish.
3. Heat 1 tablespoon oil in 12 inch nonstick frying pan using high heat until it starts to shimmer Lay half of fish in frying pan, sugar side down, and press lightly to make sure even contact with pan. Cook until edges of fillets are opaque and bottoms are mildly browned, two to three minutes. Using 2 spatulas, flip fillets. Cook on second side until thickest part of fillets is firm to touch and fish flakes easily, two to three minutes. Move fish to platter and tent with aluminium foil. Repeat with 1 tablespoon oil and remaining fish.
4. Stir lime juice and remaining 1 tablespoon oil into sauce and sprinkle with salt and pepper to taste. Move fish to individual serving plates, leaving any collected juices behind on platter. Ladle small amount of sauce over fish and drizzle with scallion greens. Serve with rest of the sauce and lime wedges.

POMPANO IN GREEN SAUCE (PÁMPANO EN SALSA VERDE)

Yield: Servings 6 as a first course

Ingredients:

- ¼ teaspoon cumin seeds
- ¼ teaspoon peppercorns
- ½ teaspoon salt
- 2 pompano, each approximately 1¼ pounds (570 g)
- Juice of 1 big lime

The sauce

- ⅛ teaspoon dried mexican oregano, yucatecan if possible
- ⅓ cup (85 ml) olive oil
- ⅓ cup (85 ml) water
- ½ green pepper, seeds and veins removed, roughly chopped
- 1 pound (450 g) green (unripe) tomatoes, roughly chopped
- 1 serrano chile, roughly chopped
- 1 tablespoon mild white vinegar
- 2 garlic cloves, roughly chopped
- 3 sprigs flat-leaf parsley, roughly chopped
- 3 sprigs fresh cilantro, roughly chopped
- 6 scallions, roughly chopped
- Salt to taste

Directions:

1. Have the fish cleaned, leaving the heads and tails on.
2. Grind the spices together dry, and mix with the lime juice.
3. Prick the fish all over with a coarse-tined fork and rub the seasoning in well. Set aside, in an ovenproof dish, to season for minimum ½ hour.
4. Preheat your oven to 300° f (150° c).
5. Place the water and vinegar into your blender jar and put in the sauce ingredients apart from the oil a little at a time, blending after each addition until you have a slightly textured mixture.
6. Place a little of the oil under the fish, pour the sauce over the fish with the remaining oil, and bake, loosely covered, for approximately twenty minutes. Turn the fish over cautiously and bake for another fifteen minutes, coating with the sauce occasionally.
7. Note: this dish must be prepared and cooked immediately or the sauce will discolor.

RAW FISH MARINATED IN LIME JUICE (CEVICHE)

Yield: Servings 6

Ingredients:

- ¼ cup (65 ml) olive oil
- ½ teaspoon dried mexican oregano
- ½ teaspoon salt, or to taste
- 1 pound (450 g) skinned fillets of sierra (kingfish)
- 12 ounces (340 g) tomatoes, finely chopped (2 scant cups/475 ml)
- 3 or 4 canned serrano chiles en escabeche
- Freshly ground pepper
- Juice of 6 or 7 big limes (1¼ to 1½ cups/3fifteen to 375 ml), diluted with approximately ½ cup (125 ml) water

To serve

- 1 small avocado, cut
- 1 small purple onion, cut into rings
- 2 tablespoons chopped cilantro

Directions:

1. Chop the fish into little cubes, approximately ½ inch (1.5 cm), and cover them with the lime juice. Set the fish aside on the bottom of the fridge until the fish loses its transparent look and becomes opaque, approximately three hours. Mix the pieces occasionally so that they get uniformly "cooked" in the lime juice.
2. Put in the tomatoes with the remaining ingredients.
3. Set the ceviche aside on the bottom of the fridge for minimum 1 hour to season. (you should serve it chilled, but not so cold that the oil congeals.)
4. Before you serve, top each portion with slices of avocado and onion rings and drizzle with a little chopped cilantro, if you wish. Best eaten the same day.

RICE WITH SHRIMP (ARROZ A LA TUMBADA CON CAMARONES)

Yield: Servings 4 as a main course, 6 as a first course

Ingredients:

- ¾ cup (185 ml) finely chopped white onion

- 1 cup (250 ml) fruity (but not extra virgin) olive oil
- 1 small red bell pepper, cleaned of veins and seeds, thinly cut
- 1 teaspoon dried mexican oregano
- 1½ cups (375 ml) long-grain unconverted white rice, washed and drained
- 1½ pounds (675 g) medium shrimps, unshelled (weighed without heads)
- 12 ounces (340 g) tomatoes, finely chopped (about 2 cups/500 ml)
- 2 garlic cloves, finely chopped
- 2 heaped tablespoons roughly chopped cilantro
- 2 tablespoons roughly chopped chives
- 2 tablespoons roughly chopped mint
- About 5 cups (1.25 l) water or fish broth
- Salt to taste

Directions:

1. Heat the olive oil in a deep—about 5 inches (13 cm) deep—flameproof casserole. Put in the shrimps and a good drizzle of salt, and stir-fry using high heat for approximately one minute. Remove using a slotted spoon and save for later. In the same oil fry the tomatoes, onion, pepper, and garlic on moderate heat until well amalgamated—about five minutes.
2. Mix in the rice, put in the water with salt to taste, and bring to its boiling point. Cover the pan and cook on moderate heat for approximately 8 minutes. Put in the shrimps and herbs and carry on cooking, covered, still on moderate heat, until the rice is soft—about ten minutes. The consistency must be soupy.

SALMON WITH ROASTED SALSA VERDE

Yield: Servings 4

Ingredients:

- ¼ cup minced fresh cilantro
- 1 (1¾ to 2 pound) skin on salmon fillet, 1½ inches thick
- 1 jalapeño chile, stemmed, halved, and seeded
- 1 poblano chile, stemmed, seeded, and chopped
- 1 tablespoon lime juice, plus lime wedges for serving

- 1 teaspoon ground coriander
- 2 tablespoons plus 2 teaspoons extra virgin olive oil
- 2 teaspoons chopped fresh oregano
- 3 garlic cloves, peeled
- 3 scallions, chopped
- 8 ounces tomatillos, husks and stems removed, washed well, dried, and quartered
- Salt and pepper

Directions:

1. Adjust oven racks to lowest position and 6 inches from broiler element and heat broiler. Coat baking sheet with aluminium foil. Toss tomatillos, poblano, jalapeño, 1 tablespoon oil, garlic, oregano, coriander, ¼ teaspoon salt, and ¼ teaspoon pepper together, then spread onto readied sheet. Broil vegetables on upper rack until tomatillos and jalapeños are browned, ten to twelve minutes, stirring once in a while.
2. Move broiled vegetables to blender and allow to cool slightly. Put in 2 tablespoons cilantro, scallions, lime juice, and 1 tablespoon oil and blend until the desired smoothness is achieved, approximately one minute. In the meantime, place clean rimmed baking sheet on lower oven rack and heat oven to 500 degrees.
3. Cut salmon crosswise into 4 fillets. Using sharp knife, make 4 or 5 shallow slashes, approximately an inch apart, through skin of each fillet, being cautious not to cut into flesh. Pat salmon dry using paper towels, rub with remaining 2 teaspoons oil, and sprinkle with salt and pepper.
4. Reduce oven temperature to 275 degrees and remove preheated baking sheet. Cautiously place salmon, skin side down, on baking sheet. Roast on lower rack until center is still translucent when checked with tip of paring knife and records 125 degrees (for medium rare), 9 to 13 minutes. Move salmon to plates, spoon some of sauce over top and drizzle with remaining 2 tablespoons minced cilantro. Serve with rest of the sauce and lime wedges.

SEARED SHRIMP WITH TOMATOES, LIME, AND AVOCADO

Yield: Servings 4

Ingredients:

- ⅛ teaspoon sugar
- ¼ cup minced fresh cilantro
- 1 avocado, halved, pitted, and diced
- 1 pound tomatoes, cored, seeded, and slice into ½ inch pieces
- 1 tablespoon lime juice, plus lime wedges for serving
- 1½ pounds extra big shrimp (21 to 25 per pound), peeled and deveined
- 1–2 teaspoons minced canned chipotle chile in adobo sauce
- 2 tablespoons vegetable oil
- 3 garlic cloves, minced
- 6 scallions, white and green parts separated and cut thin
- Salt and pepper

Directions:

1. Toss tomatoes, scallion whites, cilantro, garlic, chipotle, and ¾ teaspoon salt together in container. In separate container, toss shrimp with sugar, ¼ teaspoon salt, and ¼ teaspoon pepper.
2. Heat 1 tablespoon oil in 12 inch frying pan using high heat until just smoking. Put in half of shrimp to pan in single layer and cook, without moving, until spotty brown on one side, approximately one minute. Move shrimp to big container (they will be underdone). Repeat with remaining 1 tablespoon oil and shrimp.
3. Return now empty frying pan to high heat, put in tomato mixture and lime juice, and cook until tomatoes are slightly softened, approximately one minute. Mix in shrimp with any collected juices and cook until shrimp are thoroughly cooked and hot, approximately one minute. Move shrimp to big platter and drizzle with avocado and scallion greens. Serve with lime wedges.

SHREDDED FISH TAMIAHUA (SARAGALLA DE PESCADO)

Yield: Servings 6

Ingredients:

- ¼ cup (65 ml) finely chopped white onion
- ¼ cup (65 ml) water
- ¼ teaspoon coriander seeds, crushed

- ½ teaspoon salt, or to taste
- ½-inch (1.5-cm) piece of cinnamon stick, crushed
- 1 small ancho chile
- 1 teaspoon capers, washed, strained, and roughly chopped
- 1½ tablespoons raisins
- 12 peppercorns, crushed
- 2 cups (500 ml) cooked and firm-fleshed shredded fish (approximately 1 pound/450 g)
- 2 garlic cloves
- 2 serrano chiles, or any fresh, hot green chile, finely chopped
- 3 tablespoons light olive oil
- 6 green olives, pitted and finely chopped
- About 6 ounces (180 g) tomatoes, finely chopped (approximately 1 cup/250 ml)

Directions:

1. Take away the seeds and veins from the ancho chile, cover with water, and simmer for five minutes. Soak for another five minutes, then drain and put in to the blender jar. Put in the crushed spices, salt, garlic, and water and blend, putting in more water only if required, to a loose paste.
2. Heat the oil in a heavy frying pan and fry the paste for approximately one minute. Put in the tomatoes, onion, serrano chiles, olives, capers, and raisins. Fry on moderate heat for approximately five minutes, stirring occasionally, for approximately five minutes. Mix in the shredded fish and cook for five minutes longer.
3. Tweak the seasoning and serve either hot or cold, with freshly made tortillas.

SHRIMP A LA DIABLA

Yield: Servings four to 6

Ingredients:

- ¼ cup chopped fresh cilantro or parsley
- 1 (8 ounce) can tomato sauce
- 1 cup water
- 1 onion, chopped fine
- 1 tablespoon lime juice, plus lime wedges for serving

- 1 tablespoon minced canned chipotle chile in adobo sauce
- 2 pounds extra big shrimp (21 to 25 per pound), peeled and deveined
- 2 tablespoons extra virgin olive oil, plus extra for serving
- 2 teaspoons dried oregano
- 3 garlic cloves, minced
- 8 dried guajillo chiles, stemmed, seeded and torn into ½ inch pieces (1 cup)
- Salt and pepper

Directions:

1. Toast guajillo chiles in Dutch oven on moderate heat, stirring regularly, until aromatic, 2 to six minutes; move to container.
2. Heat oil in now empty pot over moderate high heat until it starts to shimmer Put in onion and ½ teaspoon salt and cook until tender, approximately five minutes. Mix in garlic, chipotle, and oregano and cook until aromatic, approximately half a minute. Mix in tomato sauce, water, and toasted chiles, bring to simmer, and cook until chiles become tender, approximately ten minutes.
3. Move mixture to blender and pulse until smooth, approximately half a minute. Return sauce to now empty pot and mix in shrimp. Cover and cook over moderate low heat until shrimp are thoroughly cooked and completely opaque, five to seven minutes.
4. Move shrimp to separate plates. Stir cilantro and lime juice into sauce and sprinkle with salt and pepper to taste. Ladle sauce over shrimp, sprinkle with extra oil, and serve with lime wedges.

SHRIMP BALLS (ALBÓNDIGAS DE CAMARONES)

Yield: Servings 6

Ingredients:

- 1½ pounds (675 g) small shrimps, shelled, cleaned, and roughly chopped

The tomato broth

- ⅛ teaspoon coriander seeds
- ⅓ cup (85 ml) finely chopped white onion
- 1 cup (250 ml) nopales, cooked

- 1 cup (250 ml) peeled, diced potatoes (about 6 ounces/180 g)
- 1½ cups (375 ml) peeled and diced chayote (approximately eight ounces/225 g)
- 1½ pounds (675 g) tomatoes, finely chopped (approximately four cups/1 l)
- 2 teaspoons salt, or to taste
- 3 garlic cloves, finely chopped
- 3 tablespoons vegetable oil
- 4 cups (1 l) water
- 5 peppercorns

Shrimp ball seasoning

- ¼ teaspoon coriander seeds
- ¼ teaspoon peppercorns
- ½ ancho chile, veins and seeds removed
- ½-inch (1.5-cm) piece of cinnamon stick, broken up
- 1 tablespoon vegetable oil
- 1½ garlic cloves
- 1½ teaspoons salt, or to taste
- 3 tablespoons water

Directions:

1. Place the shrimps into the freezer for approximately 2 hours, until they are slightly frozen (this will make it easier to grind them in the blender or food processor).
2. In the meantime, prepare the tomato broth. In a wide, heavy pan, heat the oil and fry the tomatoes, onion, and garlic, stirring them occasionally and scraping the bottom of the pan, until they are reduced to a thick sauce. Put in the 4 cups (1 l) of water, salt, peppercorns, and coriander seeds and bring to its boiling point. Put in the potatoes and cook for approximately ten minutes, then put in the chayote and cook until nearly soft, approximately fifteen minutes more. Put in the nopales and just heat through. Tweak the seasoning.
3. Prepare the seasoning for the shrimp balls by first soaking the ancho chile in hot water for fifteen minutes, then drain and put in a blender jar. Crush the coriander seeds, peppercorns, and cinnamon stick. Put in the spices to the blender jar, together with the salt, garlic, and water, and blend to a paste. Heat the oil and fry the seasoning paste using high heat for approximately 2 minutes. Set aside.

4. Combine the slightly frozen shrimps to a quite smooth consistency. Put in the fried seasoning and work it in well with your hands. Lightly grease your hands, then make the mixture into balls approximately 1¼ inches (3.5 cm) in diameter—there must be 18 of them. Cautiously place the shrimp balls into the simmering broth, then cover the pan and continue simmering for approximately fifteen minutes, turning them once during the cooking time.
5. Serve the shrimp balls in deep soup bowls, with sufficient the broth and vegetables.

SHRIMP CREPES WITH PASILLA SAUCE (CREPAS DE CAMARÓN EN CHILE PASILLA)

Yield: Servings 6 as a first course

Ingredients:

- ⅓ cup (85 ml) vegetable oil
- ½ teaspoon granulated sugar
- 1¼ cups (315 ml) grated chihuahua cheese or muenster
- 1½ cups (375 ml) thick sour cream, plus extra for serving
- 1½ pounds (675 g) small shrimps cooked and peeled
- 1½ pounds (675 g) tomatoes, broiled
- 12 thin crepes, approximately 5½ inches (14 cm) in diameter, prepared in accordance with any standard crepe recipe
- 2 tablespoons crudely chopped white onion
- 6 pasilla chiles, wiped clean, seeds and veins removed
- Salt to taste

Directions:

1. Preheat your oven to 350° f (180° c).
2. Heat a griddle or comal and toast the chiles lightly, turning them occasionally so that they do not burn. Crush the chiles into a blender jar, put in the tomatoes and onion, and blend to a smooth sauce.
3. Heat the oil in a big frying pan. Put in the sauce, sugar, and salt, and cook the mixture on moderate heat, stirring it occasionally to prevent sticking. You will probably have to

cover the pan with a lid, as the sauce splatters rather fiercely. After about ten minutes the sauce will have thickened and seasoned. Set it aside to cool a little.

4. Mix the sour cream well into the sauce and allow it to continue to heat through for one minute or so.
5. Combine the shrimps into 1 cup (250 ml) of the sauce. Put a little of the mixture in each of the crepes and roll them up loosely. Put the crepes side by side on an ovenproof serving dish and pour the rest of the sauce over them.
6. Drizzle the grated cheese over the sauce and put some dollops of sour cream around the edge of the dish. Allow the crepes heat through in your oven and the cheese melt. Serve instantly.
7. Note: the crepes and sauce can always be made the day before—the sauce freezes very well. They can be filled several hours ahead and the rest of the sauce added just before they go into the oven.

SHRIMP FAJITAS

Yield: Servings 4

Ingredients:

- ⅛ teaspoon cayenne pepper
- ¼ cup minced fresh cilantro
- ½ cup Mexican crema
- 1 big red onion, halved and cut thin
- 1 teaspoon cumin seeds
- 1 teaspoon minced canned chipotle chile in adobo sauce
- 1 teaspoon sugar
- 1½ pounds medium big shrimp (31 to 40 per pound), peeled, deveined, and tails removed
- 12 (6 inch) flour tortillas, warmed
- 2 red bell peppers, stemmed, seeded, and cut thin
- 2 tablespoons lime juice, plus lime wedges for serving
- 2 tablespoons water
- 4 garlic cloves, peeled and smashed
- 6 tablespoons vegetable oil

- Salt and pepper

Directions:

1. Whisk 3 tablespoons oil, lime juice, garlic, chipotle, sugar, ½ teaspoon cumin seeds, 1 teaspoon salt, ½ teaspoon pepper, and cayenne together in big container. Put in shrimp and toss to coat. Cover and place in your fridge for half an hour

2. Heat 1 tablespoon oil in 12 inch nonstick frying pan over moderate high heat until it starts to shimmer Put in bell peppers, onion, water, remaining ½ teaspoon cumin seeds, and ½ teaspoon salt and cook until peppers are tender and onion is browned, approximately eight minutes. Move to serving container and sprinkle with salt and pepper to taste.

3. Wipe out frying pan using paper towels. Remove garlic from shrimp marinade and discard. Heat 1 tablespoon oil in now empty frying pan using high heat until just smoking. Put in half of shrimp to pan in single layer and cook until spotty brown and edges turn pink, one to two minutes. Remove pan from heat and flip each shrimp over using tongs. Cover and let shrimp stand off heat until just thoroughly cooked, one to two minutes; move to container and cover to keep warm.

4. Repeat with remaining 1 tablespoon oil and remaining shrimp. Toss shrimp with cilantro and serve with vegetables, warm tortillas, crema, and lime wedges.

SHRIMPS IN PUMPKIN SEED SAUCE (CAMARONES EN PIPIÁN)

Yield: Servings 6 to 8

Ingredients:

- ½ small white onion, roughly chopped
- ⅔ cup (165 ml) thick sour cream
- 1 cup (250 ml) hulled, raw pumpkin seeds (approximately four ounces/115 g)
- 1 small bunch cilantro, roughly chopped
- 1 tablespoon unsalted butter
- 1 teaspoon salt, or to taste
- 1½ pounds (675 g) medium-size shrimps, unshelled
- 2½ cups (625 ml) cold water, roughly

- 4 fresh serrano chiles or any fresh, hot green chiles, roughly chopped with seeds

Directions:

1. Shell and devein the shrimps and save for later. Place the shells, tails, and heads, if any, into a deep cooking pan, put in the water with salt, and cook on moderate heat for approximately twenty minutes, to extract the flavor and make a light broth. Strain and discard the shells, saving for later the cooking liquid. Allow the liquid to cool a little. Put in the shrimps and cook over gentle heat for approximately 3 minutes, or until they are just turning opaque. Drain the shrimps, saving for later the broth.

2. In a heavy, ungreased frying pan, toast the pumpkin seeds lightly, stirring them frequently, until they start to swell up and start to pop about—do not allow them to brown. Set them aside to cool and then grind them finely in a coffee/spice grinder. (alternatively they can just be added to the blender with the broth in the next step, but the sauce will not be as smooth.)

3. Put the shrimp broth, pumpkin seeds, cilantro, chiles, and onion in a blender and blend together until the desired smoothness is achieved.

4. Melt the butter in a heavy deep cooking pan. Put in the mixed pumpkin seed sauce and cook over very low heat while stirring and scraping the bottom of the pan continuously, for approximately 3 minutes. Mix in the sour cream, tweak the seasoning, and just heat through—about three minutes. Then put in the shrimps and heat through for another five minutes. The sauce must be of a medium consistency. Serve instantly.

5. Serve with fresh, hot tortillas or crusty french bread. Despite the temptation to do so, it is better not to serve it on top of rice or all that lovely sauce will be sopped up and lost.

SHRIMPS PICKLED IN RED CHILE SAUCE (CAMARONES EN ESCABECHE ROJO)

Yield: Servings 6 to 8 as a first course

Ingredients:

The sauce

- ¼ teaspoon dried mexican oregano
- ⅓ cup (85 ml) roughly cut white onion
- ½ cup (125 ml) olive oil
- 1 pound (450 g) medium shelled and cooked shrimps
- 1¼ cups (315 ml) mild white vinegar
- 2 mexican bay leaves
- 3 garlic cloves, roughly cut
- 3 whole cloves, crushed
- 5 ancho chiles, wiped clean, seeds and veins removed
- 8 peppercorns, crushed
- Salt to taste

Directions:

1. Heat the oil in a frying pan and fry the chiles lightly on both sides. Tear into pieces. Put in the onion and garlic to the frying pan and fry until translucent. Drain and move to the blender jar together with the chiles, ¼ teaspoon oregano, the peppercorns, and cloves.
2. Heat the vinegar and pour it over the ingredients in the blender jar. Set aside to soak for approximately ten minutes, then blend to a smooth, thick consistency. No more liquid must be necessary, but if it is then put in vinegar, not water (see note).
3. Reheat the oil and put in the sauce, with the bay leaves, additional ⅛ teaspoon oregano, and salt. Once the mixture in the pan begins to bubble, reduce the heat and carry on cooking the sauce for approximately fifteen minutes, stirring it occasionally to prevent sticking. Place a lid over the pan, as the thick sauce will splatter about fiercely.
4. Leave the sauce in your fridge to ripen for minimum 1 day before you use it.
5. Dilute the sauce with a little water, heat, and put in the shrimps for just long enough to heat them through.

SPICY GRILLED SHRIMP SKEWERS

Yield: Servings 4

Ingredients:

- ¼ teaspoon cayenne pepper

- ½ teaspoon ground cumin
- ½ teaspoon salt
- ½ teaspoon sugar
- 1 jalapeño chile, stemmed, seeded, and chopped
- 1 tablespoon chopped fresh cilantro
- 1 teaspoon lime zest plus 5 tablespoons juice (3 limes)
- 1½ pounds extra big shrimp (21 to 25 per pound), peeled, deveined, and butterflied
- 3 tablespoons extra virgin olive oil
- 6 garlic cloves, minced

Directions:

1. Mix lime zest and juice, oil, jalapeño, cilantro, garlic, cumin, salt, and cayenne in big container. Measure out 2 tablespoons marinade and set aside for serving.
2. Pat shrimp dry using paper towels, put in to remaining marinade, and toss to coat. Cover and place in your fridge for fifteen minutes. Thread marinated shrimp firmly onto four 12 inch metal skewers, alternating direction of heads and tails. Drizzle 1 side of shrimp skewers with sugar.
3. FOR A CHARCOAL GRILL: Open bottom vent fully. Light big chimney starter filled with charcoal briquettes (6 quarts). When top coals are partly covered with ash, pour uniformly over half of grill. Set cooking grate in place, cover, and open lid vent fully. Heat grill until hot, approximately five minutes. FOR A GAS GRILL: Set all burners to high, cover, and heat grill until hot, approximately fifteen minutes. Leave primary burner on high and turn other burner(s) to low.
4. Clean cooking grate, then constantly brush grate with well oiled paper towels until black and shiny, five to ten times. Put shrimp, sugar side down, on hotter part of grill and cook until mildly charred, three to four minutes. Flip skewers and slide to cooler part of grill. Cover and carry on cooking until shrimp are consistently pink, one to two minutes.
5. Holding skewers with potholder, use tongs to slide shrimp off skewers into moderate container. Put in reserved marinade and toss to coat. Move shrimp to platter before you serve.

STEAMED CLAMS WITH CHORIZO

Yield: Servings 4

Ingredients:

- 1 (28 ounce) can diced tomatoes
- 1 cup beer
- 1 onion, chopped fine
- 1 tablespoon vegetable oil
- 2 serrano chiles, stemmed and cut thin
- 2 tablespoons minced fresh cilantro
- 3 garlic cloves, minced
- 4 pounds littleneck clams, scrubbed
- 8 ounces Mexican style chorizo sausage, casings removed
- Lime wedges

Directions:

1. Heat oil in Dutch oven on moderate heat until it starts to shimmer Put in chorizo and cook, breaking into ½ inch pieces with wooden spoon, until starting to brown, approximately five minutes. Move chorizo to paper towel–lined plate, leaving fat in pot.
2. Put in onion to fat left in pot and cook over moderate high heat until tender, five to seven minutes. Mix in serranos and garlic and cook until aromatic, approximately half a minute. Mix in tomatoes and their juice and beer. Decrease the heat to moderate and simmer until slightly thickened, about eight to ten minutes.
3. Increase heat to high and mix in clams and reserved chorizo. Cover and cook, stirring once, until clams have opened, four to 8 minutes.
4. Using slotted spoon, move clams to serving container or individual bowls; discard any clams that haven't opened. Stir cilantro into broth, then pour broth over clams. Serve with lime wedges.

STUFFED BLUE CRABS (JAIBAS RELLENAS)

Yield: Servings 6 as a first course

Ingredients:

- ¼ cup (65 ml) plus 3 tablespoons olive oil
- ½ teaspoon salt, or to taste
- ⅔ cup (165 ml) finely chopped white onion
- 1 garlic clove, finely chopped
- 1½ tablespoons big capers, washed
- 1½ tablespoons finely chopped flat-leaf parsley
- 12 ounces (340 g) tomatoes, finely chopped (about 2 scant cups/475 ml)
- 2 serrano chiles, finely chopped
- 2 tablespoons salt
- 6 tablespoons thoroughly ground, toasted bread crumbs
- 8 big blue crabs

Directions:

1. Drop the crabs into boiling, salted water and cover the deep cooking pan. Bring them to its boiling point and cook them for approximately 3 minutes. Remove and drain.
2. When they are sufficiently cool to handle, remove the heart-shaped breastplate and pry off the big back shell, keeping it undamaged. Scrape out any fat and eggs that have remained in the shell, as well as those in the crab itself. Set them aside.
3. Scrub 6 of the shells well and set them aside. Take away the meat from the crabs and set it aside. Preheat your oven to 350° f (180° c).
4. Heat the ¼ cup (65 ml) olive oil in a frying pan and fry the garlic and onion until they barely start to turn golden. Put in the tomatoes, parsley, chiles, capers, and salt, and cook the mixture over a moderate heat until it is almost dry—5 to 8 minutes. Mix in the crabmeat and take out of the heat.
5. Fill the crab shells with the crabmeat mixture, drizzle with the bread crumbs and remaining 3 tablespoons olive oil, and put the shells in your oven just long enough to heat them through.
6. Turn on the broiler and brown the surface of the stuffing.

STUFFED FISH (PESCADO RELLENO)

Yield: Servings 6

Ingredients:

- ⅓ cup (85 ml) fresh lime juice
- 1 pound (900 g) tomatoes, finely chopped (about 2⅔ cups/665 ml)
- 1¼ cups (315 ml) finely chopped white onion
- 2 tablespoons butter
- 2 tablespoons finely chopped flat-leaf parsley
- 2 tablespoons olive oil
- 6 garlic cloves
- 6 small red snappers (approximately 12 ounces/340 g each), one for each person
- 6 tablespoons melted butter
- 8 ounces (225 g) cooked crabmeat
- 8 ounces (225 g) raw scallops
- 8 ounces (225 g) raw shrimps, peeled and deveined
- Salt and pepper to taste

Directions:

1. Have the fish cleaned, leaving the head and tail on. Have as much of the backbone removed as you can to make a good pocket for stuffing the fish without completely opening it up.
2. Crush the garlic and mix it to a paste with the salt, pepper, and lime juice. Prick the fish all over on both sides with a coarse-tined fork and rub the paste in well—inside and out. Set the fish aside to season for minimum 1 hour.
3. Preheat your oven to 350° f (180° c) and prepare the stuffing.
4. Melt the butter with the oil in a frying pan and cook the onion until translucent. Put in the tomatoes and cook them over quite high heat until some of the juice has vaporized.
5. Chop the shrimps into halves and the scallops into four equivalent portions. Put in them, with the parsley and seasoning, to the tomato mixture and allow to cook on moderate heat until the scallops and shrimps are just soft—about ten minutes. Mix in the crabmeat.
6. Stuff each fish with approximately ½ cup (125 ml) of the filling and sew it up. Put half of the butter into a shallow ovenproof dish, put the fish side by side, and drizzle them with the rest of the butter. Cover the dish and bake until the fish are soft—about twenty minutes.

VERACRUZ RED SNAPPER (HUACHINANGO A LA VERACRUZANA)

Yield: Servings 6 as a first course

Ingredients:

- ¼ cup (65 ml) plus 3 tablespoons olive oil
- ¼ teaspoon dried mexican oregano
- ½ teaspoon salt, or to taste
- 1 cup (250 ml) thinly cut white onion
- 1 teaspoon salt, or to taste
- 12 pitted green olives or stuffed with red pepper, cut into halves
- 2 big garlic cloves, cut
- 2 jalapeño chiles en escabeche, cut into strips, or whole chiles largos
- 2 mexican bay leaves
- 2 pounds (900 g) tomatoes, finely chopped (about 5⅓ cups/1.335 l)
- 2 tablespoons big capers
- 2 tablespoons fresh lime juice
- A 3-pound (1.35-kg) red snapper

Directions:

1. Preheat your oven to 325° f (165° c).
2. Have the fish cleaned, leaving the head and tail on. Prick the fish on both sides with a coarse-tined fork, rub in the salt and lime juice, and set it aside in an ovenproof dish to season for approximately 2 hours.
3. Heat ¼ cup (65 ml) oil in a frying pan and fry the onion and garlic, without browning, until they are tender. Put in the tomatoes, with the remaining ingredients, to the pan and cook the sauce over brisk heat until it is well seasoned and some of the juice has vaporized—about ten minutes. Pour the sauce over the fish.
4. Drizzle the rest of the 3 tablespoons oil over the sauce and bake the fish for approximately twenty minutes, loosely covered, on one side. Turn the fish over very cautiously and carry on baking it until it is just soft—about twenty minutes. Baste the fish regularly with the sauce during the cooking time.

YUCATECAN SOUSED FISH (SIERRA EN ESCABECHE)

Yield: Servings 6

Ingredients:

Preparing the fish

- ¼ cup (65 ml) fresh lime juice
- 1 cup (250 ml) water
- 1 teaspoon salt
- 6 1-inch- (2.5-cm-) thick steaks of sierra or salmon (about 3 pounds/1.35 kg)

Step 1

- ½ cup (125 ml) water
- ½ cup (125 ml) wine vinegar
- ½ teaspoon coriander seeds, crushed
- ½ teaspoon cumin seeds, crushed
- ½ teaspoon dried mexican oregano, yucatecan if possible, toasted
- ½ teaspoon granulated sugar
- ½ teaspoon peppercorns, crushed
- ½-inch (1.5-cm) piece of cinnamon stick, broken up
- 10 small garlic cloves, toasted, peeled and left whole
- 2 garlic cloves
- 2 mexican bay leaves
- 2 whole allspice, crushed
- 2 whole cloves, crushed
- Salt to taste

Step 2

- ½ cup (125 ml) olive oil
- ¾ cup (185 ml) wine vinegar
- 1¼ cups (315 ml) water

Step 3

- ½ cup (125 ml) vegetable oil
- 4 cups (1 l) thinly cut purple onions, blanched
- 6 güero chiles, toasted but not skinned

Directions:

1. Pour the water, lime juice, and salt over the fish and set it aside for an hour, turning it once during that time.
2. Pulverize the spices in an electric grinder or mortar. Crush the 2 garlic cloves and grind them until a paste is achieved with the spices. Place the spice-garlic paste into the deep cooking pan with the remaining ingredients in step 1 and bring the mixture to its boiling point. Put in the oil, vinegar, and water and once again bring the mixture to its boiling point. Set aside and keep hot.
3. Dry the fish slices meticulously. Heat the oil in a frying pan and fry them about five minutes on each side. They must be barely cooked. Put them in a serving dish and pour the hot souse over them. Put in the chiles and onions. Set the fish aside to season for minimum 1 hour in the souse.
4. Serve at room temperature.

Egg dishes

Eggs are popular in breakfast recipes in Mexico. We Mexicans like to make delicious egg dishes by combining leftovers from the previous day, and a few eggs. Below are a few of my favourite egg recipes.

Breakfast Burritos

Yield: Servings 6

Ingredients:

- ¼ cup half and half
- 1 jalapeño chile, stemmed, seeded, and minced
- 1 red bell pepper, stemmed, seeded, and chopped
- 1 red onion, chopped fine
- 1 tablespoon unsalted butter
- 3 scallions, cut thin
- 6 (10 inch) flour tortillas
- 6 ounces cheddar cheese, shredded (1½ cups)
- 6 ounces Mexican style chorizo sausage, casings removed
- 8 big eggs
- Salt and pepper

Directions:

1. Cook chorizo in 12 inch nonstick frying pan over moderate high heat, breaking up meat with wooden spoon, until starting to brown, approximately five minutes. Put in onion, bell pepper, and jalapeño and cook until vegetables become tender, approximately five minutes; move to container.
2. Beat eggs, half and half, ½ teaspoon salt, and ⅛ teaspoon pepper with fork in container until meticulously blended and mixture is pure yellow; do not overbeat. Wipe out frying pan using paper towels, put in butter, and melt on moderate heat. Put in egg mixture and, using heat resistant rubber spatula, continuously and tightly

scrape along bottom and sides of frying pan until eggs start to clump and spatula leaves trail on bottom of frying pan, 1½ to 2½ minutes.

3. Decrease the heat to low and gently but continuously fold eggs until clumped and slightly wet, thirty to 60 seconds. Remove the heat, gently fold in cheddar, scallions, and chorizo mixture; if eggs are still underdone, return frying pan to moderate heat for no longer than half a minute.

4. Cover tortillas in damp dish towel and microwave until warm and flexible, approximately one minute. Place warm tortillas on counter. Mound egg mixture across center of tortillas, close to bottom edge. Working with one tortilla at a time, fold sides then bottom of tortilla over filling, pulling back on it tightly to tighten it around filling, then carry on rolling firmly into burrito. Serve instantly.

Bricklayer's Eggs

Yield: Servings 4

Ingredients:

- ¼ cup fresh cilantro leaves
- ¼ cup warm water
- ½ small onion, chopped coarse
- 1 big poblano chile, stemmed, seeded, and chopped
- 1 jalapeño chile, stemmed and halved
- 1 tablespoon unsalted butter, cut into 4 pieces and chilled
- 1 teaspoon ground coriander
- 2 garlic cloves, peeled and smashed
- 2 teaspoons lime juice
- 2 teaspoons minced fresh oregano or ½ teaspoon dried
- 4 ounces tomatillos, husks and stems removed, washed well, dried, and quartered
- 5 teaspoons vegetable oil
- 8 big eggs
- Salt and pepper

Directions:

1. Adjust oven rack 6 inches from broiler element and heat broiler. Coat rimmed baking sheet with aluminium foil. Toss tomatillos, poblano, onion, jalapeño, 1 tablespoon oil, garlic, oregano, coriander, ¼ teaspoon salt, and ¼ teaspoon pepper together, then spread onto readied sheet. Broil vegetables until browned, ten to twelve minutes, stirring once in a while.

2. Move broiled vegetables to food processor. Put in warm water, cilantro, and lime juice and pulse until crudely ground, ten to fifteen pulses. Sprinkle with salt and pepper to taste. (Sauce can be placed in your fridge for maximum 2 days; reheat in microwave and adjust consistency with extra water as required before continuing.)

3. Heat remaining 2 teaspoons oil in 12 or 14 inch nonstick frying pan using low heat for five minutes. In the meantime, crack eggs into 2 small bowls (4 eggs per container) and sprinkle with salt and pepper.

4. Increase heat to moderate high and heat until oil is shimmering. Put in butter and swiftly swirl to coat frying pan. Working swiftly, pour 1 container of eggs in 1 side of frying pan and second container of eggs in other side. Cover and cook for a couple of minutes.

5. Remove frying pan from heat and allow it to stand, covered, approximately 2 minutes for runny yolks (white around edge of yolk will be barely opaque), approximately 3 minutes for tender but set yolks, and approximately four minutes for medium set yolks. Slide eggs onto warm plates and top with sauce. Serve instantly.

Country Eggs (Huevos Rancheros)

Yield: Servings 1

Ingredients:

- ½ cup (125 ml) Salsa of Choice
- 2 big eggs
- 2 small tortillas
- 2 tablespoons vegetable oil

Directions:

1. Heat the oil in a frying pan and fry the tortillas lightly on both sides, as you would for enchiladas—they should not become crunchy. Drain them using paper towels and put them on a warmed dish.
2. In the same oil, fry the eggs, then put them on the tortillas.
3. Cover the eggs with the warmed sauce and serve instantly.

Eggs Poached In A Chile-Tomato Broth (Huevos En Rabo De Mestiza)

Yield: Servings 6

Ingredients:

- ⅓ cup (85 ml) vegetable oil
- 1½ cups (375 ml) thinly cut white onion
- 12 big eggs
- 2 pounds (900 g) tomatoes, broiled
- 3 cups (750 ml) water
- 6 slices queso fresco
- 7 poblano chiles, charred and peeled, cleaned, and slice into thin strips
- Salt to taste

Directions:

1. Heat the oil in a big frying pan and cook the onion until translucent—about two minutes. Put in the chile strips to the pan and allow them to cook for approximately 3 minutes, stirring regularly to prevent sticking.
2. Combine the broiled tomatoes for a few seconds—do not overblend—and put in them to the onion-chile mixture. The sauce should have some texture. Allow them to cook over quite high heat for approximately ten minutes, or until the sauce is well seasoned and has reduced fairly. Put in the water and salt and carry on cooking for one minute or so more.
3. Crack the eggs, one at a time, onto a saucer and cautiously slide them into the hot broth. Position the slices of cheese on top. Cover the dish with a lid and let the eggs poach very gently until set—six to eight minutes.

Eggs Scrambled With Tortilla Crisps And Pasilla Sauce (Huevos Revueltos Con Totopos Y Salsa De Chile Pasilla)

Yield: Servings 1

Ingredients:

- ¼ cup (65 ml) vegetable oil
- 1 tablespoon crumbled queso fresco
- 1 tablespoon finely chopped white onion
- 1½ small tortillas, cut into strips and dried
- 2 big eggs
- 3 tablespoons salsa de chile pasilla, at room temperature
- Salt to taste

Directions:

1. Heat the oil in a big frying pan and fry the tortillas until they are just crisp and a light golden brown.
2. Leaving the crisps in the pan, drain off all but approximately 1 tablespoon of the oil.
3. Beat the eggs with the salt and put in them to the crisps in the pan. Mix the eggs on moderate heat until they are set.
4. Serve the eggs topped with the sauce and sprinkled with the onion and cheese.

Eggs With Dried Beef (Machacado De Huevo)

Yield: Servings 6

Ingredients:

- 3 tablespoons melted lard
- 4 ounces (115 g) machaca (dried and shredded salted beef)
- 8 big eggs

Directions:

1. Place the dried beef into a container, cover with cold water, and soak one minute to tenderize slightly. Drain, then squeeze to extract as much water as you can. Shred the beef crudely.
2. Heat the lard in a frying pan, mix in the beef, and fry lightly until the moisture has vaporized—do not brown—about three minutes.
3. Break the eggs into the mixture—do not beat beforehand—stir, and stir until they are set and curdy, approximately 2 minutes. Serve the eggs instantly with the tomato sauce.
4. The beef is usually salty enough that no extra salt must be required, but that is a matter of taste.

The tomato sauce

Ingredients:

- ½ cup (125 ml) finely chopped white onion
- 1¼ pounds (570 g) tomatoes
- 1½ tablespoons lard
- 7 dried piquín chiles
- Salt to taste

Directions:

1. Chop the tomatoes into four equivalent portions along the length and, using the coarse side of the grater, grate the flesh and seeds of each section until you have only the skin left in your hand—take care not to grate your knuckles or nails in the process. Save all the juice that exudes. You should have about 2 cups (500 ml) of juicy flesh with seeds.
2. Heat the lard in a big frying pan, put in the onion, the chiles, and salt, and fry on moderate heat until translucent—about two minutes. Put in the grated tomatoes and carry on cooking using high heat until seasoned—about fifteen minutes, or until you have a juicy, textured sauce. Serve warm.

Eggs With Epazote And Chiles (Huevos Con Epazote Y Chile)

Yield: Servings 2

Ingredients:

- ⅓ cup (85 ml) tightly packed, roughly chopped epazote
- ⅔ cup (165 ml) water
- 3 tablespoons vegetable oil
- 4 big eggs
- 6 serrano chiles, broiled until tender and roughly chopped
- Salt to taste

Directions:

1. Place the water into your blender jar, put in the chiles, epazote, and salt, and blend to a rough-textured consistency.
2. Heat the oil in a big frying pan, break the eggs into it, put in a little salt, and stir just to combine. Cook the eggs on moderate heat, folding them over so that they cook uniformly until well set. Pour the sauce over the eggs and carry on cooking, without stirring, still on moderate heat, until the sauce has reduced and seasoned a little—about two minutes.

Farmhouse Scrambled Eggs (Huevos Revueltos Del Rancho)

Yield: Servings 1

Ingredients:

- 1 tablespoon crème fraîche or thick sour cream
- 1 tablespoon finely chopped white onion
- 2 big eggs
- 2 small tortillas
- 2 tablespoons vegetable oil
- 3 tablespoons salsa de chile pasilla
- A slice of queso fresco
- Salt to taste

Directions:

1. Heat the oil in a big frying pan and fry the tortillas lightly on both sides. They should not get crunchy. Drain them on the paper toweling and put them onto a warmed plate.
2. In the same oil, cook the sauce for a few seconds using high heat.
3. Beat the eggs lightly with the salt and put in them to the sauce in the pan. Mix the eggs until they are set.
4. Serve the eggs on top of the tortillas and top with the cheese, onion, and crème fraîche or sour cream.

Green Chile And Potato Frittata

Yield: Servings 6

Ingredients:

- ½ teaspoon ground cumin
- 1 onion, chopped fine
- 1 pound Yukon Gold potatoes, unpeeled, cut into ½ inch pieces
- 12 big eggs
- 2 poblano chiles, stemmed, seeded, and slice into ½ inch pieces
- 2 tablespoons extra virgin olive oil
- 2 teaspoons minced canned chipotle chile in adobo sauce
- 2 teaspoons minced fresh oregano or ½ teaspoon dried
- 3 garlic cloves, minced
- 3 tablespoons chopped fresh cilantro
- 3 tablespoons half and half
- 4 ounces Monterey Jack cheese, cut into ¼ inch pieces (1 cup)
- Salt and pepper

Directions:

1. Adjust oven rack 6 inches from broiler element and heat broiler. Toss potatoes, 1 tablespoon oil, and ¼ teaspoon salt together in container. Cover and microwave until potatoes are translucent around edges, five to seven minutes, stirring midway through microwaving.

2. In the meantime, beat eggs, half and half, cilantro, ¾ teaspoon salt, and ½ teaspoon pepper with fork in container until meticulously blended; do not overbeat.

3. Heat remaining 1 tablespoon oil in 10 inch ovensafe nonstick frying pan on moderate heat until it starts to shimmer Put in poblanos and onion and cook until tender, approximately eight minutes. Mix in hot potatoes, then mix in garlic, oregano, chipotle, and cumin and cook until aromatic, approximately half a minute.

4. Put in egg mixture and, using heat resistant rubber spatula, continuously and tightly scrape along bottom and sides of frying pan until big curds form and spatula leaves trail on bottom of frying pan, but eggs are still very wet, approximately 3 minutes. Shake frying pan to spread eggs uniformly. Drizzle with Monterey Jack and softly push into eggs with spatula.

5. Broil until frittata has risen and surface is puffed and spotty brown, two to three minutes; when cut into with paring knife, eggs must be slightly wet and runny. Remove frying pan from oven and let frittata rest for five minutes. Using oven mitts (frying pan handle will be hot), run spatula around frying pan edge to loosen frittata, then cautiously slide it out onto serving plate. Serve warm or at room temperature.

Huevos Rancheros

Yield: Servings 4

Ingredients:

- ¼ cup extra virgin olive oil
- ⅓ cup minced fresh cilantro
- ½ cup chopped canned green chiles
- 1 avocado, halved, pitted, and diced
- 1 onion, chopped
- 1 tablespoon lime juice
- 1 tablespoon packed brown sugar
- 2 (28 ounce) cans diced tomatoes
- 3 scallions, cut thin
- 3 tablespoons chili powder
- 4 garlic cloves, cut thin
- 4 ounces pepper Jack cheese, shredded (1 cup)

- 8 (6 inch) corn tortillas, warmed
- 8 big eggs
- Salt and pepper

Directions:

1. Adjust oven rack to middle position and heat oven to 500 degrees. Coat rimmed baking sheet using parchment paper. Drain tomatoes in fine mesh strainer set over container, pushing using a rubber spatula to extract 1¾ cups tomato juice; discard extra juice. Whisk sugar and lime juice into tomato juice.

2. In separate container, mix onion, chiles, oil, chili powder, garlic, ½ teaspoon salt, and drained tomatoes. Spread tomato mixture uniformly over readied sheet. Roast until charred in spots, thirty-five to forty minutes, stirring midway through baking. (Tomato juice mixture and roasted vegetables can be placed in your fridge separately for maximum one day; reheat vegetables in microwave for 45 seconds and bring juice to room temperature before continuing.)

3. Reduce oven temperature to 400 degrees. Mix roasted vegetables and tomato juice in 13 by 9 inch baking dish, sprinkle with salt and pepper to taste, and drizzle uniformly with pepper Jack. Using spoon, make 8 indentations (2 to 3 inches wide) in tomato mixture. Crack 1 egg into each dent and season eggs with salt and pepper.

4. Bake until egg whites are just starting to set but still have some movement when dish is shaken, thirteen to 16 minutes. Move dish to wire rack, tent with aluminium foil, and allow it to sit for five minutes. Drizzle with avocado, scallions, and cilantro. Serve instantly with warm tortillas.

Mexican Breakfast Sandwiches

Yield: Servings 4

Ingredients:

- ¼ cup jarred cut jalapeños, plus 2 teaspoons brine
- ¼ cup mayonnaise
- ⅓ cup refried beans
- 1 avocado, halved, pitted, and slice into ½ inch pieces
- 1 plum tomato, cored and diced into ½ inch pieces

- 1 teaspoon minced canned chipotle chile in adobo sauce
- 4 big eggs
- 4 kaiser rolls
- 6 slices bacon
- Salt and pepper

Directions:

1. Adjust oven rack 6 inches from broiler element and heat broiler. Position rolls split side up on rimmed baking sheet. Mix mayonnaise and chipotle in container. In separate container, gently mix refried beans, avocado, tomato, and jalapeño brine.
2. Cook bacon in 12 inch nonstick frying pan on moderate heat until crunchy, 7 to 9 minutes. Move to paper towel–lined plate, allow to cool slightly, then break each slice in half.
3. Broil rolls until a golden-brown colour is achieved, one to three minutes, rotating sheet midway through broiling. Flip rolls and broil until just crisp on second side, one to two minutes.
4. Crack eggs into 2 small bowls (2 eggs per container) and sprinkle with salt and pepper. Pour off all but 1 tablespoon fat from frying pan and heat on moderate heat until it starts to shimmer Working swiftly, pour 1 container of eggs in 1 side of frying pan and second container of eggs in other side. Cover and cook for a minute. Remove frying pan from heat, and allow it to sit, covered, fifteen to 45 seconds for runny yolks (white around edge of yolk will be barely opaque), 45 to 60 seconds for tender but set yolks, and about two minutes for medium set yolks.
5. Spread chipotle mayonnaise on roll tops and refried bean mixture on roll bottoms. Slide 1 egg onto each bottom. Top with bacon, cut jalapeños, and bun tops. Serve instantly.

Mexican Scrambled Eggs (Huevos Revueltos A La Mexicana)

Yield: Servings 1

Ingredients:

- 2 big eggs

- 2 serrano chiles or to taste, finely chopped
- 2 tablespoons finely chopped white onion
- 2½ tablespoons vegetable oil
- 4 ounces (115 g) tomatoes, finely chopped (about ⅔ cup/165 ml)
- Salt to taste

Directions:

1. Heat the oil in a frying pan and mix in the chopped ingredients with salt to taste. Cook for a minute.
2. Lightly beat the eggs with a little salt and mix into the tomato-chile mixture. Stir on moderate heat until set.
3. Serve instantly with hot tortillas.

Mexican Scrambled Eggs With Totopos (Huevos Revueltos Con Totopos Y Jitomate)

Yield: Servings 4

A perfect brunch recipe.

Ingredients:

- ¼ cup (65 ml) vegetable oil, plus more for frying
- 3 tablespoons finely chopped white onion
- 4 to 6 serrano chiles, finely chopped
- 6 big eggs
- 6 tortillas, each cut into 6 triangular pieces and dried
- 8 ounces (225 g) tomatoes, finely chopped (approximately 1⅓ cups/335 ml)
- Salt to taste
- Vegetable oil for frying

Directions:

1. Heat the oil in a big frying pan and fry the tortilla pieces, one half at a time, so they cook uniformly. They must be just a little crisp but not too brown. Drain using paper towels and keep warm.

2. Heat the ¼ cup oil, then put in the chopped ingredients to the pan and cook on moderate heat for five minutes, stirring the mixture occasionally.
3. Beat the eggs with the salt and put in them, with the dried tortilla pieces, to the pan. Cook while stirring, until the eggs are set but not too dry.
4. The dish must be eaten instantly.

Migas

Yield: Servings 4

Ingredients:

- 1 jalapeño chile, stemmed, seeded, and minced
- 1 onion, chopped fine
- 1 red bell pepper, stemmed, seeded, and chopped fine
- 2 ounces baked tortilla chips, broken into ½ inch pieces (1 cup)
- 2 tablespoons minced fresh cilantro
- 2 tablespoons unsalted butter
- 3 garlic cloves, minced
- 3 ounces pepper Jack cheese, shredded (¾ cup)
- 8 big eggs
- Salt and pepper

Directions:

1. Melt 1 tablespoon butter in 12 inch nonstick frying pan on moderate heat. Put in onion, bell pepper, and jalapeño, cover, and cook until tender and mildly browned, approximately eight minutes. Mix in garlic and cook, uncovered, until aromatic, approximately half a minute; move to container.
2. Beat eggs, tortilla chips, ¼ teaspoon salt, and pinch pepper with fork in container until meticulously blended; do not overbeat. Wipe out frying pan using paper towels, put in remaining 1 tablespoon butter, and melt on moderate heat. Put in egg mixture and, using heat resistant rubber spatula, continuously and tightly scrape along bottom and sides of frying pan until eggs start to clump and spatula leaves trail on bottom of frying pan, 1½ to 2½ minutes.

3. Decrease the heat to low and gently but continuously fold eggs until clumped and slightly wet, thirty to 60 seconds. Remove the heat, gently fold in pepper Jack, cilantro, and vegetable mixture; if eggs are still underdone, return frying pan to moderate heat for no longer than half a minute. Sprinkle with salt and pepper to taste. Serve instantly.

Nopal Cactus With Egg (Nopales Con Huevo)

Yield: Servings 4

Ingredients:

- ⅓ cup (85 ml) finely chopped white onion
- 1 pound (450 g) nopales (about 3½ cups/875 ml) cleaned and diced
- 2 garlic cloves, finely chopped
- 2 tablespoons lard or vegetable oil
- 3 big eggs
- 4 serrano chiles, finely chopped
- 8 ounces (225 g) tomatoes, finely chopped (approximately 1⅓ cups/335 ml)
- Salt to taste

Directions:

1. Heat the lard in a frying pan and put in the remaining ingredients (except the eggs). Put in salt to taste. Cover the pan and cook on moderate heat, shaking the pan occasionally, for approximately twenty-five minutes—until the mixture is dry and well seasoned.
2. Break the eggs into the nopales and stir quickly until set.

Oaxacan Scrambled Eggs (Salsa De Huevo)

Yield: Servings 2

Ingredients:

- ¼ teaspoon salt, or to taste
- ⅓ cup (85 ml) chopped nopales, freshly cooked (not necessary)

- ½ cup (125 ml) water
- 1 big sprig epazote
- 1 garlic clove, roughly chopped
- 1 or 2 fresh serrano chiles or any fresh, hot green chile, charred
- 10 ounces (285 g) tomatoes, broiled
- 2 tablespoons roughly chopped white onion
- 3 big eggs
- 3 tablespoons vegetable oil

Directions:

1. Combine the unskinned tomatoes with the chile, onion, garlic, and salt. Heat 1 tablespoon of the oil in a frying pan and fry the mixture for five minutes, stirring occasionally. Dilute with the water, put in the epazote and nopales, and cook on moderate heat for a couple of minutes more. Set aside.
2. Heat the rest of the oil in a heavy pan. Beat the eggs for a short period of time with a little salt and cook very lightly in the oil, turning them continuously, until they are just set. Put into the sauce, stirring continuously for a few minutes, and cook for approximately 3 minutes more.

Scrambled Eggs With Tomato, Onion, And Jalapeño

Yield: Servings 6

Ingredients:

- 1 jalapeño chile, stemmed, seeded, and minced
- 1 small onion, chopped fine
- 1 tomato, cored and slice into ¼ inch pieces
- 12 big eggs
- 2 tablespoons chopped fresh cilantro
- 2 tablespoons unsalted butter
- 3 ounces queso fresco, crumbled (¾ cup)
- 6 tablespoons half and half
- Salt and pepper

Directions:

1. Toss tomato with ⅛ teaspoon salt in container, then move to paper towel–lined plate and allow to drain for fifteen minutes.
2. In the meantime, melt 1 tablespoon butter in 12 inch nonstick frying pan on moderate heat. Put in onion and jalapeño, cover, and cook until tender and mildly browned, six to eight minutes; move to container.
3. Beat eggs, half and half, ¾ teaspoon salt, and ¼ teaspoon pepper with fork in container until meticulously blended and mixture is pure yellow; do not overbeat. Wipe out frying pan using paper towels, put in remaining 1 tablespoon butter, and melt on moderate heat. Put in egg mixture and, using heat resistant rubber spatula, continuously and tightly scrape along bottom and sides of frying pan until eggs start to clump and spatula leaves trail on bottom of frying pan, 1½ to 2½ minutes.
4. Decrease the heat to low and gently but continuously fold eggs until clumped and slightly wet, thirty to 60 seconds. Remove the heat, gently fold in vegetable mixture and ½ cup queso fresco; if eggs are still underdone, return frying pan to moderate heat for no longer than half a minute. Drizzle with drained tomato, remaining ¼ cup queso fresco, and cilantro. Sprinkle with salt and pepper to taste. Serve instantly.

SCRAMBLED EGGS WITH CHORIZO, ONION, AND JALAPEÑO

Omit tomato and step

Directions:

1. Substitute 8 ounces Mexican style chorizo sausage, casings removed, for butter in step 2.
2. Cook chorizo in frying pan on moderate heat, breaking up meat with wooden spoon, until thoroughly browned, about eight to ten minutes, before you put in onion and jalapeño.
3. Substitute shredded cheddar cheese for queso fresco and 2 thinly cut scallions for cilantro.

Scrambled With Chorizo (Huevos Revueltos Con Chorizo Eggs)

Yield: Servings 1

Ingredients:

- 1 chorizo, approximately 2 ounces (60 g)
- 2 big eggs
- Salt if required

Directions:

1. Heat the pan. Skin the chorizo and crumble it into the pan. Allow it to cook gently—if the heat is too high it will burn swiftly—until the fat has rendered out of the meat. Drain off all but 2 tablespoons of the fat.
2. Break the eggs into the pan and stir until set. Put in salt if required.
3. Serve instantly.

Spicy Chilaquiles With Fried Eggs

Yield: Servings 4

Ingredients:

- 1 onion, chopped fine
- 1 tablespoon unsalted butter, cut into 4 pieces and chilled
- 1 teaspoon minced canned chipotle chile in adobo sauce
- 1½ cups chicken broth
- 16 (6 inch) corn tortillas, cut into 8 wedges
- 2 (8 ounce) cans tomato sauce
- 2 tablespoons chili powder
- 2 tablespoons chopped fresh cilantro
- 3 garlic cloves, minced
- 4 ounces queso fresco, crumbled (1 cup)
- 6 tablespoons plus 2 teaspoons extra virgin olive oil
- 8 big eggs
- Salt and pepper

Directions:

1. Adjust oven racks to upper middle and lower middle positions and heat oven to 425 degrees. Spread tortillas uniformly over 2 rimmed baking sheets. Sprinkle each sheet with 2 tablespoons oil and ¼ teaspoon salt and toss until uniformly coated. Bake, stirring once in a while, until tortillas are golden brown and crunchy, fifteen to twenty minutes, switching sheets midway through baking.

2. Heat 2 tablespoons oil in Dutch oven on moderate heat until it starts to shimmer Put in onion and cook until tender, approximately five minutes. Mix in chili powder, garlic, and chipotle and cook until aromatic, approximately half a minute. Put in tomato sauce and broth, bring to simmer, and cook, stirring once in a while, until flavors meld, approximately ten minutes. Remove pot from heat.

3. Heat remaining 2 teaspoons oil in 12 or 14 inch nonstick frying pan using low heat for five minutes. In the meantime, crack eggs into 2 small bowls (4 eggs per container) and sprinkle with salt and pepper.

4. Increase heat to moderate high and heat until oil is shimmering. Put in butter and swiftly swirl to coat frying pan. Working swiftly, pour 1 container of eggs in 1 side of frying pan and second container of eggs in other side. Cover and cook for a couple of minutes.

5. Remove frying pan from heat and allow it to stand, covered, approximately 2 minutes for runny yolks (white around edge of yolk will be barely opaque), approximately 3 minutes for tender but set yolks, and approximately four minutes for medium set yolks.

6. While eggs finish cooking, return sauce to brief simmer over moderate high heat. Remove the heat, mix in toasted tortillas, cover, and allow it to sit until tortillas have become tender slightly, 2 to five minutes. Split tortilla mixture among separate plates and drizzle with queso fresco. Slide eggs on top, drizzle with cilantro, and serve instantly.

Sweet Potato And Chorizo Hash

Yield: Servings 4

Ingredients:

- ½ cup heavy cream
- ½ teaspoon ground cumin

- ¾ teaspoon minced fresh thyme or ¼ teaspoon dried
- 1 onion, chopped fine
- 1 pound russet potatoes, peeled and slice into ½ inch pieces
- 1 pound sweet potatoes, peeled and slice into ½ inch pieces
- 1 tablespoon minced fresh chives
- 1 tablespoon vegetable oil
- 1½ teaspoons minced canned chipotle chile in adobo sauce
- 3 garlic cloves, minced
- 8 big eggs
- 8 ounces Mexican style chorizo sausage, casings removed
- Salt and pepper

Directions:

1. Toss russet potatoes, sweet potatoes, oil, ½ teaspoon salt, and ¼ teaspoon pepper together in container. Cover and microwave until potatoes are translucent around edges, 7 to 9 minutes, stirring midway through microwaving.
2. In the meantime, cook chorizo in 12 inch nonstick frying pan over moderate high heat, breaking up meat with wooden spoon, until starting to brown, approximately five minutes. Mix in onion and cook until onion becomes tender and mildly browned, five to seven minutes. Mix in garlic, chipotle, thyme, and cumin and cook until aromatic, approximately half a minute.
3. Mix in cream and hot potatoes. Using back of spatula, gently pack potatoes into frying pan and cook uninterrupted for a couple of minutes. Flip hash, 1 portion at a time, and lightly repack into frying pan. Repeat flipping process every few minutes until potatoes are well browned, six to eight minutes.
4. Remove the heat, use spoon to make 4 indentations (2 to 3 inches wide) in hash, pushing hash up into center and around edges of frying pan (bottom of frying pan must be uncovered in each divot). Crack 2 eggs into each dent and sprinkle with salt and pepper. Cover and cook over moderate low heat until whites are just set and yolks are still runny, four to 8 minutes. Drizzle with chives and serve instantly.

Tomato And Corn Tostadas With Baked Eggs

Yield: Servings 4

Ingredients:

- ½ teaspoon ground coriander
- 1 cup refried beans, warmed
- 1 onion, halved and cut thin
- 1 teaspoon ground cumin
- 1½ cups fresh or thawed frozen corn
- 1½ pounds cherry tomatoes, halved
- 2 ounces queso fresco, crumbled (½ cup)
- 2 tablespoons plus ¾ cup vegetable oil
- 2 teaspoons minced canned chipotle chile in adobo sauce
- 2 teaspoons minced fresh oregano or ½ teaspoon dried
- 3 garlic cloves, minced
- 3 tablespoons chopped fresh cilantro
- 8 (6 inch) corn tortillas
- 8 big eggs
- Salt and pepper

Directions:

1. Adjust oven rack to middle position and heat oven to 500 degrees. Coat rimmed baking sheet with aluminium foil. Toss tomatoes, corn, onion, 2 tablespoons oil, garlic, chipotle, oregano, cumin, coriander, ½ teaspoon salt, and ¼ teaspoon pepper together, then spread onto readied sheet. Roast vegetables, stirring once in a while, until tomatoes become tender and skins start to shrivel, ten to fifteen minutes. Remove sheet from oven.

2. In the meantime, using fork, poke center of each tortilla three to four times (to stop puffing and allow for even cooking). Heat remaining ¾ cup oil in 8 inch heavy bottomed frying pan on moderate heat to 350 degrees. Coat second rimmed baking sheet with multiple layers of paper towels.

3. Working with one tortilla at a time, put in to hot oil and place metal potato masher on top to keep tortilla flat and submerged in oil. Fry until crunchy and mildly browned, 45 to 60 seconds (no flipping is necessary). Move fried tortilla to paper towel–covered sheet. Repeat with the rest of the tortillas. Drizzle with salt.

4. Using spoon, make 8 indentations (2 to 3 inches wide) in tomato mixture. Crack 1 egg into each dent and season eggs with salt and pepper. Bake until egg whites are just set and yolks are still runny, five to seven minutes, rotating sheet midway through baking.

5. Spread 2 tablespoons warm refried beans over each tostada, then top with vegetables and eggs. Drizzle with queso fresco and cilantro and serve instantly.

Vegetable Recipes

Vegetables and their dishes are usually fir first course on the Mexican table. However, these also make for a great main course, if the serving size is big enough.

BLACK BEAN BURGERS WITH CHIPOTLE AND CORN

Yield: Servings 6

Ingredients:

- ¼ cup finely chopped red bell pepper
- ¼ cup minced fresh cilantro
- ½ teaspoon salt
- ¾ cup fresh or thawed frozen corn
- 1 cup panko bread crumbs
- 1 shallot, minced
- 1 tablespoon minced canned chipotle chile in adobo sauce
- 1 teaspoon ground cumin
- 2 (fifteen ounce) cans black beans, washed
- 2 big eggs
- 6 tablespoons vegetable oil

Directions:

1. Heat 1 tablespoon oil in 12 inch nonstick frying pan over moderate high heat until it starts to shimmer Put in corn and cook, stirring once in a while, until kernels start to brown and pop, three to five minutes; allow to cool slightly.
2. In the meantime, purée 2½ cups beans in big container with potato masher until mostly smooth. In separate container, whisk eggs, chipotle, cumin, salt, and 1 tablespoon oil together. Stir egg mixture, corn, panko, bell pepper, cilantro, shallot, and remaining beans into mashed beans until blended. Split mixture into 6 equivalent portions and lightly pack into an inch thick burgers.
3. Adjust oven rack to middle position and heat oven to 200 degrees. Heat 2 tablespoons oil in now empty frying pan on moderate heat until it starts to shimmer Cautiously lay

3 burgers in frying pan and cook until thoroughly browned on both sides, four to five minutes per side.

4. Move burgers to paper towel–lined plate and keep warm in oven. Repeat with remaining 2 tablespoons oil and 3 burgers and serve.

CAULIFLOWER IN AVOCADO SAUCE (COLIFLOR EN AGUACATE)

Yield: Servings 6

Ingredients:

The cauliflower

- 1 pound (450 g) cauliflower, trimmed of the outer leaves
- 1 teaspoon salt
- A big pinch of aniseeds, tied in a small piece of cheesecloth

The guacamole

- ½ teaspoon salt or to taste
- 2 avocados
- 2 fresh serrano chiles or any hot, fresh green chiles
- 2 tablespoons finely chopped white onion
- 3 sprigs cilantro
- 8 ounces (225 g) tomatoes, broiled

The topping

- 2 ounces (60 g) queso fresco, crumbled (about ⅓ cup/85 ml)

Directions:

1. Wash the cauliflower well and split it into florets. Bring a big pan of water to a rolling boil. Put in the cauliflower, aniseeds, and salt and cook until just soft—about five minutes after returning to the boil. Drain and allow to cool.

2. While the cauliflower is cooking, make the guacamole. Crush the chiles, cilantro, onion, and salt to a paste in a blender. Put in the tomatoes and blend a second or so longer. Skin the avocados and purée until the desired smoothness is achieved. Put in the mixed ingredients and mix thoroughly.

3. To serve as a vegetable dip, put the guacamole in a small container and top with the crumbled cheese. Place the container onto a big platter, on which you have arranged the cauliflower.

4. To serve as a vegetable dish or salad, put the cauliflower in a single layer on a shallow serving dish. Mask with the guacamole and top with the crumbled cheese.

CHEESY STUFFED POBLANOS

Yield: Servings four to 6

Ingredients:

- ⅛ teaspoon cayenne pepper
- ¼ cup minced fresh cilantro
- 1 cup water
- 1 onion, chopped fine
- 1 recipe Fresh Tomato Salsa
- 1 tablespoon ground cumin
- 1 tablespoon juice
- 1 tablespoon minced fresh oregano or 1 teaspoon dried
- 1 tablespoon vegetable oil
- 1 teaspoon chili powder
- 1 teaspoon grated lime zest plus
- 2 (fifteen ounce) cans pinto beans, washed
- 2 cups fresh or thawed frozen corn
- 4 garlic cloves, minced
- 4 ounces Monterey Jack cheese, shredded (1 cup)
- 4 ounces sharp cheddar cheese, shredded (1 cup)
- 8 big poblano chiles
- Salt and pepper

Directions:

1. Adjust oven racks to upper middle and lower middle positions and heat oven to 425 degrees. Coat 2 rimmed baking sheets with aluminium foil and set wire rack in each. Using potato masher, purée half of beans with water in container until mostly smooth.

2. Heat oil in 12 inch nonstick frying pan on moderate heat until it starts to shimmer Put in onion and cook until tender, approximately five minutes. Mix in garlic, cumin, oregano, chili powder, lime zest, ½ teaspoon salt, and cayenne and cook until aromatic, approximately half a minute. Put in mashed bean mixture and cook, stirring continuously, until nearly all liquid has vaporized, three to five minutes.

3. Mix in corn and remaining beans and cook until warmed through, approximately 2 minutes. Remove the heat, mix in Monterey Jack, cheddar, cilantro, and lime juice. Sprinkle with salt and pepper to taste.

4. Leaving stem undamaged, cut slit along the length down 1 side of each poblano. Microwave poblanos in covered container until just flexible, approximately 2½ minutes. Lightly pry open poblanos, remove seeds, and stuff uniformly with bean cheese mixture. Lay poblanos, stuffed side up, on readied sheets. Bake until soft, switching and rotating sheets midway through baking, thirty to forty minutes. Serve with salsa.

CHICKPEA CAKES WITH CHIPOTLE LIME CREAM

Yield: Servings 6

Ingredients:

- ½ teaspoon grated lime zest plus
- ¾ cup panko bread crumbs
- 1 cup fresh or thawed frozen corn
- 1 cup sour cream
- 1 garlic clove, minced
- 1 tablespoon juice
- 1 tablespoon minced canned chipotle chile in adobo sauce
- 2 (fifteen ounce) cans chickpeas, washed
- 2 big eggs

- 2 teaspoons ground coriander
- 3 tablespoons minced fresh cilantro
- 4 scallions, cut thin
- 7 tablespoons vegetable oil
- Salt and pepper

Directions:

1. Whisk ½ cup sour cream, chipotle, lime zest and juice, and ¼ teaspoon salt in container; cover and place in your fridge until serving.
2. Heat 1 tablespoon oil in 12 inch nonstick frying pan over moderate high heat until it starts to shimmer Put in corn and cook, stirring once in a while, until kernels start to brown and pop, three to five minutes. Mix in coriander and garlic and cook until aromatic, approximately half a minute; allow to cool slightly.
3. Pulse chickpeas inside a food processor to crude paste, approximately 12 pulses. Whisk eggs, 1 teaspoon salt, and 2 tablespoons oil together in medium container. Mix in panko, scallions, cilantro, remaining ½ cup sour cream, cooked corn, and processed chickpeas until blended. Split mixture into 6 equivalent portions and lightly pack into an inch thick patties.
4. Adjust oven rack to middle position and heat oven to 200 degrees. Heat 2 tablespoons oil in now empty frying pan on moderate heat until it starts to shimmer Cautiously lay 3 patties in frying pan and cook until thoroughly browned on both sides, three to five minutes per side.
5. Move patties to paper towel–lined plate and keep warm in oven. Repeat with remaining 2 tablespoons oil and 3 patties. Serve with chipotle lime cream sauce.

CHILE POBLANO STRIPS (RAJAS DE CHILE POBLANO)

Yield: Servings 6

Ingredients:

- ¼ cup (65 ml) vegetable oil
- 1 cup (250 ml) thinly cut white onion
- 12 small poblano chiles, charred and peeled
- Salt to taste

Directions:

1. Remove stems, seeds, and veins from the chiles and chop the flesh into strips about 3 inches (8 cm) long and just less than ½ inch (1.5 cm) wide.
2. Heat the oil in a big frying pan, put in the onion, and cook until translucent—about two minutes. Put in the chile strips and salt, cover the pan, and cook, shaking the pan occasionally, for approximately 8 minutes. Serve hot.

CHILES STUFFED WITH CORN AND CREAM (CHILES RELLENOS DE ELOTE CON CREMA)

Yield: Servings 6

Ingredients:

- ¼ cup (65 ml) unsalted butter
- ⅓ cup (85 ml) water, if required
- 1¼ cups (315 ml) finely chopped white onion
- 12 small poblano chiles, charred, peeled, and cleaned, or 12 ancho chiles, seeds and veins removed, soaked in hot water for fifteen minutes
- 2 cups (500 ml) thick sour cream or crème fraîche
- 2 garlic cloves, finely chopped
- 3 tablespoons finely chopped epazote
- 4 cups (1 l) corn kernels (if frozen, measure before defrosting)
- 8 ounces (225 g) queso fresco, cut into thick slices
- About 3 ounces (85 g) chihuahua cheese or mild cheddar, grated (approximately 1 heaped cup/275 ml)
- Salt to taste

Directions:

1. Melt the butter in a big frying pan and fry the onion and garlic gently, without browning, until soft—about two minutes. Put in the corn kernels and salt, then cover the pan and cook over gentle heat until the kernels are soft. If the corn is very dry, put in about ⅓ cup (85 ml) water. Cooking time is ten to fifteen minutes, depending on

whether fresh or frozen corn is used. Put in the epazote and tweak the seasoning. Set aside to cool a little.

2. Preheat your oven to 350° f (180° c).

3. Clean the chiles cautiously, leaving the top and stem undamaged. Fill the chiles well with the corn mixture. Place a slice of cheese in the middle of the filling (the chiles must be fat but open).

4. Put the chiles in a single layer in a shallow ovenproof dish into which they will just fit easily. Pour over the sour cream and bake until well thoroughly heated, then drizzle with the grated cheese and carry on baking until the cheese is melted.

CHILES STUFFED WITH ZUCCHINI (CHILES RELLENOS CON CALABACITAS)

Yield: Servings 6

Ingredients:

- ¼ teaspoon dried mexican oregano
- ½ tablespoon fresh lime juice
- ⅔ cup (165 ml) finely chopped white onion
- 1½ pounds (675 g) zucchini, trimmed and slice into ¼-inch (.75-cm) cubes (about 5¼ cups/1.313 l)
- 2 garlic cloves, finely chopped
- 2 tablespoons fruity olive oil
- 2 tablespoons unsalted butter
- 2 tablespoons wine vinegar
- 2½ tablespoons vegetable oil
- 6 medium poblano chiles, peeled and cleaned, ready for stuffing
- 6 ounces (180 g) queso fresco, crumbled (approximately 1 cup/250 ml)
- Salt to taste

The topping

- 6 radish flowers
- Romaine lettuce leaves

Directions:

1. Heat 1½ tablespoons of the oil in a heavy frying pan. Put in 2 tablespoons of the onion and half the garlic and fry gently without browning for a couple of minutes. Put in the zucchini and salt, cover the pan, and cook on moderate heat, shaking the pan occasionally so the mixture does not stick, until the zucchini is just done— approximately eight minutes. (squash differ in moisture content. In this recipe they should steam in their own juices, but if they seem too dry, put in a little water; if too juicy, remove the lid and reduce the liquid.)

2. While the mixture is still warm, put in the remaining chopped onion, the rest of the garlic, and the oregano, vinegar, lime juice, olive oil, and cheese. Adjust the seasoning.

3. Fill the chiles until they are full but will still meet at the opening. There must be about ⅓ to ½ cup (85 to 125 ml) of the stuffing left over, depending, of course, on the size of the chiles. Fasten each opening using a toothpick.

4. Melt the butter and remaining 1 tablespoon oil together in a frying pan. Put in the stuffed chiles and fry them on moderate heat, flipping them over gently so the stuffing does not fall out, until mildly browned.

5. Position the chiles on a serving dish and top with lettuce and the radish flowers. Drizzle with the rest of the stuffing. They can be served either hot or at room temperature as a first course.

CHILES WITH CHEESE (CHILE CON QUESO)

Yield: Servings 6

Ingredients:

- ¾ cup (185 ml) whole milk
- 1 cup (250 ml) thinly cut tomatoes
- 1½ cups (375 ml) thinly cut white onions
- 3 tablespoons water
- 5 tablespoons vegetable oil
- 8 ounces (225 g) chihuahua, asadero, or muenster cheese, thinly cut
- fifteen green anaheim chiles, charred, peeled, and slice into strips (do not remove seeds;)

- Salt to taste

Directions:

1. Heat the oil in a deep frying pan and cook the onion using low heat until translucent—about two minutes.
2. Put in the tomatoes with the chile strips to the pan with salt. Cover and cook on moderate heat for approximately five minutes. Put in the milk and water and allow the mixture to cook for a few minutes more.
3. Just before you serve, put in the cheese to the chile mixture. Serve the moment the cheese melts.
4. Note: this must be eaten the moment it is prepared. However, you can always prepare the chile-tomato mixture well ahead and put in the cheese at the final moment.

CORN AND BLACK BEAN TORTILLA TART

Yield: Servings four to 6

Ingredients:

- ¼ cup extra virgin olive oil
- ¾ cup vegetable broth
- 1 (fifteen ounce) can black beans, washed
- 1 jalapeño chile, stemmed, seeded, and minced
- 1 onion, chopped fine
- 1 teaspoon ground cumin
- 1 teaspoon lime juice
- 2 big plum tomatoes, cored and slice into ¼ inch pieces
- 2 ounces queso fresco, crumbled (½ cup)
- 2 tablespoons minced fresh cilantro
- 2½ cups fresh or thawed frozen corn
- 3 garlic cloves, minced
- 4 (10 inch) flour tortillas
- 4 scallions, cut thin
- 6 ounces cheddar cheese, shredded (1½ cups)
- Salt and pepper

Directions:

1. Adjust oven rack to middle position and heat oven to 400 degrees. Heat 1 tablespoon oil in 12 inch nonstick frying pan over moderate high heat until it starts to shimmer Put in corn and cook, stirring once in a while, until kernels start to brown and pop, three to five minutes. Move to big container and allow to cool slightly. Mix in tomatoes, scallions, 1 tablespoon cilantro, and lime juice, and sprinkle with salt and pepper to taste.

2. Wipe frying pan clean using paper towels. Put in 1 tablespoon oil and onion to frying pan and cook on moderate heat until tender, three to five minutes. Mix in jalapeño, garlic, and cumin and cook until aromatic, approximately half a minute. Mix in beans and broth and cook until liquid has nearly vaporized, five to seven minutes. Move mixture to big container and purée beans with potato masher until mostly smooth. Sprinkle with salt and pepper to taste.

3. Coat rimless or inverted baking sheet using parchment paper. Softly brush both sides of tortillas with remaining 2 tablespoons oil. Put 1 tortilla on readied sheet. Spread one-fourth of mashed beans over top, leaving ½ inch border around edge. Drizzle with one-fourth of corn mixture, one-fourth of cheddar, and one-fourth of queso fresco. Repeat with the rest of the tortillas, beans, corn, cheddar, and queso fresco to make layered tart.

4. Bake tart until cheese is melted and slightly brown, twenty to twenty-five minutes. Allow to cool on baking sheet for five minutes, then slide onto cutting board using parchment; discard parchment. Drizzle remaining 1 tablespoon cilantro over top. Cut into wedges before you serve.

CORN COOKED WITH EPAZOTE (ESQUITES)

Yield: Servings 6

Ingredients:

- 1½ teaspoons salt, or to taste
- 2 serrano chiles or any fresh, hot green chiles, finely chopped
- 2 tablespoons unsalted butter
- 3 heaped tablespoons chopped epazote leaves
- 3 tablespoons lard or vegetable oil

- 6 small ears of corn

Directions:

1. Cut through each ear of corn at the stalk end and remove all the leaves and silks. Chop the ears into slices approximately 1½ inches (4 cm) thick.
2. Heat a heavy pan into which the corn will just fit in a single layer. Melt the butter and lard together in the pan, then put in the corn, salt, and chiles. Cover the pan and cook the corn on moderate heat, shaking the pan occasionally and turning the corn over once, until it is soft and slightly browned—about fifteen minutes. Mix in the epazote for the last three minutes of the cooking time.

CORN FUNGUS WITH ZUCCHINI (CUITLACOCHE CON CALABACITAS ESTILO QUERÉTARO)

Yield: Servings 6

Ingredients:

- ¼ cup (65 ml) vegetable oil
- ½ teaspoon salt, or to taste
- 1 cup (250 ml) corn kernels
- 1 garlic clove, chopped
- 1 heaped tablespoon roughly chopped epazote leaves
- 1 pound (450 g) cuitlacoche, shaved from the corn cob and roughly chopped (approximately four cups/1 l)
- 1 pound (450 g) zucchini, trimmed and diced small (about 3½ cups/875 ml)
- 2 big scallions, finely chopped
- 2 jalapeño chiles, serrano chiles, or any fresh, hot green chiles, cut into fine strips

Directions:

1. Heat the oil in a big frying pan and fry the scallions and garlic gently, without browning, until tender. Put in one-fourth of the diced zucchini and cook for a few seconds over a quite high heat, turning continuously, then put in another quarter, and so on. When all the zucchini is in the pan, fry for a few minutes more.

2. Put in the corn kernels by degrees, similarly you did the zucchini. Put in the cuitlacoche similarly. Put in the chile strips and salt, then cover the pan and cook over a low heat while stirring occasionally, until the vegetables are soft—about fifteen minutes. (the vegetables should remain moist and cook in their own juices, but if they do get rather dry, drizzle liberally with water.)
3. When almost cooked, put in the epazote leaves and simmer a few seconds longer.

CORN WITH CREAM, CHILES, AND CHEESE (ELOTE CON CREMA)

Yield: Servings 6

Ingredients:

- ¼ cup (65 ml) butter
- ⅔ cup (165 ml) finely chopped white onion
- 1 garlic clove, finely chopped
- 1 teaspoon salt, or to taste
- 4 ounces (115 g) chihuahua cheese, in small cubes, approximately 1 cup (250 ml)
- 5 poblano chiles, charred, peeled, and seeds removed
- About 4 cups (1 l) corn kernels (frozen is fine)
- thick sour cream

Directions:

1. Preheat your oven to 350° f (180° c).
2. Melt the butter in an ovenproof frying pan and cook the onion and garlic using low heat until translucent.
3. Chop the chiles into thin strips, put in them to the pan, and cook them, covered, approximately five minutes.
4. Put in the corn and salt to the chile mixture. Cover firmly with a lid and put in your oven to bake for about twenty minutes. Put in the cheese just before the end of baking time.
5. Serve hot, with the sour cream. This dish is best eatenimmediately after it's cooked, as the cheese gets tough when reheated.

FRESH CORN TORTE (TORTA DE ELOTE)

Yield: Servings 6

Ingredients:

- ½ cup (125 ml) granulated sugar
- 1 teaspoon baking powder
- 4 big eggs, separated
- 4 ounces (115 g) unsalted butter, softened (¼ cup/65 ml)
- 5 cups (1.25 l) field corn kernels
- A little milk
- Salt to taste
- thick sour cream

Directions:

1. Put a heavy baking sheet in your oven and preheat to 350° f (180° c).
2. Grease an ovenproof dish roughly 9 by 9 by 2 inches (23 by 23 by 5 cm) and drizzle with toasted, thoroughly ground bread crumbs.
3. Put about one third of the corn into a blender or food processor, putting in only enough milk to loosen the cutting blades of the blender and blend the corn to a rough consistency. Put in the rest of the corn by degrees and keep stopping the machine regularly to release the blades. Set the mixture aside.
4. Beat the butter and sugar together until they are fluffy.
5. Put in the egg yolks one by one to the creamed mixture and keep beating until they are thoroughly combined in. Put in the salt and the corn mixture and beat once more.
6. Beat the egg whites until they are stiff and fold them into the mixture with the baking powder. Pour into the prepared dish. Put the dish on the hot baking sheet in your oven and bake for approximately 1 hour or until springy to the touch.
7. Serve instantly with thick sour cream, crème fraîche, or a salsa of your choice.

HUARACHES WITH POBLANOS, BELL PEPPERS, AND QUESO FRESCO

Yield: 6 huaraches; serves four to 6

Ingredients:

- ¾ cup Mexican crema
- ¾ cup vegetarian refried pinto beans, warmed
- 1 recipe Pickled Shallot and Radishes (recipe follows)
- 1½ ounces queso fresco, crumbled (⅓ cup)
- 1¾ cups hot tap water
- 2 cups (8 ounces) masa harina
- 2 poblano chiles, stemmed, seeded, and slice into ¼ inch wide strips
- 2 red bell peppers, stemmed, seeded, and slice into ¼ inch wide strips
- 3 tablespoons vegetable oil
- Salt

Directions:

1. Heat 1 tablespoon oil in 12 inch nonstick frying pan over moderate high heat until it starts to shimmer Put in poblanos, bell peppers, and ½ teaspoon salt and cook, stirring once in a while, until peppers become tender and mildly browned, ten to twelve minutes; move to container and cover to keep warm. Wipe frying pan clean using paper towels.

2. In the meantime, mix masa harina and 1 teaspoon salt in medium container, then mix in water using a rubber spatula. Use your hands to knead mixture in container until soft, sticky dough forms, one to two minutes. Cover dough using a damp dish towel and allow it to sit for five minutes.

3. Adjust oven rack to middle position, set wire rack in rimmed baking sheet, set sheet on oven rack, and heat oven to 200 degrees. Coat second baking sheet using parchment paper. Move dough to clean counter, form into ball, then divide uniformly into 6 pieces. Roll each piece into 5 inch long rope, place on parchment covered sheet, and cover using a damp dish towel.

4. Cut sides of 1 quart zipper lock bag, leaving bottom seam undamaged. Put 1 piece dough on 1 side of plastic bag and fold other side over top. Push dough into ⅛ inch thick oval with the help of a pie plate. Take the plastic off, return shaped dough to sheet, and cover with damp towel. Repeat with remaining 5 pieces dough.

5. Put in 2 teaspoons oil to now empty frying pan and place over moderate high heat until it starts to shimmer Lay 2 pieces dough in single layer in frying pan and cook until dark spotty brown on first side, four to six minutes. Flip dough and carry on cooking

until crunchy on second side, 2 to 4 minutes. Move huaraches to wire rack in oven and repeat with remaining 4 teaspoons oil and 4 pieces dough in 2 more batches.

6. Spread refried beans uniformly over huaraches, leaving ¼ inch border around edge. Top uniformly with pepper mixture, drizzle uniformly with queso fresco, and sprinkle with crema. Serve with Pickled Shallot and Radishes.

PICKLED SHALLOT AND RADISHES

Yield: About 1 CUP

Ingredients:

- ⅛ teaspoon salt
- ¼ cup lime juice (2 limes)
- 1 shallot, cut thin
- 1 teaspoon sugar
- 5 radishes, trimmed and cut thin

Directions:

1. Mix all ingredients in container. Place in your fridge for maximum 2 days.

OAXACAN CHILE STRIPS (RAJAS DE CHILE ESTILO OAXAQUEÑO)

Yield: Servings 6

Ingredients:

- ½ cup (125 ml) thinly cut white onion
- ½ cup (125 ml) whole epazote leaves
- 1½ cups (375 ml) whole milk
- 12 ounces (340 g) queso fresco, muenster cheese, teleme, or jack, cut into thick slices
- 3 tablespoons vegetable oil
- 9 chiles de agua, or 3 small poblano chiles, or anaheim chiles, charred, peeled, cleaned, and slice into strips
- Salt to taste (depending on the cheese)

Directions:

1. In a heavy frying pan approximately 10 inches (25 cm) in diameter, heat the oil, put in the onion and unchopped epazote leaves, and fry until they wilt, stirring occasionally—about two minutes. Put in the chile strips and salt and fry for approximately 3 minutes, stirring occasionally.
2. Over low heat, progressively mix in the milk, then put in the pieces of cheese and cook until they melt. Serve hot.

PEA PUDDING (BUDÍN DE CHÍCHARO)

Yield: Servings 6

Ingredients:

- ½ cup (125 ml) granulated sugar
- 1 teaspoon salt
- 1½ teaspoons baking powder
- 2 pounds (900 g) frozen or fresh cooked peas
- 3 big eggs, separated
- 4 ounces (115 g) chihuahua or muenster cheese, grated (approximately 1 scant cup/ 235 ml)
- 6 ounces (180 g) rice flour, sifted (approximately 1½ cups/375 ml)
- 6 ounces (180 g) unsalted butter (⅔ cup/165 ml)

To serve

- A sauce made by combining 2 cups (500 ml) fresh orange juice with ¾ cup (185 ml) finely chopped walnuts

Directions:

1. Preheat your oven to 500° f (260° c). Butter an 8-inch square baking dish.
2. Pass the peas through the medium disk of a food mill or process in a food processor. Melt the butter and let cool.
3. Setting the egg whites aside, beat the egg yolks until thick. Put in the sugar and carry on beating until well blended. Beat in the rice flour alternately with the butter.

4. Mix in the pea pulp, salt, and cheese, mix thoroughly, and put in the baking powder.

5. Beat the egg whites until they are stiff and fold them into the mixture. Pour the mixture into the prepared dish. Put the dish on a baking sheet and bake for about ten minutes. Then lower the oven temperature to 350° f (180° c) and carry on cooking for approximately 45 minutes. The budín must be tender and spongy to the touch—the top and sides well browned, but the inside moist.

6. Serve instantly, with the orange and walnut sauce to accompany it.

CARROT PUDDING (BUDÍN DE ZANAHORIA)

Yield: Servings 6

Ingredients:

- 2 pounds (900 g) cooked carrots

Directions:

1. Follow the above recipe, omitting the cheese and putting in ½ cup (125 ml) raisins.

2. This can either be eaten hot as a coffee cake or served as a dessert with a thin syrup and the addition of ¼ cup (65 ml) rum poured over it just before you serve.

POBLANO CHILES STUFFED WITH MEAT (CHILES RELLENOS DE PICADILLO)

Yield: Servings 6

Ingredients:

The picadillo

- ¼ cup (65 ml) lard or vegetable oil
- ½ white onion, cut
- ½-inch (1.5-cm) piece of cinnamon stick, broken into little pieces
- ⅔ cup (165 ml) finely chopped white onion
- 1¼ pounds (565 g) tomatoes, roughly chopped (about 2¾ cups/685 ml)

- 2 garlic cloves
- 2 heaped tablespoons cubed acitrón or chopped candied fruit
- 2 pounds (900 g) boneless pork with some fat, cut into 1-inch (2.5-cm) cubes
- 2 tablespoons blanched and slivered almonds
- 3 garlic cloves, finely chopped
- 3 heaped tablespoons raisins
- 5 whole cloves
- 8 peppercorns
- Salt to taste

The tomato broth

- 1¼ pounds (565 g) tomatoes, roughly chopped (about 2¾ cups/685 ml)
- 1-inch (2.5-cm) piece of cinnamon stick, broken into two pieces
- 2 garlic cloves, roughly chopped
- 2 mexican bay leaves
- 2 tablespoons lard or vegetable oil
- 3 cups (750 ml) reserved pork broth
- 3 sprigs fresh thyme, or ¼ teaspoon dried
- 3 tablespoons roughly chopped white onion
- 4 whole cloves
- 6 peppercorns
- Salt to taste

The chiles

- 6 poblano chiles, charred and peeled

The batter

- ¼ teaspoon salt
- 4 big eggs, separated
- About ⅓ cup (85 ml) all-purpose flour
- Vegetable oil for frying

Directions:

1. Place the meat into a big deep cooking pan with the cut onion, garlic, and salt and barely cover with water. Bring the meat to a simmer and carry on cooking using low heat until the meat is soft—about forty minutes. Leave the meat to cool in the broth. When cool, strain the meat, saving for later the broth. First shred and then cut the meat to a medium texture—there must be about 3 cups (750 ml).
2. Skim the broth.
3. Melt the lard in a big frying pan and cook the chopped onion and garlic until translucent—about two minutes.
4. Put in the meat and allow it to cook until it starts to brown, approximately eight minutes.
5. Crush the spices roughly and put in them, with the remaining picadillo ingredients, apart from the tomatoes, to the meat mixture. Cook the mixture a little time longer.
6. Combine the tomatoes for a short period of time and put in them to the mixture in the pan. Carry on cooking the mixture using high heat for approximately ten minutes, stirring it occasionally to prevent sticking. Put in salt to taste. It must be moist but not juicy.
7. To prepare the tomato broth: blend the tomatoes with the onion and garlic until the desired smoothness is achieved.
8. Melt the lard in a wide pan and fry the mixed tomatoes using high heat for approximately 3 minutes, stirring to stop sticking. Put in the remaining ingredients, apart from the broth and salt, and cook them using high heat for approximately five minutes, stirring.
9. Put in the pork broth and carry on cooking the broth on moderate heat for approximately ten minutes. By that time it will be well seasoned and reduced fairly— but still a broth rather than a thick sauce. Put in salt as required.
10. To prepare the chiles: make a slit in the side of each chile and cautiously remove the seeds and veins. Be careful to leave the top of the chile, the part around the base of the stem, undamaged.
11. Stuff each chile with approximately ½ cup (125 ml) of the picadillo until they are well filled out but the cut edges still come together.
12. To prepare the batter: heat the oil in a deep frying pan.
13. In the meantime, beat the egg whites until they are firm, but not too dry. Put in the salt and egg yolks one at a time, beating well after each addition.
14. Prepare one chile at a time: pat the chile completely dry (or the batter will not adhere) and drizzle them mildly with flour. Coat with the batter.

15. Fry in the hot oil, turning it occasionally, until the batter turns a deep golden color—about two minutes.

16. Drain the chiles using paper towels and put them in the tomato broth—it should come about midway up the chiles—to heat through using low heat. Serve instantly.

17. Note: you can prepare the stuffing and the sauce the day before, and clean the chiles. But do not put the stuffing into the chiles until about 2 hours before cooking.

18. If you do prepare the chiles 2 hours ahead, do not put them into the broth. Put them on a rimmed cookie sheet lined with multiple layers of paper toweling, and reheat in a 350° f (180° c) oven for approximately twenty minutes (5 minutes if filled with cheese, below). This method has the added advantage that the paper absorbs fairly a lot of the grease. Then put the chiles in the broth or pour broth over and serve with hot tortillas.

Variation: Chiles rellenos de queso (chiles stuffed with cheese)

Poblano chiles and anchos can be used for this recipe.

Follow instructions for the above recipe for preparing the chiles, and stuff them with strips of cheese instead of picadillo. Any cheese that melts easily will do the job, but try queso oaxaca or chihuahua cheese for a more authentic Mexican taste.

POTATO FRITTERS WITH ZUCCHINI AVOCADO SLAW

Yield: Servings 4

Ingredients:

- ½ teaspoon ground coriander
- 1 avocado, halved, pitted, and slice into ½ inch pieces
- 1 big egg, lightly beaten
- 1 cup vegetable oil
- 1 garlic clove, minced
- 1 jalapeño chile, stemmed, seeded, and minced
- 1 pound zucchini, shredded
- 1 red bell pepper, stemmed, seeded, and chopped
- 1 teaspoon grated lime zest plus 2 tablespoons juice
- 2 scallions, white parts minced and green parts cut thin

- 2½ pounds russet potatoes, unpeeled
- 6 tablespoons minced fresh cilantro
- 8 ounces Cotija cheese, crumbled (2 cups)
- Salt and pepper

Directions:

1. Prick potatoes all over with fork, place on plate, and microwave until soft, eighteen to twenty-five minutes, turning potatoes over after ten minutes. Cut potatoes in half and allow to cool slightly. Scoop flesh into big container and purée with potato masher until no lumps remain; allow to cool for about ten minutes.

2. In the meantime, wrap zucchini in clean dish towel and squeeze out surplus liquid. Mix dried zucchini, avocado, bell pepper, ¼ cup cilantro, scallion whites, jalapeño, lime zest and juice, garlic, ¼ teaspoon salt, and ¼ teaspoon pepper in container; cover and place in your fridge until serving.

3. Stir Cotija, egg, coriander, remaining 2 tablespoons cilantro, scallion greens, ½ teaspoon salt, and ¼ teaspoon pepper into cooled potato. Split mixture into 8 equivalent portions and lightly pack into ¾ inch thick patties, approximately 3 inches wide.

4. Adjust oven rack to middle position and heat oven to 200 degrees. Set wire rack in rimmed baking sheet and line with triple layer of paper towels. Heat oil in 12 inch nonstick frying pan on moderate heat until it starts to shimmer Cautiously lay 4 patties in oil and cook until a golden-brown colour is achieved and crisp on both sides, approximately 3 minutes per side, adjusting heat as required so oil bubbles around edges of patties.

5. Move fritters to prepared rack and keep warm in oven. Repeat with remaining fritters using oil left in pan. Serve fritters warm with zucchini avocado slaw.

SKILLET RICE AND BEANS WITH CORN AND TOMATOES

Yield: Servings four to 6

Ingredients:

- ¼ cup minced fresh cilantro
- ½ teaspoon dried oregano

- 1 cup long grain white rice, washed
- 1 onion, chopped fine
- 1 tablespoon lime juice
- 1 tablespoon minced canned chipotle chile in adobo sauce
- 1 teaspoon ground coriander
- 1 teaspoon ground cumin
- 1½ cups fresh or thawed frozen corn
- 12 ounces grape tomatoes, quartered
- 2 (fifteen ounce) cans black beans, washed
- 2 cups vegetable broth
- 3 tablespoons extra virgin olive oil
- 4 garlic cloves, minced
- 5 scallions, cut thin
- Salt and pepper

Directions:

1. Heat 1 tablespoon oil in 12 inch nonstick frying pan over moderate high heat until it starts to shimmer Put in corn and cook, stirring once in a while, until kernels start to brown and pop, three to five minutes. Move corn to container and sprinkle with salt and pepper to taste.
2. Put in 1 tablespoon oil, onion, and ½ teaspoon salt to now empty frying pan and cook over moderate high heat until tender, approximately five minutes. Mix in garlic, chipotle, cumin, coriander, and oregano and cook until aromatic, approximately half a minute. Mix in beans, broth, and rice and bring to simmer. Cover, decrease the heat to low, and simmer gently, stirring once in a while, until liquid is absorbed and rice is soft, approximately fifteen minutes.
3. In the meantime, mix tomatoes, scallions, cilantro, lime juice, and remaining 1 tablespoon oil in container and sprinkle with salt and pepper to taste.
4. Remove the heat, drizzle corn over rice. Cover and allow it to sit for five minutes. Lightly fluff rice with fork and sprinkle with salt and pepper to taste. Drizzle tomato mixture over rice and beans before you serve.

SOPA SECA WITH SPINACH AND CHICKPEAS

Yield: Servings 4

Ingredients:

- ½ teaspoon ground cumin
- 1 (fifteen ounce) can chickpeas, washed
- 1 onion, chopped fine
- 1 pound curly leaf spinach, stemmed and chopped coarse
- 1 tablespoon ancho chile powder
- 2 ounces queso fresco, crumbled (½ cup)
- 2 tablespoons minced fresh cilantro
- 2 teaspoons minced fresh oregano or ½ teaspoon dried
- 2 tomatoes, cored and slice into ½ inch pieces
- 2½ cups vegetable broth
- 3 garlic cloves, minced
- 3 tablespoons vegetable oil
- 4 ounces Monterey Jack cheese, shredded (1 cup)
- 8 ounces vermicelli, broken in half
- Salt and pepper

Directions:

1. Toast pasta and 1 tablespoon oil in Dutch oven over moderate high heat while stirring continuously, until most of pasta is browned, four to six minutes; move to paper towel–lined plate.
2. Put in remaining 2 tablespoons oil, onion, and ¼ teaspoon salt to now empty pot and cook on moderate heat until tender, approximately five minutes. Mix in garlic, chile powder, oregano, and cumin and cook until aromatic, approximately half a minute.
3. Mix in broth, chickpeas, toasted pasta, ¼ teaspoon salt, and ½ teaspoon pepper. Increase heat to moderate and bring to vigorous simmer. Cover and cook, stirring frequently, until pasta is just soft, about eight to ten minutes.
4. Remove the cover, mix in spinach 1 handful at a time, and cook until spinach is mostly wilted, four to six minutes. Remove the heat, mix in tomatoes. Drizzle Monterey Jack over top, cover, and allow it to sit until cheese is melted, approximately 3 minutes. Drizzle with queso fresco and cilantro before you serve.

STEAMED CACTUS PADDLES OTUMBA (NOPALES AL VAPOR ESTILO OTUMBA)

Yield: 2½ cups (625 ml), enough to fill 12 tacos

Ingredients:

- 1 big scallion (1 big cebolla de rabo in mexico), finely chopped
- 1 pound (450 g) prepared nopales, cut into little cubes (about 3½ cups raw/875 ml)
- 1 teaspoon salt, or to taste
- 2 big sprigs epazote, roughly chopped
- 2 garlic cloves, finely chopped
- 2 jalapeño chiles or any hot, fresh green chiles (seeds and veins left in), thinly cut
- 2 tablespoons vegetable oil

Directions:

1. Heat the oil in a large, heavy deep cooking pan and fry the garlic, without browning, for a few seconds. Put in the remaining ingredients, apart from the epazote. Cover the pan and cook over low heat while stirring the mixture occasionally, until the nopales are nearly soft; their viscous juice will exude.
2. Take away the lid from the pan and carry on cooking over slightly higher heat until all sticky liquid from the nopales has dried up—about twenty minutes total, depending on how soft the nopales are. Mix in the epazote three minutes before the end of the cooking time.
3. To serve, fill a freshly made hot tortilla with some of the nopales and put in a little crumbled queso fresco, if you wish.

STUFFED (POBLANO) CHILES IN WALNUT SAUCE (CHILES EN NOGADA)

Yield: Servings 8

Ingredients:

- ⅓ cup (85 ml) raisins

- ⅓ cup (85 ml) skinned and slivered almonds
- ⅔ cup (165 ml) water
- 1 garlic clove
- 1 pound (450 g) apples, peeled, cored, and cut into little cubes (approximately 1¾ cups/435 ml)
- 1 pound (450 g) peaches, peeled, pit removed, and cut into little cubes (approximately 1½ cups/375 ml)
- 1 pound (450 g) pears, peeled, cored, and cut into little cubes (approximately 1¾ cups/435 ml)
- 1 ripe plantain (approximately eight ounces/225 g), peeled and cut into little cubes (approximately 1 cup/250 ml)
- 1 slice white onion
- 12 ounces (340 g) pork tenderloin, finely chopped, approximately 1 cup (250 ml)
- 3 tablespoons pork lard
- 3 tablespoons sugar
- 6 ounces (180 g) tomatoes, broiled
- 8 big poblano chiles, charred, peeled, seeds and veins removed
- Salt to taste

The batter

- ¼ teaspoon salt
- 4 big eggs, separated
- Flour for dusting the chiles
- Vegetable oil for frying

To decorate

- ½ cup (125 ml) flat-leaf parsley leaves
- 1 cup (250 ml) pomegranate seeds

Directions:

1. Place the pork into a large, heavy frying pan, put in the water and salt, cover, and cook using low heat until soft—about twenty-five minutes. You may need to put in slightly more water, depending on how soft the pork is. The meat must be moist but not juicy. Put in the lard and fry on moderate heat for approximately 3 minutes.

2. Combine the tomatoes with the onion and garlic and put in to the pan. Cook over quite high heat until almost dry—about five minutes.
3. Mix in the remaining ingredients apart from the chiles and cook using low heat—covered for the first ten minutes—stirring occasionally to prevent sticking—about twenty minutes. The fruit must be soft but not mushy. Set aside to cool.
4. Fill the chiles well—each should take about ½ cup (125 ml). Then follow the recipe <u>Poblano Chiles Stuffed With Meat</u> for coating and frying them. Drain thoroughly using paper towels. Cover each chile with the sauce and garnish with the pomegranate seeds and parsley.

The walnut sauce

Ingredients:

- ¼ teaspoon salt
- ⅔ cup (165 ml) medium dry sherry
- About ½ cup (125 ml) whole milk (raw if possible)
- About 72 fresh walnuts, shelled, peeled, and roughly chopped

Directions:

1. Immediately before frying the chiles, blend the walnuts with the milk and mix in the sherry and salt. The sauce will be slightly textured.
2. Note: while these chiles are best cooked and served instantly, they could be prepared ahead up to the point of stuffing and frying. They can then be reheated in a 350° f (180° c) oven on a cookie sheet lined with paper toweling to absorb some of the surplus oil. They do not freeze successfully.

STUFFED CHAYOTES (CHAYOTES RELLENOS)

Yield: Servings 6

Ingredients:

- ⅔ cup (165 ml) finely chopped white onion
- ⅔ cup (165 ml) thick sour cream, or more to taste
- 12 small strips of queso fresco or chihuahua cheese

- 2 garlic cloves, finely chopped
- 2 heaped tablespoons unsalted butter
- 2 teaspoons salt
- 3 chayotes, approximately 1 pound (450 g) each
- 4 big eggs, well beaten with salt and pepper
- 6 ounces (180 g) queso fresco, crumbled (approximately 1 cup/250 ml)

Directions:

1. Cover the whole chayotes with boiling salted water, bring them to its boiling point, and then allow them to cook covered on moderate heat until they are just soft—around half an hour.
2. Drain the chayotes and allow them to cool. When they are sufficiently cool to handle, cut into halves and remove the pithy core and almond-like seeds. (eat the seed before anybody else does.) Scoop out the flesh cautiously, leaving the outside skin undamaged. Mash the flesh well and leave it to drain in a colander for a few minutes, since the chayotes here are very watery. Place the chayote shells upside down to drain.
3. Preheat your oven to 400° f (205° c). Melt the butter in a frying pan and cook the onion and garlic on moderate heat until translucent. Put in the eggs and stir them as you would scrambled eggs until they are just set.
4. Then put in the mashed chayote flesh and allow the mixture to dry out a little for one minute or so using low heat.
5. Mix the crumbled cheese into the mixture, and stuff the reserved chayote shells. Put in your ovenproof dish.
6. Place the strips of cheese and sour cream on top of the filled shells and heat them through in your oven for approximately fifteen minutes before you serve. (do not attempt to eat the shell.) I do not recommend freezing.

VEGETABLES IN OAXACAN PUMPKIN SEED SAUCE (LEGUMBRES EN PIPIÁN OAXAQUEÑO)

Yield: Servings 6

Ingredients:

- ¼ teaspoon cumin seeds
- 1 ancho chile
- 1 garlic clove
- 1 pound (450 g) nopales, diced (about ⅔ cups/665 ml), and crisp-cooked (about 3½ cups/825 ml)
- 2 big sprigs epazote or one toasted avocado leaf
- 2 chilcosle or guajillo chiles
- 2 teaspoons salt, or to taste
- 3 tablespoons vegetable oil
- 4 cups (1 l) cold water, roughly
- 8 ounces (225 g) raw, unhulled pumpkin seeds (about 2¾ cups/685 ml)
- 8 ounces (225 g) shelled, barely cooked peas (about 2 cups/500 ml)

Directions:

1. Place the seeds into a heavy frying pan on moderate heat. Turn them continuously until they are uniformly browned, keeping a lid handy, as they are likely to pop about fiercely. Set them aside to cool.

2. Take away the seeds and veins from the ancho chile; leave the chilcosles of guajillos whole. Cover the chiles with water and simmer them for five minutes, then allow them to soak for five minutes longer. Drain and move to a blender jar. Put in the garlic and 1 cup (250 ml) of the water to the chiles and blend until the desired smoothness is achieved.

3. When the toasted seeds are cool, grind them, together with the cumin—if possible in a coffee/spice grinder—until they are rather fine but still have some texture. Move to a container and mix in the remaining 3 cups (750 ml) of water until the desired smoothness is achieved. Pass through the medium disk of a food mill or strainer and save for later. (note: there will be fairly a lot of debris of the husks left in the food mill.)

4. Heat the oil in a large, heavy pan. Put in the chile sauce through a strainer, pushing down to extract as much of the juice as you can. Reduce the heat and fry the chile sauce, scraping the bottom of the pan continuously, until it has reduced and seasoned—about two minutes.

5. Slowly mix in the pumpkin seed sauce and cook using low heat for approximately twenty minutes, stirring and scraping the bottom of the pan occasionally as it

continues to thicken. Put in the salt and vegetables and heat them through for fifteen minutes longer, putting in the epazote or avocado leaf just before the end of the cooking time. (when the sauce is perfectly cooked, pools of oil form on the surface.)

6. Serve hot, with freshly made tortillas.

VEGETARIAN TAMALE PIE

Yield: Servings 6 to 8

Ingredients:

- ¼ cup minced fresh cilantro
- 1 (fifteen ounce) can pinto beans, washed
- 1 onion, chopped coarse
- 1 tablespoon chili powder
- 1 tablespoon minced canned chipotle chile in adobo sauce
- 1 tablespoon vegetable oil
- 1 teaspoon dried oregano
- 1 zucchini, cut into ½ inch cubes
- 1½ cups coarse ground cornmeal
- 1½ cups fresh or thawed frozen corn
- 2 (28 ounce) cans diced tomatoes, drained with 2 cups juice reserved
- 2 (fifteen ounce) cans black beans, washed
- 4 cups water
- 4 garlic cloves, chopped coarse
- 4 teaspoons lime juice
- 8 ounces Monterey Jack cheese, shredded (2 cups)
- Salt and pepper

Directions:

1. Adjust oven rack to middle position and heat oven to 475 degrees. Coat rimmed baking sheet with aluminium foil. Toss tomatoes, onion, garlic, oil, and ½ teaspoon salt together in container, then spread onto readied sheet. Roast vegetables, stirring once in a while, until edges are dark brown, thirty-five to forty minutes.

2. Remove vegetables from oven and decrease oven temperature to 375 degrees. Move roasted vegetables and any collected juices to blender. Put in chipotle, chili powder, lime juice, and reserved tomato juice and pulse until sauce is slightly lumpy, about eight to 10 seconds. Season sauce with salt and pepper to taste. Mix sauce, black beans, pinto beans, corn, zucchini, cilantro, and oregano in 13 by 9 inch baking dish and top uniformly with Monterey Jack.

3. Bring water to boil in big deep cooking pan using high heat. Put in ¾ teaspoon salt, then slowly pour in cornmeal, whisking vigorously to stop lumps from forming. Decrease the heat to moderate high and cook, whisking continuously, until cornmeal starts to tenderize and mixture thickens, approximately 3 minutes. Remove the heat, sprinkle with salt and pepper to taste. Spread warm cornmeal mixture uniformly over casserole using a rubber spatula, pushing it to edges of baking dish.

4. Cover dish using foil and bake for half an hour Remove foil and carry on baking until crust is starting to brown and filling is bubbling, half an hour. Allow to cool for about ten minutes before you serve.

ZUCCHINI COOKED IN MICHOACÁN STYLE (CALABACITAS GUISADAS ESTILO MICHOACÁN)

Yield: Servings 6

Ingredients:

- ¼ cup (65 ml) vegetable oil
- ⅓ cup (85 ml) finely chopped white onion
- ⅓ cup (85 ml) roughly chopped epazote leaves
- 12 ounces (340 g) tomatoes, broiled
- 2 garlic cloves
- 2 pounds (900 g) zucchini, trimmed and diced (approximately seven cups/1.75 l)
- 2 serrano chiles, charred
- Salt to taste

Directions:

1. Heat the oil in a large, deep frying pan and put in the zucchini, onion, epazote, and salt. Stir thoroughly, cover the pan, and cook on moderate heat, stirring once in a while, until just soft—about ten minutes.

2. Blend together the tomatoes, chiles, and garlic and mix into the zucchini mixture. Cook on moderate heat, uncovered, until the zucchini is tender and the tomato sauce has been absorbed, approximately fifteen minutes. The vegetables must be moist but not too juicy. Adjust the seasoning and serve instantly.

ZUCCHINI FRITTERS WITH CILANTRO LIME SAUCE

Yield: Servings 4

Ingredients:

- ¼ cup all purpose flour
- ¼ cup minced fresh cilantro
- ½ cup sour cream
- 1 garlic clove, minced
- 1 tablespoon juice
- 1 tablespoon minced fresh oregano or 1 teaspoon dried
- 1 teaspoon grated lime zest plus
- 1 teaspoon ground coriander
- 1½ pounds zucchini, shredded
- 2 big eggs, lightly beaten
- 2 jalapeño chiles, stemmed, seeded, and minced
- 2 scallions, minced
- 6 ounces Monterey Jack cheese, shredded (1½ cups)
- 6 tablespoons vegetable oil
- Salt and pepper

Directions:

1. Toss shredded zucchini with 1 teaspoon salt and allow to drain in fine mesh strainer for about ten minutes. Whisk sour cream, 2 tablespoons oil, 2 tablespoons cilantro, lime zest and juice, ¼ teaspoon salt, and ¼ teaspoon pepper together in container; cover and place in your fridge until serving.

2. Cover zucchini in clean dish towel, squeeze out surplus liquid, and move to big container. Mix in Monterey Jack, eggs, jalapeños, scallions, oregano, coriander, garlic, ¼ teaspoon pepper, and remaining 2 tablespoons cilantro. Drizzle flour over mixture and stir to blend.

3. Adjust oven rack to middle position and heat oven to 200 degrees. Set wire rack in rimmed baking sheet and line with triple layer of paper towels. Heat 2 tablespoons oil in 12 inch nonstick frying pan on moderate heat until it starts to shimmer Drop scant ¼ cup portions of batter into frying pan and use back of spoon to press batter into 2½ inch wide fritters (you should fit about 6 fritters in pan at a time). Cook until thoroughly browned and mildly crunchy on both sides, approximately five minutes per side.

4. Move fritters to prepared rack and keep warm in oven. Wipe frying pan clean using paper towels and repeat with remaining 2 tablespoons oil and remaining batter. Serve fritters warm with lime cilantro sauce.

ZUCCHINI STUFFED WITH FRESH CORN (CALABACITAS RELLENAS DE ELOTE)

Yield: Servings 6

Ingredients:

- 1½ cups (375 ml) salsa ranchera, omitting the onion
- 1½ pounds (675 g) zucchini—choose 6 fat ones
- 2 big eggs
- 2 heaped cups (525 ml) corn kernels
- 2 tablespoons milk
- 3 tablespoons unsalted butter, softened
- 6 ounces (180 g) queso fresco, crumbled (approximately 1 cup/250 ml)
- Salt to taste

Directions:

1. Preheat your oven to 350° f (180° c). Have ready two shallow ovenproof dishes, mildly greased.

2. Clean and trim the zucchini. Cut them into halves along the length and scoop out the inner flesh, leaving a shell about ½ inch (1.5 cm) thick. Discard the pulp or reserve for future use. Put the zucchini in the dish and set aside while preparing the filling.
3. Combine the corn, eggs, milk, and salt to a coarse mixture. Do not put in more liquid unless absolutely necessary to release the blades. Mix about three quarters of the cheese into the corn mixture, saving the rest for the topping.
4. Fill the zucchini shells with the corn stuffing, which will be fairly runny. Drizzle with the rest of the cheese and dot with the butter. Cover the dish and bake until the squash is soft—about thirty minutes. Serve covered with the tomato sauce.

ZUCCHINI WITH CREAM (CALABACITAS CON CREMA)

Yield: Servings 6

Ingredients:

- ½ cup (125 ml) crème fraîche or thick sour cream
- ½ teaspoon salt, or to taste
- 1/2-inch (1.5-cm) piece of cinnamon stick
- 1½ pounds (675 g) zucchini, trimmed and diced (about 5¼ cups/1.313 l)
- 12 ounces (340 g) tomatoes, finely chopped (2 scant cups/500 ml)
- 2 sprigs fresh mint
- 2 whole serrano chiles
- 4 sprigs cilantro
- 4 whole cloves
- 6 peppercorns

Directions:

1. Place the squash into a heavy pan with the other ingredients.
2. Cover the pan with a firmly fitting lid and cook the mixture using low heat, scraping the bottom of the pan and stirring the mixture well occasionally so that it does not adhere.
3. If the vegetables are drying up too much, put in a little water. It will take approximately thirty minutes cook.

Beans,& Rice

BEANS

Frijoles (dried beans) are easily one of the most important ingredients in the Mexican diet, and no Mexican kitchen is complete without a variety of these. Below are a few of my favourite recipes.

"Dirty" Beans (FRIJOLES A LA HUACHA)

Yield: Servings approximately 10

Ingredients:

- ¼ cup (65 ml) pork lard
- ¼ habanero chile or any fresh, hot green chile, finely chopped
- 1 pound (450 g) black turtle beans cooked, 3½ to 4 cups/875 ml to 1 l, with broth
- 2 tablespoons finely chopped white onion
- 7 big mint leaves, roughly chopped

Directions:

1. Melt the lard and fry the onion and chile, without browning, until tender.
2. Combine the beans with 1½ cups (375 ml) of the broth they were cooked in until the desired smoothness is achieved, and put in them to the pan. Fry the beans until they reduce to a thick paste, approximately ten minutes, putting in the chopped mint leaves near the end of the cooking time. Fry for a few minutes longer before you serve.

"Pot" Beans (FRIJOLES DE OLLA)

Yield: Servings 10

Ingredients:

- ⅓ cup (85 ml) roughly cut white onion

- 1 pound (450 g) dried beans—black (about 2¼ cups/565 ml) or pinto (about 2½ cups/625 ml)
- 2 big sprigs epazote, only if black beans are used
- 2 tablespoons pork lard
- Salt to taste
- ten to 12 cups (2.5 to 3 l) hot water, roughly

Directions:

1. Wash the beans in cold water and allow them to run through your hands to ensure there are no small stones or pieces of earth among them. Place them into a pot and cover with the hot water. Put in the onion and lard and bring to its boiling point, then reduce the heat and let the beans simmer, covered, until they are just tender and the skins are breaking open—approximately four hours for black beans and 2½ for other varieties, although it is very difficult to be precise. (much will depend on the age of the beans, how long they have been stored, and if they have dried out too much, and on the efficiency of the pot or pan in which you are cooking them.) Put in the salt and carry on cooking using low heat for another ½ hour or more, until the beans are completely tender.
2. For black beans, put in the epazote just before the end of the cooking time, as it tends to lose flavor if cooked too long.
3. These beans will keep in your fridge for approximately 2 days. They can also be frozen up to approximately three months.

Charra And Drunken Beans (FRIJOLES A LA CHARRA AND FRIJOLES BORRACHOS)

Yield: Servings 6

Ingredients:

- ¼ medium white onion, cut
- 12 ounces (340 g) tomatoes, finely chopped (about 2 rounded cups/525 ml)
- 2 small garlic cloves, cut
- 2 tablespoons melted lard
- 3 serrano chiles, finely chopped

- 3 thick strips bacon (approximately four ounces/115 g)
- 4 big sprigs cilantro
- 4 ounces (115 g) pork rind
- 6 cups (1.5 l) water
- 8 ounces (225 g) pink or pinto beans (approximately 1¼ cups/315 ml)
- Salt to taste

Directions:

1. Chop the pork rind into little squares and put with the beans, onion, and garlic into a bean pot.
2. Put in the water and bring to its boiling point. Reduce the heat, cover the pot, and let the beans cook gently until they become soft—approximately 1½ hours.
3. Put in the salt and cook, uncovered, for another fifteen minutes.
4. Chop the bacon into little pieces and cook it gently in the lard in a frying pan until it is slightly browned. Remove using a slotted spoon and save for later.
5. Put in the tomatoes, chiles, and cilantro to the pan and cook the mixture over quite high heat for approximately five minutes, until reduced and seasoned.
6. Put in the tomato mixture and bacon pieces to the beans and allow them to cook together, uncovered, using low heat for approximately fifteen minutes.

Sonora Bean Puree (FRIJOLES MANEADOS SONORENSES)

Yield: Servings 10

Ingredients:

- ½ small white onion, roughly cut
- ⅔ cup (165 ml) whole milk
- 1 cup (250 ml) plus 3 tablespoons vegetable oil
- 1 pound (450 g) pinto or california pink beans (about 2½ cups/625 ml)
- 1 tablespoon salt, or to taste
- 3 ancho chiles, wiped clean
- 8 ounces (225 g) asadero or chihuahua cheese, or mild cheddar, jack, or domestic muenster, cut into ½-inch (1.5-cm) cubes
- twelve to 14 cups (3 to 3.5 l) hot water, roughly

Directions:

1. Run the beans through your hands slowly, picking out any small stones or pieces of dirt that might be among them. Wash in cold water and put into a big flameproof bean pot.

2. Put in 12 cups (3 l) of the hot water, the onion, and the 3 tablespoons oil and bring to a simmer. Cover the beans and continue simmering until they are just starting to tenderize and the skins are splitting open—approximately 1 hour (depending on how dry the beans are). Put in the salt and carry on cooking until the beans are tender and mushy, approximately 30 minutes; there must be some broth in the pot. If the broth reduces too much during the cooking time, then put in more water. Put the remaining oil—1 cup (250 ml)—into a casserole. Place the casserole into the oven and set the temperature at 350° f (180° c).

3. In the meantime, put one third each of the beans and milk into a blender jar with a little of the broth and blend until the desired smoothness is achieved. Repeat twice to use up the beans and milk.

4. By the time the beans have been mixed, the oil must be super hot; if not, leave in your oven for a few minutes longer. When the oil is ready, stir the bean puree into the casserole and put back into the oven to cook, uncovered, until the edges are just drying out and the mixture is reduced—approximately 1 hour fifteen minutes.

5. After you put the bean puree into the oven, slit the chiles open, remove the veins and seeds, and toast lightly on both sides on a warm griddle or comal. Tear the chiles into fine strips and put in to the bean puree.

6. At the end of the cooking time, put in the cheese and return the casserole to the oven until the cheese has melted—about ten minutes. Serve instantly.

Veracruz Refried Beans (FRIJOLES REFRITOS A LA VERACRUZANA)

Yield: about 3 cups (750 ml)

Ingredients:

- 2 jalapeño chiles, finely chopped
- 2 tablespoons finely chopped white onion

- 3 tablespoons lard or vegetable oil
- 8 ounces (225 g) cooked black beans, with broth

Directions:

1. Heat the lard in a big frying pan, put in the onion and chile, and fry on moderate heat for a minute.
2. Put in the beans and their cooking liquid and fry over quite high heat, mashing to a textured paste—about fifteen minutes.

Well-Fried Beans (FRIJOLES REFRITOS)

Yield: Servings 6

Ingredients:

- 2 tablespoons finely chopped white onion
- 6 tablespoons pork lard (⅓ cup/85 ml)
- 8 ounces (225 g) beans cooked as for frijoles de olla, 3½ to 4 cups/875 ml to 1 l, with broth

Directions:

1. In a very heavy frying pan—approximately 10 inches (25 cm) in diameter—heat the lard and fry the onion, without browning, until tender. Put in 1 cup (250 ml) of the beans and their broth and purée well as you cook them using high heat. Slowly put in the rest of the beans, slowly and gradually, mashing them all the time until you have a coarse puree.
2. As the puree starts to dry out and sizzle at the edges, it is ready to be used for the recipes calling for frijoles refritos.

Yucatecan Sieved Beans (FRIJOLES COLADOS YUCATECOS)

Yield: Servings about 6

Only in southeastern mexico—yucatán, campeche, and quintana roo—are beans sieved before they are fried to a smooth paste. Since this is time-consuming, they could be mixed (not in a food processor) to a smooth consistency.

Ingredients:

- ¼ cup (65 ml) roughly cut white onion
- 1 habanero chile or any fresh, hot green chile, left whole and wiped clean
- 2 big stems epazote
- 3 tablespoons pork lard
- 8 ounces (225 g) black turtle beans, cooked

Directions:

1. Melt the lard in a large, heavy frying pan and cook the onion, without browning, until translucent.
2. Combine the beans with their broth and put in to the frying pan with the whole chile, and epazote, and cook over quite high heat until the beans form a loose paste that plops off the spoon—about fifteen minutes (depending, of course, how much liquid there is with the beans in the first place). Make sure you stir and scrape the bottom of the pan occasionally so the beans do not adhere.

RICE

We Mexicans love a good hearty rice meal in the afternoon.

White Rice (ARROZ BLANCO)

Yield: Servings 6

Ingredients:

- ⅓ carrot, scraped, trimmed, and thinly cut (not necessary)
- ⅓ cup (85 ml) vegetable oil
- 1 garlic clove, finely chopped
- 1½ cups (375 ml) long-grain unconverted white rice
- 2 tablespoons peas (not necessary)

- 3 tablespoons finely chopped white onion
- 3½ cups (875 ml) well-salted light chicken broth
- Salt to taste

Directions:

1. You will require a heavy-bottomed, flameproof pan approximately four inches (10 cm) deep and 9 inches (23 cm) across.
2. Pour hot water to cover over the rice and allow it to stand for approximately five minutes. Drain the rice and wash well in cold water. Shake the strainer well and leave the rice to drain for a few minutes.
3. Heat the oil. Give the rice a final shake, put in it to the pan, and stir until all the grains are well covered with the oil. Fry until just turning color, then put in the onion and garlic and fry a little time longer until these two ingredients are translucent, stirring and turning almost continuously so that they cook uniformly and do not cling to the pan. The whole process should take about ten minutes—depending, of course, on the size of the pan—and it must be done using high heat or it will take too long and the rice will become mushy in the final stage.
4. Tip the pan to one side and drain off any surplus oil (strain and place in your fridge to use again). Put in the broth, carrot, peas, and salt to taste and cook uncovered on moderate heat—do not stir again—until the liquid has been absorbed and small air holes seem in the rice—about ten minutes. Cover the rice with a piece of terry cloth and then cover with a firmly fitting lid so that none of the steam can escape. Set aside in a warm place for approximately twenty minutes, so it can carry on cooking and the grains will expand.
5. Before you serve, loosen the rice using a fork from the bottom. Serve, if you wish, topped with a sauce, gravy, or any other topping of your choice.

"LUXURY RICE CAKE" (PASTEL DE LUJO)

Yield: Servings 6

Ingredients:

The meat filling

- ¼ green bell pepper, seeded and finely chopped

- ⅓ cup (85 ml) finely chopped white onion
- ¾ cup (185 ml) water
- 1 tablespoon big capers, washed and drained
- 1 tablespoon raisins
- 12 ounces (340 g) boneless chicken, finely chopped (not ground)
- 12 small pitted green olives, roughly chopped
- 6 ounces (180 g) boneless stewing pork with some fat, finely chopped (not ground)
- 8 ounces (225 g) tomatoes, finely chopped (approximately 1⅓ cups/335 ml)
- A pinch of granulated sugar
- Salt to taste

The seasoning for the meat

- ½ cup (125 ml) medium dry sherry
- ½-inch (1.5-cm) piece of cinnamon stick, crushed
- 1 tablespoon vinegar
- 1 whole clove, crushed
- 16 peppercorns, crushed
- 2 garlic cloves, toasted and peeled
- 2 whole allspice, crushed

The rice mixture

- ½ cup (125 ml) milk
- 1 cup (250 ml) long-grain unconverted white rice cooked with water, making approximately four cups (1 l)
- 1 tablespoon sugar
- 1 tablespoon thoroughly ground toasted bread crumbs
- 2 big eggs, well beaten
- 2 tablespoons unsalted butter, softened
- 3 cups (750 ml) corn kernels
- Salt to taste

Directions:

1. Preheat your oven to 350° f (180° c).

2. Mix all the ingredients for the meat in a container. Put into an ungreased big frying pan using low heat.

3. Grind the spices together in a spice grinder to a powder.

4. In a small container, crush the garlic with the vinegar and put in the ground spices. Stir this well into the meat in the frying pan and carry on cooking, uncovered, on moderate heat until the meat is soft and the juices have vaporized—about twenty minutes.

5. Take away the frying pan from the heat, mix in the sherry, and allow to cool a little.

6. Put about one third of the corn into your blender with the milk and blend until the desired smoothness is achieved. Slowly put in the rest of the corn by degrees, blending well after each addition. Mix the corn into the rice with the eggs, butter, sugar, and salt.

7. In an ovenproof dish approximately four inches (10 cm) deep, spread half of the rice and corn mixture. Cover the rice uniformly with the meat mixture and then spread with the rest of the rice and corn mixture. Drizzle the bread crumbs over the top of the rice and bake until well thoroughly heated—about thirty minutes. Serve as soon as you can.

8. Note: the meat mixture and rice can be cooked a few hours ahead, but the corn must be mixed at the final moment since it tends to sour easily when mixed.

DRY ANGEL HAIR PASTA "SOUP" (SOPA SECA DE FIDEO)

Yield: Servings 6

Ingredients:

- ¼ cup (65 ml) vegetable oil
- ½ cup (125 ml) chicken broth
- 1 garlic clove, roughly chopped
- 1 pound (450 g) tomatoes, roughly chopped (about 3 cups/750 ml)
- 2 tablespoons roughly chopped white onion
- 2 to 3 ounces (60 to 85 g) grated chihuahua cheese or mild cheddar
- 4 chipotle chiles en adobo, roughly chopped
- 8 ounces (225 g) angel hair pasta
- Salt to taste

To serve

- ¾ cup (185 ml) crème fraîche or thick sour cream

Directions:

1. Preheat your oven to 350° f (180° c). Grease a 1-quart (1-l) casserole or 8 by 8-inch (20 by 20-cm) ovenproof dish minimum 2 inches (5 cm) deep.
2. Heat the oil in a large, deep frying pan and fry the angel hair pasta until a deep golden color, approximately 3 minutes. (they brown swiftly, so flip them over cautiously occasionally so that they do not break up.) Drain off all but about 2 tablespoons of the oil.
3. Combine the tomatoes with the onion and garlic and put in to the pan. Fry using high heat to reduce, stirring well and scraping the bottom of the pan to prevent sticking, approximately five minutes or until the mixture is almost dry. Put in the broth and salt, cover the pan, and cook using low heat until the liquid has been absorbed—8 to ten minutes.
4. Turn the pasta into the prepared dish. Push the pieces of chile into the mixture at 1½-inch (4-cm) gaps. Cover loosely, and bake until the pasta is just starting to shrink away from the sides of the pan and is bubbling.
5. Drizzle the cheese on top and put back into the oven until the cheese has melted but not browned. Serve, topping each portion with a little of the crème fraîche.

Green Rice (ARROZ VERDE)

Yield: Servings 6

Ingredients:

- ⅓ cup (85 ml) vegetable oil
- ½ cup (125 ml) cold water, more if required
- 1 garlic clove, roughly chopped
- 1 small bunch flat-leaf parsley
- 1½ cups (375 ml) long-grain unconverted white rice
- 2 poblano chiles, seeds and veins removed, roughly chopped (not charred)
- 2 tablespoons roughly chopped white onion
- 2½ to 3 cups (625 to 750 ml) light chicken broth

- 3 big romaine lettuce leaves
- 3 sprigs cilantro
- Salt to taste

Directions:

1. Prepare a heavy-bottomed pan approximately four inches (10 cm) deep and 9 inches (23 cm) across.
2. Cover the rice with hot water and allow to soak for approximately five minutes. Drain in a strainer, then wash well in cold water and leave to drain for a few minutes.
3. Heat the oil in the pan. Give a final shake to the rice in the strainer and mix it into the oil. Fry over a very high heat flipping the rice meticulously occasionally, until it is a pale golden color. Tip the pan to one side, holding back the rice using a spatula, and drain off about 3 tablespoons of the oil.
4. Pour the ½ cup (125 ml) of water into a blender jar. Put in the greens, chiles, onion, and garlic and blend until the desired smoothness is achieved, putting in more water only if absolutely necessary to release the blades of the blender.
5. Put in the mixed ingredients to the rice and fry using high heat, stirring continuously and scraping the bottom of the pan, until the rice is almost dry. Put in the broth and salt to taste and cook on moderate heat until all the liquid has been absorbed and small air holes seem in the surface of the rice—about fifteen minutes.
6. Cover the pan with a lid or foil and cook for five minutes longer. Turn off the heat. Cover the rice with a piece of terry cloth and set aside to carry on cooking in its own steam for twenty minutes to half an hour.

LENTILS WITH PINEAPPLE AND PLANTAIN (LENTEJAS CON PIÑA Y PLÁTANO)

Yield: Servings 6

Ingredients:

- ½ medium-size ripe plantain (about ½ pound/225 g), peeled and slice into thick rounds
- 1 garlic clove, roughly chopped
- 1 thick slice pineapple, peeled, cored, and cut into little cubes
- 1½ tablespoons vegetable oil

- 2 tablespoons roughly chopped white onion
- 4 ounces (115 g or ½ rounded cup/125 ml) brown lentils
- 6 cups (1.5 l) cold water
- 8 ounces (225 g) tomatoes, finely chopped (about 3 cups/750 ml)
- Salt to taste

Directions:

1. Wash the lentils in cold water and drain. Cover with the cold water and bring to its boiling point, then reduce the heat and simmer until soft—2½ to three hours, depending on how dry they are. Drain and reserve the broth—there must be approximately 1½ cups (375 ml); put in water if required to make up to this amount.
2. Combine the tomatoes with the garlic and onion until the desired smoothness is achieved. Heat the oil and fry the tomato puree over a high heat for approximately 3 minutes, stirring continuously and scraping the bottom of the pan. Reduce the heat, put in the pineapple and plantain, and carry on cooking for five minutes more.
3. Put in the lentils and 1½ cups (375 ml) of the reserved broth to the pan, then put in the salt and cook until the fruit is soft—about twenty minutes (the lentil mixture must be neither too thick nor too runny).

Mexican Rice (ARROZ A LA MEXICANA)

Yield: Servings 6

Ingredients:

- ¼ small white onion, roughly chopped
- ⅓ cup (85 ml) vegetable oil
- 1 garlic clove, roughly chopped
- 1 small carrot, scraped and thinly cut (not necessary)
- 1 whole sprig parsley (not necessary)
- 1½ cups (375 ml) long-grain unconverted white rice
- 2 tablespoons peas (not necessary)
- 8 ounces (225 g) tomatoes, roughly chopped (approximately 1½ cups/375 ml)
- About 3½ cups (875 ml) well-salted chicken broth
- Salt to taste

Directions:

1. For this quantity you will need a heavy-bottomed, flameproof pan approximately four inches (10 cm) deep and 9 inches (23 cm) across.

2. Pour hot water to cover the rice well and allow it to stand for approximately five minutes. Drain the rice and wash well in cold water, then shake the strainer well and leave the rice to drain for a few minutes.

3. Heat the oil. Give the rice a final shake and mix it into the oil until the grains are well covered, then fry until just turning color, stirring and turning the rice over so it will cook uniformly and will not cling to the pan. This process should take about ten minutes—depending, of course, on the size of the pan—but it must be done using high heat or the rice will become mushy in its final stage. Tip the pan to one side and drain off any surplus oil or drain rice in a fine strainer.

4. Combine the tomatoes, onion, and garlic until the desired smoothness is achieved—there must be approximately 1 cup (250 ml). Put in the puree to the fried rice, then, continuing to cook using high heat, stir and scrape the bottom of the pan until the mixture is dry.

5. Put in the broth, carrot, peas, and parsley. Put in salt as required, then stir thoroughly (do not stir again during the cooking time). Cook on moderate heat, covered, until the liquid has been absorbed and small air holes seem in the rice. This will take about ten minutes. Take away the pan from the heat and cover the rice with a piece of terry cloth. Cover with a firmly fitting lid so that no steam can escape, and set aside in a warm place for approximately twenty minutes, so the rice can carry on cooking in its own steam and the grains will expand.

6. Before you serve, loosen the rice using a fork from the bottom.

Stewed Lentils (LENTEJAS GUISADAS)

Yield: Servings 6

Ingredients:

For cooking lentils

- 1 medium carrot, trimmed, scraped, and cut
- 1 medium white onion, finely chopped

- 2 garlic cloves
- 2 güero chiles, largos, or jalapeños, or any fresh, hot green chiles
- 2 slices white onion
- 2 tablespoons roughly chopped cilantro
- 3 tablespoons vegetable oil
- 8 cups (2 l) cold water
- 8 ounces (225 g) or 1 heaped cup/265 ml brown lentils
- 8 ounces finely chopped tomatoes (approximately 1⅓ cups/335 ml)
- Salt to taste

For serving

- 2 tablespoons finely chopped white onion

Directions:

1. Wash the lentils in cold water, then drain and put into a big deep cooking pan with the carrot, onion, and water. Bring to its boiling point, reduce the heat, and simmer until soft, 2½ to three hours, depending on the quality of the lentils. They must be very brothy.
2. Heat the oil in a frying pan and mildly brown the garlic. Discard the garlic, then, in the same oil, fry the chopped onion gently, without browning, until soft, approximately one minute. Put in the chopped tomatoes and cook using high heat, stirring continuously and scraping the bottom of the pan, until the mixture has reduced to a sauce—about three minutes.
3. Put in the tomato sauce to the lentils, with salt to taste, and cook on moderate heat for fifteen minutes longer. Cut a cross on the bottom of the chiles and put in them to the lentils. Cook for another fifteen minutes, then put in the cilantro and cook for five minutes longer. Spread the onion over the bowls of stewed lentils.

Soups

Personally, I feel Mexican soups are better than those from any other part of the world. Below are a few of my favorite Mexican sou recipes.

ANGEL HAIR PASTA IN TOMATO BROTH (SOPA DE FIDEO AGUADA)

Yield: Servings 6

This soup is easy to prepare, and easy on the wallet. Naturally, it is quite common on the Mexican dinner table.

Ingredients:

- ¼ cup (65 ml) roughly chopped white onion
- 1 garlic clove, roughly chopped
- 12 ounces (340 g) very ripe tomatoes, roughly chopped (2⅓ cups/585 ml)
- 2 sprigs flat-leaf parsley
- 3 to 4 tablespoons chicken fat or vegetable oil
- 4 ounces (115 g) angel hair pasta
- 7 cups (1.75 l) light chicken broth

Directions:

1. Heat the fat in a big frying pan and put in the whole bundles of pasta without breaking them up. Fry until the pasta is a deep golden brown, stirring all the time and ensuring not to burn. Drain off all but about 2 tablespoons of fat in the pan.
2. Combine the tomatoes with the garlic and onion until the desired smoothness is achieved. Put into the fried pasta and carry on cooking over very high heat approximately four minutes, stirring and scraping the bottom of the pan, until the mixture is almost dry. Put in the broth and the parsley and bring to its boiling point. Reduce the heat and simmer until the pasta is tender. Adjust the seasoning. (it should take about twenty minutes to cook and season well.)

AVOCADO SOUP (SOPA DE AGUACATE)

Yield: Servings 6

Ingredients:

- 2 big avocados, or enough to yield 2 cups (500 ml) pulp
- 6 cups (1.5 l) well-seasoned caldo de pollo
- Chipotle chiles adobados, torn into little pieces
- Small tortilla squares, fried crisp as for totopos

Directions:

1. Chop the avocados into halves. Take away the pits and scoop out the flesh.
2. Put 2 cups (500 ml) of broth in a blender jar, put in the avocado pulp, and blend to a smooth puree. Put into the remaining broth in the pan and just heat it through gently. Do not allow it to boil.
3. Serve the soup instantly, topped with the tortilla squares and pieces of chipotle chile.

BLACK BEAN CHILI

Yield: Servings 6 to 8

Ingredients:

- ⅛ teaspoon baking soda
- ½ cup minced fresh cilantro
- 1 (28 ounce) can crushed tomatoes
- 1 onion, chopped
- 1 pound (2½ cups) dried black beans, picked over and washed
- 1 pound white mushrooms, trimmed and broken into rough pieces
- 1 tablespoon minced canned chipotle chile in adobo sauce
- 1 tablespoon mustard seeds
- 1 tablespoon packed light brown sugar
- 2 bay leaves
- 2 red bell peppers, stemmed, seeded, and slice into ½ inch pieces
- 2 teaspoons cumin seeds

- 2½ cups vegetable broth
- 2½ cups water, plus extra as required
- 3 tablespoons chili powder
- 3 tablespoons vegetable oil
- 9 garlic cloves, minced
- Lime wedges
- Salt and pepper

Directions:

1. Adjust oven rack to lower middle position and heat oven to 325 degrees. Pulse mushrooms in food processor until consistently crudely chopped, approximately 10 pulses; set aside.
2. Toast mustard seeds and cumin seeds in Dutch oven on moderate heat, stirring continuously, until aromatic, approximately one minute. Mix in oil, onion, and processed mushrooms, cover, and cook until vegetables release liquid, approximately five minutes. Remove the cover and carry on cooking until liquid has vaporized and vegetables are browned, 5 to ten minutes.
3. Mix in garlic and chipotle and cook until aromatic, approximately half a minute. Mix in chili powder and cook, stirring continuously, until aromatic, approximately 1 minute (do not let mixture burn). Mix in broth, water, beans, sugar, bay leaves, and baking soda and bring to simmer, skimming foam from surface as required. Cover, move pot to oven, and cook for an hour.
4. Mix in tomatoes and bell peppers, cover, and carry on cooking in oven until beans are fully soft, approximately 1 hour longer. (If chili starts to cling to bottom of pot or looks too thick, mix in extra water as required.)
5. Take the pot out of the oven and discard bay leaves. Mix in cilantro and sprinkle with salt and pepper to taste. Serve with lime wedges.

BLACK BEAN SOUP

Yield: Servings 6

Ingredients:

- ⅛ teaspoon baking soda

- ½ teaspoon red pepper flakes
- 1 big carrot, peeled and chopped fine
- 1 pound (2½ cups) dried black beans, picked over and washed
- 1½ tablespoons ground cumin
- 2 bay leaves
- 2 big onions, chopped fine
- 2 tablespoons cornstarch
- 2 tablespoons lime juice
- 2 tablespoons water
- 3 celery ribs, chopped fine
- 3 tablespoons extra virgin olive oil
- 4 ounces ham steak, trimmed
- 5 cups water, plus extra as required
- 6 cups chicken broth
- 6 garlic cloves, minced
- Salt and pepper

Directions:

1. Put water, beans, ham steak, bay leaves, and baking soda in big deep cooking pan with tight fitting lid. Bring to boil over moderate high heat, skimming foam from surface as required. Mix in 1 teaspoon salt, decrease the heat to moderate low, cover, and simmer briskly until beans are soft, 1¼ to 1½ hours (if after 1½ hours beans are not soft, put in 1 cup more water and carry on simmering until soft); do not drain beans. Discard bay leaves. Move ham steak to cutting board, allow to cool slightly, then cut into ¼ inch pieces; set aside.

2. Heat oil in Dutch oven over moderate high heat until shimmering. Put in onions, carrot, celery, and ½ teaspoon salt and cook, stirring once in a while, until vegetables become tender and mildly browned, twelve to fifteen minutes. Decrease the heat to moderate low, put in garlic, cumin, and pepper flakes and cook, stirring continuously, until aromatic, approximately 3 minutes. Mix in broth, scraping up any browned bits. Mix in beans and bean cooking liquid, bring to simmer, and cook, stirring once in a while, until flavors meld, approximately 30 minutes.

3. Ladle 1½ cups beans and 2 cups liquid into food processor or blender, pulse until smooth, and return to pot. Mix together cornstarch and water in small container until

blended, then progressively stir half of cornstarch mixture into soup. Bring to boil over moderate high heat while stirring once in a while, until fully thickened. If soup is still thinner than desired once boiling, stir remaining cornstarch mixture to remix and progressively stir mixture into soup; return to boil to fully thicken. Remove the heat, mix in lime juice and ham. Sprinkle with salt and pepper to taste and serve.

BREAD SOUP (SOPA DE PAN)

Yield: Servings 6

Ingredients:

- ½ cup (125 ml) vegetable oil, more if required
- 1 cup (250 ml) thinly cut white onion
- 1 pound (450 g) tomatoes, thickly cut
- 10 peppercorns
- 2 garlic cloves, thinly cut
- 2 medium plantains (approximately 1 pound/450 g), peeled, quartered, and slice into 3-inch (8-cm) lengths
- 2 whole allspice
- 2 whole cloves
- 2-inch (5-cm) piece of cinnamon stick
- 4 cups (1 l) stale bread cubes, if possible sourdough
- 4 hard-cooked eggs, cut
- 4 ounces (115 g) carrots, scraped and thinly cut (approximately 1 cup/250 ml)
- 4 ounces (115 g) green beans, trimmed and slice into thirds
- 4 ounces (115 g) unsalted butter (approximately 1 cup/250 ml)
- 6 cups (1.5 l) chicken broth
- 6 sprigs fresh thyme or ¼ teaspoon dried
- 8 ounces (225 g) potatoes, peeled and slice into ½-inch (1.5-cm) slices (approximately 1¼ cups/315 g)
- Large pinch of saffron
- Salt to taste

Directions:

1. Preheat your oven to 300° f (150° c).
2. Put the bread cubes on a baking sheet in a single layer and bake until they are crisp on the outside but not dried all the way through—twenty minutes to half an hour.
3. Heat some of the oil in a big frying pan and melt a portion of the butter in it. Fry the bread cubes lightly until a golden-brown colour is achieved, putting in more oil and butter as required (if you put in it all at once, the bread cubes will absorb it and become soggy). Drain and set aside, saving for later the oil in the pan.
4. Heat the chicken broth, and when it comes to its boiling point, put in the beans and carrots and simmer until just soft—ten to fifteen minutes. Drain the vegetables and save for later. Put in the thyme, salt, and spices to the broth and simmer for approximately ten minutes. Strain and reserve the broth—there must be about 5 cups (1.25 l).
5. Reheat the oil in which the bread was fried, putting in about ½ cup (125 ml) more as required, and fry the cut potatoes on both sides until thoroughly browned; remove and drain. In the same oil, fry the plantain slices until a golden-brown colour is achieved; remove and drain. Fry the cut tomatoes, onion, and garlic together until soft, then remove and save for later.
6. Preheat your oven to 350° f (180° c). Grease an ovenproof dish, ideally 8½ by 13½ by 2 inches. Spread alternate layers of the vegetables and the tomato mixture in the dish. Cover with the bread cubes and top with the slices of egg. Pour the broth over and bake for approximately fifteen minutes.
7. Serve instantly in deep bowls.

CARNE ADOVADA

Yield: Servings 6

Popular in New Mexico, my hometown, this is the soup that I grew up with, and every slurp is one of nostalgia.

Ingredients:

- ¼ cup minced fresh cilantro
- ¼ cup raisins
- ⅓ cup chili powder
- ½ cup brewed coffee, hot

- 1 cup water
- 1 tablespoon minced canned chipotle chile in adobo sauce
- 1 teaspoon dried oregano
- 1 teaspoon grated lime zest plus 1 tablespoon juice
- 2 cups chicken broth
- 2 onions, chopped fine
- 3 tablespoons all purpose flour
- 3 tablespoons vegetable oil
- 4 pounds boneless pork butt roast, pulled apart at seams, trimmed, and slice into 1½ inch pieces
- 6 garlic cloves, minced
- Salt and pepper

Directions:

1. Adjust oven rack to lower middle position and heat oven to 325 degrees. Mix hot coffee and raisins in small container, cover, and allow it to sit until raisins are plump, approximately five minutes. Mix chili powder, flour, and oregano in separate small container. Pat pork dry using paper towels and sprinkle with salt and pepper.
2. Heat 1 tablespoon oil in Dutch oven over moderate high heat until just smoking. Brown half of pork on all sides, 7 to ten minutes; move to moderate container. Repeat with 1 tablespoon oil and remaining pork.
3. Pour off all but 2 tablespoons fat from pot and decrease the heat to moderate. Put in onions and cook until tender, approximately five minutes. Mix in garlic and chipotle and cook until aromatic, approximately half a minute. Mix in spice mixture and remaining 1 tablespoon oil and cook, stirring continuously, until aromatic, approximately 1 minute (do not let spices burn). Mix in broth, water, and raisin coffee mixture, scraping up any browned bits.
4. Process sauce in blender until the desired smoothness is achieved, one to two minutes. Return sauce to now empty pot. Mix in browned pork and any collected juices and bring to simmer. Cover, move pot to oven, and cook until pork is soft and sauce becomes thick, approximately 2 hours, stirring midway through cooking.
5. Take the pot out of the oven and mix in cilantro and lime zest and juice. Sprinkle with salt and pepper to taste and serve.

CHEESE BROTH (CALDO DE QUESO SONORENSE)

Yield: Servings 6

Ingredients:

- ⅓ cup (85 ml) cut white onion
- 1 anaheim chile, charred and peeled
- 1 pound (450 g) big tomatoes
- 1 small garlic clove, finely chopped
- 12 fine strips queso fresco or muenster cheese
- 12 ounces (340 g) red bliss or waxy new potatoes
- 2 tablespoons vegetable oil
- 5 cups (1.25 l) beef broth
- Salt to taste

Directions:

1. Peel the potatoes and cut them into 1-inch (2.5-cm) squares. Bring the broth to its boiling point, put in the potatoes, and allow them to cook on moderate heat for about ten minutes. They must be just cooked.
2. Cut a thin slice off the top of each tomato and grate the flesh on the coarse side of a grater. In a very short time you will have the skin of the tomato left flat in your hand. Do not forget to grate the flesh from the top slices.
3. Heat the oil in a big frying pan and lightly fry the onion and garlic, without browning, until translucent. Put in the tomato pulp and cook the sauce over brisk heat for five minutes, by which time it will have thickened fairly and be well seasoned. Put in the tomato sauce to the broth and potatoes.
4. Take away the seeds from the chile and cut it into strips. Put in the chile strips to the broth and allow it to cook on moderate heat for five minutes. Put in salt as required. Just before you serve, put in the cheese. Serve the soup as the cheese melts.

CHICKEN AND CHICKPEA SOUP

Yield: Servings 6 to 8

Ingredients:

- 1 (fifteen ounce) can chickpeas, washed
- 1 tablespoon vegetable oil
- 1 teaspoon minced fresh oregano
- 1½ pounds bone in split chicken breasts, trimmed
- 1½ teaspoons minced fresh thyme or ½ teaspoon dried
- 2 carrots, peeled and cut ½ inch thick
- 2 onions, chopped fine
- 2 tablespoons all purpose flour
- 2 teaspoons minced canned chipotle chile in adobo sauce
- 2 zucchini, cut into ½ inch pieces
- 3 tablespoons minced fresh cilantro
- 5 garlic cloves, minced
- 8 cups chicken broth
- Salt and pepper

Directions:

1. Pat chicken dry using paper towels and sprinkle with salt and pepper. Heat oil in Dutch oven over moderate high heat until just smoking. Brown chicken lightly, two to three minutes per side; move to plate.
2. Put in onions and carrots to fat left in pot and cook on moderate heat until tender and mildly browned, about eight to ten minutes. Mix in garlic, chipotle, and thyme and cook until aromatic, approximately half a minute. Mix in flour and cook for a minute. Slowly whisk in broth, scraping up any browned bits, and bring to simmer.
3. Return browned chicken and any collected juices to pot, decrease the heat to low, cover, and simmer gently until chicken records 160 degrees, fifteen to twenty minutes.
4. Move chicken to cutting board and allow to cool slightly. Using 2 forks, shred chicken into bite size pieces; discard skin and bones. In the meantime, stir zucchini and chickpeas into soup and simmer until zucchini is just soft, 5 to ten minutes.
5. Stir shredded chicken into soup and simmer until thoroughly heated, approximately 2 minutes. Remove the heat, mix in cilantro and oregano and sprinkle with salt and pepper to taste and serve.

CHICKEN AND VEGETABLE BROTH (CALDO TLALPEÑO)

Yield: Servings 6

Ingredients:

- ½ cup (125 ml) cooked and skinned chickpeas
- 1 avocado, cubed
- 1 cup (250 ml) cooked and shredded chicken
- 1 garlic clove, roughly chopped
- 1 tablespoon lard or vegetable oil
- 2 big sprigs epazote
- 2 chipotle chiles, dried or canned, torn into strips
- 2 tablespoons roughly chopped white onion
- 4 ounces (115 g) carrots (about 2 medium)
- 4 ounces (115 g) tomatoes, roughly chopped (approximately 1 cup/250 ml)
- 6 cups (1.5 l) caldo de pollo (Chicken Soup)
- 6 lime wedges
- 8 ounces (225 g) green beans

Directions:

1. Trim the beans and cut them in two. Trim and scrape the carrots and slice into rounds. Blend together the tomatoes, onion, and garlic. Heat the lard in a moderate-sized frying pan, put in the mixed ingredients, and fry on moderate heat for approximately 3 minutes.
2. Heat the caldo de pollo (Chicken Soup) in a big deep cooking pan, put in the vegetables, chickpeas, and tomato mixture, and cook on moderate heat until soft—about fifteen minutes.
3. Put in the epazote and chiles and cook for approximately five minutes more.
4. Serve the soup in deep bowls, putting in some of the shredded chicken and topping with the avocado. Lime wedges are passed separately.

CHICKEN POSOLE VERDE

Yield: Servings 6 to 8

Ingredients:

- 1 onion, chopped fine
- 1 tablespoon chopped fresh oregano or 1 teaspoon dried
- 12 ounces tomatillos, husks and stems removed, washed well, dried, and quartered
- 2 (fifteen ounce) cans white or yellow hominy, washed
- 2 jalapeños, stemmed, halved, and seeded
- 2 tablespoons vegetable oil
- 2½ cups fresh cilantro leaves and stems, trimmed (2 bunches)
- 3 garlic cloves, minced
- 4 pounds bone in chicken thighs, trimmed
- 4½ cups chicken broth
- Salt and pepper

Directions:

1. Adjust oven rack to lower middle position and heat oven to 300 degrees. Pat chicken dry using paper towels and sprinkle with salt and pepper. Heat 1 tablespoon oil in Dutch oven over moderate high heat until just smoking. Brown half of chicken, approximately five minutes per side; move to plate. Repeat with remaining 1 tablespoon oil and remaining chicken. Allow to cool slightly, then remove skin.

2. Pour off all but 1 tablespoon fat from pot; put in onion and ¼ teaspoon salt and cook on moderate heat until tender, approximately five minutes. Mix in garlic and oregano and cook until aromatic, approximately half a minute. Mix in 4 cups broth, scraping up any browned bits, and bring to simmer. Nestle browned chicken into pot together with any collected juices. Cover, move pot to oven, and cook until chicken is soft, approximately 1 hour.

3. Take the pot out of the oven, move chicken to cutting board, and allow to cool slightly. In the meantime, process tomatillos, jalapeños, cilantro, and remaining ½ cup broth in blender until the desired smoothness is achieved, approximately half a minute. Stir tomatillo mixture and hominy into stew, bring to simmer on moderate heat, and cook until flavors meld, ten to fifteen minutes.

4. Using 2 forks, shred chicken into bite size pieces; discard bones. Stir shredded chicken into stew and cook until thoroughly heated, approximately 2 minutes. Sprinkle with salt and pepper to taste and serve.

CHICKEN TORTILLA SOUP

Yield: Servings 6 to 8

Ingredients:

SOUP

- ½ jalapeño chile
- 1 big white onion, quartered
- 1 sprig fresh oregano
- 1 tablespoon minced canned chipotle chile in adobo sauce
- 1½ pounds bone in split chicken breasts, trimmed
- 2 tablespoons vegetable oil
- 2 tomatoes, cored and quartered
- 4 garlic cloves, peeled
- 8 (6 inch) corn tortillas, cut into ½ inch wide strips
- 8 cups chicken broth
- 8 sprigs fresh cilantro
- Salt

GARNISHES

- 1 ripe avocado, halved, pitted, and slice into ½ inch pieces
- 8 ounces Cotija cheese, crumbled (2 cups)
- Fresh cilantro
- Lime wedges
- Mexican crema
- Minced jalapeño chile

Directions:

1. Adjust oven rack to middle position and heat oven to 425 degrees. Toss tortilla strips with 1 tablespoon oil, spread onto rimmed baking sheet, and bake, stirring once in a while, until deep golden brown and crisp, approximately 14 minutes. Flavor mildly with salt and move to paper towel–lined plate.
2. In the meantime, bring broth, 2 onion quarters, 2 garlic cloves, cilantro sprigs, oregano sprig, and ½ teaspoon salt to simmer in Dutch oven over moderate high heat. Put in

chicken, decrease the heat to low, cover, and simmer gently until chicken records 160 degrees, fifteen to twenty minutes. Move chicken to cutting board and allow to cool slightly. Using 2 forks, shred chicken into bite size pieces; discard skin and bones. Strain broth through fine mesh strainer; discard solids.

3. Process tomatoes, jalapeño, chipotle, remaining 2 onion quarters, and remaining 2 garlic cloves in food processor until the desired smoothness is achieved, approximately half a minute, scraping down sides of container as required. Heat remaining 1 tablespoon oil in now empty pot over moderate high heat until shimmering. Put in tomato onion mixture and ⅛ teaspoon salt and cook, stirring regularly, until mixture has darkened in color and liquid has vaporized, approximately ten minutes.

4. Mix in strained broth, scraping up any browned bits, and bring to simmer. Cook until flavors meld, approximately fifteen minutes. Mix in shredded chicken and simmer until thoroughly heated, approximately 2 minutes. Remove the heat, sprinkle with salt and pepper to taste. Put some tortilla strips in bottom of individual bowls and ladle soup over top. Serve, passing garnishes separately.

CHILI CON CARNE

Yield: Servings 6

Ingredients:

- ⅓ cup masa harina
- 1 cup canned crushed tomatoes
- 1 onion, chopped fine
- 2 tablespoons cumin seeds
- 2 tablespoons lime juice
- 2 teaspoons dried oregano
- 3 dried ancho chiles, stemmed, seeded, and torn into ½ inch pieces (¾ cup)
- 3 dried New Mexican chiles, stemmed, seeded, and torn into ½ inch pieces (¾ cup)
- 4 jalapeño chiles, stemmed, seeded, and minced
- 4 pounds boneless beef chuck eye roast, pulled apart at seams, trimmed, and slice into an inch pieces
- 5 garlic cloves, minced

- 8 cups water
- 8 slices bacon, cut into ¼ inch pieces
- Salt and pepper

Directions:

1. Toast ancho and New Mexican chiles and cumin in Dutch oven on moderate heat, stirring regularly, until aromatic, 2 to six minutes; move to spice grinder. Put in oregano and grind to fine powder. Move spice mixture to container and mix in ½ cup water.

2. Cook bacon in now empty pot over moderate low heat until crisp, approximately ten minutes. Move bacon to paper towel–lined plate using slotted spoon. Pour off and reserve rendered fat in container.

3. Pat beef dry using paper towels and sprinkle with salt and pepper. Heat 1 tablespoon bacon fat in now empty pot over moderate high until just smoking. Brown half of beef on all sides, 7 to ten minutes; move to container. Repeat with 1 tablespoon bacon fat and remaining beef.

4. Heat 3 tablespoons bacon fat in now empty pot on moderate heat until shimmering. Put in onion and cook until tender, approximately five minutes. Mix in jalapeños and garlic and cook until aromatic, approximately one minute. Mix in chile paste and cook until aromatic, approximately 2 minutes. Mix in 7 cups water, tomatoes, and lime juice and bring to simmer. Mix in crisp bacon and browned beef and any collected juices and simmer until meat is soft and juices are dark, rich, and beginning to thicken, approximately 2 hours.

5. Mix masa harina and remaining ½ cup water in container to make paste. Increase heat to moderate, mix in masa harina mixture, and simmer until it becomes thick, 5 to ten minutes. Sprinkle with salt and pepper to taste and serve.

CHILLED TOMATO SOUP

Yield: Servings 4

Ingredients:

- ½ cup Mexican crema
- 1 garlic clove, quartered

- 1 shallot, peeled and halved
- 1 slice hearty white sandwich bread, crust removed, torn into an inch pieces
- 1 teaspoon sherry vinegar, plus extra for seasoning
- 1 teaspoon sugar, plus extra for seasoning
- 3 tablespoons minced fresh cilantro
- 3½ pounds tomatoes, cored and chopped coarse
- 5 tablespoons extra virgin olive oil
- Salt and pepper

Directions:

1. Toss tomatoes with ½ teaspoon salt and allow to drain in fine mesh strainer, set over container to reserve drained liquid, for an hour. Toss drained tomatoes with shallot, garlic, and sugar in separate container. Put in bread to drained tomato liquid, allow to soak for a minute, then mix into tomatoes.

2. Move half of mixture to blender and process for half a minute. With blender running, slowly sprinkle in 3 tablespoons oil until super smooth, approximately 2 minutes. Strain through fine mesh strainer into big container, using rubber spatula to help pass soup through strainer. Repeat with remaining mixture and remaining 2 tablespoons olive oil; strain into container.

3. Mix in vinegar and sprinkle with salt and pepper to taste. Cover and place in your fridge until chilled and flavors meld, minimum 2 hours or maximum 2 days.

4. Before serving, season soup with salt, pepper, extra sugar, and extra vinegar to taste. Mix in 2 tablespoons cilantro. Decorate individual portions with remaining 1 tablespoon cilantro and sprinkle with crema.

CREAM OF SQUASH FLOWER SOUP (CREMA DE FLOR DE CALABAZA)

Yield: Servings 6

Ingredients:

- ⅓ cup (85 ml) finely chopped onion
- ⅔ cup (165 ml) crème fraîche or heavy cream
- 1 big garlic clove, roughly chopped

- 1 pound (450 g) squash flowers, cleaned and finely chopped (approximately eight cups/2 l, tightly packed)
- 2 poblano chiles, charred, peeled, cleaned, cut into little squares, and lightly fried
- 3 tablespoons unsalted butter
- 3½ cups (875 ml) light chicken broth
- Salt to taste
- The reserved flowers

Directions:

1. Melt the butter, put in the onion and garlic in a deep deep cooking pan, and cook gently until translucent—do not brown. Put in the chopped flowers and salt, cover the pan, and cook using low heat until the flowers are fairly soft—ten to fifteen minutes. Set aside a scant ½ cup (125 ml) of the flowers.
2. Combine the remaining flowers with 1½ cups (375 ml) of the broth and return to the pan. Put in the remaining broth and cook using low heat for approximately 8 minutes.
3. Mix the cream into the soup and heat gently until it starts to simmer. Adjust seasoning and serve topped with the unblended flowers and the chile pieces.

DRIED FAVA BEAN SOUP (CALDO DE HABAS)

Yield: Servings 6

Ingredients:

- ⅔ cup (165 ml) roughly chopped white onion
- 10 sprigs fresh cilantro, roughly chopped
- 2 garlic cloves, roughly chopped
- 2 tablespoons vegetable oil
- 2 teaspoons salt, or to taste
- 8 ounces (225 g) dried, peeled yellow fava beans (approximately 1½ cups/375 ml)
- About 10 cups (2.5 l) hot water
- About 8 ounces (225 g) tomatoes, finely chopped (1⅓ cups/333 ml)

To serve

- 2 pasilla chiles, fried and crumbled

- 6 tablespoons fruity olive oil

Directions:

1. Wash the beans well, picking out any loose pieces of skin or fiber.
2. Heat the oil in a heavy-bottomed pot and fry the beans, with the onion and garlic, until they are mildly browned and the onion and garlic are translucent. Put in the tomatoes and fry using high heat, stirring continuously, until the mixture is almost dry—about three minutes. Put in the water, cilantro, and salt and let the soup cook using low heat until the beans are mushy and almost disintegrated—about 3½ hours.
3. Serve each container with a tablespoon of the olive oil and some crumbled pasilla chile on top.

DRIED SHRIMP CONSOMMÉ (CONSOMÉ DE CAMARÓN SECO)

Yield: Servings 6

Ingredients:

- 1 garlic clove, left whole
- 1 mulato or 2 pasilla chiles
- 4 to 5 cups (1 to 1.25 l) water
- 6 cascabel or 4 guajillo chiles
- 8 ounces (225 g) mexican dried shrimps

To serve

- Finely chopped white onion
- Lime quarters
- Roughly chopped cilantro sprigs

Directions:

1. Wash the uncleaned shrimps in cold water and drain, cover the shrimps with 2 cups (500 ml) of the water, and bring them to a simmer. Cook for a minute, then take out of the heat and set them aside to soak for five minutes longer—no more, as the shrimps soon lose their flavor. Drain the shrimps and reserve the cooking water.

2. Take away the stems from the chiles and veins and seeds from half of them. Place the chiles into a deep cooking pan, cover with water, and simmer for approximately five minutes, or until tender (time varies, depending on how dry the chiles are). Turn off the heat and set aside to soak for approximately five minutes longer. Drain, discard the water in which they were cooked, and move to a blender jar with 1 cup (250 ml) of fresh water and the garlic. Blend until the desired smoothness is achieved.

3. Clean the shrimps by removing the legs, tails, and heads, but do not peel. Split the cleaned shrimps into two parts. Roughly break up or cut one half and save for later. Move the other half with the shrimp debris to the blender jar. Put in the water in which they were cooked and blend as smooth as you can.

4. Place the chile sauce and the mixed shrimps into a large, heavy deep cooking pan, bring to a simmer, and cook, stirring all the time and scraping the bottom of the pan, for approximately 3 minutes. Put in 1 more cup (250 ml) of the water, bring back to a simmer, and carry on cooking using low heat for approximately five minutes. Pass the mixture through a fine sieve. Put in the shrimp pieces and carry on cooking for five minutes, no longer. The soup must be rather thick, but dilute with water if you want.

5. Serve in small cups and pass the toppings separately.

FISH SOUP (CALDO MICHI)

Yield: Servings 6

Ingredients:

- ¼ cup (65 ml) vegetable oil
- ¼ teaspoon dried mexican oregano
- ½ cup (125 ml) thinly cut white onion
- ⅔ cup (165 ml) loosely packed frutas en vinagre or an equivalent amount of sour pickles plus 2 slices lime
- 10 ounces (285 g) cut tomatoes, approximately 1½ cups (375 ml)
- 2 zucchini (about 6 ounces/180 g), trimmed and slice into rounds
- 2½ pounds (1.125 kg) whole catfish or carp
- 3 garlic cloves, left whole
- 3 jalapeño chiles en escabeche, roughly chopped
- 3 medium carrots (approximately four ounces/115 g), scraped and cut

- 8 big sprigs cilantro, roughly chopped
- 8 cups (2 l) chicken broth
- Salt and freshly ground pepper to taste

Directions:

1. Wash and dry the fish well. Chop the body into 1-inch (2.5-cm) slices and the head, if used, into four pieces. Sprinkle with salt and freshly ground pepper.
2. Heat the oil in a large, heavy pan and fry the fish pieces very lightly; the flesh should just turn opaque. Remove and save for later.
3. In the same oil, fry the tomatoes, onion, and garlic together until the onion is tender and the mixture has a saucelike consistency. Put in the broth, carrots, zucchini, oregano, chiles, and frutas en vinagre (or substitutes) to the pan and cook until the vegetables are just soft, approximately twenty minutes. Put in the fish pieces and simmer until the flesh flakes easily from the bone—about ten minutes.
4. Take away the pan from the heat and put in the chopped cilantro. Serve the soup accompanied by freshly made tortillas.
5. Note: this soup may be prepared a few hours ahead of time, but put in the fish pieces about ten minutes before you serve. It will not freeze.

FRESH CORN AND POBLANO SOUP (SOPA DE ELOTE Y RAJAS)

Yield: Servings 6

Ingredients:

- ¾ cup (185 ml) whole corn kernels, for putting in later
- 2 tablespoons roughly chopped white onion
- 3 cups (750 ml) milk
- 3 small poblano chiles, charred, peeled, cleaned of veins and seeds
- 3 tablespoons butter
- 6 heaped tablespoons queso fresco or substitute, crumbled
- 8 ounces (225 g) tomatoes, broiled
- About 3 cups (750 ml) corn kernels, or 1½ 10-ounce (285-g) packages frozen corn
- Salt to taste

Directions:

1. Combine the tomatoes and onion and save for later.
2. Chop the cleaned chiles into thin strips. Melt the butter in a big deep cooking pan and fry the chiles gently for approximately 2 minutes—they should not brown. Put in the mixed tomatoes to the chile strips and cook the mixture for approximately five minutes on moderate heat until the sauce has reduced a little.
3. Combine the 3 cups of corn, with the milk, at high speed to a very smooth consistency. This will probably have to be done in two stages. Place the corn mixture through the medium disk of a food mill or strainer and mix it in very progressively into the tomato sauce, stirring all the time.
4. Put in the whole kernels and salt and cook the soup using super low heat—it should just simmer—for approximately fifteen minutes.
5. Put in a little cheese to each container before pouring the hot soup into it.

FRESH CORN SOUP (SOPA DE ELOTE)

Yield: Servings 6

Ingredients:

- ¼ cup (65 ml) butter
- ½ teaspoon salt, or to taste
- 1 cup (250 ml) water
- 2 poblano chiles, charred, peeled, and cleaned, then diced and for a short period of time fried
- 3½ cups (875 ml) milk or light chicken broth
- 4 cups (1 l) fresh corn kernels (approximately 1½ pounds/675 g frozen corn)
- 6 small tortillas, cut into little squares, dried, and fried
- 6 tablespoons crumbled queso fresco

Directions:

1. Combine the corn with the water at high speed until you have a smooth puree. Place the puree through the medium disk of a food mill or a coarse strainer.

2. Melt the butter in a big deep cooking pan but do not allow it to get too hot. Put in the corn puree and allow it to cook on moderate heat for approximately five minutes, stirring all the time.

3. Put in the milk and the salt to the mixture and bring it to its boiling point. Reduce the heat and let the soup simmer for approximately fifteen minutes, stirring it occasionally to prevent sticking. By this time it will have thickened somewhat.

4. Put about ½ tablespoon diced chile and 1 tablespoon of crumbled cheese into each container. Pour the hot soup over them and put the crisp tortilla squares on top.

GARLIC AND BREAD SOUP (SOPA DE AJO Y MIGAS)

Yield: Servings 6

Ingredients:

- ⅓ cup (85 ml) vegetable or light olive oil, roughly
- 2 big eggs
- 2 big sprigs epazote
- 4 garlic cloves, cut
- 6 cups (1.5 l) strong chicken broth
- 6 thick slices french-type bread, if possible sourdough
- Salt to taste, if required
- Veins from 3 pasilla chiles, mildly toasted

Directions:

1. Preheat your oven to 300° f (150° c).
2. Put the bread slices on a baking sheet in a single layer and bake until they are crisp on the outside but not dried all the way through—about 30 minutes.
3. Heat a little of the oil in a heavy pan and fry the bread on both sides until very crisp and golden brown, putting in more oil as required. Drain on paper toweling and set aside to keep warm.
4. Put in or make up to 1 tablespoon of oil in the pan, and cook, rather than fry, the garlic on low heat so that it flavors the oil. Take away the garlic and discard. Pour a little of the broth into the pan, swirl it around, and put in to the remaining broth.

5. Heat the broth to a simmer in a deep cooking pan. Beat the eggs lightly with a teaspoon of oil and, stirring continuously in a circular motion, put in to the broth. Put in the epazote and simmer until the eggs are set. Adjust the seasoning, then put in the fried bread and simmer for half one minute, no longer.

6. Serve in deep soup bowls, with a crouton in each container, and top with chile veins to taste.

GREEN CORN SOUP (SOPA VERDE DE ELOTE)

Yield: Servings 6

Ingredients:

- ¼ cup (65 ml or about 2 ounces/60 g) unsalted butter
- ½ cup (125 ml) finely chopped white onion
- ⅔ cup (165 ml) green peas, fresh or frozen
- ⅔ cup (165 ml) tomate verde, cooked and drained
- 1 teaspoon salt, or to taste
- 2 small garlic cloves, finely chopped
- 2 small poblano chiles, charred and peeled
- 3 big romaine lettuce leaves, roughly chopped
- 4½ cups (1.125 l) corn kernels
- 5 cups (1.25 l) light chicken broth
- 6 big sprigs cilantro
- 6 tablespoons sour cream, commercial or homemade
- crisp-fried tortilla pieces

- **To serve**

Directions:

1. Melt the butter in a big deep cooking pan and fry the onion and garlic until translucent.

2. Combine the tomate verde until the desired smoothness is achieved. Put into the onion in the pan and fry using high heat for approximately 3 minutes, stirring continuously.

3. Place the corn kernels into a blender jar (one third at a time) with 2 cups (500 ml) of the chicken broth and the peas, cilantro, chiles, and lettuce leaves and blend until fairly smooth. Pass this puree through the medium disk of a food mill or strainer, then put in to the pan and cook over quite high heat for approximately 3 minutes, stirring and scraping the bottom of the pan continuously, since the mixture tends to stick.

4. Put in the remaining broth and the salt and cook the soup using low heat until it thickens and is well seasoned—about twenty minutes.

5. Serve in soup bowls with a big spoonful of the sour cream and a drizzling of tortilla pieces for each serving.

LEEK SOUP (SOPA DE PUERROS)

Yield: Servings 6

Ingredients:

- ¼ cup (65 ml) finely chopped flat-leaf parsley
- 2 tablespoons unsalted butter
- 2 tablespoons vegetable oil
- 4 cups (1 l) finely chopped leeks, white and soft green part only
- 5 hard-cooked eggs
- 6 cups (1.5 l) light chicken broth
- Salt and freshly ground pepper to taste

The topping

- Fried bread croutons or crisp-fried tortilla pieces

Directions:

1. Heat the butter with the oil in a large, heavy deep cooking pan and fry the leeks and parsley slowly until just soft, without browning—approximately eight minutes. Put in 5 cups (1.25 l) of the chicken broth and cook on moderate heat until the leeks are soft—approximately eight minutes.

2. Shell the eggs and separate the whites from the yolks. Cut the whites fine and save for later. Combine the yolks, with the remaining broth, until the desired smoothness is

achieved and put in with the chopped whites to the soup. Season and carry on cooking for another ten minutes, or until the leeks are completely tender and well seasoned.

3. Serve the soup with croutons or crisp-fried tortilla pieces.

LENTIL AND CHORIZO SOUP

Yield: Servings 6 to 8

Ingredients:

- ⅛ teaspoon ground cloves
- 1 onion, chopped fine
- 1 pound (2¼ cups) brown lentils, picked over and washed
- 1 tablespoon all purpose flour
- 1 tablespoon red wine vinegar, plus extra for seasoning
- 1 teaspoon ground cumin
- 1½ pounds Mexican style chorizo sausage, pricked with fork multiple times
- 2 bay leaves
- 2 tablespoons ancho chile powder
- 2 tablespoons extra virgin olive oil
- 3 carrots, peeled and slice into ¼ inch pieces
- 3 garlic cloves, minced
- 3 tablespoons minced fresh cilantro
- 7 cups water
- Salt and pepper

Directions:

1. Put lentils and 2 teaspoons salt in heatproof container. Cover with 4 cups boiling water and allow to soak for half an hour Drain thoroughly.
2. Heat oil in Dutch oven over moderate high heat until just smoking. Brown chorizo on all sides, six to eight minutes; move to plate. Decrease the heat to low and put in onion, carrots, 1 tablespoon cilantro, and 1 teaspoon salt to fat left in pot. Cover and cook, stirring once in a while, until vegetables are very tender but not brown, fifteen to twenty minutes. If vegetables start to brown, put in 1 tablespoon water to pot.

3. Mix in chile powder, garlic, cumin, and cloves and cook until aromatic, approximately 2 minutes. Mix in flour and cook for a minute. Slowly whisk in water, scraping up any browned bits, and bring to simmer. Put in browned chorizo with any collected juices and bay leaves, decrease the heat to low, cover, and simmer gently until lentils are soft, fifteen to twenty minutes.

4. Discard bay leaves. Move chorizo to cutting board, allow to cool slightly, then halve along the length and slice ¼ inch thick. Stir chorizo into soup and simmer until thoroughly heated, approximately 2 minutes. Remove the heat, mix in vinegar and remaining 2 tablespoons cilantro. Sprinkle with salt, pepper, and extra vinegar to taste and serve.

LENTIL SOUP (SOPA DE LENTEJAS ESTILO QUERÉTARO)

Yield: Servings 6

Ingredients:

- ¼ cup (65 ml) finely chopped white onion
- 1 big scallion, green part included, quartered
- 1 cup (250 ml) chicken broth
- 1 garlic clove, roughly chopped
- 1 jalapeño chile, or 2 serrano chiles, or any fresh, hot green chile, thinly cut
- 2 tablespoons vegetable oil
- 3 big sprigs cilantro
- 4 to 6 ounces (1fifteen to 180 g or ½ rounded cup/125 ml) small brown lentils
- 6 cups (1.5 l) water, roughly
- 8 ounces (225 g) nopales (about 3 medium-size cactus paddles), cleaned of prickles and cut into little squares (approximately 1¾ cups/ 440 ml)
- 8 ounces (225 g) tomatoes, roughly chopped (1½ cups/375 ml)
- Salt to taste

Directions:

1. Wash the lentils well and drain. Place them into a pan with 6 cups (1.5 l) of cold water. Bring to its boiling point, then reduce the heat and cook on low heat until mushy— about three hours for mexican lentils, 2 hours for american.

2. Cover the cactus pieces with cold water, put in ½ teaspoon of the salt and the scallion, and simmer until just soft—about twenty minutes. Wash in cold water and drain, discarding the onion.

3. Combine the tomatoes with the garlic until the desired smoothness is achieved. Set aside.

4. Heat the oil in a frying pan and fry the onion and chile gently, without browning, until they are tender. Put in the tomato puree and fry for another three minutes or so over a high heat while stirring continuously, until the mixture is almost dry. Put into the lentils with the chicken broth and nopales. Cover the pan and cook using low heat for approximately twenty minutes, then put in the cilantro and cook for a minute longer. Salt to taste.

MEATBALL SOUP WITH RICE AND CILANTRO

Yield: Servings 6 to 8

Ingredients:

- ¼ teaspoon ground cumin
- ½ jalapeño chile, stemmed, halved, and seeded
- ½ onion, quartered
- 1 big egg
- 1 cup long grain white rice
- 1 small zucchini, cut into ½ inch pieces
- 1 tablespoon vegetable oil
- 1½ teaspoons minced fresh oregano or ½ teaspoon dried
- 2 carrots, peeled and slice into ½ inch pieces
- 2 tomatoes, cored and quartered
- 3 garlic cloves, minced
- 5 tablespoons minced fresh cilantro
- 8 cups chicken broth
- 8 ounces 90 percent lean ground beef
- 8 ounces ground pork
- Salt and pepper

Directions:

1. Bring 4 cups water to boil in Dutch oven. Put in rice and ¾ teaspoon salt and cook, stirring once in a while, for eight minutes. Drain rice through fine mesh strainer, wash with cold water, and drain once more.

2. Use your hands to mix half of parcooked rice, ground beef, ground pork, 3 tablespoons cilantro, egg, one third of garlic, oregano, cumin, 1 teaspoon pepper, and ½ teaspoon salt together in big container until meticulously blended. Pinch off and roll mixture into 1 tablespoon size meatballs (about 40 meatballs total) and position on rimmed baking sheet.

3. Process tomatoes, onion, jalapeño, and remaining garlic in food processor until the desired smoothness is achieved, approximately half a minute, scraping down sides of container as required. Heat oil in now empty pot over moderate high heat until shimmering. Put in tomato onion mixture and cook, stirring regularly, until mixture has darkened in color and liquid has vaporized, approximately ten minutes.

4. Mix in broth and carrots, scraping up any browned bits, and bring to simmer. Cook until carrots are nearly soft, approximately ten minutes. Mix in zucchini and remaining parcooked rice, then gently put in meatballs and simmer until meatballs are thoroughly cooked, ten to twelve minutes. Remove the heat, mix in remaining 2 tablespoons cilantro and sprinkle with salt and pepper to taste and serve.

MEXICAN BEEF AND VEGETABLE SOUP

Yield: Servings 6 to 8

Ingredients:

- ½ teaspoon ground cumin
- 1 (14.5 ounce) can diced tomatoes, drained
- 1 onion, chopped
- 1 pound boneless beef chuck eye roast, trimmed and slice into an inch pieces
- 1 tablespoon minced fresh oregano or 1 teaspoon dried
- 1 tablespoon vegetable oil
- 1 zucchini, cut into ½ inch pieces
- 10 ounces red potatoes, unpeeled, cut into an inch pieces
- 2 bay leaves

- 2 carrots, peeled and slice into ½ inch pieces
- 2 cups chicken broth
- 2 ears corn, husks and silk removed, cut into an inch rounds
- 2 tablespoons minced fresh cilantro
- 4 cups beef broth
- 5 garlic cloves, minced
- Salt and pepper

Directions:

1. Pat beef dry using paper towels and sprinkle with salt and pepper. Heat oil in Dutch oven over moderate high heat until just smoking. Brown beef on all sides, five to seven minutes; move to container.
2. Put in onion to fat left in pot and cook on moderate heat until tender, approximately five minutes. Mix in garlic, oregano, and cumin and cook until aromatic, approximately half a minute. Mix in beef broth, chicken broth, tomatoes, and bay leaves, scraping up any browned bits, and bring to simmer. Mix in browned beef with any collected juices, decrease the heat to low, cover, and simmer gently for half an hour
3. Mix in carrots and potatoes and simmer, uncovered, until beef and vegetables are just soft, twenty to twenty-five minutes. Mix in zucchini and corn and simmer until corn is soft, 5 to ten minutes.
4. Remove the heat, discard bay leaves. Mix in cilantro and sprinkle with salt and pepper to taste and serve.

PORK POSOLE ROJO

Yield: Servings 8 to 10

Ingredients:

- 1 (14.5 ounce) can diced tomatoes
- 1 (5 pound) bone in pork butt roast
- 1 tablespoon minced fresh oregano or 1 teaspoon dried
- 1½ cups boiling water
- 2 big onions, chopped coarse
- 2 tablespoons vegetable oil

- 3 (fifteen ounce) cans white or yellow hominy, washed
- 3 dried ancho chiles, stemmed and seeded
- 5 garlic cloves, minced
- 6 cups chicken broth
- Salt and pepper

Directions:

1. Adjust oven rack to lower middle position and heat oven to 300 degrees. Trim thick skin and surplus fat from meat and cut along muscles to split roast into big pieces of various sizes; reserve bones. Season pork with salt and pepper.

2. Heat oil in Dutch oven on moderate heat until shimmering. Put in onions and ¼ teaspoon salt and cook until tender, approximately eight to ten minutes. Mix in garlic and cook until aromatic, approximately half a minute. Put in pork and bones and cook, stirring frequently, until meat is no longer pink on outside, approximately eight minutes. Mix in broth, tomatoes and their juice, oregano, and ½ teaspoon salt and bring to simmer, skimming foam from surface as required. Cover, place pot in oven, and cook until pork is soft, approximately 2 hours.

3. In the meantime, soak anchos in container with boiling water until tender, approximately twenty minutes. Process anchos and soaking liquid in blender until the desired smoothness is achieved, approximately half a minute. Strain through fine mesh strainer into container, using rubber spatula to help pass chili mixture through strainer. Measure out and reserve ¼ cup ancho mixture for serving.

4. Take the pot out of the oven, move pork to cutting board, and allow to cool slightly; discard bones. While pork cools, stir hominy and remaining ancho mixture into pot and bring to simmer on moderate heat. Decrease the heat to low, cover, and simmer gently until flavors meld, approximately 30 minutes.

5. Using 2 forks, shred pork into bite size pieces. Stir shredded pork into stew and cook until thoroughly heated, approximately 2 minutes. Flavor it with reserved ancho mixture, salt, and pepper to taste and serve.

SOUP OF THE SEVEN SEAS

Yield: Servings 6 to 8

Ingredients:

- 1 onion, quartered
- 1 pound big shrimp (26 to 30 per pound), peeled, deveined, tails removed, and shells reserved
- 1 pound mussels, scrubbed and debearded
- 1 pound russet potatoes, peeled and slice into ½ inch pieces
- 1 tablespoon dried oregano
- 1½ pounds skinless catfish fillets, cut into 2 inch pieces
- 2 (8 ounce) bottles clam juice
- 2 bay leaves
- 2 ears corn, husks and silk removed, cut into an inch rounds
- 2 tablespoons minced fresh cilantro
- 2 teaspoons ground cumin
- 2 teaspoons sugar
- 3 dried ancho chiles, stemmed, seeded, and torn into ½ inch pieces (¾ cup)
- 3 garlic cloves, peeled
- 3 tablespoons vegetable oil
- 5 cups chicken broth
- Lime wedges
- Salt and pepper

Directions:

1. Toast anchos in Dutch oven over moderate high heat, stirring regularly, until aromatic, 2 to six minutes; move to food processor. Put in onion, garlic, oregano, cumin, sugar, bay leaves, and 1 teaspoon pepper to processor and pulse until crudely chopped, approximately fifteen pulses.
2. Heat oil in now empty pot over moderate high heat until shimmering. Put in ancho mixture, shrimp shells, and ½ teaspoon salt and cook, stirring regularly, until mixture has darkened in color and shrimp shells have turned bright pink, two to three minutes. Mix in broth and clam juice, scraping up any browned bits, and bring to simmer. Cook until flavors meld, approximately ten minutes. Strain broth through fine mesh strainer; discard solids. Return strained broth to again empty pot and bring to simmer.
3. Mix in corn and potatoes and simmer until potatoes are soft, about eight to ten minutes. Increase heat to moderate high, mix in mussels, cover, and simmer briskly

until most mussels have opened, three to four minutes (discard any unopened mussels). Using slotted spoon, move mussels, potatoes, and corn to individual bowls.

4. Return broth to gentle simmer using low heat. Put in catfish and shrimp to pot, cover, and cook until catfish and shrimp are opaque throughout, approximately 3 minutes. Remove the heat, gently mix in cilantro and sprinkle with salt and pepper to taste. Ladle broth, shrimp, and catfish over mussels and vegetables. Serve with lime wedges.

SOUR "LIMA" SOUP (SOPA DE LIMA)

Yield: Servings 6

Ingredients:

- ¼ cup (65 ml) finely chopped chile dulce or green pepper
- ¼ teaspoon dried mexican oregano, yucatecan if possible, toasted
- ⅓ cup (85 ml) finely chopped white onion
- ½ lima agria or substitute fresh lime
- 10 garlic cloves, toasted
- 1½ tablespoons lard or chicken fat
- 2 chicken breasts with skin and bones
- 4 chicken gizzards
- 6 chicken livers (approximately eight ounces/225 g)
- 6 peppercorns
- 8 cups (2 l) water
- 8 ounces (225 g) tomatoes, finely chopped (1⅓ cups/335 ml)
- Salt to taste
- twelve tortillas, cut into strips and dried
- Vegetable oil for frying

To serve

- ⅓ cup (85 ml) habanero chiles, charred and finely chopped
- ¾ cup (185 ml) finely chopped white onion
- 6 thin slices lima agria

Directions:

1. Place the water into a soup pot. Put in the garlic, oregano, peppercorns, and salt. Heat to a simmer and cook for approximately ten minutes. Put in the gizzards and cook for fifteen more minutes.
2. Put in the chicken breasts and carry on cooking for another fifteen minutes. Put in the livers and cook for ten more minutes, or until the meats are soft.
3. Strain the broth and set it aside. Take away the meat from the breasts and shred. Cut the livers, remove the gristle from the gizzards, and cut them. Keep the meats hot.
4. Heat the lard in a frying pan and lightly fry the onion and pepper until they are soft, but not browned. Put in the tomatoes to the mixture in the pan, and cook for approximately five minutes on moderate heat. Put into the broth and allow it to simmer uncovered for approximately five minutes. Put in salt as required. Put in a little of the chopped and shredded meats to each container.
5. Squeeze the juice of the ½ lima agria into the broth. Drop the squeezed lima shell into the broth for a few seconds only, then remove. Keep the broth warm.
6. Heat the oil in a frying pan and fry the tortilla strips until they are crunchy. Drain them on the toweling, and while they are still super hot, drop some of them into the broth in each soup container.
7. Pass the chopped onion, the chiles, and slices of lima separately.

SPICY BUTTERNUT SQUASH SOUP WITH CHIPOTLE

Yield: Servings four to 6

Ingredients:

- ¼ cup pepitas, toasted
- ½ cup heavy cream
- ½ teaspoon ground cumin
- 1 (3 pound) butternut squash, halved along the length and widthwise, seeds and fibers removed and reserved
- 1 big shallot, chopped fine
- 1 tablespoon honey
- 2 tablespoons minced fresh cilantro
- 2 teaspoons minced canned chipotle chile in adobo sauce
- 4 tablespoons unsalted butter

- 6 cups water, plus extra as required
- Salt and pepper

Directions:

1. Melt 2 tablespoons butter in Dutch oven on moderate heat. Put in shallot and cook until tender, two to three minutes. Put in squash seeds and fibers and cook, stirring once in a while, until butter turns orange, approximately 4 minutes.
2. Mix in water and 1 teaspoon salt and bring to boil. Reduce to simmer, place squash cut side down in steamer basket, and lower basket into pot. Cover and steam squash until it is completely soft, thirty to forty minutes.
3. Using tongs, move cooked squash to rimmed baking sheet. When sufficiently cool to handle, use big spoon to scrape cooked squash from skin; discard skin. Strain steaming broth through fine mesh strainer into 4 cup liquid measuring cup. You should have minimum 3 cups of broth; if short, put in water.
4. Working in batches, puree cooked squash with 3 cups broth until the desired smoothness is achieved, one to two minutes. Return puree to clean pot. Mix in heavy cream, honey, chipotle, cumin, and remaining 2 tablespoons butter. Return to brief simmer, putting in additional broth (or water) as required to adjust soup's consistency. Mix in cilantro and sprinkle with salt and pepper to taste. Decorate individual bowls with pepitas before you serve.

SPICY PINTO BEAN SOUP

Yield: Servings 6

Ingredients:

- 1 jalapeño chile, stemmed, halved, and seeded
- 1 onion, quartered
- 1 tablespoon dried oregano
- 1 tablespoon minced canned chipotle chile in adobo sauce
- 2 bay leaves
- 2 tomatoes, cored and quartered
- 3 dried ancho chiles, stemmed, seeded, and torn into ½ inch pieces (¾ cup)
- 3 garlic cloves, peeled

- 3 tablespoons vegetable oil
- 7 cups chicken broth, plus extra as required
- 8 ounces (1¼ cups) dried pinto beans, picked over and washed
- Salt and pepper

Directions:

1. Dissolve 1½ tablespoons salt in 2 quarts cold water in big container or container. Put in beans and soak at room temperature for minimum 8 hours or maximum one day.
2. Drain beans and wash well. Toast anchos in Dutch oven over moderate high heat, stirring regularly, until aromatic, 2 to six minutes; move to blender. Put in tomatoes, onion, garlic, jalapeño, chipotle, and oregano and pulse until smooth, approximately half a minute.
3. Heat oil in now empty pot over moderate high heat until shimmering. Put in ancho mixture and 1 teaspoon salt and cook, stirring regularly, until mixture has darkened in color and liquid has vaporized, approximately ten minutes. Mix in broth, scraping up any browned bits. Mix in beans and bay leaves and bring to simmer. Decrease the heat to low, cover, and simmer gently until beans are soft, one to 1½ hours.
4. Discard bay leaves. Working in batches, process soup in clean, dry blender until the desired smoothness is achieved, one to two minutes. Return soup to again empty pot, adjust consistency with extra broth as required, and sprinkle with salt and pepper to taste and serve.

TARASCAN BEAN AND TORTILLA SOUP (SOPA TARASCA TIPO CONDE)

Yield: Servings 6

Ingredients:

- ¼ teaspoon dried mexican oregano
- 1 garlic clove
- 1 pound (450 g) tomatoes, broiled
- 2 tablespoons roughly chopped white onion
- 2½ cups (625 ml) chicken or pork broth
- 3 ancho chiles, cleaned of seeds and then cut into thin strips and fried

- 3 small tortillas cut into strips, fried crisp as for totopos
- 3 tablespoons lard or vegetable oil
- 6 ounces (180 g) queso fresco, thinly cut
- 8 ounces (225 g) cooked pink or pinto beans (about 3½ to 4 cups; 875 ml to 1 l) with broth
- Salt as required
- thick sour cream

Directions:

1. Combine the beans, with their broth, to a smooth consistency and move to a large, heavy deep cooking pan.
2. Combine the tomatoes, garlic, and onion together to a smooth sauce. Melt the fat in a frying pan and cook the tomato mixture using high heat for approximately five minutes, then mix into the bean puree and allow it to cook on moderate heat for approximately 8 minutes, stirring it all the time.
3. Put in the broth and let the soup cook for an extra five minutes using low heat. Put in salt to taste and put in the oregano just before you serve.
4. Place a few pieces of the cheese into each container. Pour the hot soup over them and top with the chiles, some tortilla strips, and a spoonful of sour cream.
5. Note: this soup will become thick considerably as it stands and will have to be diluted with broth or water. It freezes well.

TORTILLA BALL SOUP (SOPA DE BOLITAS DE TORTILLAS)

Yield: Servings 6

Ingredients:

The soup

- ½ cup (125 ml) finely grated queso añejo (approximately 1½ ounces/45 g)
- ½ cup (125 ml) hot whole milk
- 1 big egg, well beaten
- 12 stale tortillas, dried
- 6 cups (1.5 l) tomato-chicken broth (see Next recipe)

- Approximately ¼ cup (65 ml) whole milk, cold
- Melted lard or vegetable oil for frying
- Sea salt to taste

To serve

- ⅓ cup (85 ml) prepared sour cream
- Finely chopped fresh cilantro or parsley

Directions:

1. Break the tortillas into little pieces and blend until they are like fine bread crumbs; this amount will make approximately 1 cup (250 ml). Put in the hot milk, cheese, egg, and salt and knead the dough well, then set it aside for quite a few hours or place in your fridge it overnight, to allow the tortilla particles to become tender.
2. Again knead the dough well, putting in the cold milk. Roll the dough uniformly into one long piece; split this into 12 pieces, and each piece in half once more. Roll the 24 pieces into little balls approximately 1 inch (2.5 cm) in diameter.
3. Heat the lard in a frying pan and fry the balls very gently, turning them occasionally until they are a golden brown—about five minutes. Drain thoroughly. Place the balls into the heated broth, bring to its boiling point, then decrease the heat and simmer for approximately 2 minutes.
4. Serve in individual bowls—four balls per serving—and top each using a spoonful of the cream and some chopped cilantro.

TORTILLA SOUP (SOPA DE TORTILLA)

Yield: Servings 6

Ingredients:

- ¼ cup (65 ml) roughly chopped white onion
- 1 garlic clove
- 12 ounces (340 g) tomatoes, broiled
- 12 small tortillas, cut into strips and dried
- 2 big sprigs epazote
- 3 pasilla chiles, fried crisp and crumbled

- 6 cups (1.5 l) caldo de pollo (Chicken Soup)
- 6 heaped tablespoons grated chihuahua cheese or muenster
- Vegetable oil for frying

Directions:

1. Heat the oil in a big frying pan and fry the tortilla strips until they are mildly browned but not too crunchy. Drain them on paper toweling. Pour off all but 1 tablespoon of the oil.
2. Combine the tomatoes, onion, and garlic to a smooth sauce, then put in to the oil and fry for approximately five minutes, until the sauce is well seasoned and has reduced fairly.
3. Put in the sauce to the caldo de pollo and bring to its boiling point. Adjust seasoning. Put in the tortilla strips and cook them for approximately 3 minutes.
4. Just before you serve, put in the epazote. Cook for a minute more.
5. Serve each portion topped with pieces of crumbled chile and grated cheese.
6. Note: the base could be prepared (and even stored frozen) hours ahead but the final steps, putting in tortillas and epazote, must be done a few minutes before you serve.

WHITE CHICKEN CHILI

Yield: Servings 6 to 8

Ingredients:

- ¼ cup minced fresh cilantro
- 1 pound onions, cut into an inch pieces
- 1 tablespoon ground cumin
- 1½ teaspoons ground coriander
- 2 (fifteen ounce) cans cannellini beans, washed
- 2 tablespoons vegetable oil
- 3 Anaheim chiles, stemmed, seeded, and slice into an inch pieces
- 3 cups chicken broth
- 3 jalapeño chiles, stemmed, seeded, and minced
- 3 poblano chiles, stemmed, seeded, and slice into an inch pieces
- 3 pounds bone in split chicken breasts, trimmed

- 3 tablespoons lime juice (2 limes)
- 4 scallions, cut thin
- 6 garlic cloves, minced
- Salt and pepper

Directions:

1. Pulse half of poblanos, half of Anaheims, and half of onions in food processor until consistency of lumpy salsa, ten to 12 pulses, scraping down sides of container as required; move to moderate container. Repeat with remaining poblanos, Anaheims, and onions; move to container (do not clean food processor).

2. Pat chicken dry using paper towels and sprinkle with salt and pepper. Heat 1 tablespoon oil in Dutch oven over moderate high heat until just smoking. Brown half of chicken, approximately five minutes per side; move to plate. Repeat with remaining 1 tablespoon oil and remaining chicken. Allow to cool slightly, then remove skin.

3. Pour off all but 2 tablespoons fat from pot and decrease the heat to moderate. Put in chile mixture, two thirds of jalapeños, garlic, cumin, coriander, and ¼ teaspoon salt. Cover and cook, stirring once in a while, until vegetables become tender, approximately ten minutes. Remove pot from heat.

4. Move 1 cup cooked vegetable mixture to now empty food processor. Put in 1 cup beans and 1 cup broth and pulse until smooth, approximately twenty seconds. Put in vegetable bean mixture and remaining 2 cups broth to pot and bring to simmer over moderate high heat. Nestle browned chicken into pot together with any collected juices. Decrease the heat to low, cover, and simmer gently until chicken records 160 degrees, fifteen to twenty minutes.

5. Move chicken to cutting board and allow to cool slightly. In the meantime, stir remaining beans into chili and simmer, uncovered, until beans are thoroughly heated and chili has thickened slightly, approximately ten minutes.

6. Using 2 forks, shred chicken into bite size pieces; discard bones. Stir shredded chicken and remaining jalapeño into chili and cook until thoroughly heated, approximately 2 minutes. Remove the heat, mix in lime juice, cilantro, and scallions. Sprinkle with salt and pepper to taste and serve.

Stews

PREPARATION OF CORN FOR POZOLE, MENUDO, AND GALLINA PINTA

In this section, you will find recipes for pozole, menudo, and gallina pinta. All of these recipes call for an ingredient called "prepared and cooked white corn". Dried corn with broad, white kernels is commonly known as "cacahuazintle or maiz pozolero" and is easily found in the freezer section of Latin American grocery stores. If you can't find it, or have the time and patience to make your own, here's how you go about it:

Directions:

1. Allow 1 pound (450 g) of corn to soak in cold water overnight. This step is not essential, but it helps reduce the final cooking time. Remove any bits that float to the top of the water, then strain.
2. Place the corn into a deep pot, cover well with water, put in 1 tablespoon powdered lime, and bring to a simmer—it will turn yellow. Carry on cooking uncovered using low heat for approximately fifteen minutes. Turn off the heat and set aside to cool and soak for approximately twenty minutes. When sufficiently cool to handle, wash in fresh water and rub the kernels through your hands until the rather slimy skin has been removed—you may need several changes of water until it is clean and white. With a paring knife—or strong fingernails—remove the pedicels at the top of the kernels.
3. Return the cleaned kernels to the pot and cover with water to come about 3 inches (8 cm) above the level of the corn—a little difficult because the kernels tend to float. Cook on moderate heat, covered, until the kernels open up like a flower—about three hours depending on how old and dry the corn is. Put in salt to taste.

CHICKEN STEW MIX

Yield: Servings 6 to 8

Ingredients:

- ¼ cup unsalted dry roasted peanuts
- 1 (fifteen ounce) can pinto beans, washed
- 1 jalapeño chile, stemmed
- 1 onion, quartered
- 1 pound sweet potatoes, peeled and slice into ½ inch pieces
- 1 tablespoon red wine vinegar
- 2 cups ½ inch pineapple pieces
- 2 ripe plantains, peeled, quartered along the length and cut an inch thick
- 3 dried ancho chiles, stemmed, seeded, and torn into ½ inch pieces (¾ cup)
- 3 garlic cloves, peeled
- 3 tablespoons sesame seeds, toasted, plus extra for serving
- 3 tablespoons vegetable oil
- 4 pounds bone in chicken thighs, skin removed, trimmed
- 4 scallions, cut thin
- 4½ cups chicken broth
- Salt and pepper

Directions:

1. Adjust oven rack to lower middle position and heat oven to 300 degrees. Toast anchos in Dutch oven over moderate high heat, stirring regularly, until aromatic, 2 to six minutes; move to blender. Put in ½ cup broth, 1 cup pineapple, onion, peanuts, sesame seeds, garlic, and jalapeño and pulse until smooth, approximately 60 seconds.

2. Heat oil in now empty pot over moderate high heat until shimmering. Put in ancho mixture and 1 teaspoon salt and cook, stirring regularly, until mixture has darkened in color and liquid has vaporized, approximately ten minutes. Mix in remaining 4 cups broth, scraping up any browned bits. Mix in sweet potatoes and beans and bring to simmer. Season chicken with salt and pepper and nestle into pot. Cover, move pot to oven, and cook until chicken is soft, approximately 1 hour.

3. Take the pot out of the oven and move chicken to cutting board. Let chicken cool slightly, then, using 2 forks, shred into bite size pieces; discard bones. Stir shredded chicken, plantains, and remaining 1 cup pineapple into stew and bring to simmer on moderate heat. Mix in vinegar and sprinkle with salt and pepper to taste. Serve with scallions and extra sesame seeds.

CHILE DE ÁRBOL SAUCE

Ingredients:

- 3 ounces (85 g) árbol chiles (about 2 cups/500 ml, stems only removed
- Water to cover

Directions:

1. Wash the chiles for a short period of time in cold water, drain, and cover with fresh water. Set aside to soak overnight.
2. Combine the whole chiles with the water in which they were soaking. Run the sauce through a strainer, discarding the debris. Do not put in salt (conventionally no salt is added).

MEXICAN BEEF STEW

Yield: Servings 6 to 8

Ingredients:

- ¼ cup minced fresh cilantro
- ¼ teaspoon ground cinnamon
- 1 (14.5 ounce) can diced tomatoes
- 1 cup pitted green olives, chopped coarse
- 1 jalapeño chile, stemmed, seeded, and minced
- 1 tablespoon dried oregano
- 1½ pounds red potatoes, unpeeled, cut into 1½ inch pieces
- 1½ teaspoons ground cumin
- 2 dried ancho chiles, stemmed and seeded
- 2 onions, chopped fine
- 2 red or green bell peppers, stemmed, seeded, and slice into an inch pieces
- 2 tablespoons all purpose flour
- 2 tablespoons vegetable oil
- 3 cups beef broth
- 3 garlic cloves, minced

- 4 pounds boneless beef chuck eye roast, pulled apart at seams, trimmed, and slice into 1½ inch pieces
- Salt and pepper

Directions:

1. Adjust oven rack to lower middle position and heat oven to 325 degrees. Toast anchos in Dutch oven over moderate high heat, stirring regularly, until aromatic, 2 to six minutes; move to container.
2. Pat beef dry using paper towels and sprinkle with salt and pepper. Heat 1 tablespoon oil in now empty pot over moderate high heat until just smoking. Brown half of beef on all sides, 7 to ten minutes; move to plate. Repeat with remaining 1 tablespoon oil and remaining beef.
3. Put in onions and ¼ teaspoon salt to fat left in pot and cook on moderate heat until tender, approximately five minutes. Mix in garlic, jalapeño, oregano, cumin, and cinnamon and cook until aromatic, approximately half a minute. Mix in flour and cook for a minute. Slowly whisk in broth, scraping up any browned bits. Mix in tomatoes and their juice and toasted anchos and bring to a simmer. Mix in browned beef and any collected juices, cover, move pot to oven, and cook for an hour.
4. Mix in potatoes and bell peppers, cover, and cook in oven until beef and potatoes are soft, one to 1½ hours.
5. Take the pot out of the oven and discard anchos. Mix in olives and allow it to sit until thoroughly heated, two minutes. Adjust stew consistency with hot water as required. Mix in cilantro and sprinkle with salt and pepper to taste and serve.

MOLE COOKED IN A POT (MOLE DE OLLA)

Yield: Servings 6

Ingredients:

The meat

- 2 quarts (2 l) water
- 2 teaspoons salt, or to taste
- 3 pounds (1.35 kg) pork neck bones or 3 pounds (1.35 kg) boiling beef (brisket or a shoulder cut), with bone

The seasoning sauce

- ⅛ teaspoon cumin seeds, crushed
- ½ medium white onion, roughly chopped
- 1 cup (250 ml) tomate verde, cooked and drained
- 2 garlic cloves, roughly chopped
- 3 tablespoons vegetable oil
- 4 ancho chiles, wiped clean, seeds and veins removed
- 4 pasilla chiles, wiped clean, seeds and veins removed

The vegetables

- 1 big ear of corn
- 1 small chayote (approximately eight ounces/225 g)
- 1 xoconostle, peeled and center with seeds removed
- 3 sprigs epazote
- 4 ounces (115 g) green beans
- 8 ounces (225 g) potatoes
- 8 ounces (225 g) zucchini

The garnish

- Wedges of lime and finely chopped white onion

Directions:

1. Have the butcher chop the meat and bones into serving pieces. Cover them with the water, put in the salt, and bring to its boiling point. Reduce the heat and simmer the meat, uncovered, until nearly soft—about forty minutes for the pork and 1 hour for the beef.
2. In the meantime prepare the chiles. Heat the comal and toast the chiles on both sides, ensuring not to burn. When cool they must be easy to crumble into your blender. Combine the chiles with the remaining seasoning ingredients apart from the oil until the desired smoothness is achieved.
3. Heat the oil in a frying pan and fry the sauce for approximately five minutes. Put in it to the meat.
4. Clean and trim the squash and slice into halves, then into four along the length. Trim the beans and slice into halves. Chop the corn into six pieces. Chop the chayote open

and remove the core, then cut into ¼-inch (.75-cm) wedges. Skin the potatoes and slice into cubes.

5. When the meat is soft, put in the vegetables and cook the mole slowly, uncovered, for approximately 30 minutes, or until the vegetables are cooked. Put in the epazote about five minutes before the mole is ready, and put in salt as required.

6. Serve in large, deep soup bowls, with hot tortillas, wedges of lime, and finely chopped onion on the side.

NORTHERN TRIPE SOUP (MENUDO BLANCO NORTEÑO)

Yield: Servings approximately 16

Ingredients:

- 1 head of garlic, unpeeled, cut in half horizontally
- 1½ pounds (675 g) calf's feet, cut into 4 pieces
- 5½ pounds (2.5 kg) tripe of different textures
- Optional: 3 pigs' feet, approximately 1 pound (450 g)
- Salt to taste

The corn

- 1 pound 2 ounces (500 g) pozole corn, cooked and "flowered"

The seasoning

- ⅓ cup (85 ml) water
- 1 heaped tablespoon dried mexican oregano, if possible
- 1 teaspoon cumin seeds, crushed
- 3 garlic cloves (not necessary)

To serve

- ½ cup (125 ml) toasted and powdered ancho chile
- Crumbled, dried mexican oregano
- Finely chopped white onion
- Slices of lime

Directions:

1. Wash the tripe twice in cold water, drain, and slice into two-inch (5-cm) squares. Wash the calf's and pigs' feet and drain. Put into a big stockpot or mexican earthenware olla. Fill the pot with water almost to the top—the level must be several inches above the meats. Put in the garlic and salt and put using low heat, uncovered, until it comes to a simmer. Carry on cooking for an hour, then cover and carry on cooking until the tripe and feet are soft—anywhere from 2 to 4 hours depending on the quality of the tripe.
2. Meantime, the corn must be cooking. When it is soft and has opened up, or "flowered," drain, saving for later about 3 cups (750 ml) of the broth.
3. Place the ⅓ cup (85 ml) of water into your blender jar, put in the cumin, oregano, and optional garlic, and blend until the desired smoothness is achieved.
4. When the meats are soft, put in the seasoning mixture and corn with the reserved broth. Adjust the salt, and carry on cooking uncovered until the meats are soft— approximately 1 hour more.
5. Take away the pieces of calf's foot from the broth and chop the gelatinous parts into little cubes. Return them to the pot.
6. Serve the menudo—about 2 cups (500 ml) per person is a healthy portion—in deep bowls and pass the toppings separately.

OXTAIL, PORK, AND BEAN SOUP (GALLINA PINTA)

Yield: Servings 6 to 8

Ingredients:

- ½ cup (125 ml) pinto beans
- ½ white onion, roughly cut
- 1 oxtail (1½ to 2 pounds/675 to 900 g), cut into little pieces with most of the fat removed
- 1 pound (450 g) country-style pork spareribs, cubed
- 1½ cups (375 ml) prepared and cooked white corn for pozole
- 2 ancho chiles, seeds and veins removed and mildly toasted
- 2 garlic cloves
- 2 quarts (2 l) water

- 6 peppercorns
- Salt to taste

Directions:

1. Place the oxtail into a big deep cooking pan with the onion, garlic, salt, pinto beans, and peppercorns. Cover with the water and bring to its boiling point. Reduce the heat and simmer for an hour.
2. Put in the spareribs and white corn and carry on cooking using low heat, uncovered, for another one to 1½ hours, until the meat is super soft and the beans tender. Put in salt to taste.
3. About twenty minutes before the soup is done, blend one of the chiles with a little of the broth and put in the mixture to the soup. Tear the other chile into fine strips and put in to the soup.
4. Serve in deep bowls.

PORK AND WHITE CORN SOUP (POZOLE DE JALISCO)

Yield: Servings twelve to 14

Ingredients:

- ½ pig's head, approximately 3 pounds (1.35 kg)
- 1 pound (450 g) pork neck bones
- 1 pound (450 g) white corn kernels for pozole
- 1½ pounds (675 g) boneless stewing pork
- 1½ tablespoons salt
- Approximately 14 cups (3.5 l) water

To serve

- 1 cup (250 ml) cut radishes
- 1 cup (250 ml) finely chopped white onion
- 2 cups (500 ml) finely shredded lettuce or cabbage
- chile de árbol sauce
- Wedges of lime

Directions:

1. Two days before you serve, put the corn to soak, as indicated.
2. One day before you serve, clean and prepare the white corn for cooking.
3. Chop the pork into big serving pieces and put it, with the head and bones, in cold water to soak overnight. Change the water as frequently as is practical.
4. On serving day, cover the white corn with the cold, unsalted water. Bring to its boiling point and cook, uncovered, over brisk heat until it opens up like a flower— approximately 1 hour. Do not stir the corn during this time, but, if required, skim the surface of the water occasionally.
5. Drain and cover the head with cold, unsalted water. Bring to its boiling point, then reduce the heat and allow it to simmer, uncovered, until the flesh can be removed from the bone—but do not overcook—approximately 1 hour. Set it aside to cool.
6. When the head is sufficiently cool to handle, remove all the meat and skin and cut it into serving pieces. Chop the ear up (there must be a piece for everyone) and set the eyes aside for the honored guest. Put in the pieces of head, and the broth in which it was cooked, to the corn in its pot.
7. Put in the salt. Put the meat on top of the corn and let the pozole cook, uncovered, over gentle heat for approximately 4 hours. Throughout the cooking time skim the fat from the surface. Keep some water boiling in a kettle at the side to put in to the liquid in the pan. On no account should cold water be added. The liquid must be maintained at almost the same level from start to finish.
8. Put the meat onto a serving dish so it can be divided up more easily and everyone can have the part that he likes best. Serve the pozole with the corn in large, deep bowls, with the following small side dishes to which everyone can help himself: the chile de árbol sauce, finely chopped onion, cut radishes, finely shredded lettuce, and wedges of lime.

TRIPE IN A SPICY, PICANTE BROTH (MONDONGO EN KABIK)

Yield: Servings 6

Ingredients:

The meats

- ½ head garlic, toasted and unpeeled
- 1 small calf's foot, cut into 8 pieces
- 1 tablespoon salt
- 1 teaspoon dried mexican oregano, toasted, yucatecan if possible
- 2 cups (500 ml) seville orange juice or substitute
- 2 pounds (900 g) tripe, cut into two-inch (5-cm) squares

The tomato seasoning

- ⅓ cup (85 ml) finely chopped white onion
- 1 small green pepper, cleaned and chopped into little squares
- 1 teaspoon simple recado rojo
- 2 tablespoons vegetable oil
- 3 yucatecan green chiles, güero chiles, or any fresh, hot green chiles, toasted
- 4 sprigs epazote, leaves and soft stems only, roughly chopped
- 8 ounces (225 g) tomatoes, finely chopped (about ⅓ cup/85 ml)
- Salt to taste

To serve

- ⅓ cup (85 ml) finely chopped chives
- ½ cup (125 ml) finely chopped white onion
- 6 yucatecan green chiles or any fresh, hot green chiles, cut into rounds
- Slices of lima agria or lime

Directions:

1. Rinse the tripe well, cover with the orange juice, and let soak for minimum 4 hours flipping the pieces once in a while. Scrub the pieces of calf's foot. Put into a big deep cooking pan with the garlic, oregano, and salt, and cover well with water. Bring to its boiling point, then reduce the heat and allow to cook gently for approximately three hours, or until the meat is just starting to get soft. Set aside, in the cooking liquid, in your fridge overnight.
2. The next day, drain the tripe, wash, and put in to the calf's foot, in its broth. Bring to its boiling point and cook slowly until both meats are soft—2½ to three hours.
3. In the meantime, heat the oil in a heavy pan and put in the tomatoes, onion, green pepper, and chopped epazote. Fry on moderate heat until the mixture is reduced and

seasoned, approximately eight minutes. Put in the chiles and recado rojo, together with 2 tablespoons of the meat broth, and cook for a few minutes more. Season and save for later.

4. When the meats are soft, drain, saving for later the broth. Take away the bones from the calf's foot and cut the meat, gristle, and skin (all edible) into big pieces. Place the pieces, together with the tripe, onto a warmed serving dish and set aside in a warm place.

5. If required, put in water to the reserved broth to make up to 8 cups (2 l). Put in the tomato seasoning and simmer for approximately five minutes, or until well flavored. (if there is too much fat on top of the broth, skim as required.) Serve the broth in big soup bowls; serve the meat separately.

TRIPE SOUP WITH CHILE (MENUDO COLORADO NORTEÑO)

Yield: Servings approximately 16

Ingredients:

- 1 head of garlic, unpeeled, cut in half horizontally
- 1½ pounds (675 g) calf's foot, cut into 4 pieces
- 5½ pounds (2.5 kg) tripe of different textures
- Optional: 3 pigs' feet, approximately 1 pound (450 g), each one cut into 3 pieces
- Salt to taste

The corn

- 1 pound 2 ounces (500 g) pozole corn, cooked and "flowered"

The chile

- 1 heaped tablespoon dried mexican oregano, long-leafed from nuevo león if possible
- 1 teaspoon cumin seeds, crushed
- 2 ancho chiles, seeds removed (leave the veins)
- 3 garlic cloves (not necessary)
- 3 guajillo chiles, seeds removed (leave the veins)
- About 1¼ cups (315 ml) water

To serve

- Crumbled, dried mexican oregano
- Finely chopped serrano chile
- Finely chopped white onion
- Slices of lime

Directions:

1. Wash the tripe twice in cold water, drain, and slice into two-inch (5-cm) squares. Wash the calf's and pigs' feet and drain. Put into a big stockpot or mexican earthenware olla. Fill the pot with water almost to the top—the level must be several inches above the meats. Put in the garlic and salt and set using low heat, uncovered, until it comes to a simmer. Carry on cooking for an hour, then cover and carry on cooking until the tripe and feet are soft—anywhere from two to three hours, depending on the quality of the tripe.

2. Meantime, the corn must be cooking. When it is soft and has opened up, or "flowered," drain, saving for later about 3 cups (750 ml) of its broth.

3. Place the chiles into a container, cover with cold water, and let soak for a little more than half an hour. Drain and tear into pieces.

4. Put ¼ cup (65 ml) of the water into your blender jar, put in the cumin, oregano, and optional garlic, and blend until the desired smoothness is achieved. Put in the remaining 1 cup (250 ml) of water and blend the chiles, a few at a time, until the desired smoothness is achieved. If some pieces of guajillo skin remain, pass the sauce through a strainer, pushing down hard to extract as much of the chile as you can.

5. When the meats are soft, remove the pieces of calf's foot from the broth, remove the bones, and chop the gelatinous parts into little cubes. Return them to the pot. Put in the chile sauce and corn with the reserved broth. Adjust the salt, and carry on cooking uncovered until the meats are soft—approximately 1 hour more.

6. Serve with toppings on the side.

Sides

BAKED BROWN RICE WITH BLACK BEANS AND CILANTRO

Yield: Servings four to 6

Ingredients:

- ¼ cup minced fresh cilantro
- ¼ teaspoon pepper
- 1 (fifteen ounce) can black beans, washed
- 1 cup chicken broth
- 1 green bell pepper, stemmed, seeded, and chopped fine
- 1 onion, chopped fine
- 1 teaspoon salt
- 1½ cups long grain brown rice
- 2¼ cups water
- 3 garlic cloves, minced
- 4 teaspoons extra virgin olive oil
- Lime wedges

Directions:

1. Adjust oven rack to middle position and heat oven to 375 degrees. Heat oil in Dutch oven on moderate heat until it starts to shimmer Put in onion and bell pepper and cook, stirring once in a while, until tender and thoroughly browned, twelve to fourteen minutes. Mix in garlic and cook until aromatic, approximately half a minute.
2. Mix in water and broth and bring to boiling point. Remove the heat, mix in rice and salt. Cover, move pot to oven, and bake until liquid is absorbed and rice is soft, around one hour five minutes to an hour ten minutes.
3. Take the pot out of the oven, put in beans, and fluff rice with fork to blend. Replace lid and let rice sit for five minutes. Fold in cilantro and pepper. Serve with lime wedges.

CABBAGE CARROT SLAW

Yield: Servings four to 6

Ingredients:

- ½ cup water
- ½ head green cabbage, cored and cut thin (6 cups)
- 1 big carrot, peeled and shredded
- 1 cup chopped fresh cilantro
- 1 cup cider vinegar
- 1 jalapeño chile, stemmed, seeded, and minced
- 1 onion, halved and cut thin
- 1 tablespoon sugar
- 1 teaspoon dried oregano
- 1½ teaspoons salt

Directions:

1. Whisk vinegar, water, sugar, salt, and oregano together in big container until sugar is dissolved.
2. Put in cabbage, onion, carrot, and jalapeño and toss to blend. Cover and place in your fridge for minimum 1 hour or maximum one day. Drain slaw, return to container, and mix in cilantro and serve.

CHERRY TOMATO AND AVOCADO SALAD

Yield: Servings four to 6

Ingredients:

- ½ cup fresh cilantro leaves
- ½ teaspoon ground coriander
- ½ teaspoon sugar
- 1 garlic clove, minced
- 1 poblano chile, stemmed, seeded, and slice into 2 inch long matchsticks
- 1 tablespoon red wine vinegar
- 1½ pounds cherry tomatoes, quartered
- 2 avocados, halved, pitted, and slice into ½ inch pieces

- 2 tablespoons extra virgin olive oil
- Salt and pepper

Directions:

1. Toss tomatoes, sugar, and ¼ teaspoon salt in big container and allow it to sit for half an hour Move tomatoes and any collected juices to salad spinner and spin until seeds and surplus liquid have been removed, 45 to 60 seconds, stopping to redistribute tomatoes multiple times during spinning. Return tomatoes to container. Strain ½ cup tomato liquid through fine mesh strainer into 2 cup liquid measuring cup; discard any extra liquid.
2. Bring tomato liquid, vinegar, garlic, and coriander to simmer in small deep cooking pan on moderate heat and cook until reduced to 3 tablespoons, approximately five minutes. Move to small container and let cool completely, approximately five minutes. Whisking continuously, slowly sprinkle in oil until blended.
3. Put in avocados, poblano, and cilantro to container with tomatoes. Sprinkle with dressing and lightly toss to blend. Sprinkle with salt and pepper to taste and serve.

CLASSIC MEXICAN RICE

Yield: Servings 6 to 8

Ingredients:

- ⅓ cup vegetable oil
- ½ cup minced fresh cilantro
- 1 onion, chopped coarse
- 1 tablespoon tomato paste
- 1½ teaspoons salt
- 2 cups chicken broth
- 2 cups long grain white rice, washed
- 2 tomatoes, cored and quartered
- 3 jalapeño chiles, stemmed
- 4 garlic cloves, minced
- Lime wedges

Directions:

1. Adjust oven rack to middle position and heat oven to 350 degrees. Process tomatoes and onion inside a food processor until the desired smoothness is achieved, approximately fifteen seconds. Move mixture to 4 cup liquid measuring cup and spoon off surplus as required until mixture measures 2 cups. Remove ribs and seeds from 2 jalapeños and discard; mince flesh and save for later. Mince remaining 1 jalapeño, including ribs and seeds; set aside.

2. Heat oil in Dutch oven over moderate high heat for one to two minutes. Drop 3 or 4 grains rice in oil; if grains sizzle, oil is ready. Put in rice and cook, stirring regularly, until light golden and translucent, six to eight minutes.

3. Decrease the heat to moderate. Put in garlic and reserved seeded jalapeños and cook, stirring continuously, until aromatic, approximately 1½ minutes. Mix in pureed tomato onion mixture, broth, tomato paste, and salt and bring to boiling point. Cover, move pot to oven, and bake until liquid is absorbed and rice is soft, half an hour, stirring well after fifteen minutes.

4. Take the pot out of the oven and fold in cilantro and reserved jalapeño with seeds to taste. Serve with lime wedges.

DRUNKEN BEANS

Yield: Servings 8 to 10

Ingredients:

- ¼ cup tomato paste
- ½ cup tequila
- 1 cup Mexican lager
- 1 onion, chopped fine
- 1 pound (2½ cups) dried pinto beans, picked over and washed
- 2 bay leaves
- 2 limes, quartered
- 2 ounces Cotija cheese, crumbled (½ cup)
- 2 poblano chiles, stemmed, seeded, and chopped fine
- 3 garlic cloves, minced
- 30 sprigs fresh cilantro (1 bunch)

- 4 slices bacon, cut into ¼ inch pieces
- Salt

Directions:

1. Dissolve 3 tablespoons salt in 4 quarts cold water in big container or container. Put in beans and soak at room temperature for minimum 8 hours or maximum one day. Drain and wash well.

2. Adjust oven rack to lower middle position and heat oven to 275 degrees. Pick leaves from 20 cilantro sprigs (reserve stems), mince, and place in your fridge until needed. Using kitchen twine, tie remaining 10 cilantro sprigs and reserved stems into bundle.

3. Cook bacon in Dutch oven on moderate heat until crunchy, 5 to 8 minutes; move to paper towel–lined plate. Put in onion, poblanos, and garlic to fat left in pot and cook on moderate heat until tender, five to seven minutes. Remove the heat, put in tequila and allow it to sit until vaporized, three to four minutes. Mix in 3½ cups water, beans, cilantro bundle, 1 teaspoon salt, and bay leaves and bring to boiling point using high heat. Cover, move pot to oven, and bake until beans are just soft, forty-five minutes to an hour.

4. Take the pot out of the oven. Discard bay leaves and cilantro bundle. Mix in beer and tomato paste and bring to vigorous simmer over moderate low heat. Cook, stirring regularly, until liquid is thick and beans are fully soft, approximately 30 minutes. Sprinkle with salt to taste. Serve, passing lime wedges, Cotija, minced cilantro, and reserved crisp bacon separately.

ENFRIJOLADAS

Yield: Servings four to 6

Ingredients:

- ½ teaspoon salt
- 1 jalapeño chile, stemmed, seeded, and minced
- 1 onion, chopped fine
- 1 tablespoon vegetable oil
- 1 teaspoon ground cumin
- 12 (6 inch) corn tortillas

- 2 (fifteen ounce) cans black beans, washed
- 2 cups chicken broth
- 2 scallions, cut thin
- 2 tablespoons minced fresh cilantro
- 2 tablespoons tomato paste
- 2 teaspoons chili powder
- 2 teaspoons minced fresh oregano or ½ teaspoon dried
- 3 garlic cloves, minced
- 4 ounces Monterey Jack cheese, shredded (1 cup)
- Vegetable oil spray

Directions:

1. Adjust oven rack to middle position and heat oven to 400 degrees. Process 2 cups beans and 1 cup broth inside a food processor until the desired smoothness is achieved, approximately half a minute, scraping down sides of container as required. Put in remaining beans and pulse until crudely ground, approximately 5 pulses.
2. Heat oil in 12 inch nonstick frying pan on moderate heat until it starts to shimmer Put in onion, jalapeño, and salt and cook until onion becomes tender, approximately five minutes. Mix in garlic, chili powder, oregano, and cumin and cook until aromatic, approximately half a minute. Mix in tomato paste and cook for a minute. Mix in processed beans and cook, stirring frequently, until well blended and thickened slightly, approximately 3 minutes. Let bean mixture cool slightly.
3. Spray both sides of tortillas with oil spray. Stack tortillas, wrap in damp dish towel, and place on plate; microwave until warm and flexible, approximately one minute.
4. Working with one tortilla at a time, dip into bean mixture to coat both sides and fold into four equivalent portions; shingle folded tortillas in 3 columns widthwise in 13 by 9 inch baking dish.
5. Whisk remaining 1 cup broth into remaining bean mixture and pour over tortillas. Drizzle with Monterey Jack and bake until tortillas are thoroughly heated and cheese is melted, approximately ten minutes. Drizzle with scallions and cilantro before you serve.

MANGO, JÍCAMA, AND ORANGE SALAD

Yield: Servings four to 6

Ingredients:

- ¼ teaspoon grated lime zest plus 3 tablespoons juice (2 limes)
- ¼ teaspoon red pepper flakes
- 12 ounces jícama, peeled and slice into ¼ inch pieces (1½ cups)
- 2 mangos, peeled, pitted, and slice into ½ inch pieces
- 2 oranges
- 3 tablespoons sugar
- Pinch salt

Directions:

1. Bring sugar, lime zest and juice, pepper flakes, and salt to simmer in medium deep cooking pan on moderate heat, stirring continuously, until sugar is dissolved, approximately 2 minutes. Remove the heat, mix in jícama and let syrup cool for about twenty minutes.
2. In the meantime, cut away peel and pith from oranges. Slice oranges into ½ inch thick rounds, then cut rounds into ½ inch pieces. Put oranges and mangos in big container.
3. When syrup is cool, pour over oranges and mangos and toss to blend. Place in your fridge for fifteen minutes before you serve.

MASHED SPICED PUMPKIN

Yield: Servings four to 6

Ingredients:

- ⅛ teaspoon cayenne pepper
- ¼ teaspoon ground cinnamon
- ¾ teaspoon ground coriander
- ¾ teaspoon ground cumin
- 1 (4 to 4½ pound) sugar pumpkin, halved along the length and seeded
- 1 garlic clove, minced
- 1 onion, chopped fine
- 3 tablespoons packed brown sugar

- 4 tablespoons unsalted butter
- Salt and pepper

Directions:

1. Adjust oven rack to middle position and heat oven to 375 degrees. Coat rimmed baking sheet with aluminium foil and place pumpkin halves cut side down on sheet. Roast until flesh can be easily pierced with a skewer, forty-five minutes to an hour.
2. Flip pumpkin and continue to roast for half an hour Let pumpkin cool slightly, then scoop flesh into container; discard skins. Mash pumpkin with potato masher until nearly smooth.
3. Melt butter in big deep cooking pan on moderate heat. Put in onion and ¾ teaspoon salt and cook until tender, approximately five minutes. Mix in garlic, cumin, coriander, cinnamon, and cayenne and cook until aromatic, approximately half a minute. Put in sugar and mashed pumpkin and cook, stirring regularly, until mixture is thoroughly heated, approximately 2 minutes. Adjust consistency with water as required. Sprinkle with salt and pepper to taste and serve.

MEXICAN STREET CORN

Yield: Servings 6

Ingredients:

- ¼ cup mayonnaise
- ¼ teaspoon cayenne pepper (not necessary)
- ¼ teaspoon pepper
- ¼ teaspoon salt
- ¾ teaspoon chili powder
- 1 garlic clove, minced
- 2 ounces queso fresco or Cotija cheese, crumbled (½ cup)
- 3 tablespoons minced fresh cilantro
- 3 tablespoons sour cream
- 4 teaspoons lime juice
- 4 teaspoons vegetable oil
- 6 big ears corn, husks and silk removed

Directions:

1. Mix queso fresco, mayonnaise, sour cream, cilantro, lime juice, garlic, ¼ teaspoon chili powder, pepper, and cayenne, if using, in big container. In second big container, mix oil, salt, and remaining ½ teaspoon chili powder, then put in corn and toss to coat.

2. 2A. FOR A CHARCOAL GRILL: Open bottom vent fully. Light big chimney starter filled with charcoal briquettes (6 quarts). When top coals are partly covered with ash, pour uniformly over half of grill. Set cooking grate in place, cover, and open lid vent fully. Heat grill until hot, approximately five minutes. FOR A GAS GRILL: Set all burners to high, cover, and heat grill until hot, approximately fifteen minutes. Leave all burners on high.

3. Clean and oil cooking grate. Put corn on grill (on hot side if using charcoal). Cook (covered if using gas), turning as required, until corn is mildly charred on all sides, 7 to twelve minutes. Move corn to container with mayonnaise mixture and toss to coat and serve.

QUINOA, BLACK BEAN, AND MANGO SALAD

Yield: Servings 6

Ingredients:

- ⅓ cup fresh cilantro leaves
- ½ cup extra virgin olive oil
- ½ jalapeño chile, stemmed, seeded, and chopped
- ¾ teaspoon ground cumin
- 1 (fifteen ounce) can black beans, washed
- 1 avocado, halved, pitted, and cut thin
- 1 mango, peeled, pitted, and slice into ¼ inch pieces
- 1 red bell pepper, stemmed, seeded, and chopped
- 1½ cups prewashed white quinoa
- 2 scallions, cut thin
- 2¼ cups water
- 5 tablespoons lime juice (3 limes)
- Salt and pepper

Directions:

1. Toast quinoa in big deep cooking pan over moderate high heat while stirring frequently, until quinoa is very aromatic and makes continuous popping sound, five to seven minutes. Mix in water and ½ teaspoon salt and bring to simmer. Decrease the heat to low, cover, and simmer gently until most of water has been absorbed and quinoa is nearly soft, approximately fifteen minutes. Spread quinoa onto rimmed baking sheet and allow to cool for about twenty minutes; move to big container.
2. Process lime juice, jalapeño, cumin, and 1 teaspoon salt in blender until jalapeño is finely chopped, approximately fifteen seconds. With blender running, put in oil and cilantro; continue to pulse until smooth and blended, approximately twenty seconds.
3. Put in bell pepper, mango, beans, scallions, and lime jalapeño dressing to cooled quinoa and toss to blend. Sprinkle with salt and pepper to taste. Serve, topping individual portions with avocado.

REFRIED BEANS

Yield: 3 cups; serves four to 6

Ingredients:

- ½ cup chicken broth, plus extra as required
- ½ teaspoon ground cumin
- 1 jalapeño chile, stemmed, seeded, and minced
- 1 onion, chopped fine
- 1 poblano chile, stemmed, seeded, and chopped fine
- 1 tablespoon minced fresh cilantro
- 1 tablespoon vegetable oil
- 2 (fifteen ounce) cans pinto beans, washed
- 2 teaspoons lime juice
- 3 garlic cloves, minced
- 3 ounces salt pork, rind removed, chopped fine
- Salt and pepper

Directions:

1. Process broth and all but 1 cup beans inside a food processor until the desired smoothness is achieved, approximately half a minute, scraping down sides of container as required. Put in remaining beans and pulse until crudely ground, approximately 5 pulses.

2. Heat oil in 12 inch nonstick frying pan on moderate heat until it starts to shimmer Put in salt pork and cook, stirring once in a while, until rendered and thoroughly browned, ten to fifteen minutes; discard pork, leaving fat behind in frying pan.

3. Put in onion, poblano, jalapeño, and ¼ teaspoon salt to fat left in frying pan and cook on moderate heat until vegetables become tender and starting to brown, approximately eight minutes. Mix in garlic and cumin and cook until aromatic, approximately half a minute. Mix in processed beans and cook, stirring frequently, until well blended and thickened slightly, approximately five minutes. Remove the heat, mix in cilantro and lime juice and sprinkle with salt and pepper to taste. Adjust consistency with extra hot broth as required and serve.

VEGETARIAN REFRIED BEANS

To make these beans less spicy, omit the jalapeño.

Substitute 1 cup water for ½ cup broth; put in all of water to processor in step 1. Omit salt pork and put in vegetables to pan when oil is shimmering. Put in 2 tablespoons tomato paste, ½ teaspoon dried oregano, and ½ teaspoon chipotle chile powder to pan with garlic and cumin. Adjust consistency with extra hot water as required before you serve.

RESTAURANT STYLE BLACK BEANS

Yield: Servings four to 6

Ingredients:

- 1 jalapeño chile, stemmed, seeded, and minced
- 1 onion, chopped fine
- 1 tablespoon lime juice
- 1 teaspoon ground cumin
- 1½ cups chicken broth, plus extra as required
- 2 (fifteen ounce) cans black beans, washed
- 2 ounces queso fresco, crumbled (½ cup)

- 2 slices bacon, chopped
- 2 tablespoons chopped fresh cilantro
- 3 garlic cloves, minced
- Salt and pepper

Directions:

1. Process 1½ cups beans and broth inside a food processor to crude paste, approximately twenty seconds, scraping down sides of container as required. Cook bacon in medium deep cooking pan on moderate heat, stirring once in a while, until crunchy, 5 to 8 minutes. Using slotted spoon, move bacon to paper towel–lined container and save for later.
2. Put in onion and jalapeño to fat left in deep cooking pan and cook on moderate heat until onion becomes tender, approximately five minutes. Mix in garlic and cumin and cook until aromatic, approximately half a minute. Mix in processed beans and remaining whole beans and cook, stirring frequently, until well blended and thickened slightly, fifteen to twenty minutes.
3. Remove the heat, mix in lime juice and crisp bacon and sprinkle with salt and pepper to taste. Adjust consistency with extra hot broth as required. Move beans to serving container and drizzle with queso fresco and cilantro and serve.

ROASTED WINTER SQUASH WITH CHIPOTLE AND LIME

Yield: Servings four to 6

Ingredients:

- ½ teaspoon minced canned chipotle chile in adobo sauce
- 1 (2½ to 3 pound) butternut squash
- 1 tablespoon minced fresh cilantro
- 1 teaspoon ground coriander
- 1 teaspoon ground cumin
- 2 tablespoons extra virgin olive oil
- 2 teaspoons honey
- 2 teaspoons lime juice
- 3 tablespoons unsalted butter, melted

- Salt and pepper

Directions:

1. Adjust oven rack to lowest position and heat oven to 425 degrees. Using sharp vegetable peeler or chef's knife, peel squash until completely orange with no white flesh remaining (roughly ⅛ inch deep). Halve squash along the length and scrape out seeds. Put squash cut side down on cutting board and slice crosswise ½ inch thick.

2. Toss squash with melted butter, cumin, coriander, ½ teaspoon salt, and ½ teaspoon pepper. Position on rimmed baking sheet in single layer. Roast squash until side touching sheet toward back of oven is thoroughly browned, twenty-five to thirty minutes. Rotate sheet and carry on baking until side touching sheet toward back of oven is thoroughly browned, 6 to ten minutes. Remove squash from oven and use metal spatula to flip each piece. Continue to roast until squash is super soft and side touching sheet is browned, ten to fifteen minutes longer.

3. Whisk oil, cilantro, honey, lime juice, and chipotle together in container and sprinkle with salt and pepper to taste. Move squash to serving platter, sprinkle with vinaigrette, before you serve.

SHAVED ZUCCHINI SALAD WITH PEPITAS

Yield: Servings four to 6

Ingredients:

- ¼ cup pepitas, toasted
- ½ cup chopped fresh cilantro
- ½ teaspoon grated lime zest plus 1 tablespoon juice
- 1 garlic clove, minced
- 1½ pounds zucchini
- 2 ounces queso fresco, crumbled (½ cup)
- 2 tablespoons extra virgin olive oil
- Salt and pepper

Directions:

1. Using vegetable peeler, slice zucchini along the length into super slim ribbons. Whisk lime zest and juice, garlic, ¾ teaspoon salt, and ¼ teaspoon pepper together
2. in big container. Whisking continuously, slowly sprinkle in oil until blended. Put in zucchini, cilantro, and queso fresco and toss to blend. Sprinkle with salt and pepper to taste. Drizzle with pepitas and serve instantly.

SIMPLE RICE DISHES

Yield: Servings 4

CHILE RICE

Basmati, jasmine, or Texmati rice can be substituted for the long grain rice.

Ingredients:

- 1 small onion, chopped fine
- 1 teaspoon minced canned chipotle chile in adobo sauce
- 1½ cups long grain white rice, washed
- 2 garlic cloves, minced
- 2 tablespoons unsalted butter
- 2 teaspoons ancho chile powder
- 2½ cups chicken broth
- Salt and pepper

Directions:

1. Melt butter in big deep cooking pan on moderate heat. Put in onion and cook until tender, approximately five minutes. Mix in garlic, chile powder, and chipotle and cook until aromatic, approximately half a minute. Put in rice and cook, stirring frequently, until edges start to turn translucent, approximately 2 minutes. Mix in broth and ¾ teaspoon salt and bring to boiling point. Decrease the heat to low, cover, and simmer until liquid is absorbed and rice is soft, 16 to twenty minutes.
2. Remove the heat, lay clean folded dish towel underneath lid, and let rice sit for about ten minutes. Fluff rice with fork and sprinkle with salt and pepper to taste and serve.

CILANTRO RICE

Basmati, jasmine, or Texmati rice can be substituted for the long grain rice.

Ingredients:

- 1 small onion, chopped fine
- 1½ cups fresh cilantro leaves, plus 2 tablespoons minced
- 1½ cups long grain white rice, washed
- 2 garlic cloves, minced
- 2 tablespoons unsalted butter
- 2¼ cups chicken broth
- Salt and pepper

Directions:

1. Process broth and cilantro leaves in blender until cilantro is finely chopped, approximately fifteen seconds. Melt butter in big deep cooking pan on moderate heat. Put in onion and cook until tender, approximately five minutes. Mix in garlic and cook until aromatic, approximately half a minute. Put in rice and cook, stirring frequently, until edges start to turn translucent, approximately 2 minutes. Mix in broth mixture and 1 teaspoon salt and bring to boiling point. Decrease the heat to low, cover, and simmer until liquid is absorbed and rice is soft, 16 to twenty minutes.
2. Remove the heat, lay clean folded dish towel underneath lid, and let rice sit for about ten minutes. Put in minced cilantro and fluff rice with fork to blend. Sprinkle with salt and pepper to taste and serve.

LIME RICE

Basmati, jasmine, or Texmati rice can be substituted for the long grain rice.

Ingredients:

- 1 tablespoon unsalted butter
- 1 teaspoon grated lime zest plus 2 tablespoons juice
- 1½ cups long grain white rice, washed
- 2 scallions, cut thin (not necessary)
- 2¼ cups water
- Salt and pepper

Directions:

1. Melt butter in big deep cooking pan on moderate heat. Put in rice and cook, stirring frequently, until edges start to turn translucent, approximately 2 minutes. Mix in water and 1 teaspoon salt and bring to boiling point. Decrease the heat to low, cover, and simmer until liquid is absorbed and rice is soft, 16 to twenty minutes.
2. Remove the heat, lay clean folded dish towel underneath lid, and let rice sit for about ten minutes. Put in lime zest and juice and scallions, if using, and fluff rice with fork to blend. Sprinkle with salt and pepper to taste and serve.

TOASTED CORN WITH EPAZOTE

Yield: Servings four to 6

Ingredients:

- 1 serrano chile, stemmed, seeded, and minced
- 3 tablespoons chopped fresh epazote
- 4 tablespoons unsalted butter
- 6 ears corn, kernels cut from cobs (5 cups)
- Salt and pepper

Directions:

1. Melt butter in 12 inch nonstick frying pan over moderate high heat.
2. Put in corn, serrano, and ½ teaspoon salt and cook, stirring once in a while, until corn is mildly browned, ten to fifteen minutes.
3. Remove the heat, mix in epazote and sprinkle with salt and pepper to taste and serve.

Salads

We Mexicans like to balance out all the high calorie stuff we like to eat with salads from time to time. Below are a few of my personal favourite recipes!

"Mountain" Chiles (CHILES DE LA SIERRA)

Yield: Servings 6

Ingredients:

One day ahead

- ¼ teaspoon dried mexican oregano
- ½ cup (125 ml) vinegar
- ½ cup (125 ml) water
- ½ teaspoon salt, or to taste
- 1 small white onion, thinly cut
- 2 ounces (60 g) queso añejo, romano, or sardo cheese, finely grated (about ⅔ cup/165 ml)
- 3 tablespoons vegetable oil
- 6 medium ancho chiles, wiped clean

To serve

- 1 medium tomato, cut
- 1 small white onion, thinly cut
- 6 romaine lettuce leaves

Directions:

1. A day ahead, heat an ungreased frying pan or comal on moderate heat and let the chiles heat through, flipping them over occasionally, until they have become tender and become flexible. Flatten each chile out as much as you can, then make a slit down one side and midway around the top, to which the stem is attached. Take away the seeds and veins.

2. Heat the oil in a frying pan. Pressing the inside of one chile at a time into the oil, allow it to fry for one minute or so—its color will turn to an opaque tobacco brown. (take care that the heat is not too high or the chile will readily burn.) When all the chiles have been fried, drain off the surplus oil.

3. Put in the cut onion to the frying pan and cook gently until it is translucent; do not allow it to brown. Put in the vinegar, salt, water, and chiles and simmer for approximately ten minutes, or until the chiles are completely tender. Take away the chiles from the frying pan, drain, and set them aside to cool.

4. Drizzle the inside of each chile with a little cheese. Reform them by folding the edges back in place, then set them in a single layer in a serving dish and pour the liquid from the pan over them. Drizzle them with oregano. Top with onion rings, both cooked and raw. At this point, the chiles can be left to marinate in your fridge for a day or two. Just before you serve, garnish the sides of the dish with the lettuce and tomato.

Green Bean And Zucchini Salad (ENSALADA DE EJOTE Y CALABACITA)

Yield: Servings 6

Ingredients:

- 1 small white onion, thinly cut
- 12 ounces (340 g) cooked green beans
- 12 ounces (340 g) cooked zucchini
- A well-seasoned oil and vinegar dressing

To serve

- 1 small avocado, peeled and slice into strips
- 2 peaches, peeled and cut
- Seeds of half a pomegranate, if available

Directions:

1. Chop the zucchini along the length into halves and then into four equivalent portions. Chop the beans into thirds. Combine the onion with the squash and beans in a nonreactive container.

2. Toss the vegetables in the dressing and spread onto a serving platter. Garnish the salad with the peeled and cut peaches, the avocado strips, and the pomegranate seeds.

PICKLED CHILES STUFFED WITH BEANS (CHILES EN ESCABECHE COLIMENSES)

Yield: Servings 6

Ingredients:

The chiles

- 3 tablespoons vegetable oil
- 6 medium-size poblano chiles

The pickling mixture

- ½ cup (125 ml) wine vinegar
- 1 cup (250 ml) thinly cut purple onion
- 1 medium carrot, scraped and thinly cut
- 1 teaspoon salt, or to taste
- 2 tablespoons water
- 5 garlic cloves, halved

The filling

- 12 ounces (340 g) chorizos
- 2 tablespoons pork lard
- 3 tablespoons finely chopped white onion
- 3 tablespoons grated queso ranchero seco or añejo, or sardo or romano cheese
- 8 ounces (225 g) pinto beans (or any other bean of your choice), cooked, with their broth
- About 6 ounces (180 g) tomatoes, finely chopped (approximately 1 rounded cup/265 ml)

To serve

- 6 slices queso panela or domestic muenster
- Romaine lettuce leaves to line the dish

Directions:

1. Three days ahead, heat the oil in a frying pan and fry the chiles on moderate heat, turning them occasionally, until they are blistered and thoroughly browned, approximately ten minutes. Take away the pan from the heat, cover, and let the chiles "sweat" for approximately five minutes in the pan. Take away the chiles from the pan, drain, and set them aside to cool while preparing the pickling mixture.

2. In the same oil, fry the garlic gently until mildly browned. Put in the other pickling ingredients and bring to its boiling point. Lower the heat and allow the mixture to simmer while stirring occasionally, for approximately 2 minutes. Move the contents of the pan to a glass or china container.

3. Take away the skins from the chiles (if you have fried them adequately, they should slip off easily). Cautiously slit the chiles open and remove the seeds and veins, taking care to keep the top and stem undamaged. Put in the chiles to the ingredients in the container and store at the bottom of the fridge for two or 3 days, flipping them over at gaps so they become uniformly impregnated with the seasoning.

4. On the day you plan to serve the chiles, prepare the filling. Combine the beans and their broth (do not overblend, as they must have some texture). Set aside.

5. Skin and crumble the chorizo, then heat the lard in a frying pan and cook the chorizo pieces gently—they will burn easily—until the fat has rendered out, approximately five minutes. Take away the chorizo pieces and save for later.

6. In the same fat, fry the onion gently, without browning, until translucent. Put in the tomatoes and fry for about three minutes longer. Put in the mixed beans and chorizo and fry the mixture, stirring and scraping the bottom of the pan, until it is reduced to a thick paste. Turn off the heat and allow to cool, then mix in the grated cheese.

7. Fill the chiles with the bean mixture and place them on a round platter lined with romaine lettuce leaves. Cover each chile with a strip of the cheese and the onion and carrot pieces from the pickling mixture, and serve at room temperature.

SALAD OF NOPAL CACTUS PIECES (ENSALADA DE NOPALITOS)

Yield: Servings 6

Ingredients:

The salad

- ¼ cup (65 ml) roughly chopped cilantro
- ½ teaspoon dried mexican oregano
- 2 cups (500 ml) nopal cactus pieces, cooked
- 2 tablespoons olive oil (not necessary)
- 3 tablespoons finely chopped white onion
- 4 teaspoons mild vinegar or fresh lime juice
- Salt to taste

To serve

- 1 small purple onion, cut
- 2 medium tomatoes, cut
- 4 ounces (115 g) queso fresco, crumbled (about ⅔ cup/165 ml)
- Lettuce leaves
- Strips of jalapeño chiles en escabeche

Directions:

1. Mix all the salad ingredients well and set aside to season for approximately 1 hour.
2. Coat the dish with the lettuce leaves, put the salad on top, and top with the remaining ingredients.

Stuffed Chile Salad (ENSALADA DE CHILES RELLENOS)

Yield: Servings 6

Ingredients:

The marinade

- ⅓ cup (85 ml) water
- 1 garlic clove, cut

- 1 mexican bay leaf
- 2 tablespoons vinegar
- 3 sprigs fresh marjoram or ⅛ teaspoon dried
- 3 tablespoons olive oil
- Salt to taste

The chiles

- 6 small poblano chiles, charred and peeled

The guacamole stuffing

- ½ teaspoon fresh lime juice
- 2 medium avocados
- 3 tablespoons finely chopped white onion
- Salt to taste

To serve

- Lettuce leaves
- Pomegranate seeds or chopped fresh cilantro

Directions:

1. Mix all the marinade ingredients well and set them aside.
2. Leaving the top of the chiles undamaged, slit down the side and cautiously remove seeds and veins. Place the chiles into the marinade and place in your fridge them minimum 2 days, turning them occasionally.
3. When you are ready to serve the chiles, crush the onion. Cut open the avocados and scoop out the flesh. Mash with the onion, lime juice, and salt.
4. Drain the chiles and stuff them well with the guacamole. Position on a bed of lettuce leaves on a serving dish and garnish them with the pomegranate seeds or chopped cilantro.

THE ORIGINAL ALEX-CAESAR CARDINI SALAD (ORIGINAL ENSALADA ALEX-CÉSAR CARDINI)

Yield: Servings 2

Ingredients:

- ¼ cup (65 ml) freshly grated parmesan cheese
- ¼ cup (65 ml) olive oil
- 1 big egg, raw
- 1 tablespoon fresh lime juice
- 1 teaspoon worcestershire sauce
- 10 romaine lettuce leaves, roughly
- 3 garlic cloves
- 6 anchovy fillets
- 6 half-inch (1.5-cm) rounds of stale french bread
- Salt and freshly ground pepper to taste

Directions:

1. Rinse the lettuce, spin dry, wrap in a dry towel, and set aside in your fridge to crunchy.
2. Preheat your oven to 400° f (205° c). Place the bread slices onto an ungreased baking sheet and bake until crisp—twenty minutes. Brush with 1½ tablespoons of the oil and put back into the oven to brown—about ten minutes.
3. Crush together the garlic and the anchovies and progressively put in 1 tablespoon of the oil. Spread this mixture onto the bread slices and save for later.
4. Cover the egg with boiling water and cook for a minute; the white must be opaque and just setting.
5. Place the lettuce leaves into the salad container, put in the rest of the ingredients, and toss with the egg and bread until well blended.

Yucatecan Jicama Salad (ENSALADA DE JÍCAMA YUCATECA)

Yield: Servings 6

Ingredients:

- ½ cup (125 ml) seville orange juice or substitute
- 1 big sweet orange

- 1 heaped tablespoon finely chopped cilantro
- 2 small jícamas or 1 big one (approximately 1½ pounds/675 g)
- Salt to taste

Directions:

1. Peel the jícamas with a potato peeler, cut them into approximately ¼-inch (.75-cm) cubes, and put into a nonreactive container. Put in the cilantro, salt, and seville orange juice and set aside to season for minimum 1 hour.
2. Peel and finely slice the orange. Serve the salad topped with the orange slices.

Zucchini Salad (ENSALADA DE CALABACITA)

Yield: Servings 6

Ingredients:

- ½ teaspoon mexican dried oregano
- 1½ pounds (675 g) cooked zucchini (or cauliflower, or chayote), still mildly crunchy
- A well-seasoned oil and vinegar dressing

To serve

- 1 small avocado, cut
- 4 ounces (115 g) strips of queso fresco (about ⅔ cup/165 ml)
- Green olives
- Sliced white onions wilted in lime juice

Directions:

1. Chop the squash along the length into halves and then into four equivalent portions. Split the cauliflower into flowerets, or peel and slice the chayote.
2. Combine the vegetable with the oregano and salad dressing in a nonreactive container. Spread on a serving platter and garnish with the pickled onion rings, avocado slices, olives, and strips of the cheese.

Desserts and cookies

No meal is complete without a good dessert at the end.

ALMOND SPONGE CAKE (TORTA DE CIELO)

Yield: Servings 12

Ingredients:

- ¼ teaspoon baking powder
- 1 tablespoon all-purpose flour
- 1 tablespoon brandy
- 5 big eggs, separated
- 8 ounces (225 g) granulated sugar (1 heaped cup/265 ml)
- 8 ounces (225 g) whole almonds, unskinned (approximately 1⅔ cups/415 ml)
- A drop of almond extract
- A good pinch of salt

Directions:

1. Coat the bottom of a 9-inch (23-cm) springform pan using parchment paper. Butter the paper and sides of the pan well, and dust with flour.
2. Pour hot water over the almonds so that they are well covered and allow them to soak for approximately 4 hours. (take off the skins—they should slip right off.)
3. Preheat your oven to 325° f (165° c) and place a rack on the middle level.
4. Cut the nuts roughly and grind them a little at a time in a coffee/spice grinder. They must be neither too coarse nor too fine. Set aside.
5. Beat the egg whites until they are fluffy. Put in the salt and carry on beating until they are firm. Put in the yolks one at a time and carry on beating until they are all blended.
6. Combine the dry ingredients with the almonds and, beating at a low speed, progressively put in them to the eggs. Put in the brandy and almond extract and pour the batter into the readied pan. Bake for 1¾ hours. Take away the cake from the pan or cool on a rack.

BREAD PUDDING II (CAPIROTADA 2)

Yield: Servings 6

Ingredients:

- ⅓ cup (85 ml) blanched, cut almonds or pine nuts
- ⅓ cup (85 ml) golden raisins and currants, mixed
- ⅓ cup (85 ml) granulated sugar
- ½ cup (125 ml) cubed acitrón or dried pineapple
- 2½ cups (625 ml) milk
- 2-inch (5-cm) piece of cinnamon stick
- 3 dried tortillas, 6 inches (fifteen cm) in diameter
- 4 tablespoons unsalted butter
- 5½ tablespoons vegetable oil
- fifteen slices sweet yeast bread, each roughly 6 inches (fifteen cm) long, 2 inches (5 cm) high, and ½ inch (1.5 cm) thick

The topping

- 2 tablespoons granulated sugar, roughly
- 4 big eggs, separated
- Pinch of salt

Directions:

1. Place the milk, sugar, cinnamon stick, raisins, and almonds into a deep cooking pan and bring to a simmer. Continue simmering until the sugar has melted, then allow to cool.
2. Heat 1½ tablespoons of the oil and fry the tortillas on both sides; they must be leathery. Drain using paper towels, then cut them into pieces so that they completely cover the bottom of a round baking dish.
3. Melt 2 tablespoons of the butter in 2 more tablespoons of the oil. Swiftly dip both sides of the bread slices into the mixture so they are lightly covered but do not absorb excessively. Put in the rest of the oil and butter and repeat the process for the rest of the slices. Place the pieces back into the frying pan, a few at a time, and fry using low

heat until golden on both sides. (the original recipe used up a great deal more fat because the slices were just fried. This is a more laborious method but uses less fat.)

4. Put one third of the fried bread into the readied pan in a single layer, completely covering the bottom. Pour over about one-fourth of the sweetened milk, raisins, and almond mixture, then drizzle on one third of the acitrón. Cover with an additional layer of the bread. Pour about one third of the rest of the milk and fruit uniformly onto the bread, then drizzle on a separate third of the acitrón. Repeat the layers with the rest of the ingredients and set aside for the bread to absorb the milk—about fifteen minutes.

5. Put an oven rack on the lowest shelf of the oven; preheat your oven to 350° f (180° c).

6. Beat the egg whites together until fluffy. Put in the salt and beat until stiff (you must be able to turn the container upside down without the eggs sliding out). Put in the yolks, one at a time, beating well after each one is added, until they are well blended.

7. Spread the top of the pudding uniformly with the beaten eggs, then drizzle with the sugar and set in your oven to bake for approximately 30 minutes. When cooked, all the liquid must be absorbed and the top mildly browned.

8. Serve either hot or cold.

Buñuelos From Chihuahua (BUÑUELOS CHIHUAHUENSES)

Yield: 1two 8-inch (20.5-cm) buñuelos

Ingredients:

- ¼ teaspoon cream of tartar
- ¼ teaspoon salt
- ⅓ cup (85 ml) warm water, roughly
- 1½ big eggs, lightly beaten
- 1½ tablespoons solid vegetable shortening, cut into little pieces
- 12 ounces (340 g) unbleached all-purpose flour (about 3 cups/750 ml)
- 2 teaspoons baking powder
- 3 tablespoons grated chihuahua cheese or mild cheddar
- Vegetable oil for frying

The topping

- ½ cup (125 ml) granulated sugar, roughly, mixed with 2 tablespoons ground cinnamon

Directions:

1. Sift the flour, baking powder, cream of tartar, and salt together. Mix in the cheese. Put in the shortening and rub in lightly using the tips of the fingers until it is well blended.
2. Slowly mix in the eggs and water, then knead the dough lightly until it is tender and flexible—about two minutes. Cover the dough with waxed paper and set aside for approximately 2 hours. Do not refrigerate—unless, of course, the weather is super hot and sticky.
3. Split the dough into 12 equal balls approximately 1½ inches (4 cm) in diameter. Lightly drizzle a pastry board or cloth with flour. Using a thin rolling pin, roll four of the balls of dough out super slim; they should each make a circle approximately eight inches (20 cm) in diameter.
4. Pour the oil into a heavy 10-inch (25-cm) frying pan to a depth of an inch (1.5 cm) and heat until it starts to shimmer Cautiously place a thin round of dough in the hot fat and fry until it is a deep golden color on the underside (you may need to use two spatulas near the end of the frying period to keep the buñuelo down in the fat); this should take about two minutes. Turn it over cautiously and fry the second side. (the whole process should take from 3½ to 4 minutes.) Remove and drain using paper towels. While still hot, drizzle with the sugar and cinnamon.
5. Repeat with the rest of the three circles, then roll out four more balls of dough and continue until the rest of the buñuelos have been fried.
6. Serve the buñuelos instantly or allow to cool and store in an airtight container for a few days only as they will develop a rancid flavor.

BUÑUELOS FROM THE NORTH OF MEXICO (BUÑUELOS DEL NORTE)

Yield: About 22 10-inch (25.5 cm) buñuelos

Ingredients:

The buñuelos

- ½ cup (125 ml) granulated sugar (if not using the syrup; only 1 rounded tablespoon sugar if using the syrup)
- ½ teaspoon salt
- 1 big egg, lightly beaten
- 1 cup (250 ml) cold water, roughly
- 1 pound (900 g) unbleached all-purpose flour (approximately four cups/1 l)
- 2 teaspoons baking powder
- 4 tablespoons pork lard or butter, cut into little pieces
- Vegetable oil for frying

The sugar syrup (optional)

- ½ cup (125 ml) cold water
- 1 cup (250 ml) light brown sugar
- 2½-inch (6.5-cm) piece of cinnamon stick, broken in half

Directions:

1. Place the water into a small deep cooking pan. Put in the sugar and salt and warm through using low heat until the sugar has melted. Allow the mixture cool off to lukewarm while you start the dough.
2. Sift the flour and baking powder together, then rub with the fat through your fingertips until the mixture looks like fine crumbs. Put in the beaten egg and then, progressively, the sugared water. Work the dough very hard, kneading, pulling, and throwing it down onto the table until it is smooth and elastic. Examine by making a cushion of the dough and slashing it using a knife to a depth of approximately 1 inch (2.5 cm); the dough should spring back instantly. This will take ten to fifteen minutes, depending, of course, on how much strength you put into it.
3. Push the dough out to a thick oval, then roll up into an elongated sausage shape. Tuck both ends in to make a cushion and place inside a plastic bag. Set the dough aside, in a warm place, for a minimum of three hours.
4. After the dough has rested, split up and roll into balls roughly an inch (2.5 cm) in diameter. Put the balls on a tray; cover first using plastic wrap and then with a damp towel, and set aside in a warm place for minimum 30 minutes.
5. Cover your table with a cloth. Sitting in a comfortable chair, cross your legs and place a dry, clean kitchen towel over your knee. Push one of the balls of dough tightly

between your palms until you have a circle about 2½ inches (6.5 cm) in diameter. Take the dough between the thumbs and forefingers of both hands and gently stretch it out into a bigger circle approximately four inches (10 cm) in diameter; do this in such a way that the center will be almost transparent while the edges are still thick.

6. Put the center of the dough on your knee and, using the thumbs and forefingers of both hands, gently ease out, rather than pull, and at the same time stretch, the thick edge in quick little movements, working clockwise, until you have a circle approximately 10 inches (25 cm) in diameter. Put the buñuelo cautiously onto the tablecloth to dry (you can hang them around the edge of the table, too) while you proceed with the rest of the balls of dough.

7. It will take about forty-five minutes for the buñuelos to dry out on one side. Flip them over and allow them to dry out completely on the second side. The drying process should take approximately 1 hour fifteen minutes, depending, of course, on how humid the air is. They should then feel dry and papery to the touch.

8. Pour oil to a depth of ½ inch (1.5 cm) into a large, heavy frying pan and heat until it is hot but not smoking. Spread a big tray with a twofold layer of paper toweling.

9. Put one of the buñuelos cautiously into the hot oil—it will most probably balloon up— and holding a sharp-tined fork in each hand, prick the dough in various places and lift up the edge at one side to let the air out. In perhaps 2 seconds light golden spots will seem through the dough or at the edge, the sign that the buñuelo must be turned over and cooked for a few seconds more on the other side. The buñuelo must be pale gold in color, with some creamy-colored patches. If it is too dark in color (commercially made ones usually are), reduce the heat and let the oil cool off a little before cooking the next one.

10. As each buñuelo is cooked, drain thoroughly of any surplus fat by holding it over the pan and then lay on the paper toweling to drain further. Serve instantly or keep hot if you are going to dribble them with syrup first.

11. If you are using the sugar syrup, put the ingredients for the syrup into a small deep cooking pan. Set using low heat and stir until the sugar has melted. Increase the heat and cook fast until the syrup reduces and forms a tender thread—120° f (49° c) on a candy thermometer. Dribble the syrup over the hot buñuelos before you serve.

12. Buñuelos must be kept only a few days in a cool place—they will have a rancid flavor if kept longer.

COW'S-MILK DESSERT WITH WINE AND ALMONDS (CAJETA DE LECHE ENVINADA)

Yield: Servings 6

Ingredients:

- ⅓ cup (85 ml) almonds, blanched and slivered
- ½ cup (125 ml) medium-dry sherry or madeira
- 1 pound (450 g) granulated sugar (about 2 cups/500 l)
- 3 yolks of big eggs
- 6 cups (1.5 l) milk
- A pinch of baking soda

Directions:

1. Place the milk, sugar, and baking soda into a heavy deep cooking pan and set it on moderate heat until the sugar has melted. Then raise the heat and boil it as fast as you can for half an hour Put ¾ cup (185 ml) of the milk–sugar mixture aside to cool. Beat the egg yolks until creamy and put in them to the cooled milk.
2. Continue boiling the remaining milk mixture until it becomes thick, like condensed milk. As it thickens, stir the mixture continually or it will cling to the pan. This should take about thirty minutes.
3. Turn off the heat and put in the egg mixture to the thickened milk, stirring all the time. Carry on cooking the mixture on moderate heat until it begins to come away from the bottom and sides of the pan.
4. Mix the almonds and sherry into the mixture. Pour the mixture into a serving dish and allow it to get meticulously cool before you serve.

Curds In Syrup (CHONGOS ZAMORANOS)

Yield: Servings 4

Ingredients:

- ½ cup (125 ml) dark brown sugar
- ½ tablespoon cold water

- 1 quart (1 l) milk
- 2 yolks of big eggs
- 2-inch (5-cm) piece of cinnamon stick
- Rennet (tablets or liquid) sufficient to clabber the milk (see manufacturer's instructions)

Directions:

1. Heat the milk gently to 110° f (44° c)—a little hotter than lukewarm.
2. Beat the egg yolks lightly and mix them well into the milk. Crush the tablets and allow them to dissolve in the water.
3. Pour the milk mixture into a flameproof dish minimum 3 inches (8 cm) deep and 8 (20 cm) to 10 (25 cm) inches in diameter. Mix in the rennet solution. Set the dish in a warm place until the milk has set—about thirty minutes. Next, with a pointed knife, cautiously cut across the junket, dividing it into 8 equal wedges.
4. Place the dish using low heat, and the moment the curds and whey start to separate, drizzle the brown sugar between the segments of the curd. Break up the cinnamon stick a little and put the pieces into the whey.
5. Leave the dish over the lowest possible heat for about two hours. Watch it cautiously to see that it does not come to its boiling point. If required, put an asbestos mat under the dish. The curds will get firmer as the cooking time lengthens and the sugar and whey will form a thin syrup. At the end of the cooking time, remove the dish from the heat and let cool.
6. When cool, beginning from the pointed end of each piece, roll the curd up cautiously. Place the rolled pieces onto a serving dish and pour the syrup, with the cinnamon pieces, over the chongos. Serve at room temperature.

Flambéed Mangoes (MANGOS FLAMEADOS)

Yield: Servings 2 to 3

Ingredients:

- 1 ounce (30 ml) triple sec or cointreau
- 1 ounce (30 ml) white tequila
- 1½ tablespoons granulated sugar

- 1½ tablespoons unsalted butter
- 2 manila mangoes or 1 big hayden, approximately 1 pound (450 g)
- Juice of ½ lime
- Juice of ½ orange
- Zest of ½ lime, thinly pared and julienned
- Zest of ½ orange, thinly pared and julienned

Directions:

1. Peel the mangoes, slice the flesh off the pits, and slice into thick strips. Set aside.
2. Melt the butter in a chafing dish, mix in the sugar, and continue stirring until it has dissolved. Put in the zests with the triple sec, heat the mixture, and flame it. When the flames have died down, put in the juices and cook until reduced—about two minutes.
3. Put in the mango strips and heat until the syrup starts to bubble. Put in the tequila, heat through, and flame once more. Serve instantly.

FRITTERS IN ANISE-FLAVORED SYRUP (BUÑUELOS DE VIENTO)

Yield: 12 small buñuelos veracruz

Ingredients:

The syrup

- 1½ cups (375 ml) dark brown sugar
- 3 cups (750 ml) water
- Scant ¼ teaspoon aniseeds

The dough

- ¼ teaspoon anise seeds
- ¼ teaspoon baking powder
- ¼ teaspoon salt
- 1 cup (250 ml) water
- 2 big eggs
- 3 tablespoons lard

- 4 ounces (115 g) sifted flour (approximately 1 cup/250 ml)

The buñuelos

- Vegetable oil for frying—at least 1½ inches (4 cm) deep in the pan

Directions:

1. Put in the brown sugar and aniseeds to the water in a deep cooking pan. Cook on moderate heat until the sugar has melted, and then bring it swiftly to its boiling point. Allow the syrup boil for approximately twenty minutes; by then it should have reduced to approximately 1½ cups (375 ml). Set it aside to cool.
2. Place the water, salt, aniseeds, and lard into a deep cooking pan and bring to a fast simmer. When the lard has completely melted and the mixture is still simmering, stir the flour into it swiftly. Beat the mixture, while continuing to cook it, until it shrinks away from the sides of the pan. Set it aside to cool.
3. When the dough is sufficiently cool to handle, knead it until it is fairly smooth.
4. Beat the eggs lightly and mix them into the dough, a little at a time, saving for later some of the egg until you have tested the dough. You must be able to roll it into a tender ball that will just retain its shape. Put in the rest of the egg if required.
5. Combine the baking powder into the dough.
6. In a deep frying pan heat the oil to approximately 375° f (190° c). Wet your hands well, take a piece of the dough, and roll it into a ball approximately 1½ inches (4 cm) in diameter.
7. Put the ball on your fingers—not on your palm—and flatten it to make a cake about ¾ inch (2 cm) thick. Make a big hole in the middle of the dough and drop it into the hot oil. Cook it on both sides until it is golden brown and well puffed up.
8. Take away the buñuelos from the fat using a slotted spoon and drain them on the paper.
9. Pour ¼ cup (65 ml) syrup over each serving of two buñuelos and serve instantly.

GOAT'S-MILK DESSERT (CAJETA DE CELAYA)

Yield: approximately 1 quart (1 l)

Ingredients:

- ¾ teaspoon cornstarch
- 1 quart (1 l) cow's milk
- 1 quart (1 l) goat's milk
- 1½ cups (375 ml) granulated sugar
- Scant ¼ teaspoon baking soda

The caramel

- ½ cup (125 ml) granulated sugar

Directions:

1. Place the goat's milk and 3½ cups (875 ml) of the cow's milk into a large, heavy deep cooking pan and bring to its boiling point.
2. Combine the cornstarch, baking soda, and remaining ½ cup (125 ml) of the cow's milk together and stir the mixture into the boiling milk.
3. Mix the 1½ cups (375 ml) sugar progressively into the deep cooking pan and keep stirring until it has dissolved. Carry on cooking the mixture. In the meantime prepare the coloring.
4. Caramelize the ½ cup (125 ml) sugar. Take away the milk mixture from the heat and very progressively put in the hot caramel. Take care as it will foam up alarmingly.
5. Continue boiling the mixture until it is just starting to thicken—40 to 50 minutes, depending on the depth of the cajeta in the pan. Then carry on cooking, stirring it all the time, until it forms a thread and coats the back of a wooden spoon.
6. Pour the cajeta into a dish to cool before you serve. From start to finish it will take approximately 1½ hours to cook.

Guavas Stuffed With Coconut (GUAYABAS RELLENAS DE COCADA)

Yield: 12 pieces

Ingredients:

- ⅓ cup (85 ml) fresh orange juice
- ½ cup (125 ml) water, if possible the water from the coconut
- ½ teaspoon fresh lime juice

- 12 canned or cooked fresh guava "shells"
- 2 yolks of big eggs, lightly beaten
- 8 ounces (225 g) granulated sugar (approximately 1 cup/250 ml)
- 8 ounces finely shredded coconut, roughly ½ fresh coconut
- Finely grated zest of 1 orange

Directions:

1. Melt the sugar in the water in a heavy deep cooking pan on moderate heat, then bring the syrup to its boiling point. Allow it to boil fast until it forms a thin thread—225° f (110° c) on a candy thermometer.
2. Put in the coconut to the syrup and cook it until it is transparent but not too soft— about five minutes. Set aside to cool.
3. Put in the remaining ingredients apart from the guava shells, return to the heat, and carry on cooking the mixture on moderate heat for approximately fifteen minutes, until the mixture is almost dry, scraping the bottom of the pan constantly. Set the cocada aside to cool.
4. Fill each guava shell with a big tablespoon of the cocada, covering the top of the guava shell completely.
5. Put the filled shells under the broiler and let the cocada brown a little. Take care: it will burn very swiftly. Set them aside to cool before you serve.

BREAD PUDDING (CAPIROTADA)

Yield: Servings 6

Ingredients:

- ¼ cup (65 ml) melted pork lard
- ¼ cup (65 ml) raisins
- ¼ cup (65 ml) slivered almonds or pine nuts
- ¼ cup (65 ml) vegetable oil
- 1 cup (250 ml) water
- 3 tablespoons unsalted butter, softened and cut into little pieces
- 4 bolillos, or 16 half-inch (1.5-cm) slices french bread, dried out
- 4 ounces (115 g) queso añejo or romano, finely grated

- 4-inch (10-cm) piece of cinnamon stick or 1 big fig leaf
- 8 ounces (225 g) piloncillo or dark brown sugar

Directions:

1. Preheat your oven to 350° f (180° c) and put the oven rack on the middle level.
2. Butter liberally a shallow dish just big enough to accommodate half of the bread slices in a single layer—a dish 8½ by 8½ inches (21.5 by 21.5 cm) must be perfect.
3. Pick a cookie sheet onto which all the bread slices will just fit easily. Combine the melted lard and oil and coat the cookie sheet well. Position the pieces of bread on the cookie sheet and paint the top of them liberally with the remaining oil–lard mixture. Bake for approximately ten minutes, then turn the pieces over and bake for another ten minutes, or until the bread is crisp and a deep golden color.
4. Over low heat, melt the piloncillo or sugar in the water, together with the cinnamon or fig leaf (if using the piloncillo, see the note). Bring the resulting syrup to its boiling point and cook for eight minutes only (the syrup should have some body but not be too thick).
5. Put one half of the bread slices into the prepared dish and very slowly pour about one third of the syrup onto the bread (not the dish), then drizzle with one half of the cheese, raisins, and nuts. Dot with half the butter. Cover with the rest of the bread slices and syrup and drizzle on the remaining cheese, raisins, and nuts, and dot with the rest of the butter. (note: it is particularly important to pour the syrup slowly and gradually onto the bread, waiting for each batch to be absorbed before you put in more. If you do not do this, the syrup will run to the bottom of the dish and the top layer will remain dry.) Cover the dish using foil and bake for approximately twenty minutes, by which time the bread must be tender but not mushy and the top slightly browned.
6. Serve either hot or cold.

IMPERIAL COCONUT FLAN (COCADA IMPERIAL)

Yield: Servings 6

Ingredients:

- ¾ cup (185 ml) granulated sugar

- 1 cup (250 ml) reserved coconut water
- 1 small coconut
- 2 cups (500 ml) milk
- 4 big eggs, separated
- A pinch of salt

Directions:

1. Prepare a flan mold coated with caramel.
2. Preheat your oven to 350° f (180° c).
3. Melt the sugar in the milk using low heat in a heavy deep cooking pan, then raise the heat and boil it briskly. Take care that it doesn't boil over. Once it starts to thicken, stir the mixture so that it does not cling to the bottom of the pan. After about thirty minutes, it must be the consistency of a thin condensed milk and should have been reduced to approximately 1 cup (250 ml).
4. Pierce a hole through two of the "eyes" of the coconut and drain the water from it. Set the water aside. Place the whole coconut into the oven for approximately 8 minutes. Crack it open; the flesh should come away fairly easily from the shell.
5. Pare the brown skin from the flesh with a potato peeler and grate the flesh finely; 2¼ cups (565 ml), loosely packed, will be needed for the flan.
6. Put in the grated coconut to the coconut water and boil it over brisk heat for approximately five minutes, stirring it all the time. Put in the "condensed" milk and carry on cooking for another five minutes. Set the mixture aside to cool.
7. Beat the egg yolks together until they are creamy and stir them well into the coconut mixture. Beat the egg whites until they become foamy, put in the salt, and carry on beating until they are firm but not too dry. Fold them into the mixture.
8. Pour the mixture into the prepared mold. Cover the mold with a well-greased lid and put it into a water bath. Cook the flan on the lowest shelf in your oven for approximately 1½ hours, then test to see if it is done. When it is done, let cool.

MEXICAN SHORTBREAD COOKIES (POLVORONES)

Yield: about 2 dozen cookies

Ingredients:

- ⅛ teaspoon salt
- ⅓ cup (85 ml) confectioners' sugar, roughly
- ⅓ to ½ cup (85 to 125 ml) unskinned almonds (about 2 ounces/60 g), plus 10 extra almonds
- 1 teaspoon baking powder
- 2 ounces (60 g) unsalted butter (¼ cup/65 ml), cut into little pieces
- 2 ounces (60 g) vegetable shortening or lard (¼ cup/65 ml)
- 2½ tablespoons granulated sugar
- 8 ounces (225 g) unbleached all-purpose flour (2 cups/500 ml)

Directions:

1. Preheat your oven to 350° f (180° c).
2. Spread the unskinned almonds and flour on separate cookie sheets and toast each on the top shelf of the oven or in a toaster oven until the nuts are crisp and the flour a deep creamy color—about fifteen minutes. Set both ingredients aside to cool off completely. Turn off the oven.
3. Sift the cooled flour with the salt and baking powder and put onto a marble slab or pastry board. Make a wide well in the middle of the flour. Place the cooled nuts into your blender with the granulated sugar and blend until fine, then put the mixture, together with the butter and shortening, into the center of the well in the flour and stir until the dough is crumbly, like pie crust. Place the dough onto a big square of plastic wrap and gather it into a ball, pushing the "crumbs" lightly together. Set the dough aside for a minimum of 2 hours in your fridge.
4. Preheat your oven again to 350° f (180° c). Butter a cookie sheet well.
5. Unwrap the ball of dough, and leaving the dough on top of the wrap, put another square of the wrap on the surface of the dough. Push the dough out between the wrap with quick, short movements of your rolling pin until it is about ¼ inch (.75 cm) thick; it will be very crumbly around the edges. Using a cookie cutter 2 inches (5 cm) in diameter, cut out as many cookies as you can. Gather up the rest of the dough and roll out and cut more cookies.
6. (note: the cookies must be moved to the cookie sheet on a spatula with very great care or they will break up.) Repeat until all the dough has been used up.
7. Bake the cookies on the top shelf of the oven until they are a pale golden color—ten to fifteen minutes. Drizzle them well with the confectioners' sugar and allow to cool before attempting to remove them from the sheet.

8. Cautiously remove the polvorones to an airtight container or wrap in tissue paper, as follows: cut 24 squares of tissue paper 8 by 8 inches (20 by 20 cm). Put each cookie in the center of a square and fold two sides over to cover it. Lightly bunch the ends of the paper and twist them tightly. Use scissors to chop the paper at each end into a fringe approximately 1½ inches (4 cm) deep.

Neapolitan Cheese (QUESO DE NÁPOLES)

Yield: Servings 6

Ingredients:

- ¼ cup (65 ml) granulated sugar
- ¼ cup (65 ml) thoroughly ground almonds (approximately 1½ ounces/45 g)
- 2 cups (500 ml) milk
- 4 egg whites
- A pinch of salt

Directions:

1. Prepare a flan mold coated with caramel.
2. Preheat your oven to 350° f (180° c).
3. Bring the milk to its boiling point in a heavy deep cooking pan and allow it to simmer for five minutes.
4. Put in the sugar and the almonds to the milk and allow the mixture to simmer for another five minutes. Set it aside until it is cool.
5. Beat the egg whites until frothy, put in the salt, and carry on beating until they are firm. Fold the beaten whites into the milk mixture. Pour the mixture into the prepared mold.
6. Cover the mold with a well-greased lid and set it in the lowest part of the oven in a water bath. Cook for about ninety minutes, then test to see if the queso is tightly set. When it is done, let cool.

Old-Fashioned Flan (FLAN A LA ANTIGUA)

Yield: Servings 6

This is a truly superb flan with a satiny texture.

Ingredients:

- ½ cup (125 ml) granulated sugar
- 1 quart (1 l) whole milk
- 4 big eggs
- 6 big egg yolks
- A pinch of salt
- A vanilla bean, approximately 2 inches (5 cm)

Directions:

1. Prepare a flan mold coated with caramel.
2. Preheat your oven to 350° f (180° c).
3. Heat the milk in a heavy deep cooking pan, put in the sugar, vanilla bean, and salt, and allow it to simmer for approximately fifteen minutes. The milk must be reduced by about ½ cup (125 ml). Set it aside to cool.
4. Beat the eggs and egg yolks together well. Pour them through a strainer into the cooled milk and stir thoroughly. Pour the mixture through a strainer into the coated mold. (rinse the vanilla bean, allow it to dry, and store it for use once more.)
5. Cover the mold and set it in a water bath on the lowest shelf in your oven. Cook the flan for about two hours and test to see if it is tightly set. When it is done, let cool.

Orange Flan (FLAN DE NARANJA)

Yield: Servings 6

Ingredients:

- ¾ cup (185 ml) granulated sugar
- 1 cup (250 ml) orange juice plus juice of ½ lime
- 6 big eggs, separated
- Finely grated zest of 2 oranges and ½ lime

Directions:

1. First make the caramel. Melt ½ cup (125 ml) of the sugar in a heavy pan using low heat. When it has completely melted, Increase the heat and stir the syrup using a wooden spoon until it darkens (the color will depend on how dark you prefer your caramel). Pour the caramel into a flan mold, or a 1-quart (1-l) charlotte mold, and turn it around swiftly, tipping the mold from side to side until there is a uniform coating of caramel over the bottom and midway up the sides. Set aside.
2. Preheat your oven to 350° f (180° c). If you are not using a flan mold, set a water bath on the lowest shelf of the oven (improvising with a roasting pan into which the mold will fit and putting in hot water to a depth of 1½ inches [4 cm]), or so that it will come almost midway up the side of the mold after it has been filled with the flan mixture.
3. Put in the grated zest to the juice and stir the rest of the ¼ cup (65 ml) sugar in progressively so that it dissolves.
4. Beat the egg yolks until they are thick, then, in a separate container, beat the whites until firm. Slowly put in the yolks to the whites, beating all the time. When they are meticulously blended, progressively beat in the orange juice. Allow the froth subside before pouring the mixture into the prepared mold. Grease the lid of the mold, cover, and set in the water bath. Bake until the flan is set—about 2 hours. (test by inserting a cake tester. If the blade comes out clean, then it is cooked.) Set aside to cool, not in your fridge, before attempting to unmold.

Pine Nut Or Pecan Cream (CREMA DE PIÑON O NUEZ ENCARCELADA)

Yield: Servings 6

Ingredients:

- ⅓ cup (85 ml) brandy or rum or ⅔ cup (165 ml) white wine, or to taste
- ¾ cup (185 ml) granulated sugar
- 1 tablespoon unsalted butter for the dish
- 10 ladyfingers, roughly broken up
- 2 big egg yolks, well beaten
- 2 tablespoons rice flour or cornstarch
- 3 cups (750 ml) milk
- 4-inch (10-cm) piece of cinnamon stick, roughly broken up

- 8 ounces (225 g) pine nuts or pecans (roughly 2¼ cups/565 ml), roughly chopped, plus a few whole nuts for decoration

Directions:

1. Lightly butter a shallow dish, ideally about 9 inches (23 cm) in diameter and 1½ inches (4 cm) deep.
2. Bring the milk to its boiling point, then put in the cinnamon and mix in most of the sugar, saving for later a little to grind with the nuts. Reduce the heat and stir until the sugar is melted. Stir ¼ cup (65 ml) of the warmed milk into the rice flour and work to a smooth paste. Stir this into the milk–sugar mixture and carry on cooking, stirring all the time, until it thickens slightly.
3. Grind the nuts with the reserved sugar until very fine and mix into the boiling milk mixture. Cook until the mixture has reduced and thickened—twenty minutes to half an hour. Put in approximately 1 cup (250 ml) of the hot mixture to the egg yolks and beat together well. Return to the pan and carry on cooking, stirring and scraping the bottom of the pan continuously, until the mixture thickens to the extent that you can see the bottom of the pan as you stir. (it should coat the back of a wooden spoon thickly.) Mix in about two thirds of the brandy or wine.
4. Pour half of the mixture into the prepared dish. Cover with the ladyfingers, drizzle with the remaining brandy or wine, and cover with the rest of the cream. Garnish the top with the whole nuts and set aside to cool completely—do not refrigerate—before you serve.

PINEAPPLE AND BANANA DESSERT (CAJETA DE PIÑA Y PLÁTANO)

Yield: Servings 6

Ingredients:

- 1 pineapple, approximately 4 pounds (1.8 kg)
- 1½ cups (375 ml) dark brown sugar
- 2 pounds (900 g) bananas (not too ripe)
- 2-inch (5-cm) piece of cinnamon stick
- 2-inch (5-cm) piece of cinnamon stick, broken in half

- 3 cups (750 ml) water
- Juice and zest of ½ lime

Directions:

1. Preheat your oven to 350° f (180° c).
2. Bring the brown sugar, water, and cinnamon to its boiling point in a heavy pan and allow them to continue to boil fast for approximately twenty minutes. The liquid will have reduced to approximately 2½ cups (625 ml). Take away the cinnamon stick.
3. Clean and dice the fruit and blend it with the syrup to a medium texture.
4. Pour the mixture into a shallow ovenproof dish, ideally not much more than 3 inches (8 cm) deep, and mix in the broken cinnamon stick and lime juice and zest. Set the dish in your oven and allow the mixture to cook for approximately 4 hours. From time to time, scrape the mixture from the sides of the dish and stir it well. This is particularly important near the end of the cooking period.
5. When the mixture is thick, sticky, and a rich, dark brown, move it to a small serving dish and glaze it swiftly under the broiler. Set it aside to cool.
6. Serve the cajeta with queso fresco or thick sour cream.

PUMPKIN COOKED IN RAW SUGAR (CALABAZA EN TACHA)

Yield: about 30 pieces

Ingredients:

- 1 medium pumpkin, approximately 5 pounds (2.5 kg)
- 10 guavas (not necessary), halved, seeds left in
- 1½ pounds (675 g) piloncillo or panela, broken into little pieces, just under 4 cups (960 ml) or dark brown sugar
- 3 two-inch (5-cm) cinnamon sticks
- 8 cups (2 l) water

Directions:

1. Pierce the shell-like outer rind of the pumpkin in several places to enable the syrup to penetrate the flesh and slice into pieces about 3 inches (8 cm) square, leaving the fibrous flesh and seeds inside.

2. In a wide, heavy deep cooking pan put enough water to completely cover the pumpkin. Put in the brown sugar and cinnamon sticks and bring to its boiling point. Put in the pieces of pumpkin and guavas and cook over quite high heat, moving the pieces around occasionally to prevent sticking. Cover the pan and cook for approximately fifteen minutes, then remove the lid and carry on cooking until the syrup has reduced and the flesh of the pumpkin is a rich brown.

RING COOKIES (ROSCAS)

Yield: 20 to 22 cookies

Ingredients:

- ¼ cup (65 ml) water
- ¼ teaspoon ground cinnamon or ½ teaspoon aniseeds
- ¼ teaspoon salt
- ½ teaspoon baking powder
- 2 ounces (60 g) granulated sugar (¼ cup/65 ml), plus 2 tablespoons for dusting
- 2 ounces (60 g) unsalted butter, at room temperature (¼ cup/65 ml)
- 2 ounces (60 g) vegetable shortening, at room temperature (¼ cup/65 ml)
- 2 tablespoons heavy cream
- 8 ounces (225 g) unbleached all-purpose flour (2 cups/500 ml)

Directions:

1. Sift the flour, baking powder, cinnamon, if you are using it, and salt onto a marble slab or pastry board. Make a well in the middle, and into this put the butter, shortening, ¼ cup (65 ml) of the sugar, the water, and cream. Work the ingredients in the middle with your fingers until they are completely blended and smooth.
2. Slowly work in the dry ingredients, and the aniseeds, if used, and knead the mixture well. Work the dough hard for approximately five minutes, pushing it out with the palms of your hands, using them like pedals, against the working surface until it is smooth and flexible. (if you do not work it well enough, you will not be able to make the roscas as indicated.)
3. Preheat your oven to 350° f (180° c) and set an oven rack on the top shelf. Lightly grease two baking sheets.

4. Roll the dough into balls of approximately 1¼ inches (3.5 cm) in diameter. Take one of the balls and work it under your palms (on an unfloured surface, if possible) into a rounded, even strip of dough about ¼ inch (.75 cm) in diameter. Double the strip, then press the ends together. Holding the ends tightly down onto the surface with one hand and beginning from the other end, swiftly and lightly twist the two strands together. If you have trouble rolling and twisting them, then make a simple ring with one strand of dough, rolling each ball out to a strip about ½ inch (1.5 cm) thick. Join the ends to make a circle, or "bracelet," approximately two inches (5 cm) in diameter, then place cautiously onto the readied baking sheet.

5. Begin with the rest of the balls of dough, and, when you got one baking sheet filled, bake until a deep golden color—fifteen to twenty minutes. Once you remove the cookies from the oven, drizzle them liberally with the extra sugar. Allow them to cool off meticulously before attempting to remove them from the baking sheet, then store in an airtight can or cookie jar.

SOPAIPILLAS

Yield: approximately 120 sopaipillas

Ingredients:

- ½ teaspoon salt
- 1 cup (250 ml) warm water
- 1 pound (450 g) unbleached all-purpose flour (approximately four cups/1 l)
- 2 ounces (60 g) pork lard (¼ cup/65 ml), cut into little pieces
- Confectioners' sugar and ground cinnamon for dusting
- Vegetable oil for frying

Directions:

1. Dissolve the salt in the water and allow to cool to lukewarm. Rub the fat into the flour with your fingertips until it looks like very fine bread crumbs.

2. Put in the salted water to the flour and mix the dough with your hands until it comes cleanly away from the sides of the container. Turn the dough out onto a mildly floured surface and knead and pull it out for approximately five minutes. Knead the dough

into a round cushion shape, put into a plastic bag, and set aside for a minimum of 2 hours, but if possible overnight. Do not place in your fridge

3. Cover a tray with a smooth, clean cloth. Take away the dough from the bag and knead for one minute or so on a mildly floured surface, then split into little balls roughly 1¼ inches (3.5 cm) in diameter; there must be about 30 of them. Set them onto the tray and cover with a slightly damp cloth or plastic wrap so the outside of the balls does not dry out and make a crust.

4. Prepare a small frying pan containing vegetable oil to the depth of ½ inch (1.5 cm). Prepare another tray, covered with two layers of paper toweling. You will then need an ordinary kitchen fork, a metal spatula, and a thin rolling pin.

5. Begin heating the oil using low heat while you roll out the first ball.

6. Dust your working surface very lightly. Roll one of the balls out until it is about 5½ inches (14 cm) in diameter—do not worry if the circle is a small amount uneven, as sopaipillas can be cut into any shape at all. The dough must be thin but not transparent. Chop the dough into four or even six triangular pieces—or what you will—and instantly, while the dough is still damp, put the sopaipillas into the hot oil. Keep pushing the sopaipillas down lightly using the back of a fork. If your oil is the correct heat the dough must begin to bubble and puff up in about 2 seconds. Once the sopaipillas are a light golden color on one side, flip them over and carry on cooking on the second side for a few seconds more. Remove using a slotted spoon and drain using paper towels. While they are still warm, drizzle with confectioners' sugar and ground cinnamon. Repeat the process with the remaining balls.

7. A note on heat of the oil: the oil must be heated to just below the smoking point. If the sopaipillas cook too quickly on the first side, then they will not puff up as readily. Keep regulating the heat and test if required with a small piece of the dough.

SWEET POTATO DESSERT (DULCE DE CAMOTE)

Yield: Servings 6

Ingredients:

- ¼ cup (65 ml) water
- ½ cup (125 ml) crudely chopped walnuts or pecans
- ½ cup (125 ml) granulated sugar

- ½ cup (125 ml) mixed candied and dried fruits, chopped (see note)
- 1 ounce (30 ml) dark rum
- 1 ounce (30 ml) tequila, if possible añejo
- 1 teaspoon ground cinnamon
- 1 teaspoon vanilla extract
- 2 pounds (900 g) sweet potatoes, if possible orange
- Unsweetened whipped cream or thick sour cream

Directions:

1. Three days before you serve, preheat your oven to 375° f (190° c).
2. Bake the sweet potatoes on a cookie sheet until they are fairly soft—about 2 hours. Set them aside to cool. Take away the skin and process the flesh in the food processor. There must be about 2 cups (500 ml).
3. Place the sugar and water into a big deep cooking pan and set using low heat until the sugar has dissolved. Turn the heat up and boil the syrup until it threads—225° f (110° c) on a candy thermometer.
4. Put in the pulp to the syrup and mix thoroughly. Move to a glass container. Stir in the remaining ingredients apart from for the whipped cream, cover, and leave it to ripen for minimum three days at the bottom of the fridge. (the longer the better.)
5. Turn the mixture into a serving dish and serve with unsweetened whipped cream or sour cream.
6. Note: the longer this dessert is left to flavor the better—i have even frozen it for one year and it was still excellent.

Drinks

Mexico has quite the collection of drinks. Some Mexican drinks like tequila are popular and easily available all over the world, while some other local gems are not so well known. In this section, I will talk about a few of my personal favourite drinks.

MARGARITA

Yield: Servings 1

Ingredients:

- ½ ounce (fifteen ml) triple sec
- 1 ounce (30 ml) fresh lime juice
- 1½ ounces (45 ml) white tequila
- A few ice cubes, crushed
- A little salt, either ordinary table salt or thoroughly ground rock salt
- A slice of lime

Directions:

1. Chill a big cocktail glass well. Rub the rim with a slice of lime. Place the salt onto a plate. Push the rim of the glass into it, giving it a turn to ensure that the rim is ringed with salt.
2. Place the tequila, triple sec, lime juice, and ice cubes into a cocktail shaker. Cover and shake together well. Pour the mixture through a strainer into the prepared glass, or over shaved ice if you want.

FERMENTED PINEAPPLE DRINK (TEPACHE)

Yield: about 2 quarts (2 l)

Ingredients:

- 1 cup (250 ml) light beer
- 1 pound (450 g) piloncillo, crushed, or dark brown sugar

- 1 very ripe pineapple, approximately 2 pounds (900 g)
- 2 whole allspice
- 2 whole cloves
- 4-inch (10-cm) piece of cinnamon stick
- 9½ cups (2.4 l) water

Directions:

1. Take away the stem and base of the pineapple and scrub the outside well. Cut into 1½-inch (4-cm) cubes, skin and flesh together. Crush the spices roughly and put in them, with the pineapple and 8 cups (2 l) of the water, to a big earthenware jug. Cover and set in the sun or a warm place until the mixture starts to ferment and become bubbly on top—about 3 days, depending on the temperature.
2. Put the rest of the 1½ cups (375 ml) of water and the brown sugar into a deep cooking pan and bring to a simmer. Simmer, stirring occasionally, until the sugar has melted. Allow it to cool slightly, then add, together with the beer, to the pineapple infusion and stir thoroughly. Cover the jug and leave in a warm place for 1 or 2 days longer, until it has fermented. Strain and serve very cold or over ice.

Jamaica Flower Water (AGUA FRESCA DE FLOR DE JAMAICA)

Yield: 4 cups (1 l)

Ingredients:

- ⅓ cup (85 ml) granulated sugar, or to taste
- ⅔ cup (165 ml) jamaica flowers
- 4 cups (1 l) cold water
- Granulated sugar, if required

Directions:

1. Place the flowers and 3 cups (750 ml) of water together into a deep cooking pan and bring them to its boiling point. Continue boiling the flowers for approximately five minutes over brisk heat.

2. Put in the rest of the water and the sugar and set it aside for minimum 4 hours or overnight.
3. Strain the liquid into the jug. Put in more sugar if required. Serve completely chilled.

Melon-Seed Drink (HORCHATA DE MELÓN)

Yield: Servings 1

Ingredients:

- 1 cup (250 ml) cold water
- 1½ tablespoons granulated sugar, or to taste
- 1½ teaspoons fresh lime juice, or to taste

Directions:

1. Put all the ingredients together in a blender jar and blend until super smooth.
2. Set aside in your fridge for a minimum of ½ hour, then strain through a fine strainer and serve over ice cubes.

MEXICAN EGGNOG (ROMPOPE)

Yield: 1 quart (1 l)

Ingredients:

- ¼ teaspoon baking soda
- ¾ cup (185 ml) pure cane alcohol or rum or ½ cup (125 ml) brandy, or to taste
- 1 cup (250 ml) granulated sugar
- 12 big egg yolks
- 4 cups (1 l) milk
- 4-inch (10-cm) piece of cinnamon stick or 1 vanilla bean

Directions:

1. Place the milk, sugar, cinnamon, and baking soda into a deep cooking pan. Bring to its boiling point, then reduce the heat and simmer for approximately twenty minutes, or

until the sugar has melted completely and the mixture is reduced to approximately 3 cups (750 ml). Set aside to cool a little.

2. In the meantime, beat the egg yolks until they form thick ribbons on the beater—about ten minutes, depending on the efficiency of your beater.

3. Take away the cinnamon from the milk mixture. Slowly put in the milk mixture to the egg yolks, still beating. Return to the pan and cook over low heat while stirring and scraping the bottom and sides of the pan continuously, until the mixture thickens enough to coat the back of a wooden spoon. (take care, as it can swiftly turn to scrambled eggs. At the first sign of this tragedy, pour into your blender and blend until it is smooth.) Set aside to cool to room temperature.

4. In the meantime, sterilize a 1-quart (1 l) bottle in boiling water.

5. Slowly stir the alcohol into the "custard," pour into the bottle, and use instantly or store in your fridge up to one month for future use.

SANGRITA

Yield: approximately 1½ cups (375 ml), approximately eight servings

Ingredients:

- 1¼ cups (315 ml) seville orange juice or substitute
- 3½ tablespoons grenadine syrup
- A good pinch of powdered red chile, piquín, or cayenne
- Salt to taste

Directions:

1. Mix all the ingredients well and chill. Serve in small glasses, approximately 2 ounces (60 ml) per person, together with a shot of tequila.

TEQUILA SUNRISE

Yield: Servings 1

Ingredients:

- 1 tablespoon grenadine syrup

- 1 teaspoon egg white
- 1½ ounces (45 ml) fresh lime juice
- 2 ounces (60 ml) white tequila
- Some ice cubes, crushed

Directions:

1. Chill a big cocktail glass well.
2. Place the tequila, lime juice, grenadine syrup, and egg white into a blender with the ice cubes. Combine the mixture until frothy and pour into the prepared glass.

HOT CHOCOLATE (CHOCOLATE)

Yield: approximately 1⅔ cups (415 ml)

Ingredients:

- 1½ cups (375 ml) water
- 1½-ounce (45-g) tablet of mexican chocolate

Directions:

1. Heat the water in an earthenware pot. As it comes to its boiling point, break the chocolate into it and stir until the chocolate has melted.
2. Allow it to boil gently for approximately five minutes so that all the flavor comes out, then beat it with a molinillo or blend in a blender until it is frothy.

COFFEE WITH CINNAMON AND BROWN SUGAR (CAFÉ DE OLLA)

Yield: Servings 1

Ingredients:

- ¼ cup dark-roasted, crudely ground coffee
- 1-inch (2.5-cm) piece of cinnamon stick
- 2 cups (500 ml) water

- Piloncillo or raw dark brown sugar to taste

Directions:

1. In an earthenware pot, bring the water to its boiling point. Put in the dark-roasted coffee, the cinnamon stick, and the dark brown sugar to taste.
2. Bring to its boiling point a couple of times, then strain before you serve.

ATOLES

These classic Mexican drinks are commonly enjoyed with tamales, for supper or breakfast. They are also enjoyed on their own, as a refreshment, or just to quench thirst.

CORN FOR ATOLE (ATOLE MASA)

Yield: about 2¼ pounds (1.15kg), approximately 4 cups (1 l) masa

This will be used as an ingredient in the recipes that follow.

Ingredients:

- 1 pound (450 g) white dried corn
- 6 cups (1.5 l) water

Directions:

1. Wash the corn and remove any unwanted bits and pieces, put into a deep deep cooking pan, and cover with the water. Set the pan using high heat and bring to its boiling point. Reduce the heat to moderate, cover the pan, and cook for fifteen minutes—it should cook at a fast simmer.
2. Turn off the heat and set aside to soak overnight. The next day, drain the corn and have it ground to a fine, very tender dough, masa.

Blackberry Atole (ATOLE DE ZARZAMORA)

Yield: approximately eight cups (2 l)

Ingredients:

- 1 cup (250 ml) Corn for atole
- 1 pound (450 g) blackberries
- 2 cups (500 ml) water
- About 6½ cups (1.6 l) water
- Piloncillo or raw dark brown sugar to taste

Directions:

1. Place the blackberries into a deep cooking pan with the 2 cups of water and bring to its boiling point. Reduce the heat and simmer for five minutes. Strain the blackberries into a container, pushing out as much of the flesh as you can. Discard the seeds. Set the blackberry puree aside. There must be about 3 cups of puree.
2. Dilute the masa with 1½ cups (375 ml) of the water. Put the remaining water into a mexican clay olla or heavy deep cooking pan and bring to its boiling point. Put in the diluted masa through a strainer, pushing out any lumps using a wooden spoon. Cook on moderate heat, stirring occasionally to prevent sticking, until the mixture is just starting to thicken—5 minutes.
3. Mix in the strained blackberry puree with sugar to taste and carry on cooking on moderate heat, stirring and scraping the bottom of the pan to prevent sticking, until the mixture thickens—it should make a thin coating over the back of a wooden spoon—about fifteen minutes.
4. Serve either warm or at room temperature.

CHOCOLATE-FLAVORED ATOLE (CHAMPURRADO)

Yield: about 4½ cups (1.125 l)

Ingredients:

- 2 cups (500 ml) water
- 2 tablespoons cornstarch
- 2 tablespoons granulated sugar, or to taste, depending on the chocolate
- 3 ounces (90 g) mexican drinking chocolate
- 4 cups (1 l) whole milk
- 4-inch (10-cm) piece of cinnamon stick, broken up
- Thin zest of 1 whole orange

Directions:

1. Place the water, orange zest, cinnamon, and sugar into a pan and boil swiftly for approximately twenty minutes, or until you have an infusion and the liquid has reduced by minimum 1 cup (250 ml). Put in the milk, and just before it comes to its boiling point, the chocolate. Simmer the mixture until the particles of chocolate have

thoroughly blended (mexican drinking chocolate will take longer than the others)—about ten minutes.

2. Place the cornstarch into a small container. Mix in about 2 tablespoons of the milk mixture and smooth out the lumps using the back of a wooden spoon. Put in ½ cup (125 ml) more of the milk mixture to dilute the cornstarch meticulously. Stir this into the deep cooking pan and cook until the mixture thickens slightly, stirring continuously for approximately ten minutes. Strain and serve hot.

PINEAPPLE ATOLE (ATOLE DE PIÑA)

Yield: approximately eight cups (2 l)

Ingredients:

- 1 cup (250 ml) Corn for Atole
- 1¼ pounds (565 g) cleaned and finely diced pineapple (about 3⅓ cups/835 ml)
- About 6½ cups (1.6 l) water
- Piloncillo or raw dark brown sugar to taste

Directions:

1. Put 5 cups (1.5 l) of the water into a mexican clay olla or heavy deep cooking pan, put in 1 cup (250 ml) of the diced pineapple, and bring to its boiling point.
2. In the meantime, dilute the masa with the rest of the water and put in through a strainer to the boiling water, pushing out any lumps using a wooden spoon. Cook on moderate heat, stirring and scraping the bottom of the pan to prevent sticking, until just starting to thicken—5 minutes.
3. Combine the remaining pineapple as smooth as you can and put in to the pan through a strainer, pushing out the pulp to extract as much of the flesh and juice as you can. Mix in the sugar and carry on cooking on moderate heat, stirring and scraping the bottom of the pan to prevent sticking, until the mixture thickens—it should make a thin coating over the back of a wooden spoon—about fifteen minutes.
4. Serve warm or at room temperature.

TEQUILA

Tequila is made from the distilled liquid of the baked and crushed, pineapple-like bases of the agave tequilana. It is one of those drinks that are easier bought than made at home, considering how cheap and awesome the varieties of these available in liquor stores are.

Just try the ones available in a liquor store near you, and you'll soon have a favourite. Lick the salt, swallow some tequila, then suck the lime.

ABOUT THE AUTHOR

Marissa Marie is a cook, a nutritionist, and a restaurant owner. She was raised in a small city called Los Alamos in New Mexico. Her parents loved to cook, and as a result she too fell in love with the art. Although she learnt a lot from her mother, most of her knowledge comes from self-teaching and experimentation.

Printed in France by Amazon
Brétigny-sur-Orge, FR

14652517R00288